In ecclesia non valet
hoc ego dico
hoc tu dicis,
hoc ille dicit, sed
Haec dicit Dominus.

In the church it is not decisive
what I say,
what you say,
what so and so says, rather
Thus says the Lord.

ST. AUGUSTINE
(as cited in the preface of
A. C. F. Vilmar, *Dogmatik,* V)

My Lord God, what a fine thing is a church, where the distinction exists between false and true doctrine. Indeed, that church is one which has true doctrine.

MARTIN LUTHER
Sermon from 1541
(*Weimar Ausgabe,* 49, 227, 9-12)

Those who urge us to shake ourselves free from theology and to think — and more particularly to speak and write — only what is immediately intelligible to the general public seem to me to be suffering from a kind of hysteria and to be entirely without discernment.

KARL BARTH
The Epistle to the Romans
(Preface to the Second Edition, 4)

Suffering Divine Things

Theology as Church Practice

REINHARD HÜTTER

Translated by

Doug Stott

WILLIAM B. EERDMANS PUBLISHING COMPANY
GRAND RAPIDS, MICHIGAN / CAMBRIDGE, U.K.

Originally published as
Theologie als kirchliche Praktik
© 1997 Chr. Kaiser / Gütersloher Verlaghaus, Gütersloh, Germany

English translation © 2000 Wm. B. Eerdmans Publishing Co.
255 Jefferson Ave. S.E., Grand Rapids, Michigan 49503 /
P.O. Box 163, Cambridge CB3 9PU U.K.

Printed in the United States of America

05 04 03 02 01 00   7 6 5 4 3 2 1

Library of Congress Cataloging-in-Publication Data

Suffering divine things: theology as church practice / Reinhard Hütter.
p.   cm.
Includes bibliographical references and index.
ISBN 0-8028-4688-2 (pbk.: alk. paper)
I. Theology, Doctrinal.   2. Church.   I. Title.
BT75.2.H78   2000
230′.01 — dc21   99-045553

To
The Center for Catholic and Evangelical Theology
and
Duke University Divinity School

Contents

Preface to the American Edition

This book sits squarely between the continents. Originally written in German for a German-speaking readership, it was composed in Chicago, Illinois, and in Durham, North Carolina. Yet the initial insight that animates the book occurred to me in a German backyard while I pondered Karl Barth's book on Anselm. It is therefore strange but gratifying to see this book "come back" to its place of composition.

The differences between the places just mentioned should not be allowed to hide the significant similarities between them, the most obvious being the productive and consumptive patterns of our late modern global market economy and its concomitant "cultural" by-products as designed by McDonald's, Disney, Hollywood, and the like. Yet more important, living with and among people gathered, gifted, challenged, and transformed by the gospel of Jesus Christ — a reality called "church" — has provided the primary context that gives inner coherence to this book's strange location between the continents with their different intellectual traditions and discursive habits. To be more precise, the issues at stake connecting both continents *theologically* are the church not only "after Constantinianism" but also "after modernity" and "after the state," and, even more important, theology "after dogma." The picture sketched in the introduction can easily be transferred to the American context: The way "to do theology" and to understand what one is doing when one is doing theology is caught between an unrestrained revisionism and a self-declared new, even "radical" orthodoxy, not to mention the rest of the broad spectrum reaching from contextualists, liberationists, ecologists, and feminists to mediationists (whether Tillichian or process), post-liberals (in Lindbeck's strict sense), confessionalists (Reformed, Lutheran, et al.), evangelical-catholics and other ecumenists, emerging neo-Augustinians, still existing Barthians, Niebuhrians, and liberal Protestants, and those for whom the prefix "post-" holds the irresistible attraction to wield the power of critically situating everything else from a yet more "advanced," more "critical," more "conscious" vantage point.

The way I have worked in this book has meant that I could not share in the rhetorically produced certainty characteristic of some of these movements. In light of the plethora of voices lifted up and of the accompanying noise produced I am rather haunted by the questions "What is theology" *theologically understood,* and why does contemporary theology need to face its repressed "other" — doctrine — in order to emerge coherently as that which it is fundamentally called to be, which is nothing less than a practice of the church?

We have learned from Alasdair MacIntyre that practices, which are prior to institutions, are still in need of institutions in order to be sustained over time. MacIntyre has also taught us how institutions, by becoming bureaucracies that manage idiosyncratic wills, tend to undermine and corrupt those practices that they were initially founded to facilitate and nourish. While I am painfully aware of the many theological institutions that increasingly work against the church's theological task, I am happy to dedicate the book to two institutions of theological learning and research that have not only helped this inquiry to come about but that, more importantly, have set an example for how theological institutions may and should serve the practice of theology for the sake of the gospel and the church.

Since this book's completion four years ago, important theological work has been done that is relevant to various aspects of my argument. I would have liked to engage this work in the manner of the discursive practice laid out in the following chapters. I can only acknowledge the names of those from whose work I have learned most since then: Ellen Charry, David Cunningham, David Ford, George Hunsinger, Robert W. Jenson, Bruce Marshall, Bruce McCormack, John Milbank, Oliver O'Donovan, Amy Plantinga Pauw, William Placher, Ephraim Radner, Eugene F. Rogers Jr., Kathryn Tanner, Alan Torrance, Miroslav Volf, John Webster, Anna Williams, and David Yeago. While the basic argument would still be the same, I might have worked out some of its parts in more nuanced ways, and others in even sharper and more definitive ways.

Having a German text rendered into English bears many risks. I am grateful to my colleagues Lewis Ayers, Stanley Hauerwas, Willie Jennings, Dean L. Gregory Jones, David Steinmetz, Geoffrey Wainwright, and David Yeago and my wife Nancy Heitzenrater Hütter for their advice and support, to Leslie Barnett and Chris Franks for their labors of proofreading and text hunting, to the translator for struggling with a dense German text, and to Jon Pott, editor in chief at Wm. B. Eerdmans Publishing Company, for his lively interest in this project.

In light of recent tendencies to question the centrality of the doctrine of justification for Christian faith and theology and a concomitant fashionable yet all-too-facile dismissal of Martin Luther's theology as "nominalist," "individualistic," and the deplorable beginning of all the ills of modernity, it is especially gratifying that the American version of this book appears at the time when the *Joint Declaration on the Doctrine of Justification* is being signed by the Roman Catholic Church and the churches of the Lutheran World Federation, an act that in and of itself suggests a vindication of the catholicity of Martin Luther's Reformation — *pace* his contemporary detractors. This recent event has also vindicated the ecumenical labors of Peter Brunner, Ulrich Kühn, Wolfhart Pannenberg, Otto Hermann Pesch, Albrecht Peters, Gerhard Sauter, Edmund Schlink, and Gunther Wenz in Germany; Carl Braaten, Robert W. Jenson, George Lindbeck, and David Yeago in the United States; and Theodor Dieter, Michael Root, and Risto Saarinen at the Institute for Ecumenical Research in Strasbourg, France. To all of them I am deeply indebted for understanding the profound catholicity of the Reformation and the deeply relevant implications of Luther's theology for the contemporary church as well as for a theology that is both evangelical and catholic.

Finally, I want to put the following text under a *caveat* that both its title and its cover intimate. It is poignantly expressed by Karl Barth at the very end of *Church Dogmatics* I/1 in relationship to Augustine's *The Trinity*, but is clearly pointed to all who dare to entertain the practice of theology:

> There are theologies whose authors have no need to be worried at the end, since for good reasons the "fulness of visions" has been spared them. Augustine was not in this happy position. He had run the risk and the "fulness of visions" had in fact come upon him. When this risk is run, one may come to grief. And a theologian who runs the risk may not only come to grief himself but also bring destruction on others. This explains Augustine's final prayer and also the closing words of the book: *Dominus Deus une, Deus Trinitas, quaecumque dixi in his libris de tuo, agnoscant et tui: si qua de meo, et tu ignosce, et tui. Amen.* [O Lord the one God, God the Trinity, whatsoever I have said in these books of you, may those that are yours

acknowledge; whatsoever of myself alone, do you and yours forgive. Amen. (Karl Barth, *Church Dogmatics*, I/1, 489)

Duke University Divinity School   REINHARD HÜTTER
Reformation Day
October 31, 1999
(On the Day of the Signing of the
Joint Declaration on the Doctrine of Justification
in Augsburg, Germany)

Preface

This book is the slightly reworked version of a study accepted as a Habilitationsschrift in the winter semester 1995/96 by the Theological Faculty of the University of Erlangen/Nürnberg. I would like to give special thanks to the readers, Hans G. Ulrich and Alasdair I. C. Heron.

This work is the product of a series of theological dialogues both in Germany and in the USA, and thus owes its genesis to many different critical and constructive impulses, impulses which probably cannot, however, be exhaustively reconstructed in retrospect. Specifically I would like to thank Oswald Bayer (Tübingen), James Buckley (Baltimore), Michael Cartwright (Indianapolis), Inagrace Dietterich (Chicago), Werner Göllner (Neuendettelsau), Jean Bethke Elshtain (Chicago), Stanley Hauerwas (Durham), Siegfried Hirschmann (Adelheidsdorf), L. Gregory Jones (Durham), Bruce Marshall (Northfield), Hans Reinders (Amsterdam), Gerhard Sauter (Bonn), David Tracy (Chicago), Bernd Wannenwetsch (Erlangen), Paul Wadell (Green Bay), Vítor Westhelle (Chicago), David Yeago (Columbia), Matthias Zeindler (Bern), and in addition all the participants in the Dogmatics Colloquy at the Center for Catholic and Evangelical Theology (Northfield), as well as its two founders, Carl E. Braaten and Robert W. Jenson. I would like to give special thanks to my teacher and mentor Hans G. Ulrich for his considerable support and for his unceasing dialogue over many years.

The external *conditio sine qua non* of this study was a Habilitationstipend from the Deutsche Forschungsgemeinschaft. It was also aided in its early stages by a stipend from the Association of Theological Schools in the United States and Canada, and toward the end, by the opportunity to work at the Institute for Advanced Studies of Religion at the University of Chicago

Divinity School. In this connection, special thanks are due Dr. William E. Lesher, President of the Lutheran School of Theology in Chicago, and Dean Ralph W. Klein for the equally noble and rare gesture of granting me a two-year leave of absence from my teaching duties.

I also need to thank the staff of the Jesuit Krauss-McCormick Library (LSTC), the Regenstein Library (University of Chicago), and the Perkins Library (Duke University), whose cordial and efficient support contributed considerably to my research.

Thanks also need to be given to the Gütersloher/Kaiser Verlag, and especially the editors of the series Beiträge zur evangelischen Theologie, Eberhard Jüngel and Rudolf Smend, for agreeing to publish this study. Printing costs were offset by the Zantner-Bush Stiftung (Erlangen), the Evangelical Lutheran Church of Bavaria, and the Arbeitsgemeinschaft Christlicher Kirchen — Ökumenische Centrale (Frankfurt).

I am also indebted to Siegfried Hirschmann and Peter Bartmann for reading the proofs. And last but not least, I would like to thank my wife Nancy Heitzenrater Hütter for our shared *peregrinatio,* and our children Hanna, Sara, Joshua, and Jonathan for that special salutary distraction of which only children are capable.

REINHARD HÜTTER
Chicago, Epiphany 1997

The New State of Theological Discourse: Unintelligible Profusion

Now we are going to speak a bit, no longer of God, but of theology. What a fall!

M. Bellet, Théologie Express   .

The emerging lack of clarity and unintelligible profusion which Jürgen Habermas has diagnosed with regards to society at large can also be discerned in the church and in theology.[1] At least for now, the time of the formation of schools, of the great "camps," and of their positional publications seems to be over. In a theological sense as well, we are clearly living in a time of great changes, a time of new beginnings and new ideas, but also of taking leave of the old, a time that is at once both "post" and "ante" and whose self-understanding is still being vehemently disputed. While all this is happening, however, common foundations and earlier agreements are increasingly falling away. Progress and regress, both heightened and failed communication, information overload and disinformation — all these are a signature of the time, nor do they leave theology untouched. The gulf is growing between a feeling of "anything goes" on the one hand and a return to age-old, eternal "truths" on the other. Drewermann and the *Opus Dei*, the "open" church and the "movement for no other gospel," with their incisively antithetical or even mirror-image quality and simultaneity, charac-

1

terize the present crisis in orientation and substance in both church and theology.

Similarly, an increasing lack of clarity also attaches to the question of what it means to engage in "theology" in the first place, or, expressed in what has become the virtually "canonical" expression in American English, "how to do theology." The locus, task, and character of theology — and this essentially means "systematic theology" or "dogmatics" — is now more than ever the subject of debate, though this debate itself has changed significantly since the 1970s. Earlier discussion focused on the "scientific nature" of academic theology and on what it means to engage in "theology" (Ebeling, Pannenberg, Sauter, Mildenberger, Ritschl, et al.). This earlier discourse, however, which was still relatively coherent and was carried on in a disciplined fashion, has in the meantime splintered into a multiplicity of individual opinions on how to engage in theology, opinions in part driven by specific movements, including, for example, the movement of liberation theology, the feminist movement, the psychological-therapeutic movement, the Pietist-evangelical movement, the charismatic movement, and so on. These tension-filled undercurrents are covered by a thin veneer of traditional confessional and academic theology that only in an official sense really sets the tone at universities and seminaries and in the ranks of church leadership. Were one to query theology students, pastors, and congregation members at large concerning the distribution and acceptance of these various theologies, one would quickly discover the dubious minority status of such academic and confessional theology.

At the same time, academic and confessional discussion *within* and *about* theological discourse is also becoming increasingly difficult to track. Although the framework of theology as a historically oriented discipline[2] has indeed been sundered, nothing capable of establishing a comparable consensus has appeared yet to take its place. Furthermore, a plethora of the most varied debates also contributes considerably to the difficulty in assessing developments. In addition to the Latin American discussion there is also a North American one, in which Great Britain also plays a not inconsiderable role, and a continental European one in which in its own turn the German discussion occupies its own sphere. These discussions themselves are further complicated by the multiplicity of ecclesiastical, political, and cultural force fields in which theological discourse takes place. The debates also mutually influence one another through the numerous translations of pioneering works from every possible quarter. Feminist theologies, liberation theologies, and various postmodern theologies with varying degrees of radical, critical challenges and new proposals increasingly alter this discourse into an expanding "market of possibilities." Indeed, the interpretations of theological discourse are just as varied as the individual "theologies" themselves, and as a rule reflect the latter's agenda: the feminist escape from the hegemony of androcentric consciousness; the liberation-theological critique of European-American cultural and economic hegemony; new religiosity as a commodity of meaning and reflection for the educated among the adherents of religion; psychologizing theology as an expression of vagabond religious subjectivity; or a theology critical of both society and the church which understands the present state of religion largely as the result of the oppressive privatization of the church at the dictate of modern-liberal, technocratic society.

The increasing loss of communication is not just a secondary problem in theology. Quite the contrary, it touches on the very essence of the gospel itself, which threatens to break apart between a fundamentalist monism on the one hand and a pluralism of individualistic religious randomness on the other. The problem emerging in theology is at the same time a problem for the church. The dynamic of advanced modernity[3] seems to be pushing the Protestant churches in two directions: either toward an incessantly increasing intensification of the understanding of "religion" and "faith" as essentially private gnosis or experience made "relevant" through various subject-centered activities; or toward objectified, increasingly reified forms of faith designed to counter the subversive dynamic of modernity itself,[4] as is certainly the case in biblical fundamentalism. These two Protestant reactions to modernity do share one common feature: in their wake the church as a genuine "public" is lost.

Of course, one can certainly ask what really is lost if "church" is understood simply as an association of religiously interested individuals. Indeed, under the conditions of modernity, can "church" be anything other than a private association? The opposite question can also be raised; namely, if indeed the church is nothing else than a private association of people with common interests, then does not precisely this sociological self-designation undermine the church's own self-understanding, that is, the promise entrusted to it and its mission? Does not the church then dissolve into an increasing number of private religious "clubs" reflecting the religious needs and tastes of their members? And is not the self-understanding of Protestant theology also directly at stake along with the self-understanding of the Protestant church? Sixty-five years ago the New Testament scholar Erik Peterson raised precisely these questions in an incisive and enduring fashion during a brief correspondence with the famous historian of church and dogma Adolf von Harnack. This correspondence will provide our point of departure for examining these questions.

3

PART ONE

The Issue at Stake:
Church — Doctrine — Theology

I. The Eclipse of the Church as Public —
Loss of Doctrine — the Crisis in Theology

1. The "Aroma of an Empty Bottle" — or the Church as Public:
The Harnack-Peterson Correspondence

The 1928 correspondence between Adolf von Harnack and Erik Peterson[1] provides a paradigmatic indicator for the eclipse of the Protestant church as a public sphere under the conditions of modernity, and offers two diametrically opposed responses to this problem. This correspondence is also an ideal point of departure for the following investigation because it shows in an exemplary fashion that any discussion concerning the essence and nature of the church also involves direct consequences for one's understanding of both doctrine and theology, and that the public character of the church is directly associated with the status of doctrine and with the locus and self-understanding of theology.

The point of departure for the correspondence was Harnack's essay "The Old Testament in the Pauline Letters and in the Pauline Communities," which appeared in 1928 in the *Sitzungsberichte der Berliner Akademie der Wissenschaften.* Harnack sent Peterson a copy of this work, and in a letter of thanks Peterson remarked that Harnack's study of the relationship between Scripture and scriptural tradition had actually given expression to the Catholic rather than the Protestant principle.[2] Harnack responded briefly that, at least *formally*, the Catholic principle of tradition was doubtless the better of the two, but *concretely* or *materially* had wrought considerably more and far worse havoc in history.[3] In his letter of response, Peterson delineated the contradiction between the perspective of the historian, who rejects the principle of tradition materially, and that of the dogmatician, who affirms it formally. In his view Protestant theology had already been living with this contradiction of a double truth for some time, and yet

> in the long run, this hiatus cannot be sustained; nor can one eliminate it by abandoning the old Protestant scriptural principle without introducing some new dogmatic authority to take its place. Similarly, I consider the Barthian return to the principle of scripture to be impossible, since it quite logically must issue again in strict verbal inspiration. Without any dogmatic authority, however, there can no longer be any church, and even worse, without such authority the church will be utterly ineffective. . . . What will be left is merely non-binding, general moral parenesis. . . . I can see quite clearly that this will rob the Protestant church of all influence; indeed, it will force the church to give up itself. The church ceases to be a "public" entity once it no longer commits itself to a dogmatic position.[4]

Peterson discerns the inseparable connection between the church as a public institution, on the one hand, and its binding doctrinal stance on the other.

Harnack responds by immediately addressing this connection, describing it with utter consistency according to the essence of liberal theology: "To be sure, 'what remains' is only 'a non-binding moral parenesis' — this derives from the very nature of older neo-Protestantism, which by the way is also a legitimate consequence of earlier Protestantism. . . . Protestantism must roundly admit that it neither wants to be nor can be a church like the Catholic church, that it rejects all formal authorities, and that it reckons exclusively with the impression elicited by the message of God and the Father of Jesus Christ and our Father." For Harnack, this distinctively congregationalist perspective naturally has direct consequences for doctrine and theology: "The difficulty resides in the pedagogical teaching of the catechism, since even the dogmatics taught at the university are nothing more than catechism instruction [contemporary practical theology]; in my opinion, however, it is not at all bad that each catechism teacher in Protestantism must find his or her own way. . . . I know of no other way of bringing to expression *within the scholarly discipline* just what constitutes the essence of Christianity than that which I used in my own lectures on the 'Essence of Christianity.'"[5]

6

Peterson in return points out that Harnack's view makes congregationalism the logical consequence of the Reformation. Because the Protestant church is so tightly bound to culture, any substantive collapse of a distinct cultural-political entity can potentially also bring about the collapse of the Protestant church.[6] Harnack's view simultaneously implies for Peterson that theology will abandon itself as an academic discipline and that what is known as "catechism instruction" will of necessity become dependent on some normative horizon, that is, on some sort of binding doctrine.[7]

In a final letter Harnack responds to these objections one more time in great detail and at great length, and his response again shows how church, doctrine, and theology are inseparably related. Subjecting the first to a radically new understanding necessarily generates profound consequences for doctrine and theology.

> *Rebus sic stantibus,* there are only two ways out for the "church" [in the older sense of the word]: Either one traces Protestantism back to [Greek or Roman] Catholicism, or one grounds it on absolute biblicism. *Neither of these alternatives is accessible, however, since both contradict our historic understanding,* not to speak of other considerations inhering in religion itself and even in the original, albeit imperfect point of departure of Protestantism itself. But if the older concept of the "church" is lost, so is the older concept of "dogma," and with it "dogma" as such, since dogma without infallibility means nothing. Luther's position at the Leipzig Disputation already sealed its fate, even though Luther himself never fully comprehended the implications of his own statements and never clearly articulated for himself the insufficiency of his contradictory attempt at replacing that dogma with a kind of half-biblicism. Although it was splendid that he was able to withdraw to his living faith, the resulting objective void has not been filled, nor can anything ever fill it. . . . You are quite correct when you say that if there is no longer "church," there can be only "fellowship," since theoretically there cannot be any "third" entity between "this" and the "church"; in a practical sense, various degrees of admixture will no doubt endure for a long time yet.[8]

The consequence of this ecclesiological perspective is that in Harnack's view, a Protestant theologian is one for whom "human kind and *this* religion belong together."[9] Moreover, he considers the existence of Protestant theology to be quite independent of the question regarding the future of university departments of theology, and in addition to the catechism instruction already mentioned, he considers an independent Christian philosophy of religion to be the crowning achievement of theological endeavor. With regard to the future, he insists that

> I do not know what will become of the protestant churches, but as you rightly suppose, I can only *welcome* the development that leads increasingly to independence and to a pure association based on conviction in the sense (I am not at all shy to say:) of Quakerism and Congregationalism. I am not worried about how we all may look or assert ourselves between Catholicism, Americanism, Russianism, and so on. We'll find ways and means without *ecclesiastical* absolutism [only in the living soul does absolutism have a place]. — Of course, we are still living to a considerable extent from the remnants of the institution of the Catholic church around us, as it were *from the aroma of an empty bottle,* nor do I believe that one ought to accelerate this development intentionally. . . . Let's just not become faint-hearted and reactionary and start yearning for the fleshpots of Egypt again. They're gone for good — unless, of course, we turn around and head back to Egypt.[10]

In his rich and provocative epilogue, Peterson rightly draws attention to the significance of this correspondence for the relationship between theology and church and the problems this relationship raises in Protestantism. His explications and queries there are serious and, in certain passages, are formulated with extraordinary precision, possibly a result of his return two years earlier to the "old Egyptian fleshpots," to use Harnack's pejorative-polemical phrase.[11] Precisely this move resulted in Peterson being labeled a *persona non grata* within Protestant theology; commensurately, the sharp challenge he issued *before* his conversion, one renewed by Heinrich Schlier, was now either dismissed as anticipatory crypto-Catholicism or simply ignored altogether.[12] This, however, is an ill-advised position for Protestantism to take, since it is precisely the possibility of a Protestant church and theology under the conditions of modernity that Peterson is questioning here. That is, if the Protestant church does indeed increasingly lose its public character, either politically as a state church or culturally-socially as a "people's church" (*Volkskirche*), and is forced into the mode of a private religious association, then how, especially given its own self-understanding, can it still be the *church* at all? And what consequences does this change have for church doctrine and for a theology that understands itself as an academic undertaking essentially related to the church?

It is worth examining Peterson's analysis of modern Protestantism in Germany as presented in retrospect in this epilogue to the Harnack correspondence. Precisely because Protestants have been so inclined to silence Peterson, I will allow him to speak a bit more at length in his own words.

He first points out that during the time between the correspondence and its publication, that is, between 1928 and 1932/33, a change took place in Protestantism, with an *objective*-religious tendency now acquiring a higher profile. Among other things, this inclination was concerned with reacquiring what Harnack called the "old Catholic element within early Protestantism." Although he is thinking naturally enough and especially of the theological work of Karl Barth, the list probably also includes many other theologians who during the postwar period set the tone for an entire generation of both Reformed and Lutheran thinkers.[13] He also records a new movement within the Protestant church itself, one attaching itself to the superintendent of the Prussian territorial church, Otto Dibelius. Both Dibelius and Barth are concerned with "public presence,"[14] one theologian with that of the church, the other with that of theology. Peterson believes not only that the two lapse into an ultimately fruitless dispute with one another, but also that ultimately neither initiative will prove productive in any case. Dibelius's activism cannot possibly *produce* the public character of the church if the latter does not already have such to begin with; nor can Barth's attempt at reestablishing the public character of theology have any enduring success, since ultimately it depends on the public character of the church. In Peterson's view, however, this entire aporia inheres "in the essence of Protestantism itself, whose presuppositions permit an 'institution of church' to become established which in fact has no real relationship with dogma and theology, and on the other hand is able to develop a theology that essentially ignores the concrete dogmatic problems of the 'territorial church.'"[15]

If, unlike Harnack and cultural Protestantism, one does not turn this situation into a virtue and declare it to be the intended result of the Reformation, then the Protestant church and theology have been facing a dilemma at least since the elimination of the territorial episcopate. On the one hand, one might return to the kind of "public will" attaching to the church's association with the *state*; this, however, is impossible given the concrete constitutional and political separation of church and state. The alternative would be to

flee to the concept of a specifically *ecclesiastical* public presence; this, however, necessarily raises the issue of establishing dogma of the sort found in Catholicism, and for ascribing doctrinal instructional authority to the church. The presuppositions of Protestantism also exclude these possibilities. But if there is no dogma in the true sense in the Protestant church, then neither is theology possible, for there is no theology without dogmat-

9

ics, and no dogmatics without dogma. . . . This, however, means that Protestant theology will always remain more or less the private affair of professors of theology, nor will any greater or lesser degree of ecclesiastical association on the part of this or that individual professor change this in principle.[16]

For Peterson, the most significant aspect of this dilemma involving the Protestant church and theology is not the attendant loss of political power, but the loss of dogmatic substance, which inevitably will not only increasingly alienate contemporary Protestantism from its own Reformational roots, thus opening up the door in the long run to a profusion of syncretistic developments, but also undermine and ultimately sunder the unity between the Protestant churches themselves. Two generations later, these concerns sound like daily reports that are all too familiar to us. Again in Peterson's own words:

Early Protestantism maintained a consciousness of its inherent, dialectical relationship with the mother church; even in the most extreme exaggerations of confessional polemic, it remained tied to the old church. But it was not just this polemic itself that kept it associated with the Catholic church, nor just the issue of successorship that drew the Protestant territorial bishop into a historic nexus with the bishops of the Catholic period, nor just the law of "liturgical successorship" connecting Protestant worship with the Roman mass — it was also the consciousness of sharing a common dogmatic basis with the old church in whatever articles of faith that were not being contested confessionally. This deep sense of unity in faith with regard to basic dogmatic truths was realized in the common entity of the *one* Christian-Roman Empire of the German Nation. The Formula of Concord of 1580 still explicitly confirms the Protestants' adherence to the Apostolic, Nicene, and Athanasian Creeds, and emphatically rejects "all manner of heresies and doctrines introduced into the church which do contradict these creeds." And the relationship of Protestant theology to Catholic theology then accordingly corresponds to its relationship with the dogma of the old church. Early Protestant orthodoxy was "scholastic," and was intimately tied to the problems of Aristotelian and Jesuit school theology; but it was also ascetic and mystic, and as such its piety was shaped not only by medieval, but also by the Catholic mysticism of the age of the Counter Reformation and the Baroque. At first glance, one of the most astonishing contemporary Protestant phenomena seems to be that it is alienated and uncomprehending not only when confronted with Catholicism (which in any case is certainly psychologically understandable), but when confronted with its own past in early Protestantism as well; and this is true today not only of "liberal" Protestants, but in a very general sense even of those subscribing to so-called "positive" theology. This incomprehension can probably be explained only as a result of the changed situation of Protestantism's own ontological foundation. The dissolution of the Christian state, and with it of the confessional territories, also prompted the disappearance of the public character of the Protestant church and theology, a presence once sustained by this state association and which for early Protestantism had still been the most important formative force. This disappearance, however, also loosened its dialectical relationship with the Catholic church and with Catholic theology with their peculiarly ecclesiastical public character. I believe this foundational shift is responsible for a great many of the contemporary developments within the Protestant church and Protestant theology.[17]

In Peterson's view Protestantism was already mired in a crisis of relevance even before it lost its public character once and for all, a presence that remained at least partially intact until the end of territorial church organization. The Protestant church and theology reacted to this crisis in a threefold fashion by trying to reestablish its "public relevance" through new, general points of reference: reason, inwardness, and activism. But is Peterson not essentially just enumerating here the basic points of reference for the history of Protestant theology in the nineteenth and twentieth centuries? At least in retrospect, one can see that these are the three paths on which the Protestant theology of the past thirty years has tried to demonstrate its public relevance: through a constitutive relationship first to the most recent developments of contemporary rationality; later to political activism; and more recently to religious inwardness and spirituality.

Quite apart from the question of whether and to what extent Peterson's analysis of Protestant theology is accurate, the relationship he describes between the loss of the Protestant churches' public character on the one hand and their ongoing crisis of relevance on the other is certainly worthy of our attention. This eclipse of the Protestant church as public might be one reason it is susceptible to becoming the bearer of national and other identities and projects,[18] securing for itself thus as a national or civil religion a measure of public relevance within the framework of the public arena of society at large. As the past decade shows, the increasing loss of even this status has plunged Protestantism into a renewed crisis of relevance. The point of Peterson's thesis is that this inherent crisis of relevance will not be resolved until Protestantism reclaims its "churchly" identity, that is, until the church again constitutes a specific public. Peterson's greatest service, however, is in drawing attention again to the connection between the church as a public sphere, binding doctrine, and theology, and the central significance of precisely this connection for the self-understanding of Christian theology. Put differently, *the self-understanding of theology as well as the articulation of its task in the larger sense depend not only or even primarily on this or that understanding of "academic discipline," but on the (again: theological) premises of church and binding doctrine.*

Protestant theologians can at this point raise two quite different objections to this position. The first might be raised by those who carry on the cultural-Protestant inheritance of Ernst Troeltsch and Adolf von Harnack; the second, by those who consider the new direction of Protestant theology implemented by Karl Barth to be the legitimate continuation of the essential concerns of the Reformation and of early Protestantism, albeit under radically altered intellectual and societal conditions. The first group would consider the entire complex of questions raised by Peterson to be faulty to begin with, and affirm Harnack's perspective as farsighted and actually proven by historical development.

It is at this point that the second group could observe that precisely the new understanding of Protestant theology in the 1930s, the *Kirchenkampf,* the (partial) reorganization of the territorial churches as people's churches during the postwar period, and the unbroken continuity of the Protestant theological university faculties show that a new, inherently stable, and in the sense of the Reformation theologically responsible relationship has been reached between church and theology, a relationship belatedly disproving Peterson's thesis.

With all due respect to these views, three objections suggest themselves. First, pneumatological as well as ecclesiological ambiguity inheres at the very center of the Barthian new beginning itself, one I will discuss in greater detail below.[19] This was the subject of a controversy in its own right between Peterson and Barth, and although Barth did indeed acquire important insights from it, it still left unresolved the central problem within his ecclesiology. Second, two important figures at the center of the Confessing Church, albeit each in his own way, agreed with Peterson's analysis: Dietrich Bonhoeffer and Heinrich Schlier. On September 9, 1940, Bonhoeffer wrote to Eberhard Bethge:

> We spoke about the situation of the church. It became clear to me again that the struggle over church government in fact involves the question of the possibility of the Protestant church for us, a question necessarily

> emerging from the history of the church itself. It is the question whether, after separation from papal and worldly authority in the church, an authority can be established in the church and grounded solely on the word and on confession. If such authority is not possible, then the last possibility for the Protestant church has passed by; then there really is only a return to Rome or to the state church or the path to isolation, to the "protest" of genuine Protestantism against false authorities.[20]

The question of a Protestant church government and of an authority based on word and confession implies the question of binding doctrine in the church and the question of the relationship between this doctrine and theology. The decisive part of Bonhoeffer's assessment is the alternatives he mentions in case a Protestant church based on word and confession proves to be impossible. The option of a return to a state church has in the meantime become obsolete, and contemporary developments in late modern Western societies are clearly moving toward a splintering off, an isolation of "protesting" groups. Erik Peterson and Heinrich Schlier choose the third option.[21] It is the fourth option, Bonhoeffer's own primary concern, that is at issue in the following discussion, albeit with a narrowing of the question to that concerning theology as a church practice.

The other position worth considering is that of Heinrich Schlier, a particularly troublesome witness for Protestant theology and the church, since he was not only a student of Bultmann and then Peterson's successor in New Testament at the University of Bonn, but also a pastor in the Confessing Church during the *Kirchenkampf*. In 1953 he converted to Roman Catholicism. In retrospect in his "Brief Account,"[22] which is certainly worth reading, he himself understands the *Kirchenkampf* in the Third Reich as, among other things, an "attempt to retrieve the church in the Protestant church."[23] Despite the unified struggle against the "German Christians" and against National Socialism, he believed that precisely these efforts on behalf of the church were essentially hopeless.

> It became increasingly clear that there were not only various confessions in the sense of confessional writings, but — even worse — that these confessional writings that once constituted the foundation of the Protestant churches were no longer recognized as such in the first place; and worst of all, the theological conviction that the concrete content of such confessional writings was the binding doctrine of the church was roundly rejected and vehemently decried as confessionalism. The characteristic and false counterargument was that the important element was not the confession in

13

the sense of confessional writing, but confession in the sense of confessing. Confession in the sense of confessional writing was allegedly merely a guide pointing faith in a certain direction, since faith is after all not agreement with certain articles of faith (and certainly it is not just that), but something quite different. I saw with increasing clarity, however, that this merely replaced the dogmatic principle with the charismatic principle. But the personal gift of faith, the kind of personal faith ignited in an encounter with scripture, is based on dogma, and cannot itself replace that dogma. Although charisma probably does indeed constitute the inner dynamic of the church, it is not its foundation. . . . Things have become rather quiet again in the Protestant church these days, and it almost seems as if we have become resigned with regard to these and similar fundamental questions. Within this calm, however, peculiar and yet in reality quite logical theological events are taking place. Ecclesiastical bureaucracy is making decisions in a disciplinary fashion with regard to dogma, and in theology, many have suspended from the inside the so-called formal principle of the Protestant church, namely, the canon of the Holy Scriptures, and have replaced it with the canon of the event of inspiration ignited by the word of scripture.[24]

We will later examine Schlier's position more extensively, since the enduring relevance of his assessment and of its implied question to Protestant churches and to Protestant theology is quite obvious. Schlier's conversion indicates among other things that by 1953, Peterson's query to Protestant theology and the church was still unresolved.

One might certainly object that Bonhoeffer and Schlier do, after all, represent only two isolated individuals — individuals with extreme views as well. Because Bonhoeffer's remarks represent private views expressed in a letter and made against the background of an extreme ecclesiastical and overall social situation, one should allegedly not make too much of them. Similarly, Heinrich Schlier converted in 1953, that is, before the Protestant churches of the postwar era had really "gotten going," and he converted for other theological reasons as well. In addition, the Second Vatican Council has in the meantime at least in part brought Schlier's own ecclesiological notions into question; beyond even this, ecumenical dialogues, compromises, and declarations of convergence have contributed considerably to mutual understanding and to a deepening of ecclesiological perspectives.

Although these objections are certainly justified and do indeed point out important and welcome changes and developments since Peterson's, Bonhoeffer's, and Schlier's time, ultimately they are unpersuasive. As far as the basic, central questions regarding the relationship between church, binding doctrine, and theology are concerned, everything is essentially just as un-resolved — or is once again just as unresolved — as during Peterson's day.[25] This is confirmed by a glance at a noteworthy contribution by one of the most subtly nuanced voices of the generation whose teachers studied under those theologians who, in Peterson's words, brought about the decisive reem-phasis on the "objective-religious line" of Protestantism. This particular con-tribution eloquently shows that the question of the relationship between church, binding doctrine, and theology as a distinct undertaking within the church and the academy is by no means merely a question of dated signifi-cance, but is also one of extreme relevance for the Protestant church today.

2. Theology in the People's Church: From Doctrinal Commitment to the Orientational Hermeneutics of Meaningful Living

In an ambitious and lengthy essay,[26] Johannes Fischer employs great sensibil-ity and discernment in describing the contemporary problem of Protestant theology as an academic discipline with an educational commission for the Protestant people's church, a problem for which he also suggests concrete so-lutions. He deserves our undivided attention not only because of his excellent understanding of the problem and his ambitious if highly questionable sug-gestions for a solution, but also because he reads like a thematic continuation of the Harnack-Peterson correspondence "after Barth." Here one can observe the subtle, cautious, and highly differentiated change of course of a post-Barthian to a line of perception more akin to Harnack. This is doubtless not least a result of the great external upheavals in society and church during the 1980s and early 1990s in Germany.[27] The situation of the contemporary church is not all that different from that of the 1920s, especially as regards the Protestant churches' tangible loss of public character and presence.[28] Hence Peterson's queries, after a period of alleged stability with regard to the church, are again in the air, and the fact that such changes in society are immediately also raising the question of the locus and task of theology with such extreme incisiveness suggests that Harnack's assessment remains accurate, namely, that the Protestant church ultimately understands itself from the perspective of a political-cultural identity, one from which theology then also articulates its own task. What, then, is Fischer's understanding of the relationship be-tween Christian faith, church, theology, and society at the end of the twenti-eth century?

In view of the increasing pluralization of society and individualization of religious identity and conviction, Fischer finds Christian theology — and

15

dogmatics at its center — confronted by a qualitatively new set of problems.[29] Although until now dogmatics has largely been able to take as its point of orientation a consensus concerning the basic tenets of faith within the church in the sense normally associated with Schleiermacher, that is, a consensus concerning church "doctrine," precisely this reference point is now no longer available. This situation, however, also renders obsolete the task of dogmatics in the tradition of Schleiermacher as a coherent presentation of the tenets of faith of a given church community. This same situation has resulted in an increasing pluralization of views that in their own turn are increasingly difficult to track and assess, and thus also in a lack of orientation of previously unknown proportions. Fischer believes that Protestant dogmatics serves this need for orientation by accompanying the life of faith with both reflection and criticism, and by offering aids to orientation for praxis in both church and society. The comprehensive paradigm is no longer an ontologically given reference in reality oriented either directly toward "God" and "world" or mediated through spirit or subjective feeling, but rather *communication among those who are present*. Dogmatics now assumes the role of the reflective-critical dialogue partner who discloses the content of faith from the perspective of the "spirit," that is, from the perspective of a constitutional horizon of a distinct communication nexus, in this case that of faith.[30] The "content" of Christian tradition then discloses itself within this horizon of communication such that it can serve as an orientation for life and values.

This shall suffice as a brief description of the essentials of Fischer's new conception of dogmatics as orientational hermeneutics for life and meaning. We will now show in detail that the axis "church-doctrine-theology" is of crucial significance for this new understanding of the task of theology, and that Fischer is able to understand dogmatics anew in this way only because he redefines "church" and "doctrine" in a quite specific way.

Fischer begins by examining the pluralistic developments within the "people's church" *(Volkskirche)*. The processes of increasing social differentiation and individualization within late modern society increasingly also affect the churches. "The result is a growing pluralism of inner-church consciousness, of attitudes of faith, styles of devotion, and of spiritual milieu. Although one may well lament this and yearn to return to a church with a homogeneous orientation, such a return is possible only at the price of a retreat of the church itself out of modern society and into a sectarian existence on the social periphery."[31] Fischer, however, has made hidden normative decisions in this situational description. He believes that a church with a homogeneous orientation would of necessity lapse into a peripheral existence within society, one corresponding to that of a "sect." He is using the sociological term

16

"sect" here in a way attributing objective-normative weight to it, but without justifying *theologically* why a peripheral social existence of this sort would in fact be inappropriate for the Protestant church in the first place or would contradict its mandate to proclaim the gospel and to represent the Christian faith. Rather, the value- and wish-horizon of a decidedly popular-Christian *(volkskirchlich)* manner of thinking seems already to be shaping his perception of these problems. By articulating this suspicion, I am not trying to impute to Fischer straightaway an interest in the church's preservation of self and of its standard of living, or in the "status quo" of the church's established cultural position within society. That would be beneath him. Rather, his perception of the problem seems to be addressing the concern, expressed in the sociological terminology of "sect" and "peripheral existence," which Peterson envisioned with the concept of "public."

This is also evident in his concern for the Christian faith's claim to truth, which, significantly, for Peterson was inextricably tied to the church's public character. Fischer sees this claim boxed in by a dilemma in which it can only lose. "The pluralism of faith and of religious milieu seems to be grinding away at the Christian faith's claim to truth. That claim has, as it were, gotten caught between Scylla and Charybdis. If it accommodates itself to the pluralistic trend, it perishes. If it does not, it perishes just the same."[32] Now, it should be mentioned here that these alternatives do *not* reside on the same level. The first is part of the distinct content of the Christian faith and of its temporally extended identity; the second refers only to the reality of the church in the sense of "people's church" *(Volkskirche)*, that is, to a broad societal acceptance of the Christian faith and to its explicitly or implicitly unchallenged and largely unrivaled status as a civil religion in modern society. Societies such as that in the United States whose pluralistic composition is already well advanced, however, show that while the first possibility is indeed a very real danger, the second does not really represent any compelling alternative. For the more clearly and precisely one articulates the identity of the Christian life-orientation, an orientation with which, ultimately, Fischer is certainly concerned, the lower the risk that the Christian claim to truth will disappear. The only qualification is that this claim can no longer be unequivocally represented within the framework of Protestantism organized along the lines of the "people's church" *(Volkskirche)*. But what does that matter, one might ask, unless for *emphatically theological reasons* one must advocate a certain concept of the church in which the external, visible unity of the church itself does indeed constitute an essential feature? What is Fischer's position on this? Although he is doubtless quite sensitive to the reality of the "people's church" *(Volkskirche)*, neither here nor in his book *Leben aus dem Geist*[33] does he

17

present an ecclesiology that would prevent or at least theologically justify an uncritical self-subjection to the reality of the "people's church" (*Volkskirche*). The only alternative Fischer sees to this "people's-church reality" is an abstract concept of church which dogmatics construes for itself, but which is alienated from the "reality" of the church. Given this understanding of the situation, and the observation that Protestant theology is to have some reference to this "people's church" (*Volkskirche*)[34] while still remaining an academic discipline at the university, Fischer inevitably encounters the question of the locus and self-understanding of Protestant theology, which in its own turn is essentially the question of the locus and self-understanding of Protestant dogmatics.

Fischer believes that the orientation of dogmatics toward a "doctrine" based on consensus, as was still the case for Schleiermacher[35] or, more recently, for the knowledge of faith proposed by Ingolf U. Dalferth,[36] can no longer succeed in the present environment because, according to this understanding, "church doctrine" would have to be capable of establishing such a consensus and thus implicitly of setting boundaries and determining just what is not part of that consensus. "And yet" — here Fischer marches directly into the center of the complex of problems concerning church and dogma opened up in the Harnack-Peterson correspondence —

> who can claim to do this, and by what right? . . . The example shows how problematic that seemingly so simple distinction is between believers and non-believers. Only sects are unequivocal in this regard. By contrast, the reality of the "people's church" (*Volkskirche*) from which in this country [Germany] university theology does indeed take its orientation, not least because it is training pastors for precisely this "people's church" (*Volkskirche*), is characterized by an extraordinarily broad and varied spectrum of attitudes of faith, all of which claim a place under the same roof. And precisely this situation generates the question of how there can possibly still be anything resembling "church doctrine" and thus "dogmatics."[37]

For Fischer, two central questions must be successfully addressed in order to overcome the crisis of dogmatics. "Given the pluralistic conditions currently shaping the church, how can one still uphold and represent the claim to truth? And how is dogmatics possible given the conditions of contemporary religious change and of pluralism within the church itself?"[38]

Fischer develops a response to these questions by first trying to establish a general theory that will disclose the relationship between communication and truth and then also enable him to examine the unique features of reli-

18

gious communication and truth.[39] This theory takes communication as the basic paradigm describing the reality preceding all intersubjectivity and all action. "Truth" comes about by way of the relationship between two communicative levels; put briefly and concisely, these levels are those of reason and faith. "Truth discloses itself by way of the relationship between two communicative levels, namely, between the communication in which intersubjectively it is taken as a theme in and for itself and — e.g., in the form of assertions — actually implemented, and the communication that originally discloses that to which the claim to truth is actually referring."[40] This distinction allows Fischer to distinguish on the one hand between communication and action, and on the other, between communication and intersubjectivity. Both intersubjectivity *and* action are always preceded by the reality of communication. This step is of enormous significance, since Fischer finds in communication and in the ground of its possibility that particular "reality" to which theology has also always referred and on which it has always depended. It is a point of reference which theology neither can nor must ground or establish, but rather in which theology itself is grounded.[41] "All communication is determined and made possible from within a sphere beyond that which we constitute as the object of communication either as knowledge or as action or in the form of intersubjectively asserted claims to validity."[42] Fischer calls this "dimension" "spirit," though it is not to be equated with consciousness or self-consciousness; rather, it is the transcendental ground of communication and, as such, the presupposition of intersubjectivity and action.

Still maintaining an external perspective, Fischer now specifically addresses the issue of religious communication, which, with Lübbe, he understands as the processing of contingency which is appropriated communicatively and "transcends the meaning of action."[43] Religion thus discloses the sphere upon which reason is absolutely dependent, but does so necessarily in the dialectical tension of *real nonconcreteness* on the one hand and (*qua* the always necessary communicative need for concreteness) *unreal concreteness* on the other: "All this is admittedly possible only because this sphere which *in and of itself is non-concrete* (non-concrete compared with everything constituted and disclosed as the object of communication) is connected with *concrete notions of God, of the gods or powers* through which it becomes comprehensible and which are verified to religious consciousness in the corresponding experience of spirit."[44]

In his assessment Fischer presents as the structure of religious knowledge the generalization of a specifically Protestant understanding of the relationship, one strongly reminiscent of Hegel, between *fides quae creditur* and *fides qua creditur*.

This, however, has certain consequences for the structure of religious knowledge. The latter is spread out between two poles mutually oriented toward one another, namely, between its cognitive content through which the experience of spirit becomes comprehensible on the one hand, and the experience of spirit in which cognitive content is verified on the other. These two poles are directly juxtaposed within the process of religious communication; the concrete reference to reality with and in which communication takes place is confirmed, under certain circumstances quite effusively, in the non-concrete experience of the communicatively dynamic spirit.[45]

This general theory of communication and truth takes the place of ecclesiology by rendering unnecessary any explicit and substantive reference to those particular procedures and practices that constitute the church and to that which must be proclaimed and taught in a binding fashion in the church under all circumstances. Fischer is able to circumvent this because the dual polarity of his theory of religion is itself able to shift its center of gravity from the "pole" of faith's content to the "pole" of the nonconcrete "experience of the spirit," but without in the process damaging precisely that "content." Of course, he would like to keep the experience of the spirit and the content of faith closely juxtaposed. But because there is no third place between the "content" of the Christian "tradition" and individual appropriation in the form of spiritual formulation, this content is found only in the medium of individual appropriation. That is, in both tradition and ultimately in the canon of Scripture itself we encounter only a multiplicity of appropriated "reality." Such multiplicity has not, however, as Fischer believes, always inhered in the Christian faith, but has resulted from a quite specific construction of "faith" as "appropriating inwardness," that is, as faith that in and of itself is not ecclesially constituted, but rather already encompasses within itself the eclipse of the church.[46]

Indirectly, Fischer himself encounters the aporia inherent in this understanding of faith as totally oriented toward the pole of "spirituality." "Problems arise when the various religious orientations drift so far apart that the unity within the spirit can no longer be defined in any commonly accepted content of faith, thereby also calling into question the commonality of religious communication and especially the notion of common worship. Here pluralism itself becomes a danger to church unity. The rapid growth of syncretistic tendencies in the large 'people's churches' (Volkskirchen) poses an extremely serious problem in this regard." But is this syncretism really such a new phenomenon? Is such syncretism not emerging today with such vehemence in the Protestant churches precisely because the kind of understanding of faith favored by Fischer, namely, one oriented toward the experience of religious subjectivity, has enjoyed such wide acceptance there? And when he now inquires about a "commonality of spirit" oriented not toward "the spirit's cognitive identification and classification, but toward its manifestations and effects, for example, in the sense of peace or justice,"[47] although this may well be possible in certain individual cases, it certainly will not be able to ensure any enduring church unity. For it is precisely with regard to "peace" and "justice" that especially Christian "spirits" choose different paths, since the implementation of these "concerns," too, all too often reveals fundamental and ultimately "dogmatic" differences. There is probably no way out here precisely because the aporia inheres within the concept of faith itself.

Building on Fischer's justified concern with preserving *church* (not necessarily people's-church, *volkskirchlich*) unity, one might ask whether in order to withstand precisely the kind of differences that will unavoidably emerge at various levels, the "unity of spirit" does not need an element of pathos external to itself; that is, does it not need to be determined or defined through binding acts and through a *doctrina evangelii*, a teaching of the gospel, formulated explicitly in a confession? This horizon, rather than being appropriated spiritually, itself does the "appropriating," providing the backdrop against which and from which faith experiences itself as "created" and takes its orientation. It is this horizon that first makes it possible to identify the "spirit" of Jesus Christ. And only when theology explicitly understands itself from the perspective of this horizon does Christian tradition, the tradition toward which that theology is oriented, acquire concrete, binding contours. Only such theological reference to distinct normative practices and to binding, authoritative doctrine can offer the kind of juxtaposed presence making a genuine communicative task both possible and necessary. Fischer, however, leaves the "spirit" of communication in faith totally undefined — ecclesiologically undefined at that — or utterly cripples it by implicitly elevating the reality of the "people's church" *(Volkskirche)* to normative status.

The final consequence is that Fischer is unable to escape Harnack's perspective or to offer any resistance to it. For if one follows Fischer's theoretical lead, theology must inevitably become the academically constituted hermeneutic of orientation for meaning and life. It acquires its object, namely, Christian "tradition," exclusively from its contingent position in a society and culture (still) shaped by Christian tradition. Hence Peterson's assertion remains indirectly correct that ecclesiology, authoritative or binding doctrine, and the locus and understanding of the task of theology remain inextricably connected. Any bracketing or significant modification of the first two entities of necessity generates serious consequences for theology, and that means essentially for dogmatics. And though Fischer's analysis and solutions are ultimately (and this is their great service) just as farsighted[48] and wise as Harnack's perspective over against Peterson, still they both remain, to use Fischer's own basic distinction, completely caught in the communication horizon of reason, namely, of that "which is the case," or that which can be extrapolated from the tendencies evident within society. This, however, plunges theology into an insoluble self-contradiction. As a distinct academic and church undertaking, it can now reflect thematically on itself and on its object only from the external perspective of the communication horizon; yet doing so secretly transforms it into a completely different undertaking, namely, into an academically constituted hermeneutic of orientation for meaning and life.

All evidence suggests that this brings theology back to Harnack, namely, theology on the one hand as independent philosophy of religion (Fischer's general theory of truth and communication, with its imbedded theory of religious communication), and on the other hand as catechetical dogmatics (Fischer's hermeneutics of Christian tradition accompanying the realization of faith within the horizon of communication between those present). This, however, brings us *back* to Peterson's original query.

II. The Outline of the Argument

1. The Pathos of Theology: Beginning in and with the Church

Christian faith under the conditions of modernity experiences itself in a twofold difference: on the one hand in the context of the split in Western Christendom, and on the other with regard to a modernity that understands itself to be post-Christian. This double difference makes ecclesiological self-reflection necessary in a way quite unknown to pre-Reformation Christianity.[49]

If modern and, more recently, "postmodern" theology do refer to "reality," either they unavoidably make certain implicit and anticipatory ecclesiological decisions to the extent that they understand themselves as "Christian," or ecclesiology itself must become the topic of the prolegomena of a theology that understands itself as Christian.

In the present crisis of intellectual and spiritual orientation, theology has two choices. It can continue to take its orientation largely from a comprehensive concept of reason, one that does, however, under the conditions of postmodern criticism, increasingly become an explicit "project" itself, that is,

22

an intersubjectively appropriated "construction."[50] Or theology can understand itself directly and explicitly as "poiesis," that is, as a "construction," its creator being the religious subject who within the framework of its theological constructions conceptualizes certain, in the comprehensive sense, religious experiences and makes these experiences communicable. Precisely in its open dissent between a continuation of the "project of modernity" on the one hand and its various postmodern versions on the other, the result of postmetaphysical thinking is that reason is able to recognize itself only in that which it itself (intersubjectively or conventionally) produces, but will no longer be able to recognize any reality that lacks the element of construction.

If theology follows this lead uncritically, the unavoidable consequence will be the kind of free metaphorical constructivism characterizing especially North American Protestant theology in its more progressive representatives. For a critical reason that is itself no longer criticized theologically, everything that is already thought becomes transparent as a construction, a skeptical insight to which one can respond only with a better construction. Put succinctly, when under the conditions of postmetaphysical thinking a cognitive-theoretical grounding of theology as a discipline has become obsolete, two alternatives are possible. The first is a constructivist understanding of theology grounded in the constitution of the religious subject or of religious intersubjectivity and directed toward a life orientation and a pragmatic articulation or actualization of faith. This alternative, however, is conceivable only in explicit alienation from and simultaneous dependence on that which makes it possible in the first place, namely, the existence of certain core acts and practices of the church, the biblical canon, a dense dogmatic and theological tradition of discourse, and a still extant corpus of Christian tradition, one from which postmodern theology lives without being able to catch up *theologically* with the "real presence" of the church.

The other alternative would be *explicitly pneumatological* as well as *ecclesiological* prolegomena to Christian theology, that is, a development of the pathos that makes Christian theology plausible as a distinct church practice. This will be the focus in the following investigation, in which I will try to find an alternative to the pervasive constructivism of contemporary Protestant theology. Rather than attempting a fundamentalist act of positing, however, which only veils its distinctly poietic character, I will conduct a search in the form of a theological argument that itself tries to locate and articulate the *pathos* which core church practices have always implied and which is identical with the pathos of faith itself. In it, Christian theology encounters the truth, and in affirming this pathos Christian theology acquires the freedom that overcomes the modern alternative between autonomy and

23

heteronomy. The following investigation will thus attempt to articulate and reflect upon, both pneumatologically and ecclesiologically, the perspective that unavoidably presents itself to theology, that constitutes it, to which it is subject, and by which it is defined — when indeed it distinguishes itself from faith and yet simultaneously is grounded in that which constitutes faith's perception of reality. By inquiring about the pathos of theology, that is, about that which inevitably shapes Christian theology, about that from which theology cannot escape, namely, the reality whose truth actually constitutes its freedom, we are at the same time making theology transparent as a certain *practice* that within the horizon of its own pathos can indeed operate constructively without such construction becoming its determinative operational mode.

2. Preliminary Overview

In the following section I will first clarify the terms "pathos," "poiesis," "praxis," and "practice," since these terms are of crucial importance for the systematic problems regarding the nexus between "suffering/undergoing," "activity," and "production" within the actual engagement of theology. In the analysis of the key concepts "pathos," "poiesis," and "praxis," Aristotle and the conceptual history taking him as its point of departure will play a privileged role. I will also draw from both paradigmatic sources and, especially, from more recent scholarship, since I cannot offer here an exhaustive intellectual-historical presentation of these three terms but can only introduce them with an eye on the problems attaching to the investigation itself; that is, I can concentrate on them only as regards their worth as heuristic aids for theology as a distinct church activity.[51] Especially as regards the concept of pathos, I will quite early delimit its use in rhetoric from a more specific theological version that actually is sensed more strongly in the Latin translation of "pathos" as *passio*. In so doing I will draw not only on Luther's own theology but also on the emphasis on *passio* found in several important representatives of contemporary Luther research (Wilfried Joest, Gerhard Ebeling, Oswald Bayer). With regard to the concept of praxis, I will emphasize the decisive distinction between the more comprehensive notion of "praxis" on the one hand and the quite distinct, theologically structured notion of "practice" on the other. Only this distinction gives access to a multiplicity of distinct and interconnected practices that cannot simply be subsumed under the rubric of a comprehensive "praxis" but must be considered each in and for itself and with regard to their variously specific interconnections.

Instead of directly offering a pneumatological-ecclesiological account of the connection between church, doctrine, and theology, I will first consider in the second part two contemporary proposals from Protestant theology that implicitly take issue with the perspective of problems developed in the first part. Both theologians undertake to determine the locus and task of theology within the context of the collapse of the unified paradigm of reason; that is, both imply the facticity of what today is called "postmodernity,"[52] albeit without explicitly taking it as the point of departure (and certainly not as an attribute) of their theological proposals. Rather, it is characteristic of both proposals to inquire in this context concerning the pathos of theology, that is, concerning that which defines theology as genuine theological engagement, and how in this determination theology acquires its object. Both proposals demonstrate how the question concerning the pathos of theology brings theology itself into focus as a distinct practice, though only because this simultaneously addresses the topic of "church" implicitly and in part that of "doctrine" explicitly. At the same time, however, both proposals exhibit a thoroughgoing fundamental pneumatological as well as ecclesiological deficit and, in particular, an inadequate pneumatological and ecclesiological anchoring of church doctrine over against the practice of theology itself, which actually is to be distinguished from such doctrine. Both proposals, however, nonetheless do open constructive perspectives on how theology can be understood as a distinct church practice whose specific pathos takes the place of modern foundationalist strategies.

First I will engage the proposal of the American Lutheran theologian and ecumenist George Lindbeck, whose *Nature of Doctrine*[53] has already been discussed extensively in the United States. Lindbeck's proposal is intended as an alternative to modern, subject-centered models of religion and to premodern models oriented toward metaphysics. Its understanding of religion is based on Wittgenstein's philosophy of language and on the theory of culture of the anthropologist and ethnologist Clifford Geertz. In such religion the specific relationship between distinct practices and distinct linguistic disposition constitutes the horizon that always precedes the individual subject and unavoidably shapes that subject's experiences. This brings into structural focus the pathos of theology as a distinct practice between concrete life-acts, on the one hand, and the doctrine that articulates the grammar of faith on the other. My interpretation, analysis, and critique will try to delineate the plausibility of Lindbeck's cultural-linguistic model of religion from the perspective of its ecumenical "life setting" and to articulate the connection (posited in its implied ecclesiology) between the praxis of faith, theological discourse, and church doctrine. I will show how Lindbeck's model makes it possible to understand theology as a distinct practice shaped by the central acts of language and ceremony of the church, acts with which it remains inextricably related. At the same time, however, the substantively and ecumenically shaped formal character of his proposal prevents any explicit development of theological discourse as church practice, or of the substantive pathos characterizing the church itself.

In working out the substantive aspect of the pathos of theology as church practice in the following section of Part Two, I will analyze the work of the German Lutheran theologian Oswald Bayer, who draws considerably from Kant's friend and critic Johann Georg Hamann in developing his own theology, one oriented toward Luther and critical of modernity and of its foundationalist strategies. My interpretation and analysis of his understanding of theology will show that, although he does develop the pathos of theology without contradicting Lindbeck in any substantive fashion, he is unable to resolve the considerable tension between an obviously ecclesially rooted theology, on the one hand, and the lack of any explicit ecclesiology in the concept of theology and of a correspondingly *explicated* theological understanding of the locus of theology itself within the church on the other. Without any explicit ecclesiology, without any notion of the constitutive (core) practices oriented toward that understanding of ecclesiology, and without any concept of church doctrine (to be distinguished from theology itself), the various elements of his concept of theology remain unconnected. This seriously threatens the strength of his proposal, namely, its concentration on the pathos of theology and its understanding of theology's locus in worship.

My interpretation of the proposals of Lindbeck and Bayer discloses a constructive perspective on how theology can be understood as a distinct church practice whose specific pathos can replace modern foundationalist strategies. At the same time, however, both proposals exhibit a thoroughgoing fundamental pneumatological as well as ecclesiological deficit, in particular an inadequate pneumatological and ecclesiological anchoring and delimiting of church doctrine over against the practice of theology, which is to be distinguished precisely from that doctrine.

In the investigation's third part, I will attempt to overcome this deficit by inquiring after the pneumatological and ecclesiological logic of a concept of church doctrine and church practices that from the very outset constitutes the systematic-theological horizon for developing theology as a distinct church practice. I will first demonstrate the relevance of the pneumatological-ecclesiological problematic for the self-understanding of theology by examining the controversy between Erik Peterson and Karl Barth concerning the nature of theology. This controversy shows quite succinctly that as long as theology's relationship to church doctrine remains undefined, theology itself as a church practice will remain an inherently unstable undertaking. In an attempt to clarify this issue, Peterson proposed taking a christological-ecclesiological approach, Barth a pneumatological-ecclesiological one. Because of problematic pneumatological-ecclesiological alternatives, both proposals ultimately remain unconvincing even though they do offer heuristically valuable suggestions. In the remainder of Part Three, I will develop an alternative beyond Peterson and Barth, one doing justice to the central concerns of both and simultaneously helping to overcome the pneumatological-ecclesiological deficit in Lindbeck's and Bayer's proposals in the direction of a pathic theological discursive practice.

In this pneumatological-ecclesiological reflection I will develop a notion of the church as the soteriological locus of God's actions, as a space constituted by specific core practices and church doctrine. These practices are understood pneumatologically as acts to be interpreted enhypostatically as "works" of the Spirit. Rather than being self-grounded, they participate in the being of the Spirit as the latter's work in the Spirit's mission of the triune God's economy of salvation. Within this constructive explication, I will refer to the neo-economic doctrine of the Trinity (Pannenberg, Jenson, et al.), to the *communio*-ecclesiology of Orthodox theologians (Zizioulas, Nissiotis, Staniloae), and to the proposals of various Finnish Luther scholars (Martikainen, Mannermaa, Peura) whose contributions are shaped by dialogue with Russian Orthodox theology. Luther's own theology, especially his concept of *doctrina* and core aspects of the writings *The Bondage of the Will* and "On the Councils and Churches," will also play a central role in this section.

I will first demonstrate that the trinitarian implications of the *communio*-ecclesiology make it possible to overcome the pneumatological-ecclesiological alternative between "act" and "being," "event" and "institution." I will then continue this train of thought by examining Luther's ecclesiological conception in "On the Councils and Churches," explicating the church from the perspective of certain constitutive core practices which, as the work of the Spirit in its mission of the triune God's economy of salvation, simultaneously participate in the being of the Spirit itself. With reference to Luther's concept of *doctrina*, I will show how something similar applies to church doctrine, how, commensurate with this pneumatological-ecclesiological reconstruction, core practices and church doctrine constitute the pathos of theology as church practice.

After examining in Part Three the pneumatological-ecclesiological horizon constituting the pathos of theology as a church practice, in Part Four I articulate its various aspects. I show first that the pneumatological disposition of this pathos, rather than representing theology's problematic and false restriction and lack of freedom, is actually the very core of that freedom. Building on Robert Jenson's interpretation of Luther's *The Bondage of the Will*, I explicate theology's freedom as participation in God's own freedom, which is identical with the trinitarian economy of salvation. The ground of theology's freedom emerges as its pathos, its *vita passiva* in its concrete connection with and dependence on core church practices and church doctrine, which in their own turn are to be understood as works of the Holy Spirit. By contrast, every other merely critical or negative concept of freedom remains theologically unsatisfactory because it forces us to conceptualize this freedom over against the works of the Holy Spirit. A substantive concept of freedom, however, one understood as being identical with the economy of salvation, allows us to understand the practice of theology as participation in God's own freedom.

I then develop a theologically grounded understanding of the "church *as public*" constituted through core practices and church doctrine. Not only is theology conceivable in the larger sense as a church practice within such a public entity, it is also both characteristic and necessary for the kind of public the church represents according to this pneumatological-ecclesiological model. For every public is defined by its own characteristic telos, one repeatedly explicated and reflected upon in this public within the framework of a distinct discourse practice, a practice which in its own turn participates in the telos of the public itself. I thus understand theology as a church practice entirely from the perspective of this soteriological telos characterizing the church as a public sphere. Within the framework of theology as a church practice, an account is rendered both internally and externally concerning the proclamation, life, and doctrine of the church; at the same time, an ongoing discussion continues between the church and the political, cultural, economic, religious, and intellectual configurations in which it finds itself and which are found in it as well. If the church collapses as a public sphere insofar as the normative status of the core practices and of church doctrine is abandoned, then theology also loses its locus and purpose as a distinct church practice. It is replaced by a variety of theologies bound to specific individual or group identities as a form of self-reflection or as a representative of those groups' interests, and by various forms of theological discourse predetermined by one or several other public entities and at least at first belonging primarily to those entities; such discourse can include that of "civil religion," as this characterizes the democratic community, or academic discourse on religion at modern universities. I will emphasize that although one must indeed preserve Christian theology as a contemporaneous practice with these public entities, this must always presuppose the church itself as a public as well as the characteristic theological discourse specific to the church.

In a third step I then outline the characteristic features of theology as a church practice defined from the perspective of the salvific-economic telos of the church as a public sphere. The pathos of theology as church practice consists in participating in the salvific-economic telos of the specific public that is the "church." This definition of theology as church practice yields three central characteristics of theology: the discursive-argumentative aspect, the aspect of theological perception and of theological judgment, and the presentative aspect of communication. I do not, however, present any fully developed "theory of theology as church practice," but try rather to outline briefly the implications of this pneumatological-ecclesiological understanding of theology as church practice, that is, the implications of the pathos of theology for actually engaging in this practice.

III. Considerations of Heuristics:
Pathos and Poiesis, Praxis and Practice

In this section I will introduce the concepts of "pathos," "poiesis," "praxis," and "practice," several of which were already used earlier in a more cursory fashion in formulating the problems of the present study. Because these terms constitute the heuristic conceptual framework of my investigation, it is appropriate to discuss them more explicitly at this point. Rather than presenting an overall conceptual history, however, brief remarks on that conceptual history can serve to clarify and delimit the central key terms with reference to one another. My primary interest is systematic rather than historical, that is, with identifying the theological intentions accompanying these concepts.

1. Pathos

This particular category of interpretation is the most difficult and unwieldy because the following investigation uses it in its original mode, one far removed from the mainstream of the conceptual history of "pathos" and from its contemporary usage. For "pathos . . . originally referred to any kind of suffering in the sense of undergoing or incurring as opposed to acting or doing, and outside philosophical usage especially to misfortune and bad luck." It is this original meaning with which I am here concerned, with "suffering, un-

29

dergoing" as opposed to "doing." It first entered philosophical vocabulary in this form as well, namely, in Aristotle, "as that which comes upon or happens to every existing entity."[54] In his *Metaphysics,* Aristotle closely associates this concept with those of *"accidens"* and "quality."[55] *Pathos/paschein* means first of all generally being qualified or affected in a specific way. Beginning already with the pre-Socratics, however, and extending to Plato and the Stoics, the term "pathos" is understood as referring to the affections of the soul. The concept then makes genuine history as a technical term in rhetorical theory, in the doctrine of the sublime, and in aesthetics.[56]

Heidegger was the first to return to the original meaning of the term by suggesting that one translate "pathos" as "tuning" (or "mood," *Stimmung*), albeit precisely not in the contemporary psychological sense but as a "disposition" that is simultaneously both "disposition and determination."[57] His use of "pathos" touches indirectly on the particular element in the word that I will articulate in a theologically more precise sense in what follows. In θαυμάζειν, a person is affected by being; in astonishment, that person "undergoes" or "is subject to" being. Heidegger characterizes the beginning of Greek philosophy as the pathos of astonishment, though not in the sense of a catalyst which, once philosophy was in motion, would become superfluous. "Astonishment is ἀρχή — it pervades every step of philosophy. Astonishment is πάθος."[58] Being affected by being takes place in astonishment; this means undergoing or suffering that which is, becoming aware of it or perceiving it. Heidegger's understanding of the concept of "pathos" will prove to be quite helpful in examining the pathos characterizing Christian theology.

An inquiry concerning the *archē* of Christian faith and of Christian theology brings us to the kind of pathos in question here. By drawing upon the conceptual usage in Aristotle and Heidegger, I am thus not referring to the human affections or to the pathos that is of central significance in the theory of rhetoric which has recently been developed in connection with theology in interesting ways.[59] The reference is rather to the "other" of action, that which determines or defines a person prior to all action, in all action, and against all action, that which a person can only *receive.*

According to Heidegger, the pathos of astonishment at being stands at the beginning of Greek philosophy. The biblical pathos of faith might similarly be understood from the perspective of Psalm 8. In view of the wondrous nature of creation, the psalmist asks in astonishment, "what are human beings that you are mindful of them?" God's specific action here, namely, that he is mindful of human beings, "determines" the believing psalmist in Psalm 8 and, with him, all human beings *qua* creatures.[60] The quality of a certain "determination" which a person's being acquires before God and from God (as creature, as sinner, and as new creation) is the pathos characterizing the core of Christian existence.[61]

Luther has provided the most focused and explicit theological explication of the pathic heart of Christian existence; moreover, he explicates it in a way that also understands pathos as characterizing what it means to do theology. Luther does not, however, address this under the rubric of the Greek term *pathos*, but within the terminology into which this Greek *pathos* and all its semantic variants have been translated into Latin, namely, as *passio*.[62] Theology participates in a fundamental way in this *passio* because it is essentially identical with faith.[63] It is the origin and center of Christian existence. The *vita activa* then emerges from the *vita passiva* of faith; pathos issues in poiesis and praxis while never really leaving the horizon of pathos.[64]

For Luther, the center of pathic existence is the *audire*, the receptivity that faith itself is:

> Hearing is faith; but it is faith not as the act of appropriation on the basis of some spiritual potency of its essence enabling a person to perform this act. . . . Faith appears rather as the *surrender* of any performance of actions, as the *surrender* of all potency and life formation . . . to the *operari* of God. Through faith, a person "follows" "the word"; one allows oneself to be controlled by its power. Here the *audire* is thus an antithetical concept to *operari*. . . . For Luther, the passive moment of being positioned and being silenced stands over against the *videre, capere, operari, etc.*[65]

Joest describes this *audire* as a "surrender to the presence of God himself."[66] Here the notion of *audire* as the actualization mode of pathos points directly to the decisive element of pathos within the theological context, namely, the *surrender to God's presence such that this presence defines or determines us and in so doing inevitably also defines or determines our theological discourse.*

We will inquire later whether this exhausts the notion of pathos as the latter characterizes theology. *What is certain at this point, however, is that the following discussion will concern itself with this particular theologically defined pathos, a pathos transcending both its Aristotelian-metaphysical and its Heideggerian-ontological understanding. Not only does God's action "determine" human beings qualitatively (as regards accidens), it also creates them as both creature and as new creation. This human pathos (and that of the theologian) corresponds to God's own poiesis, the poiesis of the Holy Spirit to which all theology is subjected and which is presented to theology in a quite specific way.*

Theological discourse not shaped by this specific notion of divine poiesis and thus not pathically constituted can only "objectify," that is, idolize

31

God by producing conceptual products through poietically argumentative and imaginative power, products which conceal God and justify the theological subject controlling this discourse. By contrast, theological discourse "free of works" is one shaped primarily by pathos and one in which the human being remains "de-centered."

2. Poiesis

Both "poiesis" and "praxis" are to be understood in a quite specific way as the counterconcepts to "pathos." To the extent that they, as "initiators," are antithetical to the passive notion of suffering and undergoing, they originally could be used synonymously as performance and action; the narrower confines of philosophical usage, however, soon came to differentiate between them.[67]

For Plato poiesis refers to both natural and artificial production.[68] In distinguishing between divine and human poiesis, he understands divine poiesis as producing that which one usually ascribes to nature, and human poiesis as producing that which humans make out of nature.[69]

Aristotle was the first to clarify conceptually the relationship between poiesis and praxis. He limits the term "poiesis" to artistic production and then differentiates more strongly than does Plato between this particular kind on the one hand and natural generation on the other. "That which exists in nature is generated by its own kind, and carries its own developmental principle (τέλος) within itself. The original cause of something produced as a work is found in the person who creates."[70] For Aristotle, all meaningful action is oriented toward a goal, the goal of poiesis residing outside poiesis itself, in the work (ἔργον), while the goal of praxis inheres within praxis itself (ἐνέργεια).[71] Poiesis and praxis thus share a reference to what is changeable in contradistinction to the eternal and to that which is generated naturally, to which theoria refers. They are different, however, inasmuch as the foundation of poiesis is technē, that of praxis aretē. Poiesis is generative activity whose criterion of quality resides in the work alone, while praxis is an action whose criterion of quality resides both in the action itself and in the character of the agent.

Plotinus's identification of poiesis and praxis then has far-reaching consequences. "For Plotinus, the highest One, as the origin of everything, 'creates' (ποιεῖ) not only the other, but also itself. This One's poiesis, however, does not create any work outside itself . . . but rather remains creatively with itself, observing itself, and is pure energeia and theoria."[72] In modernity, and after Hegel has once again picked up Plotinus's core intention, this results in the Marxist reversal of Hegel, namely, in praxis in the genuine sense always being understood as "poietic"; that is, human beings produce themselves first only through such "praxis."[73]

That to which poiesis actually refers is preserved and continued most directly in the concept of *poesy*, "which refers to an activity that produces something, to creation, in particular to the poetic creation, the poetic arts, the poem."[74] This is not the place, of course, to examine the history of poetics. My main concern is to articulate the theologically relevant potential contained in the concept of poesy as an explication and articulation of poiesis, a potential belonging to the core inventory of modernity, namely, the notion of human *autopoiesis*.[75] The early Fichte understood this philosophically as the subject's radical self-positing, while Hölderlin and Schelling understood it poetologically, Marx economically,[76] and social theoreticians such as Cornelius Castoriadis politologically.[77]

This poetic articulation of poiesis essentially involves a creative relationship with the world through which human beings engage themselves and in which imagination, either individual or collective, plays a central role.[78] In this context a central aspect of theology as church practice is at stake. Under the conditions of modernity with its postmetaphysical understanding of the sciences at large, one oriented specifically toward the natural sciences, theology has the opportunity of understanding itself as a poietic undertaking instead of viewing itself exclusively within the historical paradigm. In the United States of America, "constructive theology" embodies this self-understanding paradigmatically by developing structures of meaning by way of new metaphors; these in their own turn then offer horizons of meaning that function as guides for human action in the face of modern configurations in society and science. The result is a kind of metaphorical constructivism[79] through which poiesis both creates meaning and guides action. Its characteristic feature is productivity, and its criterion of quality is its degree of persuasiveness and the orientational strength of its "products."[80] The background to this is the tradition of pragmatism deriving from Emerson, a tradition understanding human praxis wholly as poiesis, indeed, as *autopoiesis*, and one the American religious historian Sidney Ahlstrom could call "American religion."[81] By giving a socially relevant dimension to a central feature of Idealism and of Romanticism, this view allows creative activity to become the formative principle of a new, democratic society.[82]

Against this background, and in view of metaphorical constructivism, the question arises regarding just what place poiesis occupies in Protestant theology. Is it on the whole to be understood primarily and perhaps even exclusively as "constructive" in the poetic sense? In that case, poiesis would be its genuine and exclusive identity. Or is it to be defined as poiesis only in connection with pathos? If so, one would have to clarify the specific relationship between the pathos and the poiesis of theology.

By understanding pathos as an integral part of poiesis, we view it as an experiential moment of the productively active (productive in the sense of the imagination) theological subject. If pathos itself remains determinative of poiesis, however, and if the poiesis of theology remains strictly oriented toward this pathos, then one can derive poiesis from pathos in a twofold manner: first as the poiesis of God underlying the pathos of both faith and theology; second as the poietic pathos of theology as a communicative-presentative church practice.

In the following discussion I will show that this location of poiesis within the actual engagement of theology determines the character of theology as specifically Christian theology. A theology understanding God's actions as the poiesis constituting the pathos of faith and of theology needs theological *phronesis,* the theological power of judgment making it capable of both theological knowledge and theological decisions. That, precisely, is not poiesis at all but dogmatic practice! In metaphorical constructivism, in contrast, poiesis replaces praxis and pathos simultaneously changes, moving anew (and secretly) toward Heidegger: the mystery of being that is best disclosed by the poet. Quite logically, here, too, dogmatics as the practice of judgment is no longer possible.

The pathos constituted by God's own poiesis, however, is something different. It is not accessible independent of the canonical witness of Scripture, nor independent of word, sacrament, or the church. It is pneumatologically specific pathos and characterizes theology in a binding fashion.

3. Praxis and Practice

Because of the complex conceptual history of the term "praxis,"[83] I will restrict the following sketch to the Aristotelian use of the term and try to clarify the latter by delimiting it in a threefold fashion. For the present study, the distinction between "praxis" and "practice" is of particular relevance inasmuch as I will examine theology as one church *practice* among others within the comprehensive *praxis* of faith.

In Aristotle the concept of "praxis" is best understood in its delimitation from the counterconcepts of "poiesis" and "theory." I have already discussed above the *distinction* between poiesis and praxis, and will here reintro-

34

duce it by way of a succinct formulation by Rüdiger Bubner. Bubner writes that "poiesis is oriented toward the objective products it produces such that at the end of the process of production, this activity has brought forth things in the world that nonetheless exist over against this very activity itself. Praxis concentrates entirely on the process of engagement or actualization in and for itself by actualizing its goal within the act. The attainment of practical goals coincides with the performance of the action such that no produced object remains after the conclusion of the praxis."[84] Simple examples quickly come to mind, such as the construction of a house as opposed to a city council meeting, and so on. Interestingly, Aristotle uses the term "praxis" to refer not only to the cooperative actions of free citizens in the polis, but also in the emphatic sense to life praxis whose goal is a happy life (εὐδαιμονία).[85] This actualization of life in the comprehensive sense is thus not poiesis, since the result of this actualization is not a "product" representing an entity independent of the activity of actualization.[86]

For Aristotle, and with him the entirety of Greek philosophy, the distinction between *theory* and *praxis* is of almost greater significance than that between poiesis and praxis. This distinction is as simple as it is profound, and has continued to exert at least indirect influence even into contemporary philosophy. "Theory" refers to the immutable and eternal, "praxis" to the mutable and variable.[87] The spheres of theory and praxis are incommensurable. Through theoretical contemplation, a person becomes aware of the order and harmony of timeless being, being residing beyond the human capacity for construction and manipulation.[88]

The final important distinction is that between *praxis* and *practice*. This distinction does not actually derive directly from Aristotle, and with it I am referring to a particular, pointed articulation of the Aristotelian concept of praxis undertaken by Alasdair MacIntyre in his book *After Virtue*. By *practice*, he understands "any coherent and complex form of socially established cooperative human activity through which goods internal to that form of activity are realized in the course of trying to achieve those standards of excellence which are appropriate to, and partially definitive of, that form of activity, with the result that human powers to achieve excellence, and human conceptions of the ends and goods involved, are systematically extended."[89] But while bricklaying and planting turnips do not qualify as "practice" according to this understanding, architecture and agriculture do. Similarly, chess, the arts and sciences, sports, politics in the Aristotelian sense, and the cultivation of family life are all "practices" in this sense. Now, MacIntyre articulates this pointed definition of "practice" with a distinct goal in mind, a goal that *cannot* be of concern in what follows, namely, the establishment of the necessity of virtues in a teleologically structured theory of action not directly dependent on Aristotelian biology and ontology.[90]

I will also draw on MacIntyre's distinction, one already anticipated in Aristotle, between a comprehensive life praxis on the one hand and specific contexts of action directed toward quite specific goods on the other.[91] Aristotle takes as his reference point the life-form of the free citizen of the polis in articulating the notion of simple "doing" and of reflected, legally recoverable action within the framework of an indefinite, broad concept of praxis; such "doing" acquires concrete contours first only in its juxtaposition with poiesis and theory. By contrast, the concept of "practice" refers in what follows to *distinct, describable, and meaningful contexts of action that are cooperatively and implicitly ordered and regulated.*[92]

With regard to Christian faith and theology, Oswald Bayer illuminates this issue nicely in his characterization of the relationship between faith and theology in Luther. According to Bayer, Luther understands the *vita passiva* of faith as a separate, comprehensive praxis, as a distinct *bios:* "Luther's understanding of theology and faith as praxis shatters in any event the Aristotelian understanding of praxis and simultaneously the attendant juxtaposition of *theoria* and *praxis.* Luther's concept of theology classifies faith neither under nor over the *vita activa* or *vita contemplativa.* For Luther . . . theology and faith constitute a *vita sui generis:* the *vita passiva.*"[93]

Of course, in this double delimitation Bayer is thinking on the one hand of the concrete life-form of the "theoretician," the *vita contemplativa,* and on the other of that of the free citizen, the *vita activa.* Faith and theology in the Reformation sense can be classified according to neither of these two life-forms.[94] Within the framework of Aristotelian terminology, he can, however, refer to a genuine *bios* (i.e., a *praxis tis*) characterized by a direct grounding in God's salvific actions. In characterizing the *vita passiva* as a separate comprehensive praxis, Bayer articulates an important Aristotelian point, namely, that of temporality. This temporality, however, does not stand in any incommensurable antithesis to eternity; the eternal God has entered into time and has "made history" in time. This alone disqualifies this God from being identified with the God of Aristotelian metaphysics; it also shatters the fundamental Aristotelian distinction between the immutable-eternal of the cosmos on the one hand and the changeable-mortal of human affairs on the other *(polis/oikos),* a distinction determinative for the entirety of ancient philosophy.

Christian faith, as a *bios sui generis,* is called forth and maintained by distinct temporal acts and procedures such as proclamation of the gospel, baptism, the Lord's Supper, and so on; its object is God's own salvific activity as carried out in the life, death, and resurrection of Jesus of Nazareth. And because both faith and theology are grounded in God's salvific action, and in the strict sense are his works, they are also bound to God's time. This is why faith and theology cannot be *contemplatio/theoria* in the strictly Aristotelian sense. Just as little, however, can they be part of the other life-form, namely, the *vita activa,* the praxis of free citizens, since this life-form is grounded in free human action rather than in God's salvific action. Faith is to be understood rather as *vita passiva,* as a *bios* grounded in God's salvific activity, a *bios* that rather than appearing in an abstract sense is grounded in and bound to specific activities of actualization; so also, then, must theology itself be understood as a specific activity inhering in precisely this *bios* of faith.

This is what I mean when in the following discussion I refer to theology as a *practice,* though also when I refer to *core church practices,* that is, complex and quite distinct contexts of action constituting and characterizing the church. These practices are grounded in a distinct *bios;* that is, they are activities of actualization inhering in a quite distinct comprehensive praxis. Whereas some of them are of constitutive significance for this praxis,[95] others are inherently necessary without being constitutive.[96] Still others can inhere within the praxis without being either necessary or constitutive.[97]

In the following discussion, "practices" will refer to activities in the sense just described. In contradistinction to "processes," their purpose and goal are not their resulting "products."[98] The "products" that do result within the framework of practices, however (such as sermons for the purpose of proclamation, catechisms for the purpose of instruction, books within the context of theological discourse), represent instances of actualization of the given practice which remain subordinated to the latter's specific purpose and must be evaluated from the perspective of that purpose.[99]

PART TWO

The Pathos of Theology and the Implied Question of Church and Church Doctrine

Instead of embarking directly on a pneumatological as well as ecclesiological reflection on the relationship between church, doctrine, and theology, in this part I will first engage the proposals of two contemporary Protestant theologians who implicitly address the problems discussed in Part One. Both theologians, George Lindbeck and Oswald Bayer, are concerned with the locus and task of theology following the collapse of the unified paradigm of reason. Both imply the existence of what is known today as "postmodernity,"[1] albeit without explicitly taking it as their point of departure or making it into an attribute of their theological proposals. Rather, both theologians inquire in this context concerning the pathos of theology, that is, concerning that which shapes theology as a genuine activity, and concerning how theology so defined acquires its object. An examination of both proposals shows how this question concerning the pathos of theology brings theology itself into focus as a distinct practice, though only because this simultaneously involves an implicit examination of "church" and an in-part explicit examination of "doctrine" or "teaching." Both proposals, however, exhibit a basic deficit manifesting itself especially in an inadequate pneumatological-ecclesiological anchoring of church doctrine over against the practice of theology, a practice that in fact is to be distinguished from doctrine. At the same time, however, the proposals of Lindbeck and Bayer open up a constructive perspective from which theol-

39

ogy can be understood as a distinct church practice whose specific pathos replaces modern strategies of ultimate grounding.

Other theological proposals could doubtless also have been chosen. I was concerned, however, with choosing two Lutheran theologians who explicitly examine the *verbum externum* as the pathos of theology. Lindbeck does so structurally with regard to religion in the larger sense, then structurally with regard to Christianity in focusing specifically on the biblical canon. By contrast, Bayer does so with regard to the promise of the gospel. In Part Three, I then focus on the economy of salvation in articulating this *verbum externum* in a pneumatological and ecclesiological reflection that takes special note of Luther's theology and draws from central impulses of Eastern Orthodox *communio*-ecclesiology. In this way I am able to overcome the deficient pneumatology of both Lindbeck and Bayer, a pneumatology which in its own turn is responsible for the absence of an ecclesiologically precise concept of doctrine or teaching. Against this background I develop in Part Four an account of theology as a church practice whose pathos can be developed from the perspective of both the Trinity and the economy of salvation, and which as a church practice participates in the telos of the public expression of the Holy Spirit.

I. The Praxis of Faith as the Pathos of Theology: George Lindbeck

The unique feature in George Lindbeck's proposal[2] is an understanding of religion developed against the backdrop of Ludwig Wittgenstein's philosophy of language and the anthropologist and ethnologist Clifford Geertz's theory of culture. He develops this cultural-linguistic model of religion by way of an ideal-typical contrast with the premodern model of religion oriented toward classical metaphysics, on the one hand, and the modern, subject-centered model of religion on the other. In Lindbeck's model the given nexus of distinct practices and a specific linguistic configuration constitute the horizon that always precedes the individual subject and of necessity structurally shapes that subject's experiences. This model structurally articulates theology as a distinct practice between the concrete activities of life on the one hand and "doctrine" on the other, the latter of which articulates the grammar of faith. In the following interpretation, analysis, and critique, I will examine the plausibility of Lindbeck's cultural-linguistic model of religion from the perspective of its ecumenical "life setting," and will delineate the relationship posited in its implicit ecclesiology between the praxis of faith, theological discourse, and church doctrine. My goal is to demonstrate how Lindbeck's model makes it possible to understand theology as a distinct practice shaped by the characteristic features of language and action, as a practice oriented toward these activities and inseparable from them. As will be seen, however, the substantively and ecumenically qualified formal character of Lindbeck's proposal precludes any explicit, concrete development of theological discourse as a church practice and of the substantive pathos characterizing the church itself.

1. Ecumenical Dialogue as Background and Cognitive Guide for the Cultural-Linguistic Proposal

The background to Lindbeck's proposal is his lengthy and intensive participation in ecumenical dialogue[3] between the Lutheran churches and the Roman Catholic churches, and in particular his specific experience within that dialogue, namely, that in many cases a consensus was possible with regard to doctrinal differences without either side having to compromise its own dogmatic and doctrinal tradition.[4] The desire to find a plausible hermeneutic of theology and doctrine that does justice to this phenomenon constitutes the immediate cognitive guide in Lindbeck's theory of religion,[5] a theory that does, however, ultimately transcend this specific concern by developing a comprehensive hermeneutic of religious speech and of a corresponding mode for doctrinal formation.

By calling his own proposal "postliberal," Lindbeck is taking issue with the contemporary Protestant understanding of religion regnant in the American theological debate. His goal is to find a third path beyond theological liberalism, that is, one beyond premodern orthodoxy and modern liberalism. In this specific sense of a delimitation from modern theological liberalism, liberalism characterized by the "turn to the subject,"[6] Lindbeck's proposal presupposes and draws on central elements of postmodernity. The background to his proposal is on the one hand Wittgenstein's "linguistic turn,"[7] the turn to the anteriority of linguistic and cultural systems, and on the other the most recent cultural-anthropological research.[8]

Lindbeck is also "postmodern" insofar as he intends to abandon the object- and subject-centered foundationalist strategies of the ultimate grounding of truth typical of modernity.[9] First, these include the notion that faith is grounded in a series of propositions concerning objects accessible to our rational perception: God, eternity, soul, incarnation, attested by supranatural revelation and the fulfillment of prophecies. Second, Lindbeck's model tries

41

to overcome the decidedly modern viewpoint according to which Christian concepts of faith represent forms of expression for experiences that basically precede these. The modernist understanding of religion characteristically locates the situation of "undergoing" a given religious experience entirely in the pre-linguistic and pre-reflective interiority of the subject, who then articulates this experience in language through constructive-poietic activity and expresses it in nondiscursive symbols. This subjective-poietic activity is the constitutive element of the expression of faith, while the religious experience itself, like Kant's "thing-in-itself," is *ineffabilis,* remaining "beyond" language in the subject. Only the latter's imaginative poiesis provides the bridge between the absolute privacy of religious experiences on the one hand and the public expression of mediated, nondiscursive beliefs on the other.

In a cognitive-methodological sense, however, it is decisive for Lindbeck that neither the theory of truth of premodern orthodoxy nor that of modern liberalism is able to conceptualize adequately the phenomenon of an interpretation or reformulation of church doctrine that would both be capable of establishing a consensus and stand in continuity with previously contradictory or mutually exclusive doctrinal positions. That is, a concrete theological and ecumenically urgent substantive problem rather than a change of fashion in philosophy and theology prompted Lindbeck to formulate his own cultural-linguistic proposal. Hence the following three "theories of religion" by no means represent merely different abstract schemata according to which theologies might be classified; rather, the typology shows that the cultural-linguistic perspective is capable of developing a new paradigm of theology and especially of ecclesiastical doctrinal propositions capable of explicating a practice whose plausibility the other two paradigms fail to account for, namely, the practice of ecumenical agreement concerning ecclesiastical doctrinal propositions.

Before examining critically the implications of Lindbeck's cultural-linguistic model of religion, I must first delimit his model more precisely from the alternatives.

2. The Two Traditional Ways of Viewing Religion

a. The Cognitive-Propositional Model:
Fides Quae Creditur *without* Fides Qua Creditur

This model places cognitive aspects completely in the foreground "and stresses the ways in which church doctrines function as informative propositions or truth claims about objective realities."[10] It understands religions as being similar to philosophy and science insofar as the latter produce worldviews commensurate with truth. Accordingly, the model also understands theology as an undertaking comprehensively and coherently formulating truth claims from sources of revelation and/or reason.

The main problem the cognitive-propositional model presents for ecumenical dialogue is that the formation of consensus creates only losers, or only a winner and a loser, a situation not only hindering consensus but contradicting the concrete experience of ecumenical consensus in the first place. Doctrinal consensus in this model means one of two things. The first is that both of the previous, contradictory doctrinal positions were false to begin with, and that a new formulation has been reached. This alternative creates only losers, since the new consensus cannot possibly be identical with the previous doctrinal positions. The second is that the consensus carries forward one or the other of the conflicting doctrinal positions, remains thus identical with that position, the consequence being that the alternative position has now been proven false. This aporetic situation arises because this model understands doctrinal positions directly in the sense of a correspondence with the truth, and does not distinguish between first- and second-order theological statements (doctrinal propositions).

b. The Experiential-Expressive Model: Fides Qua Creditur *without* Fides Quae Creditur[11]

Whereas the preliberal model understood religion in analogy to metaphysics, the liberal model understands it in analogy to aesthetics. Here Lindbeck is obviously orienting these prototypical models toward the change in European theology from pre-Kantian, classical orthodoxy to post-Kantian theology of the sort exemplified especially by Schleiermacher. Whereas the first model took its orientation from an "objective" reality, the second is characterized by the "turn to the subject" and by the latter's constitutive role for all explicit "religion." This model understands religions as different systems of expression of inner feelings and attitudes and of existential orientations. These symbolic systems have a strictly nondiscursive, nonpropositional character; that is, they make no immediate and definitive statements about reality, offering instead the interpretive expression of individual "inner," pre-reflexive "experiences." In this context different religious scholars raise the question whether all religions are not ultimately dealing with the same basic experience. In Lindbeck's own words, "there is thus at least the logical possibility that a Buddhist and a Christian might have basically the same faith, although expressed very differently."[12] This model understands theology either as being purely descriptive (second-order language) insofar as it coherently presents and interprets a given group's expressions of faith, or as being radically poietic-constructive insofar as it brings religious experience to immediate expression (first-order language) with the aid of metaphorical constructions and in so doing also interprets it.[13]

This model presents considerable difficulties for ecumenical dialogue insofar as doctrinal statements and dogmas can constantly change meaning here or can even become completely meaningless. On the one hand, this model makes even the possibility of any enduring identity of doctrinal statements extremely questionable, considering that the latter reflect merely the spatially and temporally qualified manifestations of collective religious disposition. On the other hand, ecumenical consensus through dialogue is impossible because the doctrines themselves must be the interpretive expression of religious experience in order to be "authentic" in the first place, something ecumenical dialogue can hardly provide. This model is thus useless for ecumenical dialogue, since doctrines here make no truth claims whatever, raising claims instead to "authenticity." The latter, however, is dependent on the concrete disposition of religious subjects and as such cannot possibly be the object of consensus-oriented dialogue.

3. The Cultural-Linguistic Model — Religion as Verbum Externum: *Joining* Fides Quae Creditur *and* Fides Qua Creditur

Drawing from the linguistic-philosophical work of Ludwig Wittgenstein and the cultural-anthropological method of Clifford Geertz, Lindbeck counters these two models with a third, one understanding religions "as comprehensive interpretive schemes, usually embodied in myths or narratives and heavily ritualized, which structure human experience and understanding of self and world."[14] According to this model,

> a religion can be viewed as a kind of cultural and/or linguistic framework or medium that shapes the entirety of life and thought. It functions somewhat like a Kantian *a priori*, although in this case the *a priori* is a set of acquired skills that could be different. It is not primarily an array of beliefs about the true and the good (though it may involve these), or a symbolism expressive of basic attitudes, feelings, or sentiments (though these will be generated). Rather, it is similar to an idiom that makes possible the description of realities, the formulation of beliefs, and the experiencing of inner

44

attitudes, feelings, and sentiments. Like a culture or language, it is a communal phenomenon that shapes the subjectivities of individuals rather than being primarily a manifestation of those subjectivities. It comprises a vocabulary of discursive and nondiscursive symbols together with a distinctive logic or grammar in terms of which this vocabulary can be meaningfully deployed. Lastly, just as a language (or "language game," to use Wittgenstein's phrase) is correlated with a form of life, and just as a culture has both cognitive and behavioral dimensions, so it is also in the case of a religious tradition. Its doctrines, cosmic stories or myths, and ethical directives are integrally related to the rituals it practices, the sentiments or experiences it evokes, the actions it recommends, and the institutional forms it develops. All this is involved in comparing a religion to a cultural-linguistic system.[15]

The great advantage of this model for ecumenical dialogue is obvious. Doctrines can now be understood as second-order statements in the sense of rules or regulations which themselves do not make any immediate truth claims, but which rather regulate language and activities of the first order; only the latter raise any truth claims. Lindbeck considers the decisive advantage of the cultural-linguistic perspective to be this specific referential neutrality, that is, the bracketing out of the ontological or correspondential truth of dogmas.[16]

a. Poietic Pathos within the Cultural-Linguistic Life Praxis

Lindbeck understands the pathos characterizing theology in the cultural-linguistic model as a comprehensive reality constituted by an indispensable network of language and ritualized activities. A person is always a part of these activities; they constitute the horizon that can only be replaced by a new one but never transcended.

According to this model, faith is actualized within these contexts of language and activity that themselves actualize the content of faith. As such, this model is characterized by the *inseparable juxtaposition of faith actualization and faith content, of* fides qua *and* fides quae. The engagement in faith is tied to concrete, interconnected configurations of language and behavior that always refer to the concrete content of faith. At the same time, this content of faith is comprehensible only within the referential mode of the actualization of faith itself. By contrast, the cognitive-propositional and experiential-expressive models are characterized by a strict separation of the content of faith and the actualization of faith. Whereas the former concentrates completely

45

on the establishment of the truths of faith, understanding the actualization of faith as the simple acknowledgment of these truths and subordinating it to them, the latter places the religious subject and its experience of faith at the center and understands the content of faith as a nondiscursive mode of expression of this religious subject.

The cultural-linguistic model intends to overcome this dichotomy between subject and object so typical of modernity, a dichotomy between the strict affirmation and strict negation of the allegedly correspondential truth of theological statements. Both the subject and the object are now part of a matrix constituted by distinct practices; this matrix is reproduced intersubjectively, and within the framework of specific practices accompanying it a person becomes the "subject," perceives "objects," and has "experiences." In contradistinction to the other two models, this one inherently contains a social and political component, since a religion understood in analogy to "language" and "culture" always implies specific practices and their attendant institutions, both of which together embody the specific configurations of language and fixed activities constituting any given religion.

The specifically Christian query concerning this social and political component inevitably comes upon the notion of *church*. That this ecclesiological perspective is indeed a logical implication, and yet is not explicitly examined, is a result of Lindbeck having conducted his investigation in a formal and ambivalent fashion between a general theory of religion on the one hand and an ecclesial-ecumenical hermeneutics of theological discourse and church doctrines on the other. The specific "context of discovery"[17] for the cultural-linguistic theory of religion was indeed the notion of ecumenical dialogue and its specific dynamic. For that which is perceived within his own context of discovery, however, Lindbeck offers an explanatory model that must leave implicit his own specific context of justification, namely, a "theology of the church," so that it may remain a theologically neutral model and thus be ecumenically acceptable to everyone.

The pathos characterizing Christian faith and Christian theology comes into focus first in a purely formal, external fashion. Christian faith happens in such an elementary fashion that at least formally it can no longer even be experienced as an "occurrence," since it precedes the subject, albeit not as a prelinguistic experience but as a context of praxis constituting or shaping the subject in quite distinct configurations of language and activity. In this model, pathos itself comes into focus not within distinct configurations of language and activities such as prayer or worship, but only in a purely formal fashion as the fundamentally formative horizon arising in and with this network of practices. The religious constitution of the subject is itself the elementary pathos implied by Lindbeck's model. This pathos is grounded in a comprehensive, intersubjective faith praxis, that is, in the specific configuration of language and activities of the Christian faith.

The logic of such configurations of language and activity, however, does imply that a person become a competent participant in these activities. Such participation is always *active* participation, participation that understands the inherent "grammar" or "logic" of these activities and can apply them independently. That is, the logic of linguistic and cultural competence alone already requires a *mimetic capacity*, namely, a learning of specific configurations of language and action through imitation, and a *poietic capacity*, the ability to apply and interpret. "To become a Christian involves learning the story of Israel and of Jesus well enough to interpret and experience oneself and one's world in its terms. A religion is above all an external word, a *verbum externum*, that molds and shapes the self and its world, rather than an expression or thematization of a preexisting self or of preconceptual experience."[18]

According to Lindbeck's model, the comprehensive faith praxis of Christians is constituted by specific configurations of language and activity, and can thus be described as *poietic pathos*, as a situation of unavoidably "undergoing" or being subject to that which we are, but one in which we always participate poietically. The decisive element is that this poiesis does not constitute us and posit religious faith praxis outside itself, but is to be understood rather as one, albeit central, *aspect* of a comprehensive pathos; hence the expression "poietic *pathos*."[19] This pathos resides in the structure of the specific configurations of language and fixed activities constituting the Christian faith, though it is never fully in effect without the active participation of the individual, that is, without the latter's actualizing participation. This dialectic between poiesis and pathos results from Lindbeck having emphasized structure alone, that is, the modes of *actualization* of language and action, without specifying the latter substantively. Hence the concept of experience also remains strictly bound to these contexts of language and action, that is, to concrete practices; but because Lindbeck comprehends it structurally, its content remains indeterminate and the concept itself thus *theologically* unreflected.

b. Experience

In contradistinction to the experiential and expressive model of religion, the following applies to the cultural-linguistic model: "Instead of deriving external features of a religion from inner experience, it is the inner experiences which are viewed as derivative."[20] That is, the cultural-linguistic model of religion understands experience in a way that overcomes the simple antithesis between pathos and poiesis. How, one might inquire along with Lindbeck regarding the purely poietic understanding of experience, can one ever know whether the forms of expression for certain experiences, once found, are genuinely commensurate with those experiences? Moreover, how can one speak of an experience, of a kind of event, if the latter is not already semiotically or metaphorically associated with other events and thus in principle already publicly accessible and articulated in already existing codes? An experience that is searching for its expression must rather be understood as an intimation, as the beginning of a new articulation. That is, the inviolability and subjectivity of such an experience belong not in the ineffability of our interiority, but rather on the surface as a visible and audible modification of the publicly accessible inventory of sounds, words, and images.[21] Experience is dependent on a cultural-linguistic matrix that makes the experience possible in the first place. Analogously, religious experience is first made possible by configurations of religious language and activities. Without these configurations there is no corresponding experience.[22] The prerequisite or precondition for the possibility of having certain experiences is thus the accessibility of a specific cultural-linguistic life praxis. "On this view, the means of communication and expression are a precondition, a kind of quasi-transcendental (i.e., culturally formed) *a priori* for the possibility of experience. . . . In short, it is necessary to have the means for expressing an experience in order to have it, and the richer our expressive or linguistic system, the more subtle, varied, and differentiated can be our experience."[23] Experience is thus a poiesis that is always pathically grounded; that pathos itself is of an explicitly external nature, that is, it is articulated semiotically and culturally in configurations of language and activity, a *verbum externum,* as Lindbeck puts it. Experience is part of the poietic pathos in which the "illative sense"[24] of interiorized configurations of language and activity is appropriated.

c. The Poietic Pathos of Learning Faith: The Perfection of the Saints

This praxis of poietic pathos has its concrete practitioners with their distinct skills. In this connection Lindbeck draws attention to the saints as paradigmatic embodiments of the configurations of language and activity constituting the Christian faith. The way he deals theologically with the saints is of great ecumenical significance insofar as he introduces them in a way that is identical neither with the Protestant nor with the Catholic understanding, and yet is compatible with both.

According to the Protestant understanding, the saints are those who in affirmation allow God's salvific actions to happen to them. They are thus defined as being primarily pathic, as those who let themselves be determined entirely by God's actions, which from the opposite perspective means that they stand fully within the praxis of Christian faith.[25]

There are always Christians who have developed their skills so paradigmatically in the praxis of poietic pathos that their own faith praxis becomes a point of orientation and a model for others. One can comprehend and articulate at least one central aspect of the Catholic understanding of the saints without contradicting the Protestant understanding if one considers that these "models" are of great significance for faith praxis, and that an ecclesiastical process for identifying this paradigmatic Christian competence in language and action certainly does not run counter to their capacity to serve as orientational models; quite the contrary, such a process is what first allows them to function fully as such models.[26]

According to Lindbeck's model, the decisive feature about the saints is that they perform with paradigmatic competence the praxis of poietic pathos of the Christian faith. That which happens to them as God's action and shapes them through and through, they interpret in a way that can only be concretely imitated in its own turn but never theoretically anticipated:

> Having been inwardly formed by a given tradition — by, for example, "the mind of Christ" (1 Cor. 2:16), as Paul puts it — the saint has what Thomas Aquinas calls "connatural knowledge" and by [sic] what Newman calls "the illative sense" in matters religious. This is quite different from the reflective and theoretical knowledge of the trained theologian, who employs publicly assessable rules and procedures in seeking to distinguish between the good and the bad, the true and the false. Rather, it is like the grammatical or rhetorical knowledge of a poet such as Homer, who could not enunciate a single rule in either discipline and yet was able to sense as could no one else what conformed or did not conform to the spirit, the unarticulated rules, of the Greek language. On this view, the way a religion functions once it is interiorized is much better described in expressivist than in cognitivist terms.[27]

This involves concrete judgmental practice that can only be performed or imitated with an orientation toward stories or persons (concrete models) who themselves have performed this practice paradigmatically. This understanding of saints simultaneously implies that the Christian faith can be taught and learned as a concrete praxis of specific configurations of language and activity, precisely because the cultural-linguistic model understands the Christian faith as something that is genuinely practiced.

The primary context for this is *mimetic pathos*, the imitative acquisition of the faith praxis by way of concrete models. In this sense all believers are practitioners of the Christian faith; all saints are simultaneously both students and teachers of faith, are always oriented toward models as they are themselves models for others. At the same time, however, there are paradigmatic models whose concrete capacity for judgment provides a comprehensive point of orientation. Wherever faith is practiced in this sense, theology is a practice of judgment inhering in the praxis of faith, a practice all believers perform. This is the basis of the thesis that all believers are basically theologians.

d. Learning Faith: Catechetical and Intratextual Theology

With regard to the "learning of faith" according to Lindbeck's model, it is important to understand that it is not just models who play a decisive role in this acquisition of faith praxis. *Theology* plays a quite specific role here as well, and does so precisely commensurate with the logic of the cultural-linguistic model, according to which the learning of faith takes on a dual form. The first is the initiatory learning of the central configurations of language and traditional activities of the Christian faith.[28] This type of faith acquisition might be called *catechetical learning*, and depending on context and age, it might extend over a longer or shorter period of time and perhaps also be ecclesially anchored in different ways. The goal of this process is to learn new, unfamiliar configurations of language and activities at the end of which a person has acquired a certain competence in language and behavior. This is accompanied by a process of "learning the faith," a process inherent in faith itself, one a person begins anew daily and never really completes. In this process a person develops the implications of the praxis of Christian faith in various contexts; that is, the person interprets faith with regard to precisely these contexts and maintains faith within them. According to Lindbeck's cultural-linguistic model one might call this ongoing learning of faith, one that quite naturally may coincide with the catechetical process, *peregrinational learning*, learning that is an integral part of the Christian peregrination.

Within the cultural-linguistic model, theology must thus be understood as a procedure inhering in the comprehensive praxis of faith and mediating the two forms in which faith is learned. As "catechetical theology," it is concerned with gradually accommodating a person to the faith praxis (catechetical learning); as "intratextual theology," it is concerned with maintaining the praxis of

50

Christian faith in the most varied life situations and with interpreting these situations within the context of faith praxis (peregrinational learning).

Catechetical and intratextual theology are thus the two poles of poietic pathos implied by Lindbeck's cultural-linguistic model. Catechetical theology emphasizes the aspect of pathos; its purpose is to use paradigmatic, first-order linguistic configurations (biblical stories, confessions of faith, legends of the saints) and paradigmatic behavioral guides (commandments) to transmit the logic of faith praxis. Explicit "grammatical rules" (i.e., doctrines) can play an important role in this self-interpretation of faith.[29] The pathos of catechetical theology is poietic insofar as it must take account of the context, that is, of the origin, the social, cultural, and intellectual locus of the catechumens.[30] Catechetical theology thus always has a basic pragmatic-apologetic character; it is "ad hoc" apologetics.[31]

By contrast, intratextual theology emphasizes the aspect of poiesis; its purpose is to insure an ongoing maintenance of faith in all life situations, that is, with interpreting these situations with reference to faith (drawing the world into the biblical story). This poiesis, however, always remains encompassed by the pathos attaching to the distinct configurations of language and action already provided by the praxis of faith.

With regard to ecclesiastical doctrine, catechetical and intratextual theology can be differentiated and related as follows. Whereas catechetical theology articulates the logic of faith by way of paradigmatic and normative examples and through the explicit use of (regulatory) church doctrines, and teaches the elementary and central configurations of language and action of the praxis of the Christian faith, intratextual theology operates analogically-typologically (rather than metaphorically)[32] with explicit use of church doctrine.

The learning of faith as a theological practice can thus be understood in a twofold fashion. On the one hand, it is the entry into the praxis of faith by way of paradigmatically acquired configurations of language and action; on the other, it is the ever new learning of faith through engagement with a theological interpretive practice which itself inheres in the praxis of the Christian faith. In this sense every Christian is a catechumen only once — and yet, as a saint in the Protestant sense, that person is always also a theologian in the intratextual sense.

e. Excursus: Christus Est Dominus: Performative-Propositional and Intrasystematic Truth

One of the decisive points upon which critical objections to Lindbeck's concept have focused is his theory of truth.[33] In analogy to the model of language, Lindbeck distinguishes in a religion between "vocabulary" and "grammar," with vocabulary being variable, grammar largely constant. Lindbeck understands doctrines or dogmas as a religion's grammar; as such, they comprehensively regulate the religion's individual configurations of language and activities. Lindbeck thus refers to them as "second-order propositions" or truth claims; instead of making direct statements about reality, they address "first-order propositions" or truth claims. Whereas first-order propositions are concerned with correspondential truth, that is, with truth in the sense of the ontological truth concept, second-order propositions are concerned with truth coherency, that is, with intrasystematic truth. Lindbeck believes, however, that ontological truth can be asserted only within the context of one's overall faith praxis as a life-form. The overall context of configurations of religious language and activities is accordingly "performative-propositional";[34] religious statements generate a life-form that itself has "referential" status. Ultimately, only the entire praxis of faith can correspond to its referent, and not individual statements inherent to it.[35]

Critics regularly assert that Lindbeck's performative-propositional theory of correspondence understands church doctrine or dogmas in a purely functional manner, that is, as making no immediate ontological truth claims whatever, and in so doing surrenders the universal truth claim of Christianity.[36]

This question — and the complexity attaching to it in Lindbeck's proposal — can be illustrated quite nicely in an example he himself adduces, one that in the meantime has also "made history" in the critical reception of his proposal. "Thus for a Christian, 'God is Three and One,' or 'Christ is Lord' are true only as parts of a total pattern of speaking, thinking, feeling, and acting. They are false when their use in any given instance is inconsistent with what the pattern as a whole affirms of God's being and will. The crusader's battle cry *"Christus est Dominus,"* for example, is false when used to authorize cleaving the skull of the infidel (even though the same words in other contexts may be a true utterance). When thus employed, it contradicts the Christian understanding of Lordship as embodying, for example, suffering servanthood."[37] In a positive turn, Lindbeck then concludes that "similarly, if the form of life and understanding of the world shaped by an authentic use of the Christian stories does in fact correspond to God's being and will, then the proper use of *Christus est Dominus* is not only intrasystematically but also ontologically true."[38] In this view the intrasystematic truth of *Christus est Dominus* depends on using the statement correctly and in the correct context; christological doctrines concerning "Christ's lordship" regulate this usage. Such intrasystematically correct usage is ontologically true only in the context of the overall faith praxis, and only to the extent that the latter itself corresponds to "God's being and will" by employing the normative Christian stories authentically. *Intrasystematic truth is thus a necessary but ultimately insufficient constituent part of the "whole truth," while ontological truth is always sufficient, that is, is always the "whole truth."* And yet it cannot be dogmatically regulated or argumentatively resolved. It inheres in the entire praxis of faith and in the referential character of its witness, and can be demonstrated only eschatologically.

Attentiveness is essential here to avoid misunderstanding Lindbeck's use of this example. What does it mean, one might ask, to say that the *statement "Christus est Dominus"* is false? Strictly speaking, this already is the wrong question. The real question is: What does it mean to say that the *specific speech act "Christus est Dominus"* is false? Several distinctions must be made here. First, the example is persuasive only if one implicitly presupposes that neither the theological legitimation nor the conduct of a crusade (or of any Christian "holy war"!) can be justified. How does the logic of Lindbeck's model understand the relationship between the statement and the speech act in this example?

a. As a *speech act during the cleaving of the skull,* the statement is false in the sense of being conditionally nonsensical, since it condemns either the act and the agent, or it creates an immediate connection between the act and the statement such that *Christus* does indeed lose the signifier if *Dominus* is related to what the crusader does. Or the crusader completely misunderstands *Dominus* if *Christus* is supposed to refer unequivocally to the person and work of the canonically attested Jesus of Nazareth.

b. As a *speech act during a worship service prior to the battle,* the statement is conditionally true insofar as it is a doxological and confessorial speech act, albeit one that through the overall context of the crusade does fall into a contradiction of coherence.

c. As a *theological judgment or normative doctrinal statement* functioning as a justification for exempting a crusade and its concomitant killing of infidels from ecclesiastical punishment, the statement is untrue in the sense of truth coherency, assuming a crusade cannot be justified christologically in the first place.

This survey of the various possibilities shows that a statement such as *Christus est Dominus* becomes a specific speech act only through the given context in which it is used. In all three contexts one can argue that the speech act is not true because, in various ways, neither the truth of correspondence (in [a]) nor the truth of coherence (in [a], [b] and [c]) is present. The statement *Christus est Dominus* could, however, still be true independently of this.

Here Lindbeck would counter by asking, *but who is making* this statement and in what context — and is thus making it unavoidably into a speech act? Is there a third possibility besides truth correspondence and truth coherence?

The answer is yes if with Karl Barth one assumes that God himself, in the actions of the Holy Spirit, confirms the truth of "statements," and that truth attaches to theological statements and is constituted neither through speech acts nor through ontological truth correspondence, but rather is *produced* by God's own actions in the Holy Spirit. George Hunsinger critically applies to Lindbeck's proposal Barth's core theological insight at this crucial point: "The Lindbeck proposal would seem to involve the idea that truth is not a property that pertains to sentences so much as to the forms of life in which sentences are used. It is not sentences in themselves but religious forms of life as a whole which may properly be said to correspond (or fail to correspond) to reality (i.e., ultimate reality)." Hunsinger thus identifies Lindbeck's lack of distinction between statement and speech act as a problem, and believes that Lindbeck strictly identifies the two such that "[r]eligious sentences would therefore be true only insofar as they were used in conformity with the truth of a religious form of life."[39] In response, he justifiably adduces from Barth a *theological* truth attaching to statements that is not identical with the speech acts themselves, and is grounded rather in God's own actions: "Is it [the relevant context] not finally determined by God in such a way that cultural-linguistic considerations (or any other anthropological considerations), however valid they may be on their own plane, cannot be either decisive or exhaustive?"[40] *Here Hunsinger is raising the decisive question concerning God's actions in connection with the performative aspect of theological truth:* "What is finally decisive for Barth in any consideration of the performative aspect of theological truth is not the human but the divine mode of involvement. Does not God's use of the community's theological utterances, Barth might ask, so overrule its use of them that even its most right, truthful, and orthodox usage does not guarantee that an utterance will actually be divinely attested and thus made to correspond to reality in any given situation, whether for the one who utters it or for the one to whom it may be addressed?"[41] Hunsinger adduces two substantive theological points here: first, God's actions *in the present* and over against any praxis of faith; second, God's normative and yet indirect self-mediation in the witness of the canonical Scriptures. This substantive query shifts the center of gravity from the truth of speech acts to a *theological truth attaching to statements* quite independently of any speech act. This truth, however — and here Hunsinger's query ultimately does *not* address Lindbeck's problem — is identical neither with truth coherence nor with truth correspondence, integrating rather both in a substantive theological horizon beyond Lindbeck's formal-hermeneutical model. Hence, although Hunsinger's objection is indeed justified, it transcends the capacity and intention of Lindbeck's model, which Hunsinger no longer understands analogically but rather as an explicit theological truth claim itself! Although his criticism does not really do justice to the intention and status of Lindbeck's model, it does uncover problems inhering within that model, problems I will discuss more thoroughly below. Lindbeck's model cannot address his substantively theological argumentation because Lindbeck does not explicitly understand his own model as being a part of theological discourse as church practice, and thus cannot bring the *theological* point of his own formalism to bear against Hunsinger. Within the framework of my interpretation, which follows Lindbeck's model in understanding theology as an intratextual and catechetical church practice, one can indeed pick up and constructively integrate Hunsinger's argument, since by doing so one might *theologically* ground the distinction between "statement" and "speech act," though this would presuppose an explicit and ecclesiologically explicated pneumatology.

Although Lindbeck's complex theory of truth could admittedly have been formulated more clearly, it is still theologically further along than its cognitive-propositional critics insofar as it does raise anew or articulate more succinctly the problem of correspondence by referring it to the overall praxis of faith.[42] "To what" does this praxis of faith correspond?[43] Although Lindbeck's theory of truth offers no direct answer to this, the logic of this "intratextuality" — itself developed along the lines especially of the biblical canon — would require that God's economy of salvation be addressed thematically here. The performance of the praxis of the Christian faith corresponds to the essence of God insofar as it becomes transparent for the performance of God's salvific action. That is, the specific pathos of the faith praxis, the distinct structure and substance of its configurations of language and action, corresponds to God's salvific activity insofar as it can be drawn into this activity. The performance of these configurations of language and activities thus depends on the pathos of their salvific-economic transparency. They are performatively-propositionally true insofar as they become transparent for God's salvific activity.[44] Lindbeck's critics' repeated, theologically unreflected question concerning the truth correspondence or the ontological truth of church doctrines or dogmas betrays the repression of the genuinely theological issue by old metaphysical concerns. For even if one asserts straightaway the "ontological truth" of dogmas *qua* dogmas, their truth content must either be demonstrated in the context of metaphysical argumentation — which will be extremely difficult under present philosophical conditions — or their universal truth claim must be expressed in the sense of an eschatological ontology. By taking this path, however, one displaces these doctrines for all practical purposes into the horizon in which, according to Lindbeck, they very well can function as parts of the praxis of faith itself, namely, as doxological and confessorial statements which within the framework of the overall praxis of faith and together with that praxis refer to the God who alone will demonstrate their truth.

The distinction between truth coherence and truth correspondence thus depends to a large degree on the logic of the cultural-linguistic model. The strict distinction between the two and the corresponding distinction between "vocabulary" and "grammar" can be maintained only conditionally in view of the actual complexity of the praxis of the Christian faith, and is in fact undermined by the substantive dynamic of the praxis of faith (especially if with Barth and Hunsinger one starts to take account of God's own activity); this does not, however, militate against this model as such, but only against taking the model to be more than it is, namely, an analogy whose strength is its heuristics and whose intention is ecumenical understanding.[45]

f. Church Doctrine and Academic Theology: Second-Order Discourse/the Grammar of Faith

In contradistinction to the performative-propositional actualization of the comprehensive life praxis of faith, Lindbeck understands academic theology and especially official church doctrine as discourse *about* this first-order performative-propositional actualization. Whereas the cognitive-propositional theory of religion understands theology and church doctrine as first-order expressive forms with the status of immediate truth correspondence, in the cultural-linguistic theory of religion,

> [t]echnical theology and official doctrine, in contrast, are second-order discourse about first-intentional uses of religious language. Here, in contrast to the common supposition, one rarely if ever succeeds in making affirmations with ontological import, but rather engages in explaining, defending, analyzing, and regulating the liturgical, kerygmatic, and ethical modes of speech and action within which such affirmations from time to time occur. Just as grammar by itself affirms nothing either true or false regarding the world in which language is used, but only about language, so theology and doctrine, to the extent that they are second-order activities, assert nothing either true or false about God and his relation to creatures, but only speak about such assertions.[46]

56

This strict distinction unequivocally clarifies the status of church doctrines: "Church doctrines are communally authoritative teachings regarding beliefs and practices that are considered essential to the identity or welfare of the group in question."[47] Church doctrine is thus to be understood as the implicit (operative doctrines) or explicit (official doctrines) normative "logic" or "grammar" of the Christian faith.[48] These are the rules that are decisive for the identity, welfare, and cohesion of a certain group and distinguish that group from others.

The advantage of this particular theory of doctrine for ecumenical dialogue is obvious. Dogmatic differences no longer immediately lead into a dead end of contradictory truth claims; differences can now be explained or interpreted differently, namely, as different rules referring to different things.[49] As far as official doctrines are concerned, however, the correct and in many ways fertile emphasis on the ecclesiological-political role of doctrines is a two-edged sword, since in most cases these are actually assertions that always exclude some concrete alternative; that is, as a rule they contain not only distinct affirmations but also quite concrete rejections. Although one can, of course, explain this up to a point by means of the rule theory and its normative character, because the decisive normative doctrines do also always have a dogmatic-confessorial character, and because their ecclesiastical-political implications do always directly influence the praxis of faith, they become part of the performative-propositional praxis of faith and as such always also imply a direct truth claim.

The reverse sequence, however, does indeed allow the sense of Lindbeck's model to emerge. Wherever false doctrine is rejected and the church community is broken off, this involves — so to speak *in statu nascendi* — performative-propositional activity that in further *internal* use acquires a regulatory-theoretical function. The decisive difference here derives from the various configurations of language and activity that actualize concrete "church" politics; once again, this shows clearly that Lindbeck's theory is to be understood in the sense of "inter"-church ecumenism, and that these decisive ecclesiological implications must be left out of account because the various churches understand and implement them in extremely different ways.

This understanding of church doctrine as normative *regula fidei* seems to distinguish clearly between theology and church doctrine. "There can be a great variety in the theological explanation, communication, and defense of the faith within a framework of communal doctrinal agreement." In contradistinction to operative and official doctrine, theological treatises "generally deal with everything that it is desirable to teach rather than only with that which functions as communally essential; and the explanations, justifications, and defenses of doctrine that they present are optional theological theories rather than communally normative."[50] This distinction seems cogent enough as long as one focuses on the distinction between *doctrine* and *theology*. "Explanations, justifications, and defenses" identify theology unequivocally as an independent church practice in contradistinction to the operative and official rules regulating the comprehensive praxis of faith and to the theology inhering in the praxis of faith itself. Lindbeck does, however, understand this theological discourse as an academic undertaking that in its own turn is regulatory-theoretical as the interpretation, explication, and defense of church doctrine. Would this not make it third-order discourse? Or is it ultimately nonetheless to be tied back to the comprehensive praxis of faith which, as we saw above, implies "theology" in a twofold fashion, namely, in the context of catechesis (the initiatory learning of faith) and of "intratextual theology" (the "ongoing" learning of faith)? If, as Lindbeck asserts above, theological treatises "generally deal with everything that it is desirable to teach,"[51] this statement is meaningful only if theological discourse as this productive engagement in the "explanations, justifications, and defenses" of church doctrine is itself understood as part of the comprehensive praxis of faith. As part of the comprehensive praxis of faith, concrete engagement in theological discourse always implies first-order truth claims, claims whose character clearly distinguishes them from prayers and confessions insofar as they always refer in a decisive fashion to church doctrine. This would involve understanding them as "conditionally propositional" (regulatory-theoretically conditional), though they are always intended propositionally insofar as they, as discourse practice, always participate in the comprehensive performative-propositional praxis of faith. *Hence, if Lindbeck's distinction between church doctrine and theology really is to function, it implies theological discourse as an independent church practice between church doctrine on the one hand and the (ongoing) acquisition or learning of faith on the other.*

Precisely because of this relation of theology to church doctrine, theology itself must of necessity "stand" within the praxis of faith itself to fulfill its task. "If the doctrine . . . is taken as a rule, attention is focused on the concrete life and language of the community. Because the doctrine is to be followed rather than interpreted, the theologian's task is to specify the circumstances, whether temporary or enduring, in which it applies. In the first case, as Wittgenstein might say, language idles without doing any work, while in the second case, the gears mesh with reality and theological reflection on doctrine becomes directly relevant to the praxis of the church."[52] Being able to fulfill this theological task means participating in the concrete configurations of language and activity within the community of faith, and becoming schooled in the practice of judgment that is always taking place within those configurations. Without being shaped by all these first-order performative-propositional activities, a theologian cannot fulfill this task.

Theological discourse thus stands between the two poles of learning the faith on the one hand and church doctrine on the other, between the pole of individual poietic pathos in which theological discourse participates catechetically and that of public church doctrinal articulation which theological discourse accompanies.

In order to see in greater detail how theological discourse is to be understood as a church practice between these two poles, one must first examine in greater detail what Lindbeck concisely outlines as "intratextual theology" in the final chapter of his book. Here theological discourse emerges as a practice characterized by moving back and forth between a "context of discovery" and a "context of justification."[53]

4. Intratextual Theology: Ethnology or Dogmatics?

"The task of descriptive (dogmatic or systematic) theology is to give a *normative explication* of the meaning a religion has for its adherents."[54] The apparent simplicity of this definition of the task of dogmatic theology according to the cultural-linguistic model glosses over one central point of tension, namely, that between description and normative explication. How can normative explication be the task of a "descriptive" discipline? Is it not the task precisely of a purely descriptive discipline to adhere to the concrete elements already before it? By contrast, does not an explication oriented toward a norm imply a notion of "correct" and "false" that precisely does *not* coincide with pure description, and is rather the implicate of some concrete judgment?

The logic of intratextuality might be able to explain this tension, since Lindbeck does call this particular method "intratextual," delimiting it from the extratextual method of cognitive-propositional and experiential-expressive theories of religion, both of which locate the religious meaning of a text or of a semiotic system in an external reference point, either in objective realities or in pre-linguistic experiences.[55] For intratextual theology, meaning is text-immanent; "meaning is constituted by the uses of a specific language rather than being distinguishable from it."[56]

"Among semiotic systems, intratextuality . . . is greatest in natural languages, cultures, and religions which . . . are potentially all-embracing and possess the property of reflexivity. One can speak of all life and reality in French, or from an American or a Jewish perspective; and one can also describe French in French, American culture in American terms, and Judaism in

Jewish ones. This makes it possible for theology to be intratextual, not simply by explicating religion from within but in the stronger sense of describing everything as inside, as interpreted by the religion, and doing this by means of religiously shaped second-order concepts."[57] The implications of this analogy are far-reaching, since they basically shatter the model's universal character, that is, they expose its function as a limited analogy whose limit is reached precisely at this point. Intratextual theology is itself text-immanent, that is, its own peculiarity and uniqueness is always determined by the given, specific text, and is inseparable from that text. A genuinely exhaustive and accurate description of the first-order configurations of language and action presupposes participation in precisely these activities and in their attendant practice of judgment. *Here a central element of tension emerges in Lindbeck's model between form and content. Although the model presupposes this tension on the one hand in order to function as a formal and universal model, that very tension is undermined by the impossibility of abstracting the descriptive activity from the text itself. Is this tension to be understood as applying also to the internal contradiction in the definition of the task of dogmatics?*

Lindbeck initially follows the cultural-linguistic model further and refers especially to the cultural-anthropological method of Clifford Geertz. "The theologian, like the ethnographer, should approach 'such broader interpretations and abstract analyses from the direction of exceedingly extended acquaintances with extremely small matters.'" "What the theologian needs to explicate 'is a multiplicity of complex conceptual structures, many of them superimposed or knotted into one another, which are at once strange, irregular and inexplicit, and which he must contrive somehow first to grasp and then to render.'" This view still understands theologians as ethnographers who move within a basically foreign culture, describing it from the inside down to its smallest details. A bit later, however, Lindbeck emphasizes that *theological* "thick description" does have a highly creative side as well: "There is, indeed, no more demanding exercise of the inventive and imaginative powers than to explore how a language, culture, or religion may be employed to give meaning to new domains of thought, reality, and action. Theological [thick] description can be a highly constructive enterprise."[58] Here the analogy with ethnology completely collapses, since this creative and constructive aspect of theology plays a role, indeed, becomes necessary only if theologians themselves participate in the substantive configurations of language and activities of the religion in question! One must oneself participate in the practice of judgment schooling "the illative sense" in order to actualize fully the creative and constructive aspect of theological description. Despite all "thick description" and precise acquaintance, an ethnologist — *qua* scientist — remains "outside" at this decisive point. Although an ethnologist may well anticipate and project the possibility of new solutions, still only concrete and substantive participation in the configurations of language and activities makes the concrete, creative actualization of these solutions possible. Why? Because the actualization of this concrete poiesis depends on participation in the pathos of faith; that is, it itself actualizes a moment — the reflexive moment — of the comprehensive praxis of faith. Only with reference to that which Lindbeck himself, with reference to Aquinas and John H. Newman, calls the "illative sense" of faith can his demand for an enduringly creative (poietic) and normative (pathic) intratextual theology be met.

Interestingly, Lindbeck's own further explanation of the concept of an intratextual theology confirms precisely this thesis, since he introduces the scriptural canon as its normative horizon. Here Lindbeck explicitly addresses the specific pathos of the praxis of Christian faith and accordingly also that of intratextual theology: "For those who are steeped in them, no world is more real than the ones they create. A scriptural world is thus able to absorb the universe. It supplies the interpretive framework within which believers seek to live their lives and understand reality."[59]

Lindbeck believes that this understanding of reality with the aid of Scripture follows not the logic of metaphor, but that of *typology*.

> Typology does not make scriptural contents into metaphors for extra-scriptural realities, but the other way around. It does not suggest, as is often said in our day, that believers find their stories in the Bible, but rather that they make the story of the Bible their story. The cross is not to be viewed as a figurative representation of suffering nor the messianic kingdom as a symbol for hope in the future; rather, suffering should be cruciform, and hopes for the future messianic. More generally stated, it is the religion instantiated in Scripture which defines being, truth, goodness, and beauty, and the nonscriptural exemplifications of these realities need to be transformed into figures (or types or antitypes) of the scriptural ones. Intratextual theology redescribes reality within the scriptural framework rather than translating Scripture into extrascriptural categories. It is the text, so to speak, which absorbs the world, rather than the world the text.[60]

Typology thus refers in a specific way to the poietic pathos of theological discourse. This discourse is pathic insofar as it stands in the history referred to by the canonical Scriptures, and from the perspective of this history (poietically) interprets the world. By contrast, "metaphorical" interpretation of the Bible draws the Bible into a different, comprehensive horizon and understands biblical language as metaphors or symbols referring to more comprehensive contexts and content that "actually" can be understood in other ways (conceptual illumination, scientific explanation). These biblical metaphors are themselves understood as the result of temporally conditioned, creative-religious poiesis which according to metaphorical constructivism must be replaced by new, timely, and relevant metaphors within the framework of new poietic acts. By contrast, the logic of poietic pathos oriented toward typology remains determined by the specific history of God, and writes itself into that history again and again and ever anew; poietic discourse is concerned with producing new metaphors that orient the praxis of faith anew toward that which the "old" biblical "metaphors" tried to express in their own way.[61] The pathos of intratextual theology is thus characterized by a specific, binding horizon (canonical Scripture) and by specific, binding configurations of language and action. By contrast, the pathos of extratextual theology consists in being determined by another, explicit or implicit normative horizon within which the Bible itself is understood as poiesis that must be replaced by a timely and relevant poiesis of new metaphors.

If one accepts that the *theological* "thick description" undermines the comparison with ethnology, Lindbeck's postliberal method sooner resembles the catechesis of the early church: first a person is attracted by the witness of Christians, that is, by their concrete praxis of faith (a person "comes upon" the church); is then socialized into this world by learning the configurations of language and action; and understands (learns) faith ever anew and ever more deeply by participating in its poietic pathos. The postliberal theologian is actually merely disguised as an ethnologist, and in reality turns out to be a catechetical theologian whose descriptive theology is actually the (ever new) practice and introduction to the Christian faith. In catechetical theology both elements come to bear and, as it were, meet at the center: the regulatory-theoretical introduction to the faith, that is, binding doctrine, on the one hand, and this faith's ever new interpretation of the world, that is, its activity of drawing the world into the Bible, on the other. *One can understand these descriptive and binding elements together only if one understands Lindbeck's intratextual theology as catechetical theology.* "The task of descriptive (dogmatic or systematic) theology is to give a *normative explication* of the meaning a religion has for its adherents."[62]

5. The Soteriological Center — beyond Formalized Pathos

As already seen, one of the central points of tension in Lindbeck's model is that understanding the program of theology according to the cultural-linguistic model as "thick description" calls into question two central elements of this model: first, its strict distinction between first- and second-order "language games," and second, that between "actualization" and "description." This problem also inheres in the tension between the model's seeming neutrality and formality on the one hand and the demanded "thick description" on the other. Either the mode of "thick description" remains external to the model itself, or the actualization of this "thick description" undermines the model's formality and neutrality. A consistently intratextual theology implies that its "thick description" is so encompassed and shaped by its object that it cannot examine itself thematically without at the same time examining thematically its pathic nature, that is, without understanding itself from the perspective of its object. Hence a consistently intratextual theology cannot really abstract at all from the "simple talk of God"[63] without falling into self-contradiction. Even in its methodological self-explication intratextual theology must remain *theological*, that is, explicitly oriented toward God's activity. It cannot avoid the question of its pathos.

This raises the question of the soteriological center of theological discourse. Does not the specific actualization of intratextual theology as sketched by Lindbeck in his final chapter also imply its soteriological disposition? "Drawing the world into the Bible" does, after all, mean bringing the world to ever new expression from the perspective of God's salvific activity as paradigmatically articulated in the biblical witness, and bringing it to expression with regard to the world itself such that the world is interpreted from the perspective of God's salvific activity. If this poiesis, still left within pathos, is not to be understood yet again as the poiesis of the *religious subject* that most certainly understands itself as being of a pathic disposition, that is, if this intratextuality is to be carried forward in a consistent fashion, then one must inevitably inquire concerning *the poiesis that is the determinative ground of the pathos of the praxis of faith and of theology. This raises the question of the* Spiritus Creator, *the presence of God in his creative activity, an activity that in its own turn creates its own recipient.* If intratextuality is not to break up reflexively and become fixed in formalized intersubjectivity (as the continuation and differentiation of the logic of subjectivity), then only a substantively developed pneumatology as a salvific-economic explication of the doctrine of the Trinity will be able to examine thematically the poiesis underlying the pathos of consistent, that is, soteriologically explicit, intratextuality.

The weakness in Lindbeck's model is precisely that it remains external to the practice of theological discourse that is its goal. In order to remain plausible, the intratextual method of theology would actually have to be understood and implemented *intratextually*, though admittedly this would at least initially hinder the project of ecumenical understanding. The inner logic of Lindbeck's model divides the discourse of theology into the two aspects of first-order theological configurations of language and action on the one hand and second-order reflexive, regulatory statements on the other. The comprehensive praxis of faith and life opened up by the linguistic-cultural schema is itself no longer theologically maintained, and is articulated neither ecclesiologically nor pneumatologically. This gives the model an emphatically static, and thus unhistoric, formal character, something evident not least in its failure to associate theology *theologically* with its pathic and poietic elements.[64]

This formalism is especially clear in the model's understanding of religion as verbum externum *in a purely structural rather than a substantive sense. This formalizes in a problematic fashion the soteriologically decisive core element in Lutheran theology, the result being that the reflection of intratextual theology loses its unique soteriological center; soteriology slips off into form.*

Hence, although Lindbeck's proposal does function quite well as a doctrinal hermeneutics "from the outside" between churches, and especially as a plausibility model for establishing dogmatic consensus, it does indeed stand in problematic tension with the implementation of "thick description" that is so central for the cultural-linguistic model. There is, however, a *bona fide* explanation for this whose presupposition is, however, the concrete (in this case: ecumenical) implementation of theology as church practice.

At this point one must keep firmly in mind the limited goal of Lindbeck's undertaking. His guiding interest is ecumenical dialogue, and the heuristic intention of his cultural-linguistic theory of religion stands utterly in the service of facilitating such understanding. Read from this perspective, Lindbeck's treatise exemplifies a special case of theological discourse as church practice, namely, that of ecumenical dialogue between churches. This dialogue is essentially always conducted in a substantively theological fashion, and within it, this particular tractate is to be understood as an ad hoc formalization representing pragmatic, goal-oriented hermeneutics rather than a new metatheory. Nor does this hermeneutics in its own turn understand itself as a specific theological argument. It is an argumentative invitation to understand the results of ecumenical dialogue as the results of theological discourse; the actualization of that dialogue in its own turn has led to a new regulation of decisive linguistic rules of faith allowing a consensus not contradicting old, previously contradictory linguistic rules. It is precisely this strategic interest in ecumenical dialogue that keeps Lindbeck's specific argumentation formal. This formalism is thus to be understood as a form of ecumenically occasioned reserve.[65]

From this perspective Lindbeck's proposal can be read as one *element* of theological discourse that makes sense only as an ecclesial (here: specifically ecumenical) practice; moreover, it is only with the help of a hermeneutical model understanding Christian faith in analogy to culture or language that this discourse can render an account of the character of its own doctrinal formation without thereby prejudicing theological decisions regarding content. By contrast, understanding the model as a comprehensive, universal theory of religion according to which religion represents a structural a priori in analogy to language or culture prevents any possibility for intratextual theology, and calls severely into question the model's alleged theological neutrality.[66] Here Lindbeck's proposal remains problematically ambivalent by seemingly trying to square a circle. *His proposal, however, makes sense only within a theological discourse that already understands itself as church practice; that is, it has specific ecclesiological and theological presuppositions that for specific reasons relating to dialogue remain unspoken.*

Without an *explicit* thematic articulation of these specific theological and ecclesiological presuppositions, however, he falls into a formalism that itself does not really move beyond the other two models of religion. That is, Lindbeck's model is persuasive only if one presupposes ecumenical dialogue as a paradigmatic practice of theological discourse.

A much stronger theological-substantive understanding — in this case: pneumatological-ecclesiological understanding — of the overall praxis of faith is necessary if it is to remain a hermeneutic rather than itself becoming an a priori schema of ultimate grounding; in the latter case, and in its own a priori abstractness, it will still be carrying forward the intention of the experiential-expressive model of religion even if it reverses the latter's logic.

6. Implied Ecclesiology: The Church as a Specific Context of Praxis

In reality, theology as church practice is already the necessary presupposition of Lindbeck's model. This emerges if one inverts his model and reads it as a special case of theology as church practice rather than under the aspect of a universal truth claim, and if one understands the internal contradictions attaching to the model's formalism not as a shortcoming but as being quite precisely *ecclesially* determined. Not only can one conclude this indirectly, one can also demonstrate it explicitly, since his model presupposes not only the church as an actual context of praxis, but also normative elements of an ecclesiology that in fact requires "theology" as a practice inhering in the church. The preceding discussion already demonstrates in a twofold fashion that Lindbeck's proposal is presupposing a normative ecclesiology.

1. If Lindbeck's maxim for all intratextual theology — "The Bible is to absorb reality" — really is to come to bear, then it must be realized within the framework of a "sociology" and "politology" of church practices.[67] Without firm ecclesiological anchoring, this proposal too easily falls prey to biblicism, something Lindbeck certainly does *not* intend. One of the core elements of this implied *ecclesiology* is the outline of a doctrine of Scripture that thwarts even nascent ecclesiological fundamentalism. One characteristic of church practices is that they allow the canonical Scriptures to function as witness to God's word and subject themselves to this primacy. That is, the ecclesiological anchoring of the Bible within the framework of a church doctrine of Scripture is precisely *not* an ecclesiological functionalization of the Bible, but rather its implementation as "Scripture."[68] Not understanding this from an explicitly ecclesiological perspective quickly turns the Bible itself into an abstraction, into a historical, cultural, or political phenomenon.

2. Lindbeck's model suggests that the Christian religion as *verbum externum* always presupposes its historical as well as political-social disposition as a church. The model does, after all, imply three important things: *(a)* that there is a functioning church practice of worship, prayer, and so on; in short: first-order religious linguistic praxis governed by a grammar that in its own turn is preserved in specific doctrinal formulations in the form of rules for language and action; *(b)* that there is a distinct practice of ecclesial judgment[69] deciding publicly concerning doctrinal formation; and finally *(c)* that there is a specific discursive practice of intratextual theology that moves back and forth between and participates in both first- and second-order configurations of language and action, and yet is identical with neither. Only the framework of an implicitly presupposed ecclesiology allows these elements not only to be articulated, but also to be meaningfully implemented in the first place.

Interestingly, Lindbeck's argumentation can also be reversed. His own ecclesiological vision, developed in a series of essays, implies theology as a practice necessarily inhering within the church in the sense just discussed.[70] In these essays Lindbeck engages in highly interesting ecclesiological reflections standing in a merely implied and yet immediate relation to his main work. Two mutually related features characterize these reflections: first, a sociologically formulated feature related to the present, and second, a biblical-normative one; ultimately, however, both can be comprehended historically.

In view of the overall sociocultural situation in the Western world, with its increasing secularization and religious pluralization, he sees the future of the church as being emphatically post-Constantine, including the modern "Constantine," organizational forms of the "people's church" (*Volkskirche*) in

Europe and of Christianity as "civil religion" in the USA. The future of the church as extrapolated with the tools of sociology is that of a "sect," understanding sect in a strictly *sociological* rather than theological fashion. In the sociological sense, the church will become a "sect" insofar as in an increasingly post-Christian society it will increasingly separate itself from that society and continue to maintain the traditional Christian message of the absoluteness and normative significance of God's revelation in Jesus Christ. In the theological sense, this church will of necessity be emphatically nonsectarian and essentially ecumenical, since only such a church has any real chance of survival[71] in a post-Christian society.

Within the horizon of this hypothetical prognosis (in which he, so to speak, reverses the perspective of the historian and engages in cautious futurology), he makes the early church with its ecclesiological reflections — reflections preserved in the canon — his central point of reference. For this early church was both: sociologically a sect and theologically a "catholic" or "ecumenical" community. Lindbeck takes the self-understanding of the Christians of the early church, a self-understanding cast within a people-of-God ecclesiology focused on Israel, as the guiding reference point for a future ecumenical ecclesiology; given present prognoses, this ecclesiology is of extraordinary relevance for the reality of churches in the Western world.[72]

This ecclesiological outline characterizes the church in a threefold fashion: *(a)* As a witnessing community called by God, it is inevitably directed toward the world and society around it, and yet simultaneously remains emphatically *distinct* from that world. *(b)* Its existence as a witnessing and confessing community demands an explicit learning of the faith, that is, an explicit initiation. *(c)* It is characterized by an ecumenical-catholic structure, that is, by a unity presupposing rather than excluding multiplicity, but at the same time excluding those variants contradicting the identity and calling of the church. *It is precisely this church that needs both church doctrine and "theology" as its own inherent discursive practice in order to remain the church to which it has indeed been called.*

a. Only where the church is not identical with the society around it does the theological actualization of faith, that is, the "thinking of faith," become a necessity for the church, and that in a twofold fashion: first as an internal, intersubjective consensus concerning faith, and second as the rendering of an account concerning faith itself. It is in this sense that intratextual theology is to be understood as a necessary implicate of a people-of-God ecclesiology that develops the church as a witnessing community.

b. Precisely this ecclesiology also requires an explicit and intentional learning or acquisition of faith, since "faith" is to be understood here not docetically, but as an entry into or familiarization with specific configurations of language and activities, configurations which by being understood are also *learned,* and by being learned are also *understood.* Catechesis and catechetical theology are thus inevitably the second implicate of this ecclesiology.

c. The ecumenical-catholic structure of this ecclesiology, a structure in which the balance between unity and multiplicity must continually be articulated anew, demands the formulation of normative rules that in their own turn articulate and fix ever anew the identity and continuity of the church's witness within the multiplicity of these configurations of language and activity. Church doctrine and dogmatic formulation inevitably accompany this ecclesiology because two things are at stake: an ever new relationship with the societies and cultures in which the church exists, and ever new formulations of its identity and continuity in delimitation from false doctrine. At least according to Lindbeck's model, these are the precise concerns of church doctrine and dogmatic formulation.

One further element in Lindbeck's ecclesiological reflections comes to bear indirectly here as well. By understanding the church as a "messianic pilgrim people of God" whose model is Israel's own history, Lindbeck allows this Israel-related ecclesiology to be articulated also with regard to its inherent practice of theological discourse. Just as the rabbinical practice of Torah interpretation and the tradition of that interpretation is of central significance for the existence of the synagogue (as an essential element of what actually constitutes Israel's existence), so also is the practice of theological discourse an essential element of the church understood in this way.

Lindbeck's cultural-linguistic proposal thus comes full circle. His model implies a practice of theological discourse which in its own turn presupposes the church with its concrete configurations of language and activities and church doctrine as its inherent actualization. Viewed from the other side, the church can anticipate a future in which not only does the cultural-linguistic model acquire increasing relevance, but the practice of theology it implies will itself become an essential part of the church in this sense.

7. Conclusions

If one rigorously examines the implicit understanding of theology in Lindbeck's cultural-linguistic model, one finds that "theology" is actually a rather complex phenomenon there. In connection with first-order propositions, it appears as catechetical theology and as intratextual theology; in connection with second-order propositions, it appears as the practice of dogmatic judgment. The practice of dogmatic judgment in the form of second-order propositions actually involves a type of theology that cannot be fixed in the fashion of a school; the concern is rather to ascertain "where proper grammar is to be found . . . [and] who are the competent speakers of a religious language."[73] Only when one has clearly identified as specific practices the learning of faith within its own (catechetical) logic, on the one hand, and the implementation of ecclesial doctrinal decisions on the other, can one then distinguish theology from them as a discursive church practice and examine it independently. Understood from the perspective of regulative theory, church doctrine will additionally acquire considerable importance as a result of its intimate connection with the praxis of faith in the church.

Though if it is to function at all, Lindbeck's model must already presuppose theological discourse as a church practice. Understood in an essentially *ecclesiological* fashion, the model already implies the kind of discourse that must be conceived as a specific church practice, that is, theology within the actualization of faith (*in* the grammar of faith) and as reflection *on* the grammar of faith from the perspective of the actual praxis of faith. The ecclesiology implicit in the model does contain highly interesting allusions to the connection between the praxis of faith, theological discourse, and church doctrine, opening up at the same time a perspective for understanding theology as the intersubjective poietic pathos inherent to the actualization of faith, as a practice shaped by the central configurations of language and action of the church, always related to these configurations, and inseparable from them. In this sense Lindbeck's model shows us the right path. At the same time, however, its formal character, a result of its ecumenical "life setting," inhibits any explicit development of the relationship between theology as a church practice and the substantive pathos characterizing the church itself. The task now is to follow this thread further and in so doing examine and constructively articulate the interior of what Lindbeck's cultural-linguistic model already intends theologically.

II. The Gospel as the Pathos of Theology: Oswald Bayer

In order to follow this thread concerning the substantive aspect of the pathos of theology as church practice, I will now engage the work of the German Lutheran theologian Oswald Bayer. Drawing considerably from Kant's friend and critic Johann Georg Hamann, Bayer develops a theology oriented especially toward the thinking of Martin Luther and critical of modernity's foundationalist strategies.

"*Theology emerges from worship and moves toward it.* As a specialized and specific conceptual undertaking, it is part of the auditory faith that loves God not only with all of one's heart, but also with all of one's power and vitality, and with all of one's thinking (Mk. 12:30). Understood comprehensively, theology is identical with faith."[74] This citation contains the core of Bayer's proposal to understand theology from the perspective of worship and to explicate it as an implication of auditory faith. The substantive explication of the pathos constituting theology as a church practice, an explication lacking in Lindbeck, is found in a surprisingly complementary form in this other Lutheran theologian. Bayer draws explicitly from Hamann's critical contemporaneity over against the Enlightenment to oppose, as does Lindbeck, the project of modernity and especially its *theological* implementation. The difference is that Bayer does not understand the pathos of theology in any formal-structural fashion, as does Lindbeck; instead, he explicates its substance theologically. He attempts to develop theology programmatically beyond its modern alternatives as articulated in Kant, Hegel, and Schleiermacher, alternatives understanding theology from the perspective of morality, speculation, or religious feeling, and does so with a creative reference back to Luther's own Reformation theology and from the perspective of a new consideration of the notion of auditory faith. After a series of essay collections,[75] he offered a more comprehensive account, one oriented especially toward Luther, in the recently published introductory volume to the theological series "Handbuch Systematischer Theologie," a volume whose title is both simple and, in that very simplicity, quite challenging: *Theology*.[76] Rather than presenting a comprehensive overview of his often subtle theology, I will concentrate on the *concept of theology* he develops with his own constructive, normative goals. My debate with Bayer, like that with Lindbeck, is of a primarily *heuristic* nature. A presentation of the strengths and weaknesses of his concept of theology will articulate the progress this affords beyond Lindbeck's own model, and an examination of its deficiencies will then prepare the ground for continuing the discussion beyond Bayer himself.

Anticipating for a moment, let me say that the strength of Bayer's concept of theology is its concentration on the pathos of theology; in contradistinction to Lindbeck, he develops a theologically explicit and concrete understanding of that pathos from the perspective of the concept of *promissio*, and articulates it with respect to its roots in worship and its ecclesial task as a communicative form of judgment. Unfortunately, the mostly implicit ecclesiology in his proposal weakens this strength in a disturbing way.[77] In particular, there is no comprehensive pneumatological-ecclesiological conception of church practices making it possible to relate to one another the various core elements of his concept of theology. Probably the most problematic implication of this deficit in his concept of theology is that he perceives the *doctrina,* and with it church doctrine, only within the horizon of catechetical systematics. In so doing, however, he ultimately robs theology of the pneumatological-ecclesiological framework making it possible to develop theology as a conflict discipline of precisely the sort Bayer himself envisions. Hence, although the inner complexity of his concept of theology and its anchoring in a substantively developed theological pathos is indeed impressive, its contours ultimately remain vague because its relation to church doctrine is never clarified.

1. The Fourfold Object of Theology

Building on Luther's understanding of theology, Bayer develops the object of theology completely from the perspective of the doctrine of justification. The only proper object of theology is sinful humanity and the justifying God, whereby the two adjectives "sinful" and "justifying" are to be understood as *essentia* rather than as *accidentia.* That is, they do not define more precisely a "humanity" and "God" that could actually be described in other terms as well; rather, they define the very essence of both God and humanity.[78]

Bayer believes that the concrete nature of theology's object emerges in three encounters "which cannot in any way be derived from one another or subordinated to a common concept such as God's self-revelation."[79] Bayer defines the temporally first encounter as the *law,* which convicts sin and kills. The second, decisive, and ultimate event is the *gospel,* and the third is *God's hiddenness.*[80] "There can be no talk about God or humanity or world beyond this fear and this love, beyond grace and judgment, law and gospel, faith and unfaith, death and life, or beyond that which incomprehensibly contradicts God's promise."[81] The fourth object he adduces is then the *primus usus legis,* the first use of the law, which in contradistinction to the grace of new creation is concerned with the grace of preservation.[82] This fourfold definition of theology's object lends complex, concrete content to the understanding of its pathos, content consistently characterized by soteriology.

In this basic definition theology clearly emerges first of all in the engagement in faith itself; the pathos of theology also embraces the theologian, divulging the dual polarity of theology recalling Lindbeck's distinction between theology as first-order language within the comprehensive praxis of faith, on the one hand, and second-order discourse on the other. I will examine each of these poles, first theology as the inherent actualization of the *vita passiva* characterizing every Christian, and then its academic implementation first as the doctrine of language and form with relation to the gospel, and then as the metacritique of faith itself, that is, as a conflict discipline.

2. Theological Existence within the Pathos of Faith

a. Oratio, Meditatio, Tentatio

By reconstructing Luther's understanding of theology, Bayer gains access to the pathos of theology as the linguistic performance of faith. The leitmotiv behind this access is Luther's famous remark concerning what makes a theologian a theologian in the first place: "Vivendo, immo moriendo et damnando fit theologus, non intelligendo, legendo aut speculando."[83]

Bayer takes Luther's preface to the first volume of the Wittenberg edition of his German writings as his point of departure for interpreting Luther with constructive intent. In that preface Luther uses Psalm 119 in examining thematically the three rules *oratio, meditatio, tentatio,* the tools with which theology can be properly studied. Bayer articulates Luther's concern as follows: "A theologian is someone who is interpreted by the Holy Scripture, allows himself or herself to be interpreted by it, and as someone interpreted by it interprets it for others who are afflicted or tempted."[84] He finds that prayer, meditation, and temptation refer not to private, individual events in the modern sense, but to the "course of the word through church history and world history."[85] I can agree with this without qualification if it is clear that this "course of the word" is bound to distinct church practices whose decisive feature is that they are indeed *practiced* both communally as well as individually, and are practiced *regularly* and as such constitute a self-evident characteristic of the church itself.

Oratio[86] Prayer is directed toward the triune God, mediated in the embodied word of the promise of Christ. Luther understands *oratio* as *active waiting* for God's activity, as a practice encompassing theology itself and turning attention from the theological subject to the object of theology such that the object, as the real subject, performs its salvific work in the petitioner. Passivity here means a change of subject, means giving God's activity room and allowing it to take place in oneself. It is easy to see that this contradicts the *vita activa*. What is decisive, however, is that this contradicts the *vita con-*

templativa as well. For even a vision in which the perceiving subject is emptied and ultimately comes to view God such that the subject is itself viewed — even such a vision cannot yet be understood as *vita passiva* in the full sense. The difference to the *vita passiva* of *oratio* resides at a much deeper level, for *the primary, central focus here is the soteriological articulation of God's economy of salvation. In an utterly concrete sense, God is accorded all honor here insofar as the person praying seeks to allow God to perform on him or her precisely that which God did and continuously intends to do in Christ. Vita passiva* as *oratio* is the practice in which God, rather than being separated from God's work, is rather recognized in this petition to be subject to God's salvific action. It is precisely the surrender of subjective being — in the modern sense — within the prayer of the *vita passiva* that creates the theologian in the strict sense of the linguistic actualization of faith; the beginning of all theology is this implied change of subjects in the *oratio*.

Meditatio[87] *Meditatio* is not a new aspect; its goal is rather for the *oratio* to be directed completely toward the *verbum externum* to the point that it is engaged publicly, that is, audibly. Here Luther returns to an insight of the early church that over the course of time had paled: "This refers to the practice of reading and praying aloud, and at the same time — and even more importantly — to its scriptural orientation, especially to a certain manner of dealing with the psalter."[88] Bayer succinctly articulates the decisive point here: "In meditation, a person does not listen to the interior, and does not go into himself or herself, but rather outside. . . . In this relation to God, a person is rather from the very outset already enhypostasized in the word, as it were, but is personally anhypostatic."[89] That is, such people "abide," as it were, completely in the word, and over against that word have no real substance "in themselves." In audible *meditatio*, that is, in the *meditatio* that is public precisely before me, I surrender myself completely to the word such that the word itself becomes my substance. In modern terms, I involve myself so completely in the word that it becomes my identity, that is, there is no longer any difference between me as the praying subject and the execution of the prayer itself. Precisely this logic of the externality of the *vita passiva* is to be understood pneumatologically. "For God will not give you his Spirit without the external word, so act accordingly. For he has not commanded us for nothing to write, preach, read, hear, sing, speak, etc. externally."[90] In Luther's view, then, the Holy Spirit has bound itself to specific church activities, practices with an inherently *public* character. Bayer articulates this as follows: "Hence Luther's rule of meditation . . . is on the whole nothing other than a doctrine of the Holy Spirit. The Holy Spirit, however — and on this Luther insists — has bound itself to a quite specific linguistic sphere: . . . to the sounds and letters of Holy Scripture."[91] Here Bayer turns against an understanding of theology as meditation that forces the Procrustean distinction between "private" and "public," as a result of which theology is understood as private reflection on Scripture.[92]

Tentatio[93] The *vita passiva* culminates in *tentatio,* for if everything discussed above were implemented without the reality of temptation, God's reign would already have been realized once and for all in the practice of *oratio* and *meditatio.* Luther renews the experiential concept of New Testament apocalyptic precisely by holding fast to the reality of *tentatio* as external, public temptation of faith through contradiction, attack, and persecution.[94] "God's unity, and with it the unity of reality and of its experience, do not stand before us as an unchallenged, eternal and necessary principle, but rather are challenged both factually and practically as well as in a completely 'external' fashion. Anyone who meditates on the first commandment of necessity becomes entangled in the dispute between the one and the many Lords (cf. 1 Cor. 8:5f.)."[95] To a certain extent the *vita passiva* itself becomes disputed turf. Those who expose themselves completely to God's word, that is, publicly expose themselves to it within the practices just discussed, are confronted by the powers and forces that struggle with the God of Israel and the Father of Jesus Christ for control of this *vita passiva,* powers whose goal is for a person ultimately to be enhypostasized in them and to find personal identity in them. "Temptation is . . . the touchstone of God's word, a word that demonstrates its own credibility and power in and against temptation."[96]

Experience: The Pathos of *Tentatio*   The perspective of the *vita passiva* brings the notion of "experience" into unequivocal opposition to the modern concept of experience as understood especially since Schleiermacher. For Luther, experience is not an independent, self-sufficient category, but rather one bound to Scripture and filled through concrete encounter with God's word. Experience is determined by the specific pathos characterizing the *vita passiva:* "Temptation alone teaches us to pay attention to God's word, which itself, however, is the condition for the possibility of its experience. This is why a person *has* the experience of God's word by *undergoing* it."[97] Bayer quite justifiably concludes that the experience of Scripture rather than "experience as such" makes a theologian into a theologian.[98]

Conclusion   In this interpretation of Luther, Bayer regains a central feature of an ecclesial understanding of theology, namely, the *theological* existence of all Christians actualized in the *oratio, meditatio,* and *tentatio* of the *vita passiva.* This *vita passiva* characterizes Christians and makes them into theologians, and all theology is grounded in its pathos. To experience Christian existence in this way means to be a theologian; to be this kind of theologian means to experience Christian existence in this way.

This inevitably raises the question regarding how and where Christians are concretely introduced to this mode of Christian being, and where this existence is practiced, fostered, and taught both communally and individually. That is, Luther's existence of the theologian/Christian *in oratio, meditatio,* and *tentatio* implies the necessity of concrete church practices in which this *vita passiva* comes to bear. Bayer leaves this point in uncomfortable abeyance; yet in view of the obvious and extensive lack of such practices in contemporary Protestantism, precisely this issue becomes an urgent, burning question *if* with Bayer one does indeed understand the center of Christian and thus of theological existence in this way. Luther had no difficulty in simply carrying forward his own *praxis pietatis* as a monk without explicitly having to reflect ecclesiologically on it or identify it as an explicit church practice.[99] Nor did the elimination of the institution familiarizing him with this practice really rob him of the practice itself; that is, he did not have to take ecclesiological account of the elimination of the context of this praxis. What Luther thus did not have to take into account in any explicitly ecclesiological fashion (and yet nonetheless began to do in his treatise "On the Councils and Churches"),[100] Bayer would indeed have to do under the conditions of modernity, namely, explicitly examine the distinct church practices in which the *vita passiva* is familiarized, fostered, and actualized.

This problem emerges most incisively in Bayer's brief and essentially accurate reference to Luther's "ecclesiological understanding of theology."[101] This characterization derives from the striking structural identity he perceives between the three "marks of theology" *(oratio, meditatio, tentatio)* and three of the "marks of the church" Luther adduces in "On the Councils and Churches." Just *what* this structural identity means, however, remains unclear. A brief, anticipatory reference to an ecclesiological consideration I will suggest later can clarify this critical query.[102] Bayer is correct in asserting that Luther's understanding of theology is ecclesiological, and that *oratio, meditatio,* and *tentatio* correspond to prayer, word, and discipleship in suffering. Here he encounters in Luther the explicit possibility of anchoring ecclesiologically in distinct practices the elementary and basic understanding of theology attaching to *oratio, meditatio,* and *tentatio,* and of developing that understanding from the perspective of precisely those practices. Because his interpretation is centered so exclusively on this structural parallelism, however, he is unable to anchor in any genuinely *ecclesiological* fashion theological existence as *vita passiva* in distinct "thick" contexts of church praxis. For the fulcral pneumatological-ecclesiological point of the characterization of the church in "On the Councils and Churches" never really comes to bear in Bayer's proposal; this is also why the relation of *oratio, meditatio,* and *tentatio* remains unclear in the aforementioned church characteristics (word, prayer, cross).

The decisive point seems to me to reside in the fundamental consolation that Luther's ecclesiology offers, namely, in the assurance that we will always encounter the church wherever we encounter the network of those particular, distinct practices through which God sanctifies his people. Luther refers back to the analogy of the tablets of the law, tablets that now, however, are written in the hearts of believers rather than on stone.[103] The first tablet deals with the proper knowledge of God,[104] the second with the sanctification of the body.[105] The seven marks of the church which Luther develops all refer to the first tablet and are all understood as being constitutive for the church. God sanctifies his people both through and in these activities: "That is called new holy life in the soul, in accordance with the first table of Moses. It is also called *tres virtutes theologicas*, 'the three principle virtues of Christians,' namely, faith, hope, and love; and the Holy Spirit, who imparts, does, and effects this (gained for us by Christ) is therefore called 'sanctifier' or 'life-giver.' For the old Adam is dead and cannot do it, and in addition has to learn from the law that he is unable to do it and that he is dead; he would not know this of himself."[106] The "holy Christian people" can be recognized in the world in the seven main elements of Christian sanctification according to the first tablet.[107] They have a public character and are distinct activities, or "practices" in the most comprehensive sense that can be performed or not performed. Yet Bayer's interpretation does not really offer any comprehensive "thick" reading of "On the Councils and Churches,"[108] that is, does not address each mark on its own and articulate their performance or relation to the ordained office; when he then refers to Luther's disputation thesis "ubi est verbum, ibi est ecclesia,"[109] however, his interpretation inevitably must be understood as saying that wherever the word is, so also is the church, whereby "church" then remains abstract and formless — quite unlike in "On the Councils and Churches." If by contrast one reads the thesis "ubi est verbum, ibi est ecclesia" against the background of all the characteristics Luther adduces, then the church is indeed already implied in the word, and is such as a "thick" nexus of practices without which the word itself is utterly inconceivable.

b. Catechetical Systematics:
Toward the Practice of Catechetical Meditation

Bayer's interpretation of Luther does, however, contain important allusions that can be developed ecclesiologically with regard to concrete church practices in which theology finds its "life setting" in the church. These include first of all baptismal instruction, then domestic worship, and finally communal worship.[110] For Luther, most of these practices were oriented toward the *catechism*, something Bayer articulates quite clearly: "The cultivation of catechesis with which Luther wanted to preserve the truth of the monastic life form is necessary for the salvation of every human being. . . . Knowledge of the catechism and attention to it are necessary for salvation. Faith clings to the word, to its literality. Rhythm and linguistic form are not external, but belong rather constitutively together."[111] He similarly points out that Luther expected a training in the catechism within precisely stipulated practices on a daily basis.[112] In "On the Councils and Churches" Luther identifies catechetical practice as one of the Holy Spirit's "holy possessions" characterizing the church.[113] By recalling the central position occupied by the catechism in Luther's understanding of theology as a daily actualization of the *vita passiva*, Bayer seems to be implying the necessity of a distinct practice in which the catechism has its place in this given form and fulfills a specific purpose. Explicitly, however, he concentrates only on the — certainly also — important question of catechetical *systematics* while not addressing the urgent question of the actual *church practices* in their ecclesiological context, practices corresponding to the form and content of the catechism. The question thus already arises concerning whether, for Bayer, this catechetical systematics does not rather usurp the place of church doctrine. He must "dogmatize" Luther because as far as a binding ecclesiological formulation of the *fides quae creditur* is concerned, he does not explicitly assign any ecclesiological "life setting" to church doctrine alongside Luther's catechetical systematics, systematics he understands as normative.

3. The Pathos of the Promissio

a. Theology's Constitutive Object: The Promissio

As we just saw, Bayer's understanding of theology, in strict orientation toward Luther, represents an unequivocal stance against all fundamental poiesis in theology. Rather than theology creating its object, the object forces itself

upon theology; indeed, and in an even more radical sense, that object constitutes both theology and the theologian. At its core, theology is not human
poiesis at all, but a situation of passively subjecting oneself to God's action;
that is, it is pathos. As such, however, it is simultaneously also a reflective activity, a distinct practice whose object forces itself upon it (in a way to be clarified later) such that it "suffers" or "undergoes" this object.[114] This point of
departure provides Bayer with a crucial freedom of movement over against
the dominant modern paradigm of the *homo faber* and the *homo poieticus*[115]
that creates the objects of its own reflection. If the object of theology forces itself upon the latter, indeed, if it radically creates the theologian in the first
place, then asking about the object of theology really means to become "ques-
tion-able" as a theologian, that is, inevitably to become the object of thematic
theological examination oneself. To be created as a theologian by the object
itself: this is the radical apex of Bayer's understanding of theology with which
he builds on a central aspect of Luther's theology. The pathos of this theology
is that it is based on a poiesis whose subject is precisely *not* the human being,
but rather God, and is *exclusively* God.

The center of this pathic understanding of theology is found in Bayer's
reconstruction of Luther's Reformational discovery of the gospel as a liberating linguistic act that provides assurance as a *promissio* or pledge.[116] The central point is that in the *promissio* content and statement are one; what is said
is at the same time also performed or implemented:

> Luther's great hermeneutical, in the strict sense Reformational discovery
> was that the *signum* itself is already the *res*. As he himself tells us, he made
> this discovery initially in reflection on the sacrament of penitence. In con-
> nection with absolution, saying that the *signum* itself is already the *res*
> means that the statement "I absolve you from your sins" is not a judgment
> merely confirming what already is, that is, it does not presuppose that an
> inner, divine, actual absolution or justification has already taken place;
> rather, it is itself a linguistic act constituting the content of this deed in the
> first place.[117]

As the creator's word, God's promise always actualizes that which is promised. God's speaking, God's concrete promise in the gospel is always at once
also an act: The *signum* is itself already the *res*.[118] According to Bayer, these
promissiones can be found throughout Scripture. Nevertheless, they do not
constitute an incoherent plurality of varied heterogeneous promises. Rather,
according to Bayer, a "primal promise" stands behind every *promissio*. "Every
one of God's promises repeats the primal statement of his self-introduction,

'I am your God, and thus you are my people.' Such a promise opens up to human beings a dependable fellowship in which despite the presence of danger they can already stand in freedom. . . . The gospel preamble to the Decalog, the so-called 'first commandment,' 'I am the Lord your God,' is encountered primally as the life promise applying to every human being, the promise granting space and time, history and nature. The 'first commandment' is, 'You may freely eat . . .' (Gen. 2:16)."[119] In this intertwining of covenant and creation, Bayer interprets *promissio* in connection with a doctrine of creation that in its own turn already interprets the creaturely aspect of human existence as the elementary situation of being addressed by God.[120]

The nature of *promissio* also determines the mode of its reception; that is, it necessarily implies faith as the only proper, indeed, only possible mode of its adoption: "Only if the word is promise, is faith truly faith."[121] Promise is the gift that can be received only in faith, though the gift itself is found *in* the promise, that is, is identical with its performative character: The promise actualizes the gift by being spoken and by being received in faith. Faith is thus nothing other than the conclusion to the performance of the promise. It is that toward which the promise is directed, as it were its final cause. Bayer intensifies this fulcral feature of the *promissio* as performative linguistic act with the aid of John L. Austin's theory of speech acts,[122] a topic to which I will return below.

b. The Worship Locus of the Promissiones: Proclamation of the Gospel, Baptism, Lord's Supper

Although the primary locus of these varied *promissiones* is indeed Scripture, they come to expression most immediately in the proclamation of the gospel in worship. First and foremost, Bayer finds the *promissio* in the Lord's Supper.[123] The decisive feature in the Lord's Supper is the formal uniqueness of its constitutive word of Christ; it is promise, and as such it is a performative word.[124] The pathos of theology is thus tied to a central paradigmatic practice, to a constitutive ecclesial activity, namely, the Lord's Supper. Bayer understands theology as "linguistics" insofar as it begins with this performance or activity and is always oriented back toward it.

This fixed link between theology and the *promissio* in the Lord's Supper enables Bayer to avoid three specifically modern and highly problematic notions of the relation between theology and its object, namely, the theoretical (Hegel), moral (Kant), and psychological (Schleiermacher, Feuerbach).[125] The crucial feature of these three modern models is that each is based on a specific poiesis that is either speculative, moral/value-oriented, or expressive-emotive. By contrast, by taking the *promissio* as his own point of orientation,

Bayer understands theology pathically in a twofold fashion: first as the *vita passiva* inhering within the actualization of faith itself, and second as a doctrine of language and form focused on a distinct kind of utterance (namely, performative speech acts).

c. Formal Theology as Doctrine of Language and Form[126]

Bayer both stylistically draws upon and simultaneously sharply delimits himself from Schleiermacher by defining theology as a discipline utterly dependent on God's actions as the latter manifest themselves in central language acts.[127] Academic theology differs from theology within the normal actualization of faith neither substantively nor formally, but only in the degree to which its statements are articulated and in its use of current methodological tools. Academic theology is reflexive, that is, it is well aware of its own character; it preserves its *academic* nature as theology on the one hand, and its *theological* character as an academic discipline on the other in the sense of conflict to be discussed below. Hence Bayer even understands the very academic nature of theology to be consistently pathic. In the *promissio* God's word alone has poietic power; precisely this allows it, as the object, at once also to be the subject even of theology as a scholarly discipline. Here theology acknowledges the substantively and methodically binding nature of the first commandment, effectively closing the door to any poiesis on the part of the theologian. Bayer critically delimits his own understanding from the modern turn to the subject in theology, a turn making poiesis into the constitutive feature of the perceiving subject and of its understanding.[128] By contrast, theology as a doctrine of language, word, and form[129] remains "philology" of Holy Scripture, that is, a performative activity bound to the concrete externality of the scriptural witness. For Bayer, theology exhibits this consistently philological, even grammatical feature because, as we saw, its decisive focus is found in linguistic form; *res* and *signum* coincide in the promise that offers assurance. A person receives the *res* precisely by properly comprehending the *signum* in the *fides Christi*. Because salvation inheres in the linguistic form itself, theology as second-order discourse is primarily morphology. By focusing on this linguistic form, it does justice to its object and confirms thus its own identity as an academic discipline.[130]

Bayer adduces the experience with *heresy* in demonstrating the necessity of theology as a discipline, that is, as an explicit, reflexively and methodically executed activity of faith in precisely articulated statements.[131] Precisely this demonstration, however, provokes the question concerning which "apparatus" — if not an ecclesiological one — Bayer can use to bring heresy into focus in the first place. How can heresy be identified if not through binding church doctrine that in its own turn always describes a concrete alternative as false doctrine?[132] Because theological contradiction, conflict, and dissent between theologies is the order of the day, however, one must distinguish conflicts between theologies on the one hand and between heresy and church doctrine on the other, doctrine whose binding formulation and concrete delimitation makes it possible to identify heresy as such in the first place. Otherwise, every theological conflict as such might be suspected of heresy, a situation that can only cripple theological debate. Because theology as a scholarly discipline is always involved in critical debate with other theologies, it will be clearly overtaxed unless it is distinguished from church doctrine by way of an explicit, secondary reference or orientation toward such doctrine. A problematic monism emerges in Bayer's understanding of theology as a scholarly discipline precisely because he does not address church doctrine separately. If theology really is the grammar of Holy Scripture in Luther's sense, and if Luther himself is the paradigm for engagement in such theology, then scholarly theology as a doctrine of language and form can now basically only be practiced as Luther exegesis or developed as a commentary to Luther; this, however, dogmatizes Luther's own theology. Here we touch on a central and revealing distinction between Lindbeck and Bayer. Whereas Lindbeck understands church doctrine to be the grammar of Scripture and theology to be an activity moving back and forth between Scripture and doctrine, Bayer understands theology — concretely, this means Luther's theology — to be the grammar of Scripture alongside which there is no other locus of independent logic and valency. This exposed position overtaxes theology in a hopeless way and forces it singlehandedly to assume the task of "binding and loosing," covertly turning it into church discipline. This can only cripple theological debate and undermine the specific character of theology as a scholarly discipline.[133] A contrasting model might understand scholarly or academic theology in Bayer's sense as providing proleptic clarification for church doctrines which in their own turn represent an ecclesial actualization sui generis that indeed is *not* identical with theological discourse.[134] This itself requires an explicit ecclesiological anchoring of theology as well as an understanding of church doctrine as part of an "ecclesial politic" the binding character of which is itself to be interpreted pneumatologically.[135]

Bayer now understands theology as being constitutively grounded in the *vita passiva* (its "monastic" aspect) and regulated by its methods (its "scholastic aspect"); at the same time, he understands both to be related in a mutual dynamic.[136] This position, however, requires a horizon within which theology can indeed be engaged in a context of both disagreement and conflict without at the same time always subjecting the horizon itself to discussion and debate. Bayer is unable, however, to address conceptually, on the one hand, a *doctrina evangelii* that is both antecedent to and distinct from the performance of the *promissio*, and on the other, an understanding of church doctrine that distinguishes the latter from the scholarly discipline of theology. He is unable to do so because of his problematic understanding of John L. Austin's theory of speech acts, an understanding that in its own turn results in an interpretation of Luther in which the *promissio* ultimately replaces *doctrina*.

d. Bayer, Austin,[137] and Luther

Bayer bases his entire interpretation of Luther, and thus implicitly also his own construction, on a distinction Austin makes at the beginning of his posthumously published lectures, *How to Do Things with Words*.[138] Bayer summarizes this distinction as follows:

> A constative utterance refers to content that has already been constituted; its act is that of ascertainment. The constative sentence allows that which already is to appear. It is a *logos apophantikos,* the classical judgment from the Aristotelian logic of statements. Something different occurs in the performative utterance, which Austin distinguishes from the constative utterance. It itself constitutes content; rather than confirming it as already obtaining, it posits it to begin with. . . . A performative sentence with the structure of the example "I promise you . . ." is not referring to something clearly delimited that already exists before the sentence itself and that then might appear in it as that which it already is. Rather, this sentence itself constitutes a relation and gathers within itself references of both a personal and an objective nature.[139]

In the eleventh lecture of *How to Do Things with Words,* Austin explicitly drops this seemingly clear, unequivocal distinction (except perhaps in borderline instances) between performative and constative utterances. What at the outset he called "performative verbs" he now refers to as verbs "which make explicit, as we shall now say, the illocutionary force of an utterance, or what illocutionary act it is that we are performing in issuing that utterance." By contrast, he expressly drops the notion of a purely performative utterance: "This was essentially based upon a belief in the dichotomy of performatives and constatives, which we see has to be abandoned in favour of more general *families* of related and overlapping speech acts."[140] Hence Austin's final position in his theory of speech acts is that performative verbs have a *heuristic* rather than a *constitutive* function, and the distinction between performative and constative acts can at the end of the analysis no longer simply be equated with the distinction between certain *kinds* of utterances or sentences. "The locutionary act as much as the illocutionary is an abstraction only: every genuine speech act is both."[141] The theory of speech acts is thus concerned not with classifying utterances as either performative or constative, but with examining the kinds of expressive power utterances can have.

Bayer believes that theology, as a technical or scholarly undertaking, is concerned with distinct sentences or utterances, namely, performative ones, and *not*, for example, with a distinct theological discourse tradition that understands itself as being shaped by scriptural canon and by church doctrine. The task of language analysis is to help clarify performative sentences. In relation to its object, such analysis is itself merely a constative speech activity.[142] On the basis of the strict distinction between performative and constative utterances, one Austin ultimately rejected, Bayer asserts that the gospel — the *promissio* — is not a declarative statement.[143] Rather, an assurance is genuinely assurance only if it is purely performative, that is, only insofar as it does or performs something, not insofar as it states or affirms, that is, merely ascertains.

By contrast, how does Luther's understanding of gospel and faith look from the perspective of Austin's own articulation and differentiation of the theory of speech acts? In his early period Luther undeniably concentrated quite strongly on the promissory statements accompanying the sacraments, and the enduring legacy of Bayer's study of Luther is that it explicates this with incisive clarity. If we understand the phenomenon of promissory statements from the perspective of the more precise and differentiated final version of Austin's theory of speech acts, we find that Luther concentrated on these statements not because the gospel is a distinct series of statements of a quite distinct promissory type, but because — in Austin's words — these *promissio*-formulae "make explicit . . . the illocutionary force of an utterance, or what illocutionary act it is that we are performing in issuing that utterance."[144] They make explicit the illocutionary role of the New Testament narratives and statements about Jesus; that is, they function *heuristically.*

Bayer quite rightly emphasizes that, for Luther, the illocutionary role of these utterances is of central significance. As we saw, however, it is not possible to take Austin's theory of speech acts as one's point of departure in establishing an alternative between an allegedly apophantic locutionary content of the gospel, on the one hand, and a gospel understood as creative word entirely from the perspective of its performative logic on the other, and then to play the latter off against the former. Certainly, this enables Bayer to draw a sharp line of demarcation between Luther's understanding of theology and that of the early church and medieval tradition, and to present this understanding of the gospel as a performative language act as "Luther's great hermeneutical, in the strict sense Reformational discovery."[145] In view of the former, however, it is not at all clear why Luther apparently continued to be intensively interested in the locutionary content of the gospel quite in the sense of what Bayer calls "scholastic theology."[146] In view of the latter, the question arises whether the Luther of the writing *Confession Concerning Christ's Supper* (1528), and especially the Luther of the late disputations,[147] did not possibly productively misunderstand himself.

Does this whole issue not first become plausible only by reversing Bayer's thesis? That is, that Luther understands the gospel as being primarily an utterance making a certain statement, one that on the basis of the specific character of its object always also plays an illocutionary role?[148] Because an exhaustive exegesis of Luther is not possible here, let me adduce a longer passage from the introduction to the Gospel sermons of the *Wartburg Postil,* dedicated to Albert, Count of Mansfeld, *A Brief Instruction on What to Look for and Expect in the Gospels.* I believe it shows persuasively *(a)* that the illocutionary role of the gospel, or more precisely, of the gospel *proclamation,* presupposes the locutionary content, and *(b)* that this locutionary content plays an essential illocutionary role:

> Gospel is and should be nothing else than a discourse or story about Christ, just as happens among men when one writes a book about a king or a prince, telling what he did, said, and suffered in his day. Such a story can be told in various ways; one spins it out, and the other is brief. Thus the gospel is and should be nothing else than a chronicle, a story, a narrative about Christ, telling who he is, what he did, said, and suffered — a subject which one describes briefly, another more fully, one this way, another that way. For at its briefest, the gospel is a discourse about Christ, that he is the Son of God and became man for us, that he died and was raised, that he has been established as a Lord over all things. This much St. Paul takes in hand and spins out in his epistles. He bypasses all the miracles and incidents [in Christ's ministry] which are set forth in the four gospels, yet he includes the whole gospel adequately and abundantly. . . . There you have it. The gospel is a story about Christ, God's and David's Son, who died and was raised and is established as Lord. This is the gospel in a nutshell.[149]

In Austin's terminology the gospel here is grounded entirely in its locutionary content, which does, however, play an essentially illocutionary role:

So you see that the gospel is really not a book of laws and commandments which requires deeds of us, but a book of divine promises in which God promises, offers, and gives us all his possessions and benefits in Christ. . . . When you open the book containing the gospels and read or hear how Christ comes here or there, or how someone is brought to him, you should therein perceive the sermon or the gospel through which he is coming to you, or you are being brought to him. For the preaching of the gospel is nothing else than Christ coming to us, or we being brought to him. When you see how he works, however, and how he helps everyone to whom he comes or who is brought to him, then rest assured that faith is accomplishing this in you and that he is offering your soul exactly the same sort of help and favor through the gospel. If you pause here and let him do you good, that is, if you believe that he benefits and helps you, then you really have it. Then Christ is yours, presented to you as a gift. After that it is necessary that you turn this into an example and deal with your neighbor in the very same way, be given also to him as a gift and an example.[150]

The obviously conscious synonymous use of "gospel" strongly suggests that, for Luther, the locutionary content and the illocutionary role of what is narrated (or stated) are inseparably connected, albeit in the quite specific logical sequence that makes the illocutionary character of what is narrated completely dependent on its object.

Additional support for this thesis can be found in Luther's use of the concept of *doctrina*. The gospel is a doctrine *(doctrina evangelii)* stating who Jesus Christ is and what he did and suffered. This doctrine makes statements about Jesus Christ in connection with which Luther can say that knowledge of God and knowledge of Christ are the same. Luther's explication of this *doctrina* reveals that its content includes the dogmas of Nicaea and Chalcedon as well as the doctrine of *justificatio sola fide.*

As the previous citation shows, however, this *doctrina* is for Luther always simultaneously a *promissio,* a promise, completely in the sense of Austin's final position. The gospel as *doctrina* of Jesus Christ, one making quite distinct statements about him, possesses a promissory power that is part of its essence. Saying that the gospel is a *promissio* is not to say anything about its form, but rather about its illocutionary quality. That is, speaking properly about who Jesus Christ is, what he said, did, and suffered, necessarily also — *qua* object — issues a promise, a *promissio,* to those listening. The illocutionary quality, however, depends entirely on the locutionary content, namely, *who* this Jesus is.

My conclusion is that Bayer can adduce Luther and Austin only with considerable modification of his understanding of the *promissio* as a performative speech act and of scholarly theology as a doctrine of language and form; these modifications would have to do justice to the primacy of the *doctrina evangelii*, the locutionary content of the gospel proclamation and of its binding expression in church doctrine. Of even greater importance than this question of Bayer's interpretation of Luther and Austin, however, is the *substantive* consequence for his understanding of theology. For Luther and for the theological traditions preceding and following him, theology, bound as it was to canonical Scripture, was, as a matter of course, concerned with the *doctrina evangelii;* the task was to interpret this *doctrina* from the perspective of church doctrine (and for Luther this meant especially early church dogmas). Bayer apparently eliminates this aspect entirely within the framework of theology as a scholarly discipline. True, the contrast between performative and constative utterances does allow him to rescue for such theology the faith *content* of the gospel as a performative language act in the face of massive modern criticism of that content. This apologetic strategy is indeed honorable and takes this modern criticism seriously. The question arises, however, whether this strategy, with its functionally central distinction between constative and performative utterances, does not perpetuate on the linguistic level the Kantian/neo-Protestant polemic against the *fides quae creditur,* against the *doctrina evangelii,* that is, of that which is believed in a binding fashion in faith itself. Does not his own methodical juxtaposition of *fides qua* and *fides quae* bog him down in spite of himself back in Kant's original problem, and then project precisely this problematic distinction back onto Luther?

Bayer's in this sense thoroughly modern strategy, however, is ultimately unpersuasive because the witnesses he adduces, namely, Luther and Austin, themselves understand the performative quality of certain utterances to be inseparably connected with their locutionary content. Hence, although theology can indeed make important cognitive progress by understanding itself *also* as a doctrine of the language and form of the gospel, it can do so only on the foundation of an ongoing interpretation of its locutionary content, of the *doctrina* in connection with its attendant church doctrine. Let me explicitly acknowledge here that so-called "orthodox" theologies not infrequently made the error — unlike Luther — of playing off the locutionary content against the illocutionary role of the gospel. Bayer's primary concentration on the illocutionary role of the gospel can thus be acknowledged as an important corrective to all content reification — but not at the price of a determination of the object of theology that neglects over against its performance the locutionary content of the *doctrina evangelii,* and of church doctrine, and its logical primacy.

4. Theologia Militans *as Communicative Judgment*

If the object of theology is the judging and justifying God, then the pathos of this object must characterize the reflective engagement of theology itself as a discipline. For Bayer theology is essentially a *conflict discipline* insofar as it examines thematically the conflict between God and human beings, God's challenge to human beings, the disclosure of sin in the law, and the forgiving, justifying word of the *promissio*. The object of theology is this conflict and the quite specific manner in which it is carried on in the law and the gospel; theology itself is shaped by this conflict, explicates it, and teaches it. For this reason theology must *per definitionem* give offense in a world for which this qualification can only be provocation, since the only alternative is that between judgment and repentance.[151] Within this agonistic horizon,[152] theology's explicit debate with objections is constitutive for the mode of that debate. Under the conditions of a world in which the law exposes the sinfulness of the world and the gospel promises an alien righteousness, theology can only be *theologia militans;* there is no horizon within which the gospel can be made plausible without conflict. This ties theology itself — as an academic or scholarly engagement arguing explicitly with the highest possible degree of conceptual articulation — into God's action in law and gospel and profoundly shapes it as *passio* in *oratio, meditatio,* and *tentatio.* Bayer defines engagement in this *theologia militans* more precisely as "a form of judgment inseparably bound to a specific life form."[153] This activity of judgment has its "life setting" in the existence of the justified sinner, which Bayer understands as a "critical-political existence," and is oriented toward the reality created through God's word, toward nature and history: "Such judging participation in this being as word, in this communicative being, I call a 'communicative form of judgment.' It applies not only to all areas of activity related to the church, such as preaching and instruction, pastoral care and social diaconia, mission and ecumene, but also and especially to one's dealings with nature and history in the larger sense."[154]

According to Bayer, this "communicative form of judgment" determines the structure of the debate and controversies into which the specific character of the gospel inevitably brings theology and in which theology is then to demonstrate its freedom.[155] What remains unclear is this "communication's" reference and in what way it is to be understood as "form of judgment." One possibility would be to understand "communication" from the perspective of the *promissio* such that the *promissio* itself comes to expression in that "communicative form of judgment," and to understand "form of judgment" as "placing oneself under God's judgment in law and gospel," so to speak, through the very act itself of engaging in such controversy.[156] Although this doctrine of justification has been transformed into the methodology itself, Bayer's conception does not include any ecclesial context of praxis in which this "communicative form of judgment" might be engaged concretely in the first place. Nor does this interpretation of what he means by "form of judgment" necessarily correspond to any explicit theological capacity for judgment. If the latter is indeed to be explicated, it would have to be anchored in a context of praxis in which it can be concretely practiced and engaged. This is exactly the direction he would have to take in speaking of the "praxis" of the theological discipline as "theory"[157] and in demanding the following from it: "In order to discover emergent heresy, one must develop the capacity to step back, as it were, from immediate church activities and in discourse with others try to establish substantive positions, to ascertain. . . . [Theology as a discipline] is the field of hypotheses that are presented with a specific purpose in mind and then tested in discussion according to rules previously agreed upon. These rules require that one give an account of conceptual definitions and use as well as of logical consistency of linear argumentation in a given context."[158] In consequence of this perspective Bayer actually should understand theology as a discursive practice of the church.[159]

One great advantage of understanding theology, as does Bayer, as a conflict discipline is that doing so relieves it from having to function as a comprehensively integrative system and prevents it from getting entangled in the unavoidable aporia encountered by all foundationalist strategies. This also prevents postmodern criticism of modernity from applying to his understanding of theology.[160] This proposal becomes really persuasive and useful, however, only if one understands theology as a distinct church activity concretely related to other church practices, that is, as a distinct church practice itself. An "apocalyptic theology" of the sort Bayer envisions is meaningful and possible only in connection with and deriving from an apocalyptic community and the event constituting this community, namely, worship, especially the word become flesh, the contemporaneity of Lord's Supper and word proclamation.[161] Except for the articulation of theology as a distinct practice unto itself, this is essentially Bayer's own thesis. Because his outline does not develop the church explicitly as a nexus of distinct practices, his central thesis — the anchoring of theology in worship — is not entirely persuasive.[162]

5. Theology as the Church's Discursive Practice of the Vita Passiva?

a. Implied Ecclesiology

For Bayer the center of Christian existence is an elementary theological engagement which he understands as a situation in which one is continually exposed to God's word in Scripture; Bayer takes as his reference point Luther's own understanding of the *vita passiva* as actualized in *oratio, meditatio,* and *tentatio.* Although this occurrence naturally presupposes the church, Bayer nonetheless never explicitly examines the church thematically even though it does indeed largely constitute the horizon here. "It is not the interpreter who interprets scripture, but scripture that interprets the interpreter. Scripture thus provides for its own interpretation, is its own interpreter. 'Sacra scriptura sui ipsius interpres.'"[163] The citation from Luther he adduces prior to this, however, reads as follows: "Note that the power of scripture is as follows: it is not transformed into the person who studies it, but rather transforms the person *who loves it* into itself and into its powers."[164] One might counter here that only those who love Scripture are transformed into it, not simply each and every person who studies Scripture, and that precisely this aspect does not adequately come to bear in Bayer's interpretation.[165] One might also object that the fine distinction between Bayer's general and Luther's specific formulation is in reality that Luther here *implies* an ecclesial horizon that in modernity would have to be made *explicit* if its status as a decisive feature is not to be lost. Finally, one might present the thesis that only those can love Scripture, or only those love the gospel (that is, only those believe in it as proclamation), who genuinely follow it and participate in the central practices of the church; it is *these particular* interpreters whom the Bible interprets rather than *every* individual interpreter.

In the following section Bayer does indeed draw this very conclusion: "Being interpreted by the biblical text is something that takes place only *in the church itself,* in the community of those who first hear and believe, and only then speak; 'I believed, and so I spoke' (2 Cor. 4:13). Hermeneutical and theoretical questions are essentially *pneumatological-ecclesiological;* only from the perspective of worship does an appropriate concept of 'theology' emerge."[166] This thesis addresses all the objections just presented, and appears to have answered and refuted all previous critical queries. But this is only apparently the case, for Bayer does not really develop the implications of this thesis in both directions, following rather the asymmetry between Scripture and church only in *one* direction, namely, from Scripture to the church, leaving the other side of this asymmetrical relationship unresolved. Saying that someone "is in-

89

terpreted by the biblical text" is itself an ecclesiological-normative statement relating to central practices in which we repeatedly are exposed to the "incarnate word" such that it interprets us anew. Being interpreted by Scripture is not some sort of magic inherent to the Bible, but the implicate of the engagement of central church (and especially worship-related) practices in whose context we learn to love the Bible. *Only an explicitly developed reference to worship as a specific church practice that itself is developed ecclesiologically establishes the context in which the specific pathos of "being interpreted by Scripture" can be actualized in the different individual practices.*

b. Toward an Understanding of Theology as a Discursive Practice of the Church

Bayer's proposal does, however, contain important points of departure for addressing this deficit. He explicitly points out that

> what precedes both knowledge and action is language — that particular language that creates faith, the word of Christ. Because Christians owe their freedom to this word, they never really gain control of that freedom. Rather than bringing about that freedom or acquiring it, it is given and spoken to them. To this end, they need someone else, someone who promises it to them in the name of Jesus in concrete situations and in a concretely particular form; that is, they need the *church. The church is where distinct language acts take place,* in baptism, the Eucharist, in proclamation, in personal dialogue. It is also the response to this word in prayer, hymn, educational work (understood in the comprehensive sense of world experience discussed above).[167]

Here Bayer formulates *in nuce* an ecclesiology oriented toward Luther's "On the Councils and Churches" and focused on central activities.[168] He includes theology in these ecclesiological considerations: "The education or training of Christians not only emerges from the language acts that create faith, but also turns back toward them to reflect upon them retrospectively as past events and proleptically as future events in new situations. *This activity is theology.*"[169]

Bayer's initial anchoring of theology as a conceptual activity within the church lends to his concept of theology a distinct, bipolar freedom of movement. The theological discipline is *theology* in its relation to the elementary language acts "in which law and gospel concretely come to bear as both binding and liberating."[170] *A scholarly and academic discipline* is theology depending on its relation to these elementary language acts. As such, it is character-ized in a twofold fashion. First, it is characterized by its "engagement in the scientific or scholarly methods of its time, that is, within a conceptually real-ized contemporaneity."[171] Second, it is related in a critical-regulative fashion to heresy or heterodoxy (i.e., it is a scientific or scholarly discipline precisely as dogmatics). "In order to discover emergent heresy, one must develop — cultivate — the capacity to step back, as it were, from immediate church ac-tivities and in *discourse* with others try to establish *substantive positions*. To this end, one must objectify the immediate occurrence of these language acts and make them the object of reflection, must isolate them in segments in or-der to analyze and compare them in commensurable increments."[172] Through this theology faith learns "to understand itself, to distinguish itself from unbelief and, especially, from heresy or heterodoxy, and to make itself comprehensible to as many people as possible."[173]

The central task of theology is thus to foster the self-understanding of faith, the ability to distinguish unbelief and heterodoxy, and the ability to mediate faith to others. Here Bayer programmatically and confidently describes the locus and ecclesial task of theology. Because he explicates neither the relation to wor-ship nor to the language acts of the church within the framework of an ex-plicit ecclesiology, however, the danger remains that the "incarnate word" might ultimately nonetheless remain "private." One can avoid this danger only by developing the church itself *ecclesiologically as* the public of the "in-carnate word" in tension with other publics.

c. The Ambivalent Place of Church Doctrine

Because ecclesiology and its relation to theology is explicated only in a lim-ited fashion, doctrine and its function for theology also remain unclear. Bayer does in any case write that "the locus and task of Protestant theology in the present can be determined only by considering the relation between on the one hand the truth claims of modern thinking, and on the other the truth claim of Luther's Reformational theology and of the Lutheran confessional writings, a claim recognized by the church order in every Lutheran church and commensurate with that order in the vows of ordination."[174] For Bayer, however, the experience with heresy makes theology as a discipline necessary, *not* church doctrine.[175] This, however, robs theology of the freedom of move-ment so necessary for it — within the horizon of church doctrine — and co-vertly turns theology itself into the locus of church doctrine itself.[176] But if dogmatics — and the discipline of theology is in Bayer's understanding noth-ing other than this — usurps the place of church doctrine, it becomes impossible as a conflict discipline, since only a separately implemented ecclesiastical teaching authority can open up the space in which theology can be developed as a conflict discipline. Bayer himself blocks this access by relating Protestant theology primarily to the intellectual history of modernity and then failing to develop any ecclesial-theological debate with Roman Catholic and Eastern Orthodox theology, to mention but the two most important. This is indeed consistent if one understands — as Bayer seems to do — the truth claim of Luther's theology itself in the sense of dogma such that, although one must indeed consider it over against the truth claims of modernity, one must no longer necessarily do so over against the truth claims of other ecclesial traditions. Hence it is not surprising, and yet has far-reaching consequences for his concept of theology, that his proposal articulates no constitutive relation to the dogma of the early church (a matter of course for both Luther and earlier Lutheran orthodoxy) or to ecumenical or theologically controversial dialogue at large.[177] This confessionally narrow focus and the constitutive relation to modernity is thus a questionable and in its own turn ecclesiologically problematic feature of his understanding of theology.

The absence of any concept of church doctrine oriented toward his concept of theology may derive not least from Bayer's problematic focus on performance with regard to the concept of *promissio*. For only if one assumes that a performance quality does indeed attach to certain constative utterances of the *doctrina evangelii*, and yet that this quality cannot be separated from that which is stated and rather depends precisely on it, can church doctrine continue to secure and fortify this *doctrina evangelii* against false teaching — precisely for the sake of its performance. If by contrast the content of the gospel is reserved for catechetical systematics alone, church doctrine cannot become the enduring point of reference and orientation for theology as a scholarly discipline, the consequence being that theology inevitably is forced into a doctrinal function and is thus severely hampered in fulfilling its real task.

6. *Conclusion:* Sic et Non

Bayer's substantive concept of theology, developed entirely from the perspective of pathos, generates a powerful tension between an *implicitly* ecclesiologically anchored theology, on the one hand, and the absence of any *explicit* ecclesiology within that concept of theology or any correspondingly *explicated* theological articulation of the place of theology in the church on the other. From the perspective of Lindbeck's understanding of the cultural-linguistic disposition of any articulation in speech of the Christian faith, and

Bayer's own understanding of the explicit, language-bound disposition of that faith and its enduring ties to certain statements, the question arises whether one necessary implication of his understanding of theology would not have to be a genuinely ecclesiological understanding of these central linguistic activities themselves. Moreover, this absence of any explicit consideration of how theology relates to church doctrine destabilizes any concrete ecclesial features of that understanding of theology, and neglects an important part of its pathos.[178] Within the concrete implementation of Bayer's conception, the interpretation of Luther thus seems *implicitly* to usurp the place that should rightfully and *explicitly* belong to *church doctrine*. One reason for this may be that Bayer has made the interpretation of Luther into the foundation of his own understanding of theology without reference to any of the ecumenical dialogues or agreements between Catholics and Lutherans.[179] Although his Pauline-Reformational understanding of theology is indeed critical, it is not self-critical insofar as it might have to prove itself in ecclesial discourse either ecumenically or within the forum of theological controversy. Rather, he simply presupposes this understanding as a confessional axiom and articulates it with a focus on a — necessary and certainly clarifying — controversy with modern strategies of secularization, but does not articulate it with regard to the *church*, that is, ecumenically *and* with reference to theological controversy.[180] Although he does advocate an intertwining of the monastic and scholastic aspects of theology, he does not develop this concept of theology in any living and dialogical debate with patristic or contemporary Catholic and Orthodox views. The price is high for concentrating so exclusively on a specific construction of Luther's theology, one that is itself never ecumenically examined, proven, or justified, and yet in whose light everything else is tested; at central junctures he precisely does *not* expose himself to any *ecclesial* controversy, and instead moves toward controversy only in critical debate with modernity.

The unquestionable strength of Bayer's outline is its concentration on the pathos of theology, a pathos he develops — in distinction to Lindbeck — in a theologically explicit fashion from the perspective of the *promissio*-concept and in reference to its origin in worship and its church task as a communicative form of judgment. The absence of any explicit ecclesiology, however, threatens the understanding of theology he envisions. *Only an explicitly ecclesiologically understood concept of church practices allows one to follow his central thesis further and to articulate concretely oratio, meditatio, tentatio as individual and communal practices, and to understand academic theology as a discursive practice oriented toward precisely those practices in its role as a "communicative form of judgment" that proves itself in the forum of conflict.*

Summary and Transition

Both theologians explicate the pathos of theology from the perspective of the *verbum externum*. Lindbeck does so first of all structurally from the perspective of the comprehensive life praxis of "religion" at large, then structurally as well with more specific reference to Christianity, albeit articulated from the perspective of the scriptural canon. By contrast, Bayer explicates it substantively from the perspective of the proclaimed gospel, the *promissio*. Both proposals demonstrate how the question of the pathos of theology allows the latter to emerge as a distinct practice; this is the case, however, only because both also simultaneously examine the church implicitly, and in Lindbeck's case, church doctrine explicitly. Both proposals, however, exhibit an ecclesiological deficit and especially an inadequate ecclesiological anchoring of church doctrine over against the separate practice of theology. At the same time, however, both proposals do indeed offer constructive points of departure for understanding how theology can be conceived as a distinct church practice whose pathos replaces modern foundationalist strategies.

Drawing from the positive impulses in Lindbeck's and Bayer's proposals, I will, in the following third part, develop from the perspective of God's salvific economy the pneumatological and ecclesiological aspects of this *verbum externum* with reference especially to Luther's theology and with the aid of central impulses from the *communio* ecclesiology of Eastern Orthodoxy. I hope to develop a perspective enabling us to overcome the problems attaching to Lindbeck's and Bayer's proposals within the framework of a pneumatologically grounded and ecclesiologically articulated *verbum externum*. Against this background I will then focus in Part Four on theology as a church practice whose pathos can be developed from the perspective of the Trinity and from that of the economy of salvation, a theology that then participates in the telos of the public of the Holy Spirit.

PART THREE

The Church's Rooting in the Spirit: The Core Practices and the *Doctrina Evangelii*

I. Church Doctrine as the Pathos of Theology: The Peterson-Barth Controversy[1]

My intention is to articulate critically, from the perspective of the Trinity and the economy of salvation, the relationship between church and theology, and to develop the pathos of theology explicitly from both a pneumatological and ecclesiological perspective. This point of departure is oriented specifically toward the economy of salvation, and I will first examine its relevance vis-à-vis the two dominant pneumatological-ecclesiological alternatives within the framework of Western theology, that is, *institution* and *charisma*. Within the context of my inquiry, this juxtaposition becomes highly relevant for understanding the relationship between the church, church doctrine, and theology as church practice. The controversy between Erik Peterson and Karl Barth concerning the nature and task of theology as a church activity in its relation to church and dogma exemplifies the debate between the two alternatives of institution and charisma, alternatives still providing the two basic options for Western theology since the Reformation. This particular controversy demonstrates that theology as a church practice can only remain an unstable undertaking as long as its relationship with church doctrine is not clarified, and also demonstrates that the two alternatives similarly are unpersuasive because both remain pneumatologically deficient in their "either/or." In an attempt to provide clarity, Peterson took a christological-ecclesiological path, Barth by contrast a pneumatological-ecclesiological one. Their mutual critiques both adduce significant reasons for not following either of them. At the same time, however, neither of their counterproposals is able to refute the other's objections persuasively. The debate between these two theologians shows that a determination of the nature of theology as a church practice will depend to a significant degree on one's understanding of the relationship between theology and church doctrine. In its own turn, determining this latter relationship requires that one clarify theologically — and in Barth we can already see that this means from the perspective of the *Trinity* — the relationship between pneumatology and ecclesiology in a way doing justice to the salvific-economic mission of the Holy Spirit and its work. In the remainder of Part Three, I will thus develop a pneumatological-ecclesiological perspective beyond the unsatisfactory Peterson/Barth alternative that nonetheless does justice to the central concerns of both and at the same time aids in overcoming the pneumatological and ecclesiological deficits we found in Lindbeck and Bayer, the goal here being a pathic theological discursive practice.

1. Erik Peterson's Query, "What Is Theology?": Theology in the Pathos of Dogma

In his 1925 tractate "What Is Theology?" Erik Peterson sharply attacked Barth's early dialectical theology as exemplified especially in Barth's famous lecture, "The Word of God and the Task of the Ministry."[2] There Barth understands theology as the continual movement of an unresolvable tension between the task of proclaiming God's word on the one hand and the human impossibility of doing justice to this task through human power alone on the other. The seriousness of theology consists in withstanding this tension and in not giving up, and rather to move continually back and forth "in" it.[3] From the perspective of the absolute diastasis between God and human being, Barth understands theology as the dialectical examination of this diastasis in a person's theological existence. By contrast, Peterson understands theology directly from the perspective of its object, which has mediated itself undialectically and yet in an authoritative and concretely binding fashion.

Although Peterson does applaud Barth for reclaiming Protestant theology as a serious public activity of the church, he nonetheless strikes at the heart of dialectical theology by accusing it of lacking any concrete object, which in this case meant any binding dogmatic foundation, and that it was concerned only with an endless dialectical game of possibilities. The seriousness of dialectical theology was false and only masked its self-relatedness. In contradistinction to the false seriousness of the dialectician, God's seriousness is completely undialectical: "For precisely this is part of God's seriousness, namely, that his is concretely visible and is present in an utterly undialectical fashion, *is present,* for example, in the form of final judgment as confessed by the Christian faith."[4] Peterson's critical point over against early dialectical theology is that he juxtaposes dialectics with myth, which narrates in a nonbinding fashion and can be developed dialectically in rather arbitrary ways. From this perspective dialectics is essentially free work on myth — and thus ultimately poiesis[5] — while for him, theology is essentially obedience.[6] Peterson is focusing here on the passivity of the theological subject. Revelation encounters a person such that, as is the case in theology as well, only faith and obedience are commensurate with it, that is, essentially undialectical concurrence. Dialectics comes into play only when the point of departure is two indispensable subjects, God and human being, who stand in a relationship of unresolvable tension and in infinite dissimilitude, and then one of these subjects must now also reflexively actualize this tension in the activity of theologizing.

The Undialectical, Concrete Character of Revelation   As with Barth, Peterson's axiomatic point of departure for theology is the idea of revelation. Only the nature of revelation itself can determine the character of theology. This apparent agreement, however, already contains the central difference between Peterson and early dialectical theology. Because according to Peterson an undialectical and concrete character is to be attributed to revelation, so also is theology concerned in an undialectical way with concrete knowledge. For Peterson, the concrete character of revelation derives from its being already "given" in dogma and sacrament. He views dogma and sacrament parallel insofar as neither directly continues the incarnation itself; rather, both are "given" in a certain way by Christ, the sacrament through its institution, dogma as an implication of the teaching authority conferred upon the church.[7] Hence dogma, as the "extension" of Christ's discourse about God, itself talks about God in a binding, instructive way demanding obedience.[8] On the basis of this determination of dogma, dogma itself exhibits a binding challenge to all human beings. In the incarnation God himself has "pressed up hard against the very body of human beings," something which Peterson believes is expressed concretely in the existence not primarily of the sacrament or kerygma, but of dogma.[9] The heart of his understanding of "dogma" is that, in dogma itself, a positive legal claim from within the very body of Christ is over every human being. Peterson does, however, wish to distinguish between dogma and law: "Although Christ has indeed freed us from the law, he has not freed us from obedience. The moment dogma disappears, we again become subject to the law."[10] So in Peterson's view it is precisely dogma that opposes any human dogmatization. For without dogma, theology is defenselessly exposed to the law of human doctrinal opinion and school convictions. Theology does not need to dogmatize its claims precisely because dogma itself is actually what continues Christ's instructing discourse about God.

Scripture and Prophecy Does this mean that Peterson subordinates the biblical canon to dogma and sacrament? By no means. He emphatically identifies Holy Scripture as a nonderivative authority. "For as inspired scripture, it is a primary authority. This is why the Bible, too, does not belong to the church in the same way dogma belongs to the church."[11] The biblical canon is thus the irreducible counterpart to the church; as the word of God, it comes to expression through pneumatic exegesis and proclamation in the church itself. Peterson understands Scripture itself, however (the New Testament), in contrast to dogma, not as the extension of the incarnation; that is, it has no sacramental character itself. "The Bible in and of itself, prophetic speech in the larger sense and its attendant exegesis and proclamation, can never fix this distinction between the old and new covenant by itself. In other words, because Christ as the *incarnate* spoke about God, he cannot adequately be rendered in the biblical word; rather, he breaks through that word and acquires a body in a different sphere of reality. The Bible is the body of the *prophetic* word; the body of God's logos, however, is not the Bible, but the church and the dogma posited with the church."[12] A fulcral feature of his understanding of "dogma" is doubtless that he speaks here not about the Lord's Supper as the body of God's logos, but about the church's teaching authority and, with it, dogma.

Church, Dogma, Theology The decisive feature of Peterson's understanding of theology is thus to view theology as being directly dependent on dogma; dogma itself, as the enactment of the church's teaching authority, represents the extension of the incarnate logos.[13] This enables him to distinguish sharply between *dogma* on the one hand and *confession* or *church doctrine* on the other, the former being the extension of God's logos, the latter the extension of the human act of faith. Although this ascribes to dogma only derived authority, it is nonetheless Christ's own authority "that is 'spoken' and expressed here."[14]

How does Peterson understand the relationship between theology and dogma? Although he does indeed clearly distinguish theology from dogma, at the same time he also brings the two into intimate proximity. "Theology continues in the form of concrete argumentation the situation in which the logos-revelation has entered formatively into dogma. The real sense of theology's argumentation, however, is shaped by the *quo iure* of divine revelation. Theology is the concrete *enactment* of the fact that God's logos spoke concretely about God such that there is concrete revelation, concrete faith, and concrete obedience."[15] Insofar as theology is understood as the argumentative continuation of the logos-revelation into dogma, its engagement or actualization is itself an act of obedience. At the same time, however, it is an act claiming binding authority; yet if we are to distinguish it from dogma at all and simultaneously distinguish it from a more widely conceived concept of theology, we must understand it as binding "church doctrine."

Taking as his point of departure this specific event of the incarnation of the logos in Jesus Christ and its extension into dogma, Peterson has thus articulated theology as the dogmatic teaching of the church. As such, theology becomes for him a specifically Christian phenomenon that is impossible in any other religion because the latter lacks any binding discourse about God that has in this way been extended into dogma.[16]

In summary, we can say that Peterson understands the nature of theology as being wholly constituted by the specific object of the incarnation. In being shaped entirely by that object, that is, by being utterly transparent over against dogma, theology participates in the logos's discourse about God. By utterly surrendering itself to the antecedent, binding discourse about God in dogma, theology becomes "theo-logy," logos about God; and precisely in so doing, theology *defers* all honor to Christ.[17] The decisive ecclesiological implication of this understanding is that the church, as the "body of Christ," represents Christ, and does so in a twofold manner: first, *qua* the teaching authority Christ transferred to the church in the form of dogma; second, through the sacrament of the Lord's Supper instituted by Christ. Basically, being a "theologian" is not simply a constitutive part of being a Christian, but rather is a special, public ecclesiastical position within the church's teaching authority; although Peterson does not address this, his overall argumentation suggests that this position is subordinated to the episcopate as the highest teaching office. Only thereby does theology for Peterson become a *specialized* discipline in the strict sense. As "dogmatics," it is the binding, argumentative interpretation of dogma and thus, expressed in scholastic terminology, the "*first* discipline."[18] Insofar as it continually makes binding statements in its argumentative interpretation of dogma, it is the discipline of the incarnate logos's own binding discourse about God as continued in church dogma. For Peterson, then, theology acquires its unique freedom and substantive speci-

99

ficity precisely by subordinating itself to the authority of dogma. If it rids it-self of these ties to dogma, it enters not the sphere of alleged academic or scientific freedom but that of subjugation to the law. The one dogma is replaced by the dogmatizing discourse of the many. Does not theology need the objective basis it finds in dogma, which in its own turn continues Christ's own discourse? Is it not from dogma alone that theology receives its substance, its authority, and its specific character as theology? These are the questions Peterson directs critically to early dialectical theology. Before I turn to Barth's response, let me first address a few critical questions to Peterson's understanding of pathos, an understanding utterly oriented toward dogma and wholly shaped by it.

Dogma without Kerygma   Although Peterson places the incarnation of the logos at the center of his reflections, he ultimately does not do justice to it because, by distinguishing so sharply between kerygma and dogma, he undermines the soteriological telos of the incarnation. Dogma, separated from kerygma, replaces it, the result being that it also lays claims to the latter's justifying legal authority. That is, dogma without kerygma inevitably becomes a new law itself. Under the form of juridical categories, dogma separated from kerygma thus becomes a form of the law rather than of salvation insofar as it makes a legal claim against human beings without promising them anything.[19] The better alternative would be to receive Peterson's challenge as follows. Dogma, understood as the implicate of the gospel, unfolds kerygma in binding doctrine. This preserves kerygma *as kerygma* by preserving its soteriological articulation in doctrinally binding formulations. By contrast, Peterson's peculiar proposal makes dogma into an end in itself, into "pure" discourse about God whose "corporeal claim" on all human beings can all too easily turn into a terrorization of conviction without its soteriological focus. This is precisely where the salutary soteriological distinction between law and gospel should come to bear. This distinction, however, implies that dogma expresses the *gospel* (and thus also the distinction between law and gospel) in binding doctrine.

Dogma without Pneuma   It is worth noting that Peterson does not in any way explicate *pneumatologically* this intertwined relationship between incarnation, church, and dogma, and understands dogma rather according to a sacramental logic alongside the Eucharist as the second extension of the incarnation mediated by the church's teaching authority. The result is that he conceives the church not pneumatologically from the perspective of the *Creator Spiritus,* but in direct and immediate continuation of the incarnate and

100

resurrected Christ. Here we encounter a "binitarian"[20] way of theological thinking similar to that which we will find in Barth's response, "Church and Theology." For both Peterson and Barth, the Holy Spirit possesses only an actualizing function. For Peterson this function is related to pneumatic exegesis in the cult, the mediation of the prophetic word. For Barth, as we will see, the Spirit stands for the self-actualization of God's word in faith.

Dogma and Theology   On the one hand, Peterson always distinguishes terminologically between dogma and theology. On the other, he tries to distance himself as far as possible from an understanding of theology as the scholarly presentation of faith, and in so doing brings dogma and theology into intimate proximity. "If church and dogma were constituted first only in the act of faith itself, then they would belong essentially to the person who believes. *The church, however, is not the body of the believer, but the body of Christ.* Dogma is not a concretion of the act of faith — and theology thus not a doctrine of faith — but of the logos."[21] By entirely subordinating theology to dogma as the central aspect of the church's teaching authority, he also essentially eliminates the notion that every believer is also a "theologian." Nor is this surprising, since only if faith and with it theology are from the outset understood *soteriologically* is theology of significance as an inherent actualization of faith. For Peterson, *real* theology exists only as an explicit "ecclesiastical estate." His understanding of theology also implies the eclipse of theology as a discursively proceeding church practice.

We encounter in Peterson the same problem as earlier in Bayer. If theology as dogmatics coincides completely with binding church doctrine, one can no longer do justice to a theological discourse in which one can question, interpret, criticize, and argue in ongoing debate with different theological positions. This always immediately equates theological dispute or dissent with doctrinal conflict. Only if church doctrine (dogma), theological doctrine (dogmatics), and theological discourse are meaningfully distinguished *theologically* from one another is theology as a church practice *not* overtaxed. One curious consequence of Peterson understanding theology exclusively from the perspective of dogma is that his own tractate cannot be understood as a genuine theological statement since it is not concerned with any direct and binding interpretation of dogma.

Sic et Non and the Strength of Peterson's Query   Peterson maneuvered himself into a problematic in-between position. His view of things contradicted his own church existence; he had to either retreat or move much farther forward, and he did the latter by converting to Roman Catholicism.[22] This move does not, however, justify dismissing Peterson's challenge to Protestant theology as a merely crypto-Catholic attack.[23] It remains an extremely significant query as long as the relation between church, church doctrine, and theology as church practice in Protestant theology cannot get beyond its basic rejection in theological liberalism, on the one hand,[24] or the aporia inherent in dialectical theology on the other.[25]

Over against dialectical theology, Peterson unequivocally and emphatically insisted that theology already finds its object in a completely undialectical but binding fashion in the dogma of the church, and that by being engaged in obedience to that dogma as an argumentative interpretation of the latter, theology itself acquires the status of binding church doctrine.

In the present study I will take up Peterson's thrust as a query to contemporary Protestant theology, and will try to do justice to this query myself by understanding theology as a distinct church practice. Peterson's emphasis on obedience within the actualization of theology appears to be a *particula veri* of his approach. To what extent, however, is this obedience to be understood as an inherent rather than merely external aspect of that faith such that theology, as an actualization of faith, becomes the presupposition or prerequisite of this obedience?[26] The unquestionable strength of Peterson's tractate is that by confronting Protestant theology with this incisive question, it points out that the question of "church and theology" and of the relation between theology and church doctrine is of decisive significance for theology's self-understanding as a church activity. The core problem in Peterson's own response turns out to be that the pathos of theology is articulated by means of an incarnation-theological understanding of dogma such that it is in danger of disappearing entirely, as the following, pointed statement shows: "The subject of theology is not the professor of theology, but primarily Christ and secondarily the church."[27] Although this is essentially correct, Peterson does not do justice to the fact that theology is at the same time always performed by human beings who are themselves also sinners and as such are always in need of God's forgiveness — including when they engage in theology, a point Barth vehemently brings to bear over against Peterson. Unfortunately, Barth's own rejoinder exhibits several central — and similarly pneumatological — weaknesses, prompting us to go beyond both Barth and Peterson *by following an explicit pneumatology in understanding the binding nature of church doctrine as the work of the Holy Spirit in the time of God's oikonomia, and to interpret this work of the Holy Spirit as an inherent part of the pathos in which theology is grounded.* First, however, I will examine Barth's own rejoinder to Erik Peterson's tractate "What Is Theology?"

2. Karl Barth's Response, "Church and Theology": The Pneumatological Grounding of Church Doctrine and Theology

Karl Barth and the entire group of dialectical theologians, which at this time still included Bultmann and Gogarten, felt the substantive power and incisiveness of Peterson's attack.[28] Barth's response, "Church and Theology,"[29] is a fascinating *sic et non* in which he directs incisive questions at Peterson's understanding of dogma and at his way of relating theology and dogma. At the same time, Barth himself explicitly counters Peterson by relating dogma to *kerygma* and by interpreting dogma itself as *church* doctrine, referring then in his pneumatology to God's presence and activity in the Spirit.

Barth initially agrees with Peterson that there are indeed authoritative entities — he calls them "mediate forms" — through which theology receives its object. He immediately gives his argumentation a dialectical turn, however, by confronting the "immediacy of God's eternal and omnipresent word and Spirit in which its [theology's] *freedom* is grounded"[30] with theology's own *concrete* obedience to *concrete* authority. This already prefigures the basic structure of Barth's rejoinder; the matrix of concrete authority constituting the human witness to God's word is countered by the immediacy of God's word and of his authoritative self-expression. *Tertium non datur.* The mediate forms prove to be only indirectly "mediate" as traces of God's self-disclosure, rather than in the strict sense that God's self-disclosure should be understood as being bound to those forms. How does Barth proceed with his response?

Barth calls into question the monolithic hierarchy of authority "logos-dogma-theology" by drawing attention to the complex reality of authority relationships even in contemporary Roman Catholic dogmatics at that time.[31] Although he does agree with Peterson that "dogmatics" presupposes binding church doctrine,[32] he then immediately insists on speaking about *concrete* obedience to *concrete* authorities, that is, about a multilevel network of authoritative voices.[33] By acknowledging in this fashion "mediate" authoritative entities to which theology is concretely obedient, Barth manages to break through Peterson's close connection of logos, dogma, and theology and to place dogma into the sphere of church doctrine — together with other, similar significant entities such as canon, the teaching of the Fathers, and the church's need of the moment, to all of whom theology is also to render concrete obedience.

Here, however, Barth already effects a noteworthy shift in the understanding of "obedience." *Concrete* obedience is the actualization of a specific theological existence. By entering into a specific relation with different authorities, a given theologian concretizes obedience through engaging in his or her specific mode of theologizing. "Obedience" is now no longer the simple enactment or actualization of the *vita passiva* over against dogma, but rather is a specific actualization of the theological subject. The center of gravity of obedience shifts slightly but decisively between Peterson and Barth. Peterson is concerned with a kind of theological engagement in which, although one does indeed argue and interpret authoritatively, there is no capacity of judgment concerning how in the multilayered network of authorities "concrete" obedience is rendered such that it is always utterly irreducibly this or that concrete obedience of this or that concrete theologian; that is, the obedience of theological engagement can always be measured, as it were, "from the outside" against the standard of dogma. This is not possible in Barth's understanding of concrete obedience. For him, obedience is an "immediate" obedience to God in which the concrete authority of the mediate forms merely guides one's own capacity of judgment, with whose help one renders concrete obedience through concrete evaluation. One evaluative judgment must here be juxtaposed by another evaluative judgment, and both must then prove themselves in public ecclesial debate within the horizon of the network of different authorities — which is nothing other than *theological discourse* itself.

In a further dialectical move, Barth affirms that theology does indeed live from dogma, but only *also* from dogma insofar as the church possesses authority. On the one hand, this authority is to be unequivocally affirmed over against other entities such as, for example, "history," and yet on the other it is to be theologically articulated, since it is, after all, the authority of the *church.* For Barth, however, the authority of the church is a secondary, christologically qualified authority in a threefold fashion. It is temporal, relative, and formal authority, and as such, remains unalterably different from its origin, Jesus Christ, who is the real authority.[34] The deciding feature here is the relational aspect constituting church authority. "Church authority is not authority in and of itself, but rather in *relation* to the *real* authority of the Lord in his glory."[35] The *ius divinum* derives from Christ's authority and finds its human correspondence in the establishment of a *ius humanum.* The key feature in the relationship between the two, however, is the *diastasis* between them. Even if this *ius humanum* is indeed established, Barth still believes one must continue to pray for the Holy Spirit to lead the church to complete truth. What Peterson conceives in strict continuation of the incarnate logos in unbroken continuity, Barth conceives in a fundamental diastasis (God — human being; heaven — earth) in which the various elements, although certainly related to one another, nonetheless remain strictly separated within this relationship. Church doctrine (of necessity also including the determination of the canon) is the more or less obedient human response to God's action, and is in no way part of that action itself.

The concrete obedience of the church is a human action, a "responding" action of the church toward Christ and the Spirit, for according to Barth, the word and Spirit together constitute the concrete point at which the mediate authority of the church subordinates itself visibly and concretely to the immediate authority of Christ. This concretely grounds and demarcates the secondary authority of the church. The church actualizes its obedience and authority in this concrete subordination to the word and Spirit.

This relationship between "word" and "Spirit" characterizes Barth's pneumatological logic. The Holy Spirit is God's action that in full freedom joins the witnessing human word such that it communicates itself to the listener as truth, that is, such that the listener hears it as God's word. The scriptural witness remains the condition for the possibility of any revelatory self-attestation of God and simultaneously its norm. The Holy Spirit is then this revelatory self-attestation itself, that is, the synonym for God's self-announcement in the person who hears the witness.[36]

Two things are important here: first, *that* Barth seriously brings pneumatology to bear over against Peterson's proposal, and second, *how* he does this. While the former is an unequivocal and important step forward, the latter remains a questionable undertaking, since Barth's proposal makes the Holy Spirit into the principle of God's revelatory self-presentation and self-mediation that is to resolve the problem of mediation generated by the diastasis in the first place. In the process, he connects this principle with the subjectivity of the individual believer. As it turns out, for trinitarian reasons Barth cannot envision here any public work of the Spirit, that is, any work that the *Creator Spiritus* creates beyond a *testimonium internum*.[37] The remaining course of Barth's argument shows that his pneumatological solution itself becomes a problem insofar as he applies Chalcedonian logic in determining more precisely the "locus of the conscious concrete authority."[38]

Barth localizes this concrete authority in a "third" place between God's logos and Spirit, on the one hand, and "the religious opinions and outpourings of the human subject" on the other.

> In this center, the church knows and confesses God through God's own perfect grace, albeit within human limitations according to the measure of the faith granted to it, the sinning church. Here the church perceives and proclaims God's word, albeit in weak human words. Here it makes decisions *iure divino*, albeit thereby establishing *ius humanum*. Here the infallibility of what is given by God and the fallibility of what human beings receive as little constitute a mutually exclusive antithesis as does the constancy of the covenant of grace — a covenant into which the individual is taken up — with the daily

penitence that individual needs precisely as such. In this center position, "there is" concrete authority, and "there is," alongside the other things subsumed under this concept, also dogma. That it is Christ who bestows this upon the church does not prevent it from in fact also residing in the extension of the human act of faith, or that it is also a confession of faith.[39]

Barth defends the open quality of this center position, which for him is synonymous with the "dialectic" of theology, with the aid of Chalcedonian logic, which he transfers from Christology to the logic of divine and human action. At Chalcedon the focus was on the claim that in the one person of Christ the divine "and" the human nature are together without being fused into a "third" nature and without the one absorbing the other. In Barth's use, however, the focus shifts to the claim that the divine act of revelation "and" the human act of responding witness come together always anew on the grounds of God's initiative.

> In the "and" with which theology combines in words what it cannot combine in thought because that combination can be made only in the act of the divine Word and Spirit, in this "and" lies the theological "taking" of the revelation "seriously." Only one who could say Jesus Christ, that is, could say God become flesh, God and man, in *one* word, and that word a true word, could pride himself on *not* being a "dialectical theologian." But the history of dogma teaches us and the christological dogma, especially that of Chalcedon, requires of us not to will what man cannot will in reason. And what holds here holds for the whole of theology. . . . [T]heology is in its whole course at best *Prolegomenon,* preface. Theology speaks the preamble for that which ultimately God himself must say — and will say. Just so far can theology "take" revelation "seriously."[40]

The first problem here is that Barth now no longer brings to expression any of the specific dogmas or church doctrines or other concrete authorities, since they involve merely "aspects" of that unstable "center" of the always anew coming together of God's action and human witness in the Spirit. The second problem is that Barth transfers the logic of Chalcedon to the entirety of theology. What doubtless constituted a meaningful regulative in a substance-ontological context does not in an action-determined context automatically apply. First, the unequivocal referent, one already given in the christological context, is obviously missing in this kind of problematic action-determined nexus of "God and human being." Second, this model reduces the person and work of the Holy Spirit in a highly problematic fashion. The crucial problem of the "center" thus conceived is that it is unstable, that is, that it lacks any un-equivocal referent, quite unlike the original christological "life setting" of the Chalcedonian definition. For dogma is "accessible" here only as the event of encounter between divine action in Spirit and word, on the one hand, and the human confession of faith on the other. The construction does not provide for the Holy Spirit to tie itself to such a confession or for such a confession to express human action "in" the Spirit such that the confession itself might be understood as a work of the Holy Spirit.

This can be seen quite clearly in the example Barth adduces to illustrate the dialectic of theology as the actualization of its eschatologically provisional nature.

> All our discourse, statements, speaking, and argumentation in theology can only *refer* or *relate* to *God's* address to human beings that took place and continues to take place in Christ, an address we are neither competent nor capable of *articulating* or *actualizing* ourselves. . . . There are allegedly monasteries in whose refectories the place of honor receives a *full place setting* at every meal and yet is then left *unoccupied!* This unoccupied status of *the* place where the decisive word should be spoken is the meaning of dialectics in theology.[41]

The problem with this example is the following: Barth interprets the eschatological provisionality of the "empty place," which refers strictly to the parousia of Jesus Christ, such that it contradicts Christ's promised presence in the work of the Holy Spirit. Barth's suggestion that "the church has reason to let the *promise suffice*"[42] begs the question of what we are now to think of the promise of the presence and work of the Holy Spirit. *Would it not mean precisely that, by orienting ourselves toward the promises, we are to expect and recognize God's work in the Holy Spirit also "in" the work of the church itself, that is, in the incarnate word and in the kerygmatic authority unique to it, and, moving further, in the binding doctrine of the church that takes precisely this kerygma as its object?*

Because Barth ascribes no unique work of any concretion or duration to the Holy Spirit, eschatology must become the outstanding epiphany of the "empty" place that through conscious reproduction of absence creates a kind of presence.[43] But precisely this is the fulcral point: The work of the Holy Spirit does not leave this place empty. It is always "salutarily" occupied in word and sacrament. As a matter of fact, the Holy Spirit as comforter has occupied this place since Pentecost. As Christ's Spirit, it is Christ's consoling presence, one that generates faith even though it is not yet "seeing," and one that nonetheless assures the reliability of the *vita passiva* and relieves theology of dialectics if not of *peregrinatio.* Christ's "place" is thus never really empty. Rather, it is occupied unequivocally by Christ in the Holy Spirit, with an unequivocalness that itself is the ground of faith such that theology, too, can be engaged with the unequivocalness of faith (albeit not with the unequivocalness of eschatological perception, but neither with the equivocalness of a dialectic that must also behave as if God takes with one hand what he gives with the other).

One might certainly object to my criticism of Barth's pneumatology that while it may well hold true with regard to his lecture "Church and Theology," it cannot be maintained in light of the entire thirteen volumes of Barth's *Church Dogmatics,* since there Barth did indeed decisively develop his thinking particularly regarding the relation between pneumatology and ecclesiology. It is not easy to refute an apparently cogent objection such as this, since doing so obviously would transcend the limitations of this inquiry. Nonetheless, I do believe one can counter that this objection itself is unpersuasive, and that the *Church Dogmatics* can very well be read as the development of a theological intuition already anticipated at the core of Barth's response to Peterson's query.

Let me remind the reader that my discussion of the Peterson-Barth controversy at this point in my inquiry is not intended to exhaustively clarify a specific issue in the history of theology. Rather, its goal is to illuminate a central *theological* issue, one coming to expression in what is for Western theology, especially since the Reformation, a paradigmatic alternative: the playing off against one another of *institution* and *charisma* in determining the relation between church, church doctrine, and theology. It is ultimately of no consequence for the heuristics of this inquiry into the relation between church, church doctrine, and theology whether the *Church Dogmatics* overcomes the pneumatological deficit in Barth's response to Peterson or not. Because, however, in what follows I do indeed presuppose that deficient pneumatology prevents both Barth and Peterson from overcoming the alternative of institution and charisma, I will adduce at least two reasons for not searching in the *Church Dogmatics* for a solution to this particular problem.

1. Reference can be made first to the fundamental continuity between the "dialectical" Barth and the Barth of what is known as the "Anselmian" turn with regard to the comprehensive underlying logic of action between God and human beings, one expressed most articulately in the motif of the "absent center." This motif of a "center" that as such cannot be spoken or stated but can only be circumscribed either in dialectics (as a radicalized analogy) or in analogy (as ameliorated dialectic),[44] is found not only in the second edition of the *Epistle to the Romans*[45] but also as early as the famous

essay "The Word of God and the Task of the Ministry."[46] Despite the explicit introduction of pneumatology, however, it then remains, as noted above, the fundamental, determinative motif in Barth's response to Peterson, reappearing quite clearly again with intensified articulation in Barth's later doctrine of baptism.[47]

The consequence of this diastatic determination of the relation between God and human beings within the framework of a comprehensive logic of action involving two irreducible subjects is precisely this "absent center," a center that can be filled only again and again in the joint acting of these two subjects. Yet because precisely this center must always become a new event grounded in God's sovereignty — and thus also in his faithfulness — it can only be remembered and anticipated but never really apprehended.[48] If indeed all human action per se can at best refer either anticipatorily or in response to this event, and yet if God's action in principle has never nor will it ever tie itself to any human action, then God's actions can be conceived only as becoming evident as God's self-manifestation in the interiority of the believer. For Barth, the meaning and goal of pneumatology is to render a theological conception of this manifestation of the "event" in which God's action joins human action freely, that is, again and again. This is documented in the *Church Dogmatics,* where Barth defines the Holy Spirit "as the subjective side in the event of revelation."[49]

> In both the Old Testament and New the Spirit of God, the Holy Spirit, is very generally God Himself to the degree that in an incomprehensibly real way, without on this account being any the less God, He can be present to the creature, and in virtue of this presence of His effect the relation of the creature to Himself. . . . God creates it [this relation] by His own presence in this creature and *therefore as a relation of Himself to Himself.* The Spirit of God is God in His freedom to be present to the creature, and therefore to create this relation, and therefore to be the life of the creature. . . . It is God's reality in that God Himself becomes present to man not just externally, not just from above, but also from within, from below, subjectively. *It is thus reality in that He does not merely come to man but encounters Himself from man.*[50]

The Holy Spirit is God's self-manifestation in the creature as God's free act, an act that is enacted ever anew and that in its own turn encounters itself. The decisive feature here is that God's self-relation to and from the creature is essentially world-less, that is, is at its core of the utmost immediacy in which God relates to himself.[51]

Turning now from the first to the final volume of the *Church Dogmatics,* the fragment on the doctrine of baptism, the inner continuity of this relation resurfaces when Barth understands baptism by the Spirit and that by water to be related as word and answer, and yet at the same time radically distinguished between the two. God makes his presence known to a person from the interior, or subjectively, in the baptism of the Spirit, prompting the person to respond with the act of witness and prayer, namely, baptism by water. This construction stands in unbroken continuity with the earlier diastatic logic of the *Epistle to the Romans,* according to which God's actions have no "worldly" form and can be attested in a worldly fashion *only* in the form of human action.[52] As Walter Kreck has shown, this comes to expression again in a striking way and with its ultimate consequences at the end of Barth's own life: "Shortly before his death, Barth remarked in a small circle that *he would no longer, as was yet the case in Church Dogmatics I/1, speak about the three forms of God's word.* And he then characterized proclamation with the metaphor of the ringing of the server at mass, a ringing that announces the transformation of the mass but does not itself execute it."[53] This draws the ultimate conclusion of the basic idea by making the gospel proclamation itself, in addition to baptism and Lord's Supper, into the responsive witness to the *testimonium Spiritus internum.*

These samples show that once the diastatic logic of action is axiomatically presupposed, a specific understanding of pneumatology follows that does not allow any creaturely *poiemata* of the Holy Spirit to which the Holy Spirit might tie itself. Put succinctly: Barth's pneumatology, completely subordinated as it is to the diastatic logic of action, conceptually eliminates the possibility of precisely that which Peter Brunner stated concerning the relation of the Holy Spirit to the church in his series of theses *The Spirit and the Church:* "28. The church is the vessel of the Spirit created by the Spirit. 29. By creating the new creature, the Spirit puts itself into the church as its innermost, indestructible life. By doing so, the Spirit already bestows upon the new creature it has created a nascent but real portion of the divine life. . . . 31. God himself, as the Spirit that has been poured out, already has a dwelling here on earth for his saving and beatific concrete presence. His dwelling is the church's own nature as a creature of the Spirit."[54]

2. The way Barth unfolds the doctrine of the Trinity also supports my critique especially of the diastatic logic of action underlying his pneumatology, a logic remaining consistent from the early works of what is known as his "dialectical stage" on into his late doctrine of baptism. Because an exhaustive analysis is not possible within the limits of this inquiry, I will refer to an essay in which Robert Jenson persuasively discloses the "binitarian" struc-

ture of Barth's theology.[55] I believe Jenson is correct in identifying the pneumatological *vinculum*-doctrine as the decisive problem in Barth's doctrine of the Trinity.[56] Barth unfolds the inner-trinitarian communion of Father and Son as a two-sided communion according to which the Spirit is the communion itself. He then understands this relation between Father and Son in the communion of the Spirit as constituting the ground of possibility for God's communion with human beings in faith, as we already saw above,[57] and between the being of Christ and the being of the congregation.[58] It continues to serve him analogically for determining the relation between the sexes.[59] This reproduces at every level the logic of "two-sidedness" within the framework of the analogical relationship between the Creator and creature as developed according to the *analogia fidei*.

Within the framework of his immanent doctrine of the Trinity, Barth begins basically with the three *modes of being* of the one God in order to avoid any trace of tritheism, and yet when carrying through this immanent doctrine of the Trinity he nevertheless does indeed talk about the relation of the Father to the Son and of the Son to the Father and their communion — that is, he does indeed break through the logic of the modes of being and at least analogically introduces the logic of person. Interestingly, though, this does not apply to the Holy Spirit, who on the basis of the *vinculum*-doctrine comes into focus exclusively as a *mode*.

Here we encounter anew, if indirectly, the comprehensive underlying logic of action obtaining between two distinct and yet related subjects whose intersubjective mediation is identical with the Holy Spirit, the latter conceived as an enactment or actualization.[60] Because Barth understands the triune God as having but *one* "center of action," and because his understanding of the Holy Spirit remains wholly determined by the *vinculum*-doctrine, Barth cannot overcome the diastatic logic of action obtaining between God and human beings, and is able to articulate the Holy Spirit *only* as a *mode* rather than as *Spiritus Creator* having its own salvific-economic mission and its own work.[61]

I must break off these rather brief explications concerning pneumatology within the framework of Barth's doctrine of the Trinity. My purpose was simply to adduce two responses to the objection that my earlier critique of Barth's pneumatology in the essay "Church and Theology" is ultimately inaccurate because Barth does indeed develop his pneumatology more precisely and in greater detail in his *Church Dogmatics*. Despite its doubtless impressive explication in the *Church Dogmatics*, Barth does remain true to his earlier pneumatology in the problematic fashion I suggest.

In summary, one can say that Barth does justifiably bring God's present actions in the Holy Spirit to bear over against Peterson. Theological engagement doubtless always occurs "in" God's presence, which in its own turn is not immediately identical with dogma. Given the utter lack of any pneumatological reflection in Peterson, this is an important step forward. Whereas Peterson inquires concerning the binding and clearly identifiable object of theology, Barth makes it clear that this object is itself the preeminent subject and agent. Because he conceives pneumatology actualistically, however, he remains caught in precisely the dialectic of which Peterson accuses him. He counters Peterson's realistic extension of the incarnation into dogma with his actualistic concept of God's actions in the Spirit, occurring "again and again."

Whereas Peterson thus distances pneumatology entirely from the question of the relation between theology and dogma or church doctrine, Barth examines pneumatology thematically in a substantively appropriate and even necessary fashion as the basic context of theology, doctrine, and church. Yet Barth's specific understanding of pneumatology prevents him from developing persuasively this relational context in his response to Peterson because he ascribes to the Holy Spirit no real work of its own within the framework of the trinitarian economy of salvation. The Holy Spirit, as the mode of God's self-manifestation, is rather identical with God's action.

Hence pneumatology is both the strength and the weakness of Barth's response to Peterson. Emphasis on the Holy Spirit over against dogma does address the danger of reifying the latter; dogma is not identical with Christ, remaining rather quite separate from him. Barth's pneumatological advance, however, does not go far enough for a persuasive pneumatological determination of the relation between church, doctrine, and theology, the result being that Peterson's challenge ultimately lingers — quite unresolved — at the Protestant doorstep. I have shown that the reason for this is found both in Barth's diastatic logic of action, developed as it is according to the logic of Chalcedon, and in his specific development — possibly related to that logic — of the immanent doctrine of the Trinity, which in its own turn unfolds the Holy Spirit as the *vinculum* constituting the communion of two distinct and yet mutually related entities.

This pneumatology makes it impossible for any genuine salvific-historic work of the *Spiritus Creator* to be related to or even distinguished from the salvific-economic mission of the Son. Because of this, Barth's theology cannot really establish any firm *ecclesiological* position. Barth is unable to interpret or render ecclesiologically fruitful in any pneumatologically relevant fashion what he calls the "mediate forms," and his development of the relational nexus of church, church doctrine, and theology ultimately remains ecclesiologically unstable because the pneumatology itself remains deficient. The relation between Holy Spirit and church turns out to be the core problem. Although Barth did renew theology as a serious practice within the church, namely, as "church theology," he was himself able to develop this theology only "charismatically," that is, only in his own personal practice of it; yet he was unable to give it any pneumatological-ecclesiological foundation by demonstrating why this ecclesial discursive practice is necessary in the first place and in what way it is tied to church doctrine or makes such doctrine necessary.

Hence both Barth's christological-pneumatological actualism as well as Peterson's christological-ecclesiological realism ultimately remain unsatisfactory answers to the question concerning the relation between church doctrine and theology as a church practice. Both address the problem in the manner of a mirror image. One entirely emphasizes a christologically conceived ecclesiology in which the Holy Spirit — in relation to church doctrine — is accorded no genuine work of its own. The other counters by emphasizing the Holy Spirit, but does so entirely and exclusively within the framework of a pneumatologically conceived Christology according to which the Holy Spirit is Christ's mode of action. Here, too, the Holy Spirit is accorded no work of its own in relation to church doctrine. In juxtaposition, Barth and Peterson resemble one another in consistently fading out the *Spiritus Creator* in connection with the church and church doctrine. It is not least this common deficit that prevents one from choosing between Barth and Peterson, something evident in their "spirit-forgotten" controversy itself. That is, both are able persuasively to discredit the opposing position, yet without either being able to establish any genuinely satisfactory relation between theology and church doctrine.

The debate between the two theologians does in any case show in an exemplary fashion not only that the question of the relation between theology and church doctrine (or dogma) is of central significance for the question of the nature of theology itself as a church practice, but also that the former question can be clarified only if the relation between Holy Spirit and the church is itself clarified theologically, and as we saw in Barth, this ultimately means from a trinitarian perspective.

The remaining third part of my inquiry will try to get beyond Barthian actualism, which brings on the danger of spiritualistic individualism, and Petersonian realism, which already bears within it the seeds of ecclesiastical institutionalism, and to understand both the church and church doctrine rather as the work of the Holy Spirit. The task is to understand church doctrine in its relation to the core practices of the church as the poiesis of the Holy Spirit with which theology is pathically related. That is, theology does not constitute itself "poietically"; rather, the poiesis of the Holy Spirit constitutes the pathos of theology insofar as theology is shaped by the *poiemata* of the Holy Spirit, namely, by the core practices of the church and by church doctrine. The fulcral element here is the concrete nature of the *vita passiva*, of life in God's triune economy of salvation into which theology itself is imbedded. Theology is undertaken, engaged, performed "in" the work of the Holy Spirit, in the temporal and thus ecclesial development of God's *oikonomia*.

An explicit orientation toward the pneumatological insights of Eastern Orthodoxy should thus come as no surprise. To anticipate for a moment the perspective from which, beginning with the *Spiritus Creator*, I will examine church, doctrine, and theology, let me cite the Greek Orthodox theologian Nikos Nissiotis:

> The Spirit comes in order to found the church in time. Without Pentecost, there is no church and no presence of Christ possessing any historical reality. Only after Pentecost were the apostles able to begin their apostolic office or commission, and only then could they found the visible, organically organized, charismatic and universal communion. . . . This *new* intervention of the Holy Spirit at Pentecost is a kind of new, personal revelation of the entire triune God within history. This time, revelation proceeds from the third person of the trinity, the Paraclete of truth, the Creator Spirit of the new creation, within time, at Pentecost. . . . This *new* element should not be viewed as an independent work of the third person of the trinity alone, for this risks falling into "pneumatomonism." The new element here derives from the activity of the entire triune God . . . and consists in the Christ event, which happened once and for all, being realized and actualized in time, and thus in the establishment of a personal connection between him and all human beings. . . . The Spirit acts with Christ together and is present through him among the apostles and through them among all who believe in the kerygma.[62]

Precisely from the perspective of the *Spiritus Creator*, theology must be conceived undialectically "in" the presence of the Spirit. That is, the decisive problem is not the still-outstanding vision, but the as-yet-incomplete redemption and renewal of creation. The incompleteness of theological statements is then to be understood not from the perspective of some *epistemologically* explicated eschatological reserve and then addressed in the form of dialectics, but from the perspective of the incompleteness of God's salvific work and of the attendant reality of concrete contradiction to God's salvific activity. *The διαλέγεσθαι of theological discourse must in this sense be understood differently, not as the practice of dialectical statements that in their own turn can always be turned into questions, but as the concrete* peregrinatio *in the Spirit. The kerygma that grounds faith is unfolded in the course of this* peregrinatio; *as a genuine church practice, it unfolds that kerygma discursively, in committed argumentation and interpretation, and within the horizon of church doctrine and of the core church practices.*

II. The Pathos of Faith: Holy Spirit — Church — Theology

Within the framework of basic ecclesiological options, the Peterson-Barth controversy reflects the problematic and, in the meantime, ecumenically discussed alternative[63] between church as "institution" or as "event" and, related to this alternative, church doctrine either as an inherent aspect of the institution already given *iure divino* or as an act of confession made *iure humano* constantly anew coinciding with God's own actions. The root of the problem resides on the one hand in Peterson's identification of Christ with the institution of church and complete exclusion of the Holy Spirit, and on the other in Barth's actualistic understanding of the "together" of divine and human action in a strict diastasis between Spirit and institution.

The following discussion will draw upon Eastern Orthodox theology with regard to both pneumatology and ecclesiology, and will relate these on the one hand to Luther's pneumatology and ecclesiology and on the other to several representatives of contemporary Protestant theology. The latter can help overcome the either-or resulting from the controversy between Peterson and Barth and can assist in understanding in a distinct way church doctrine as the poiesis of the Holy Spirit, a poiesis that is a constitutive part of the pathos of theology as a church practice. At the same time, the following explications will try to develop a constructive perspective, pneumatological as well as ecclesiological, from which to overcome the exemplary deficits found in Lindbeck, Bayer, Peterson, and Barth in understanding theology as a church practice in its relation to church doctrine and to what are known as the "core practices" of the church.

I intend to make the theological assertion that in order to be a church at all, the church needs binding doctrine. I will begin with this basic consensus between Barth and Peterson and will inquire concerning the relationship — in both directions — between the creative action of the Holy Spirit on the one hand and this binding doctrine on the other. I hope to overcome the Peterson-Barth alternative by showing that the immediacy of God's salvific acts does not in fact relativize or undermine church doctrine. The latter is itself to be understood as the poiesis of the *Spiritus Creator* and thus as one aspect of God's actualized salvific activity. As such, and insofar as church doctrine is determined entirely from the perspective of the *doctrina evangelii* and remains oriented back toward it, it will always exhibit a fundamentally doxological and eschatological character.

1. The Pneumatological Dimension of the Church in the Communio-*Ecclesiology*

One important impulse for this inquiry derives from the ecumenical encounter with the *communio*-ecclesiology of Eastern Orthodox theology, the pneumatological Christology and ecclesiology underlying it, and the trinitarian concept of person. In the following, first section, I will introduce the central elements of this theology in a condensed fashion in order to establish a pneumatological as well as ecclesiological perspective from which to overcome the inability of both Peterson and Barth to rightly locate theology as a church practice in terms of its relation to church and to church doctrine. I will draw primarily from exemplary representatives of contemporary and recent Eastern Orthodox theology whose ideas have generated considerable resonance in ecumenical dialogues[64] and in the meantime have also enjoyed considerable acceptance in the works of both Protestant and Catholic systematic theology in the West.[65] These include John D. Zizioulas,[66] Nikos A. Nissiotis,[67] Dimitru Staniloae,[68] and Vladimir Lossky,[69] though I draw primarily from Nissiotis and from Zizioulas's reflections on pneumatology and ecclesiology.[70]

My intention is not to appropriate constructively the entire breadth of *communio*-ecclesiology,[71] but rather to explore the potential of the trinitarian and especially pneumatological implications of its Eastern Orthodox formulation for my own pneumatological as well as ecclesiological understanding of theology as a discursive church practice.

a. The Trinitarian God and the Pathos of Personal Being in Communion

One of the central features of contemporary trinitarian theology is the increasing attention leading Western theologians[72] are paying to the Eastern Orthodox understanding of the Trinity — one deriving from the Cappa-

116

docian Fathers and especially from Gregory of Nazianzus — as a "communion of persons" or as an onto-relational unity. The central assumption of this trinitarian perspective is the logical priority ascribed to the divine "persons," who can exist only in relation to one another and as such constitute God's deity, providing thus also the basis of God's unity. That is, the unity resides in the relation of the persons to one another rather than in some substance logically preceding these persons as whose "mode of being" the latter would then be understood.[73] Within the triune communion, each of the divine persons receives its hypostatic reality from the other two; that is, each becomes the person it is through the pathos of relationality qualifying and identifying it from the perspective of the other two divine persons. The personal being of each person thus resides in its *reception* of identity through the other two; that is, it is *pathically* constituted.[74] Wolfhart Pannenberg focuses this insight, one already anticipated in Gregory of Nazianzus, into the ecstatic aspect of the concept of person:

> Each of the three persons is ec-statically related to one or both of the others and has its personal distinctiveness or selfhood in this relation. The Father is the Father only in relation to the Son, in the generation and sending of the Son. The Son is the Son only in obedience to the sending of the Father, which includes recognition of his fatherhood. The Spirit exists hypostatically as Spirit only as he glorifies the Father in the Son and the Son as sent by the Father. . . . In the mutuality of their ec-static indwelling the life of the divine Spirit fulfils itself as love.[75]

In the communion of Father, Son, and Spirit, God's being is actualized as loving communion ecstatically and thus at the same time pathically. The eschatological telos of the economy of salvation is to provide for participation in this life of the triune God. God's pathos does not contradict his freedom here, but rather is its precise expression, namely, to actualize this freedom as love in communion. The Father's own creative ecstasy is itself pathically qualified insofar as it is qualified by the Son in the Holy Spirit, finding fulfillment then only in the triune communion. The creative ecstasy thus corresponds to an inner-trinitarian kenosis expressed in the doctrine of the perichoresis of the divine hypostases. The pathos of life in faith then means participation in the Spirit in God's triune life, that is, in the pathos constituting the love between Father, Son, and Holy Spirit. The specific salvific-economic mission of the Holy Spirit is to draw humanity and creation into this communion, a communion originally opened to the "many" through the cross and resurrection of Christ.[76] Being "in the Spirit" thus means to receive God and to be transformed into the pathos of love characterizing the life of the triune God. It is the *opus inchoatum*,[77] the nascent eschatological work of the Holy Spirit characterizing the pneumatological dimension of Eastern Orthodox ecclesiology.

b. The Two Pneumatological Aspects of the Church

The Ontological Aspect: The Church as the Poiesis of the Holy Spirit
The specific emphasis on pneumatology in Eastern Orthodox ecclesiology has christological roots. An emphatically pneumatological understanding of Christology avoids the false alternative between a christological and a pneumatological grounding of ecclesiology.[78] This view develops God's economy of salvation from a strictly trinitarian perspective; that is, it does not separate the salvific-economic mission of the Son from that of the Holy Spirit.[79] For Zizioulas, understanding this confluence of the two economies means taking seriously all the implications of the biblical assertion "that Christ was born and anointed of the Spirit, and that his entire being took place in the Spirit."[80] Actually, then, Christ is conceivable only "in the Spirit." That is, the "being" of Jesus Christ is, in its essence, utterly determined by the Spirit insofar as, in its relationality, it is utterly directed toward the Father. Jesus exists entirely in the communion of the triune God and is completely qualified by this communion; it constitutes the pathos of his being.[81] This communion was interrupted in Jesus' death on the cross, then reestablished once and for all in the resurrection of the Crucified, though such that now the (ecclesial) body of Christ — the "many" who receive the body and blood of Christ in faith — is drawn into this communion.

The fulcral pneumatological point, however, is that the Holy Spirit — as *Spiritus Creator* — creates this communion and thus also its relationality.[82] If, however, relationality itself implies receptivity, that is, being qualified by the other, then the Spirit itself is the subject of this pathos or of the poiesis corresponding to it. The work of the Holy Spirit, its poiesis, becomes concrete in the pathos characterizing it. In this sense Jesus' entire existence was shaped by a fundamental and central pathos, by his existence "in the Spirit." Similarly, the existence of the church and of every believer is pathically determined in that they are constituted by the Spirit, that is, insofar as their qualification as a work of the Holy Spirit is their pathos.

The most important implication of this pneumatological Christology is its understanding of the church as mystery, as a christological as well as pneumatological event. "Neither a christological nor a pneumatological preexisting factor brings about the existence of the church; rather, both at once constitute that existence. The chronological priority of the Christ event over against the event of Pentecost is transcended in the Spirit; indeed, the Gospel of John understands the sending of the Spirit as part of the christological events themselves. It is precisely the role of the Spirit to transcend linear history, nor does this rob the church of its christological reality. The church is the body of Christ precisely in being a 'spiritual body.'"[83] The being of the church is thus qualified both christologically and pneumatologically. The specific salvific-economic work of the Holy Spirit is to "hypostasize" the church. "In the Spirit" the church becomes an image (εἰκών) of the Trinity itself; it becomes "communion" of the triune love.[84] This work of the Holy Spirit should by no means be separated from Christ's own salvific work; rather, it should be understood as its very actualization, something abundantly evident in the assertion of Eastern Orthodoxy that the church as communion has its origin and its enduring center in the celebration of the Lord's Supper.[85]

This perspective has immediate consequences. Understanding the church as "communion" with its center and origin in the Lord's Supper allows one to overcome the ecclesiological contradiction between "institution" and "event," between "being" and "act." The church at once becomes transparent as both the body of Christ *and* as a creation of the Holy Spirit; bearing the eschatological earnest of the Holy Spirit itself, it already receives a portion in the life of the triune God. As an eschatological new creation, it can be described both as "being" and as "act." Its being always remains dependent on the presence and activity of the Holy Spirit, and remains a being in invocation of the Holy Spirit — *epicletic being,* being that is completely the *work* of the *Spiritus Creator.* At the same time, as the work of the Holy Spirit it is also characterized by duration, concreteness, and visibility, and as such is identical with distinct practices or activities, institutions, offices, and doctrines. In this way the work of the Spirit acquires its own, eschatological extension "in time."

The Eschatological Aspect   As already indicated, the Holy Spirit is not only the *Spiritus Creator* whose work the church perpetually receives as its own being, it is also the eschatological Spirit. "At the same time, the same Spirit as giver of life and as *communio* draws into history the end time, the eschaton (Acts 2), namely, God's eternal life. Here the church becomes the communion of saints in which past, present, and future, rather than being causally related, are one as the body of Christ in the communion event itself."[86]

The Lord's Supper occupies the center of *communio*-ecclesiology also because, in its performance, the *eschata* already become present within the framework of the liturgical anamnesis of God's salvific acts.

> The significant and unique feature of the church's pneumatological dimension is doubtless that this extension transcends the course of linear history by making the eschaton itself part of the anamnesis (that is, of the historic consciousness) of the church. Thus can we say in the eucharistic anamnesis that the church "remembers . . . the parousia" (cf. the anaphora in the liturgy of John Chrysostom). This is done "in the Spirit," and is so decisive that it should warn ecclesiology against applying any absolute, linear historical schema to the mystery of the church. . . . This does not devalue history in the sense, for example, of Plato, since this entire "transcendence" of history stands *in* history and is grounded *on* history; in fact, this is what first sanctifies and confirms history. The only thing devalued here is historic causality, since this views God's actions as the sole cause of the historic existence of the church.[87]

In the Lord's Supper Christ becomes so present through the Holy Spirit that the celebrating congregation is drawn into the *eschata* insofar as it receives these in the promise both in the gospel proclamation preceding the Lord's Supper and in the celebration itself of the Lord's Supper. The God present in the incarnate word is here identical with the work of the Holy Spirit. Word and sacrament are the recollected *eschata,* and as such they are the mediation of God's salvation in activities making possible and simultaneously essentially containing the congregation's believing affirmation.[88] In believing affirmation, the congregation is taken up "even now" into God's life, into the communion of Father, Son, and Holy Spirit.[89] In a certain respect, then, "faith" and "doxology" thus mean "already" "being in heaven." This is the eschatological work of the Holy Spirit characterizing its hypostatic being as person.

However, this is not the "anticipation" of something yet to come, but the pneumatic manifestation of the eschaton.[90] "By bringing the eschaton into history, the Spirit enables the church through its sacramental structures to lend presence to the eschaton in history and at the same time to point beyond history. For the Spirit incessantly points to the extraordinary 'beyond' which cannot be objectified and cannot be controlled."[91] This, too, involves pathos, namely, a state of being eschatologically qualified that is *not* however an *active* anticipation of something still to come, but rather the condition of *being* seized by the eschaton that *even now* is commencing.

c. Excursus: The Problem of Anticipation

Even though Zizioulas does speak about "anticipation" in several places in his book *Being as Communion,* his "iconic" eschatology differs from Wolfhart Pannenberg's concept of "anticipation," which is of central importance for the latter's universal-historic proposal.[92] The decisive difference is that the universal-historic perspective is a necessary consequence of the modern subject constitution, that is, that "history" constitutes the universal horizon in which the modern subject is able to conceive itself together with the unity of all that is real. Despite all emphasis on the openness of the future and the contingency of historic events, this universal-historic horizon ultimately domesticates the "future" by subordinating it to the anthropological structure of prolepsis, the universal-human disposition toward the future. The yield of this apologetic strategy for integration is impressive, since the truth of the Christian message can be demonstrated in its function as a solution to the aporia within the modern (Hegelian) concept of truth, that is, by holding together the unity, historicity, and future quality of truth. The price for apologetically rendering revelatory Christian truth plausible, however, is high, and may even be too high, since it integrates the eschaton into the logic of universal history, which in its own turn is dependent on the modern understanding of the subject. The two possible objections to this view constitute the same sort of inherent connection as do universal history and modern subjectivity.

1. The *pneumatological character of eschatology* is utterly lost in the universal-historic horizon. Taking this character seriously, however, as do Luther and Eastern Orthodox theologians, ruptures the universal-historic horizon "iconically." Whereas in the logic of "anticipation" the horizon of time or history remains stable, the pneumatic manifestation of the eschaton brings about an event rupturing any unified horizon of history such that one can speak only of ages, that is, about the old aeon and the new aeon that opposes it eschatologically and will replace it. Johannes Fischer expresses this succinctly in stating that

> within a reality conceived as a unity and with linear time, one cannot simultaneously say that something both is already and is not yet. If by contrast different times and spaces overlap, that which is new is already present insofar as it acquires form "already now" under the conditions of the old, and is at the same time future insofar as it is precisely the conditions of the old under which that which is new now appears. The framework of this ontology makes it completely clear that the key question is not that concerning reality, but that concerning the Spirit, for it is the Spirit that grants one

a portion in the new reality that commenced with Christ. Without God's Spirit, this reality remains concealed.[93]

2. *"Anticipation"* or *"prolepsis"* includes forms of activity bound to the modern constitution of the subject, that is, *modes of actualization of the modern subject* that even structurally are incommensurate with the pneumatological character of the eschaton within which the human being as new creation is the poiesis of the Holy Spirit, poiesis constituting the human being such that this identity can only be conceived as pathos. Yet the subject of any anticipation or prolepsis can only be the modern subject itself. When the Holy Spirit, though, creates individuals anew as subjects of faith by drawing them into the *eschata*, they become "persons." The believer is now primarily shaped by the reality of a distinct relationality *(Christus forma fidei)*; that is, the believer "already" subsists in faith in the communion of the triune God, and yet simultaneously "still" lives in affliction by the powers of evil.[94] This eschatological "personal being" is receptively-passively constituted, which of itself fundamentally contradicts the inherently active logic of "anticipation" and "prolepsis."

In the third volume of his *magnum opus,* the *Systematic Theology,* Pannenberg seems to effect a certain shift[95] insofar as pneumatology steps more prominently into the foreground and Eastern Orthodox theologians, especially Zizioulas and Nissiotis, seem to exert an influence not yet found in Pannenberg's early work. He now explicitly combines pneumatology and eschatology. The Holy Spirit "is not just the origin of all living things but also the source of the new life that has broken in in the resurrection of Jesus Christ and that distinguishes itself from earthly life by the fact that it is linked to the divine source of life and may thus be called a *sōma pneumatikon* and immortal (1 Cor. 15:44-45)."[96] One can basically agree with this except that the concept of "origin" does not do full justice here to the creative activity of the Spirit. This new life, as a creation of the Spirit, always remains "in the Spirit" such that the Spirit is not only the origin but also the comprehensive reality of that new life itself. Shortly thereafter, Pannenberg writes that "the gift of the Spirit has a soteriological function as an anticipation of the eschatological outpouring of the Spirit."[97] This constitutes a considerable shift in the logic of the concept of "anticipation." Rather than being an act of the human subject within the horizon of universal history commensurate with the anthropological structure of the prolepsis, it is the salvific-economic act of God's self-antecedence.[98] Admittedly, Pannenberg does then try in a certain sense to rescue his earlier concept of anticipation, at least with respect to believers, and does so with astonishing similarity to Barth's conceptual figure of the simultaneity of divine and human action.[99] The Spirit as gift permits spontaneous human participation in God's life, and thus probably also the appropriation of this gift in the self-enactment of "anticipation" in the earlier sense.[100] Pannenberg's explications concerning baptism document this succinctly:

> Baptism is not just a depiction of individual self-givenness in general along the lines of an illustration of something universal. It is the actual reconstitution of the person in the form of the sacramental sign. As an anticipatory sign of the whole life history of the baptized in terms of its end it is referred to its outworking by appropriation of its content in faith. But this outworking is itself possible only in the light of baptism, and at each moment it knows that it is a work of the Spirit who is given by baptism. In other words, the appropriation and outworking of baptism are done *by Christians*, i.e., by subjects newly constituted in the act of baptism, not subjects that are supposedly present already behind all experience and that remain the same as its contents change. For by baptism believers come into relation to the death and resurrection of Jesus Christ, and as Christ's Spirit reminds Christians of Jesus (John 14:26; 16:13ff.) he also assures them of their own identity on the basis of baptism. In this regard their new subjectivity does not have the form of a self-identity that in virtue of self-familiarity stands opposed to all that is not the self. Participation in the relation of the Son to the Father by the Spirit changes the structure of self-identity itself.[101]

Here Pannenberg approaches the notion that human pathos corresponds to the work of the Spirit, pathos making someone into a person (in Zizioulas's and Luther's sense) because now he clearly transcends the modern constitution of the self and moves instead toward "person" in the pathic sense. The only difference seems to me to be that in faith, the structure of the ego's identity is not changed, but rather is transformed such that one can now refer to the "ego" only ec-statically or, put differently, only pathically. If in faith a human being really does undergo God's creative self-antecedence in the Spirit and is created anew through this experience, then reference to anticipation is no longer possible; in faith, the human being — now as "person" — has already been displaced into the eschaton. This is why in faith that person already participates in God's future and thus "recollects" the *eschata* precisely because he or she has already been drawn into them.[102]

Yet even in the third volume of his *Systematic Theology,* Pannenberg continues to insist on the concept of "anticipation." This reflects the multidimensional attempt, one quite impressive in its consistency and conceptual articulation, to balance human prolepsis of the future on the one hand and divine self-anticipation in the Spirit on the other, and between the "already" and the "not yet" of the triune work of salvation. The purpose of the balance is to secure the framework of universal history. Within this attempt to establish a balance, however, the implications of the trinitarian economy of salvation and the strong emphasis on pneumatology constitute an element of tension already intimated in the conceptual shift toward the "divine self-anticipation." A consistent development of this aspect and of the stronger emphasis on the "already" would have led to Peter Brunner's version and to that of the Eastern Church. This, of course, would have ruptured the framework of universal history of Pannenberg's overall conception, resulting in an unresolvable difference or an ongoing contradiction within this framework, one which *cannot yet* be overcome conceptually, that is, in anticipation, and which nonetheless is *already now* being overcome epicletically in the doxology of the church.[103]

d. Conclusions

A pneumatologically conceived pathos must be understood as the central category of the trinitarian *communio*-ecclesiology, for the mystery of the "communion" is precisely this pathos, that is, the receptivity in the primary relationality qualifying us as believers. The theological ground and character of this pathos resides in the triune communion of Father, Son, and Holy Spirit. "Being a person" in the sense of "hypostasis" means to be pathically constituted through receptivity in relation to the other two hypostases. The specific pathos characterizing the mutual relationality and thus also the constitutive reality (hypostasis) of the divine persons defines the triune communion.

Creation is redeemed insofar as the triune God draws it into his communion. The eschatological goal is participation in the communion of the Father with the Son in the Holy Spirit. In the incarnation, suffering, death, and resurrection of Jesus Christ, the triune God has begun to draw creation into his communion in a completely new fashion transcending its original state. This end time is already present "in the Spirit" now in the economic mission of Jesus Christ and the Holy Spirit through the communion of the ecclesial body of Christ.[104]

In the incarnation, death on the cross, and resurrection of Jesus Christ, the triune God himself performs this pathos as economy of salvation such that the communion of creation with precisely that God is thereby reestablished. The Holy Spirit draws both humanity and the world eschatologically into this pathos of Christ. Because the Holy Spirit draws us eschatologically into the triune communion, reestablishing thereby our own relationality and "in-forming" us through faith, and because Christ himself thus becomes the "form" of faith, pathos is the mode through which this salvific activity of the Spirit is enacted in human beings. The human being is entirely the receiving party here, whereas the Spirit's own actions are genuine poiesis; for the Spirit creates a *nova creatura,* in a hidden way now, but later openly. "Pathos" is on the human side the only possible mode of redemption. A human being *undergoes* God's actions, is radically qualified anew through these actions, is justified and sanctified, and is permanently relationally shaped in substance.[105] In this pathos people become "persons," that is, they receive their essence — that which qualifies them — from communion with the triune God. The reality (hypostasis) constituted through this communion determines their "being." In this pathos, however, a human being is completely present; that is, this situation of undergoing the re-creative actions of the Creator Spirit takes place in the entire human being such that this also implies "cooperation" in the sense of being present fully as agent, something reflected in the logic of the core practices. As works of the Holy Spirit they are the pathos of the trinitarian economy of salvation that actually determines or shapes us. At the same time we are ourselves also "there as agents," that is, *actively* present in praise, confession, prayer, obedience, and discipleship.[106]

e. The "Mission" of the Church in the Trinitarian Economy: The Public of the Holy Spirit

Within the framework of a trinitarian development of this *communio-ecclesiology,* the church is thus understood both as christologically "instituted"[107] and as pneumatologically "constituted."[108] That is, the church exists as the "body of Christ" from the perspective of the eschatological meal Jesus himself established, as a concrete historic entity rather than as a "Platonic republic"[109] and simultaneously as a work of the Holy Spirit on whose ever new actions it, as its *creatura,* remains dependent. In its trinitarian constitution it is essentially *koinonia.* In this sense an inherent connection obtains between eschatological participation in the communion of the triune God in faith and ecclesial communion. The one implies the other. The ecclesial *koinonia* is God's soteriological work, and as such is grounded in the trinitarian communion, which in its own turn is concretely present in the *koinonia,* indeed, has bound itself to the *koinonia.*[110] That the triune God has attached his communion to the ecclesial *koinonia* is at the same time the "other" side of the church as a work of the Holy Spirit. Not only does God's poiesis constitute in this way the pathos of the church, this self-binding of the triune communion to the *koinonia* also constitutes its binding authority. *The binding nature of the core practices and of church doctrine, which I will discuss below, is grounded solely in God's triune self-binding to the* koinonia. *That is, this binding nature should not be understood as "reified" in se, but rather from the perspective of its trinitarian ground, namely, God's self-binding to the* koinonia. *This is also the perspective from which to understand the mission of the church. In its pathos it is the organ of actualization of the salvific-economic mission of Christ and of the Holy Spirit.*

In what follows I will explicate the mission of the church such that it constitutes the horizon within which theology can be articulated as a discursive church practice. One important point is that the church, as the *work* of the Holy Spirit, is at the same time the *mode of enactment* of the Holy Spirit's economic mission; as such, it is to be articulated as the "public" of the Holy Spirit whose telos is soteriologically determined. As the public presence of the Holy Spirit, the church serves the soteriological telos of the Holy Spirit's economic mission.

In Part Four I will argue that every public possesses a telos both defining and constituting it, and that the church, on the basis of its own genuine telos, is itself a specific public that enters into multilayered relationships of tension with other publics. Insofar as it can indeed be described as a public, its soteriological telos is what distinguishes it from other publics and identifies it as the church.[111] I will further show that the soteriological mission of the church as the public of the Holy Spirit must be understood as the specific nexus of church practices and church doctrine within which theology is to be situated as a distinct church practice itself, indeed, as an aspect inhering within the telos of this public. At the same time, I need to elaborate in what way this concrete pneumatological-ecclesiological horizon itself constitutes the pathos of theology as a church practice.

f. The Holy Spirit and the Church

First, however, I will interpret the connection between the Spirit and the church so that, by drawing from Eastern Orthodox insights, one can from the perspective of Protestant theology as well understand the core practices of the church and church doctrine as *poiemata* of the *Spiritus Creator*. My point of departure is Jesus' farewell discourse in the Gospel of John in which the Spirit is promised as Jesus' representative in the time when he himself is absent: "But the Advocate, the Holy Spirit, whom the Father will send in my name, will teach you everything, and remind you of all that I have said to you" (John 14:26, NRSV). Even though this promise focuses entirely on the activity of the Holy Spirit, it nonetheless also implies distinct practices and structures of learning and recollection as well as ways to embody communally this learning and recollection; the purpose would be to transmit it as a gift of the Holy Spirit and to make possible new learning and recollection in the light of the very transmission itself. This, however, is the task of the core church practices and of church doctrine. Through them we receive the gospel in baptism, in the Lord's Supper, in a proclamation of the gospel that is in accordance with baptism and the Lord's Supper, in catechetical instruction, and in binding doctrine. To subscribe to the continuing initiative of the Holy Spirit as *Spiritus Creator* means to understand precisely these activities as the *poiemata* through which the Spirit implements such teaching and recollection. The salvific-economic mission of the Holy Spirit is thus realized not "spiritualistically" in the immediacy of the in-spiration of Spirit into individual religious consciousnesses, but in the form of concrete church practices which as such are to be understood as the gift of the Spirit in the service of God's economy of salvation.

Taking this relationship between Spirit and church as the point of departure, one can alter slightly Kant's famous expression and say that pneumatology without ecclesiology is empty, ecclesiology without pneumatology blind. Without the Holy Spirit the church would be "blind." God the Holy Spirit, in the actualization of the trinitarian economy of salvation, as the Spirit of Christ, is the origin and goal of the church. If the church does not view itself within the horizon of God's *oikonomia,* that is, if it is not created, shaped, and guided by the Holy Spirit in its service to God's economy of salvation, it becomes "blind" by losing its unique calling. The core practices and church doctrine remind the church ever anew of its origin and goal. Through them it sees and learns what its ground and enduring focus are.

If by contrast there is no understanding of the inherent relationship between the salvific-economic work of the Holy Spirit and the being and mission of the church, or if the realization is lost that the church is the creation of the Spirit in time, then the actions of the Spirit can be seen and accessed everywhere and nowhere. Invoking the Holy Spirit then becomes an empty expression. Without concrete mediation through the core practices of the church, including church doctrine, the activity of the Holy Spirit becomes questionable. How else is the Spirit to teach and remind if not through that which Barth called the "mediate forms"? If the activity of the Holy Spirit were completely separated from these forms, the Lordship of the Holy Spirit would be a vacuum to be filled with all sorts of human projects and projections. But how are the work of the Holy Spirit and the church related in this view?

Although church doctrine and the core practices definitely do not "possess" the Holy Spirit in any way such that they simply coincide with its activity, they nonetheless do constitute the indispensable "mediate forms" of its activity through which the Holy Spirit guides the church to truth. Only in a binding context of doctrine and praxis can new insights emerge, practices be reformed, and church doctrine be articulated or rethought. Without the public established by this binding authority, Christians cannot encounter God's word anew, nor make any new discoveries; without this binding authority everything becomes the object of individual evaluation and assessment. Where everything is arbitrary, however, everything and nothing is "new." As paradoxical as it may sound, the core church practices and church doctrine, precisely in their binding nature, are essential if the Holy Spirit is to lead the church to perfect truth and teach it new things by perpetually reminding it of Jesus Christ.[112]

2. The Core Practices of the Church: Poiesis of the Holy Spirit

a. Luther's Treatise "On the Councils and the Church"

The reflections of the *communio*-ecclesiology on the relation between pneumatology and ecclesiology focus on the performance of the Lord's Supper. Does this exhaust the pneumatological development of ecclesiology, or is the Lord's Supper only *one* central intersection between pneumatology and ecclesiology next to which other, similar points of intersection might also be considered? Here a dialogue will be helpful between Luther's ecclesiology and the contemporary, ecumenically largely unanimous *communio*-ecclesiology, especially with regard to Luther's often neglected treatise "On the Councils and the Church" (1539), whose third part contains a pneumatological ecclesiology *in nuce*.

In this treatise Luther unequivocally associates pneumatology and ecclesiology by way of the concept of "works" of the Holy Spirit as tied to distinct church practices. This is no accident, for at the time of this writing Luther was engaged on two fronts: in a debate first with the ecclesiology of the "old believers" who rejected the Reformation, and second with antinomianism, an intra-Lutheran movement which in the meantime had become virulent.[113]

Luther conceives Christian existence as a process of lifelong sanctification that is the work of the Holy Spirit.[114] Renewal through the Holy Spirit, however, does not bypass God's commandment; rather, the Holy Spirit enacts that commandment anew insofar as its fulfillment becomes the mode of life of the *nova creatura:* "For Christian holiness, or the holiness common to

Christendom, is found where the Holy Spirit gives people faith in Christ and thus sanctifies them, Acts 15[:9], that is, he renews heart, soul, body, work, and conduct, inscribing the commandments of God not on tables of stone, but in hearts of flesh, II Corinthians 3[:3]."[115] Although Luther does concentrate his development of this notion entirely on the first table of commandments, which he interprets pneumatologically as well as ecclesiologically, he still views his own ecclesiological explications in the immediate light of the contents of the second table, which he also thinks is to be explicated pneumatologically: "How can he speak rightly about the words of the Holy Spirit in the first table — about comfort, grace, forgiveness of sins — who does not heed or practice the works of the Holy Spirit in the second table, which he can understand and experience, while he has never attempted or experienced those of the first table?"[116] By speaking of the *works* of the Spirit, Luther is here already betraying how he intends to develop this pneumatology in a concretely ecclesiological fashion. The Holy Spirit acts not only in the sense of a comprehensive praxis, but also performs works, that is, specific *poiemata,* which can very well be individually enumerated and which refer back to the individual commandments. This passage already makes it clear that Luther does not begin with two acting subjects, namely, the Holy Spirit on the one hand and the human subject who "realizes" these commandments on the other; he begins rather with the "works" of the Spirit, and with the notion of understanding, attempting, and experiencing the works of the Spirit. *This association of the poiesis of the Spirit and the pathos of the human subject in the works of the Spirit is by no means accidental, and at the end of this section will be interpreted pneumatologically.*

The decisive feature in Luther's ecclesiological understanding of the works of the Holy Spirit is that they are tied to specific church practices which Luther calls the seven principal parts of Christian sanctification according to the first table of commandments. These include (1) the external, orally preached word of God (which includes believing, confessing, and acting in accordance with it);[117] (2) baptism;[118] (3) the Lord's Supper;[119] (4) the office of the keys as church discipline;[120] (5) ordination and offices;[121] (6) public prayer, praise, thanksgiving, instruction;[122] and (7) discipleship in suffering.[123] The economic mission of the Holy Spirit, its soteriological work of sanctification and renewal, is performed *through* these seven activities:

> These are the true seven principal parts of the great holy possession whereby the Holy Spirit effects in us a daily sanctification and vivification in Christ, according to the first table of Moses. By this we obey it, albeit never as perfectly as Christ. But we constantly strive to attain the goal, un-

der his redemption or remission of sin, until we too shall one day become perfectly holy and no longer stand in need of forgiveness. Everything is directed toward that goal. I would even call these seven parts the seven sacraments, but since that term has been misused by the papists and is used in a different sense in Scripture, I shall let them stand as the seven principal parts of Christian sanctification or the seven holy possessions of the church.[124]

The archaic-sounding reference to "holy possessions" is to be understood here in a strictly pneumatological sense. These are the *poiemata* of the Holy Spirit through which the Spirit fulfills its salvific-economic mission. That is, God's economy of salvation, rather than being separated from the divine commandment, has to be described in its full pneumatological concreteness precisely from the perspective of the divine commandment itself.[125]

These seven "holy possessions" mark the church insofar as through them "faith knows without fail: Here, indeed, 'God's world' is present in concealment, and one can justifiably speak of 'church.'"[126] The relation between "holy possession" and "mark," however, involves an irreversible relation. Distinct activities mark the church *because* they indeed *are* "holy possessions" of the Spirit, and not vice versa! Here, too, Luther is arguing implicitly pneumatologically; insofar as the Spirit makes these "holy possessions" accessible to faith as the marks of the church, it is comforting the afflicted conscience by showing concretely where the "church" is to be found even in a time of fundamental ecclesiastical conflict. The church is grounded in precisely these "holy possessions," and as such is a work of the Holy Spirit; for the *poiemata* of the Spirit remain tied to what Luther in the broader sense also wanted to call the "seven sacraments."

This unequivocal union of pneumatology and ecclesiology has important theological consequences. First, within the framework of Luther's ecclesiologically centered pneumatology, the Holy Spirit is not some "ghost" in the modern sense, that is, some disembodied *res cogitans* "spooking around" everywhere and nowhere, nor some "divine power" that must prove itself through concrete evidence of its activity. The person of the Holy Spirit is present in its economic mission of sanctification and renewal itself. As such, however, the Spirit nonetheless remains oriented toward Christ, such that one must understand *pneumatologically* the connection between Christ's body as the Lord's Supper and the church as the body of Christ. The Holy Spirit creates the church as the body of Christ through distinct, externally perceivable activities, fulfilling with their aid its own salvific-economic mission. Second, the church is *not* some "double" reality, an erroneous assumption that has long weakened Protestant ecclesiology. Precisely the *externality* of that which constitutes the church as church is to be understood *pneumatologically.* This concrete externality of the Spirit's "holy possessions," however, in no way involves the otherwise justified distinction between the "visible" and "invisible" church.[127] Precisely the external, visible church *is* the hidden church, for only faith itself can perceive the externality of the Holy Spirit's activities at issue here; that is, they are to be *believed* as *works* of the Holy Spirit. As activities of the *Holy Spirit,* precisely their straightforward, concrete externality makes them radically "invisible" to unbelief.

b. The Marks of the Church as Core Church Practices

All of Luther's "holy possessions" involve church activities with whose execution or administration specific people are charged. Ordained office plays a preeminent if not exclusive role with regard to the first four marks, since all seven activities do imply or essentially involve all those who have been baptized or specifically the person to be baptized; that is, all these activities actively imply the concrete congregation. Most important, the existence of those who are baptized cannot in any way be conceived independent of these seven activities;[128] it has meaning only within the concrete context of all seven "holy possessions."[129] That the first four "holy possessions" are tied to ordained office corresponds not only to universal church tradition, but also to the pneumatological logic of the "holy possessions" themselves.

Before examining the pneumatological logic of the "holy possessions," one must first recall that these distinct activities actually involve "practices" in the sense discussed earlier,[130] albeit practices that are simultaneously pathically qualified. Although they do indeed refer to human activities, through them the human being "undergoes" or "is subject to" the actions of the Holy Spirit.

The question is quite justified whether the term "practice" really can be applied to all seven "holy possessions" in the first place. Certainly, all seven involve forms of cooperative human activity in the broadest sense, and standards of excellence could doubtless be identified for each of them. Yet, are there also "goods" inhering within these "practices" that are, indeed, actualized through the performance of the latter? Here we encounter a boundary indicating that any application of the term "practice" in MacIntyre's sense to the seven characteristics of the church is problematic if the term is restricted to an anthropological theory of action. If by contrast one understands "practice" as an *analogous* expression from the pneumatological perspective, one can indeed provide a satisfactory response regarding the goods inherent in

131

these practices. The seven marks of the church are *genuinely* practices only if they are understood in a strictly pneumatological fashion, something that does, however, shift their logic considerably. The Holy Spirit is now to be understood as the real subject of these practices; their teleological focus is soteriological, and the "excellence" in question involves a person's growth in faith, or sanctification.[131] Although the human being is always *present* in these activities, and is always and especially *actively present,* listening, receiving, responding, praising, and rendering obedience, still this human activity does *not* constitute these practices. Human activity is indeed always an inherent part of them, but never more than that. The disposition of all seven practices is rather such that in them the human being is always the *recipient,* that is, always remains in the mode of pathos. The human being remains the one who *through* these works of the Holy Spirit is qualified and receives a new "form," the one who thus is modeled through the Spirit of Christ, the *forma fidei.*

These practices are thus distinct activities whose point is precisely their *passivum.* The radically altered logic of these specific practices is a sign of their pneumatological constitution. In the following I will refer to these activities, in the sense of the analogous use just mentioned, as *core church practices.* They are *core* practices because other practices unique to the church can certainly also be enumerated alongside them, albeit practices in contradistinction to which these *core* practices remain constitutive for the mode of enactment of the Holy Spirit's economic mission and thus for the church itself.[132]

c. The Core Practices of the Church:
"Enhypostatic" in the Spirit

What does it mean to understand the practices of the Holy Spirit, the core practices of the church, pneumatologically? Clarification here requires that one examine the analogous reference to "practices" within the context of pneumatology.

Are these, as distinct human activities, actually "products" of the Holy Spirit separate from the being of the Spirit? Is the Holy Spirit to be understood as the condition for the possibility of human performance of these practices, that is, as the "impulse" or causative factor of something the human being then "realizes"? This particular understanding is unequivocally excluded at least by Luther's terminology, and would in any event fundamentally call into question from the perspective of the Trinity both the hypostatic being and the economic mission of the Spirit. Rather, the Holy Spirit as

sanctificator simultaneously remains the Creator Spirit, and its work is inseparable from its being, which in its own turn is identical with its mission.
Hence the core practices must ultimately be interpreted with the aid of the
concept of "enhypostasis,"[133] a concept borrowed from Christology and applied analogously here. That is, they subsist enhypostatically in the Spirit.[134]
Whereas person and work are certainly to be distinguished in the case of human beings, precisely the opposite is the case with regard to the person and
work of the Spirit. The salvific-economic mission of the Spirit cannot be distinguished from the trinitarian being of the Spirit. The *poiemata* of the Spirit,
however, the core church practices, inhere in the salvific-economic mission of
the Spirit. This is why the reference here is to the *pneumatological enhypostasis*
of the core church practices, and it is also why in a certain sense Luther could
indeed have referred to them as "sacraments."[135]

d. Summary

From the pneumatological logic developed here I argued that the church
must be understood as a nexus of core practices that at once both constitute
and characterize the church. In the form of these core practices, the church
subsists enhypostatically in the Holy Spirit, and through them the Holy Spirit
performs its economic mission, namely, the eschatological re-creation of humanity, a re-creation whose beginning is faith and whose growth is growth in
faith, transforming human beings precisely in and through ongoing affliction
by drawing them into God's eschatological communion.

Alongside these core church practices a whole series of practices inherent to the church and integral to faith can be enumerated; these exhibit a variety of relationships with the constitutive core practices. *One of these practices
is theology itself.* One can show that as an (integral) practice, it relates to all
the constitutive practices *as well as* to church doctrine such that precisely this
relation is its specific, constitutive pathos.

Before addressing the question of theology as a church practice, however, one must first ask how the core practices themselves relate to that which
most of them imply in any case, namely, "doctrine." For all the core practices
imply a normative standard, a *regula fidei.* That is, the practices imply a concern with the *correct* gospel proclamation, the *correct* administration of baptism, the *correct* performance of the Lord's Supper, and so on. Obviously, each
of these core practices can be distorted and misused, and only a standard, a
regula, can prevent this. In a reverse fashion, "doctrine" isolated from the core
practices can all too easily be reified, that is, become ersatz metaphysics in
isolation from the soteriological telos.

In the following discussion I will point out in what way doctrine, which is concerned with preserving the soteriological telos of the core church practices and which precisely as such remains oriented toward them, is *itself* shaped by this soteriological telos, and indeed in a certain sense even participates in it.

3. Church Doctrine and the Core Church Practices
— Together in the Spirit

a. Doctrina *in Luther*

Luther's understanding of *doctrina* will serve as a constructive guide for understanding doctrine in correspondence to the pneumatological ecclesiology of the core church practices. This renewed reference to Luther derives from specific theological considerations, since he understands *doctrina* in an exemplary pneumatological fashion. As the Finnish Luther scholar Eeva Martikainen has demonstrated in her important study,[136] *doctrina* for Luther refers essentially to the God who is present. In her opinion, the modern Protestant understanding of Luther deviates decisively from Luther himself.[137] The reason for this, she believes, is the implicit and uncritical adoption by Protestant Luther research in the nineteenth and twentieth centuries of the critique of metaphysics inhering in modern and especially Kantian and neo-Kantian philosophy.[138] Martikainen shows that Luther's concept of *doctrina* is neither metaphysically nor antimetaphysically directed, and is rather to be understood entirely from the perspective of its specific object, namely, the God who is present.[139] Here Luther follows scholastic usage in applying the concept *doctrina* in a twofold fashion. "*Doctrina* is both the academic discipline in general as well as given, positive theological doctrine. The scholastic term *doctrina* similarly encompassed these two meanings. The wider meaning of the designation is also especially important for interpreting specific theological doctrine, namely, the articles of faith."[140] Luther does believe that although all academic disciplines are indeed connected through a common form of concepts and terms, it is *only* through these that they are connected.[141] In each discipline, however, these terms acquire a distinct and specific meaning from the perspective of that particular discipline's object.[142]

The key feature in Martikainen's study is her emphasis on the connection between doctrine and faith in Luther. It is not faith that makes doctrine into doctrine, as assumed by some in modern Luther scholarship, but doctrine that makes faith possible. "In analogy to the intuitive concept of knowledge, Luther advocates the 'intellectual' character of faith. Using concepts from Aristotelian metaphysics, he emphasizes that faith assimilates Christ as its actual object, specifically the Christ portrayed by doctrine. The divine reality in Christ disclosed by doctrine is the 'form' of faith. When emphasizing the concrete character of faith, Luther uses the expression *Christus forma fidei,* one actually not appearing in scholastic thinking."[143]

If Christ is indeed the *forma fidei,* then precisely as such he is also the pathos of faith, that is, that which shapes faith and makes it what it is.[144] As the object of faith, however, Christ as its *forma* is not separate from it; rather, "in ipsa fide Christus adest,"[145] in faith itself Christ is present. "Faith is salvific, theological knowledge because the entire divine person is present in it, not just his characteristics or gifts, but he himself as an active person."[146] Because *doctrina* mediates the object that becomes the *forma* of faith, however, faith is to be conceived analogously to knowledge. Hence not only is the *fides quae creditur,* the object of faith, inseparable from the *fides qua creditur,* the actualization or process of faith, but the former also shapes the latter insofar as the *fides quae* as form of the *fides qua* also constitutes its nature. This view finds its ultimate articulation for Luther in the concept of the *doctrina definita.* The *doctrina* receives its own *form* from its object, and to that extent is *doctrina definita.* "At its core, theological doctrine is always salvific doctrine, and in its specific meaning and most characteristic parts refers to the present Christ and to the God at work in him, the dispenser and creator of all that is good, the victor over death and sin, the initiator of faith, and the dispenser of love."[147] As the *content* of faith, the *doctrina definita* is faith's determinate form and *therein* soteriologically directed. The formative object of faith is inseparable from this soteriological orientation. "The present God in his entire fullness is the content of justifying faith. If this content is lost or if its presentation deviates in even a single article, the salvific character of doctrine is completely lost."[148] Here Luther carries forward the patristic understanding of "doctrine" as dogma. The *doctrina evangelii* is not only the binding promise of God's free grace, as the *doctrina definita* it also has its own binding, that is, specific, object which is identical with that promise. For Luther there is no salvific promise of faith independent of the object of faith bindingly formulated — that is, under the exclusion of heretical alternatives — in the early church symbols.[149]

Martikainen's study represents an important contribution precisely because her interpretation of Luther swims against the current of modern Protestant Luther scholarship. It is doubtless no accident that her perception of this central aspect of Luther's theology is part of a comprehensive change of paradigm in Luther scholarship that occurred in the course of an intensive dialogue between Finnish Lutheran theologians and theologians of the Russian Orthodox Church.[150] What Martikainen essentially prepares but does not undertake is a trinitarian development of her thesis. To put it even more succinctly: although her important insight that the *doctrina* has as its object the God who is present is certainly historically interesting, without any explicit trinitarian explication it remains theologically irrelevant. In order to avoid, for example, the kind of alternative Hans Joachim Iwand, following Karl Barth, presents between doctrine as dogma, that is, as "God's word" on the one hand and the "human word" that witnesses to this word of God on the other, one would have to articulate from a trinitarian perspective the understanding of *doctrina* she has worked out.[151] This is the only way to find an alternative both to Peterson's understanding of dogma as well as to Karl Barth's understanding of church doctrine.

Martikainen's discussion of the relation between *doctrina definita* and Luther's doctrine of the Trinity provides a useful point of departure for a trinitarian explication of *doctrina*. She begins by quite rightly focusing on the central position pneumatology occupies in Luther's trinitarian theology.[152] "Like Christ, so also is the Holy Spirit the true God, namely, the Holy Spirit associated with both the doctrine of justification and ecclesiology in the symbol explicated by the church. God himself sees to it that human beings appropriate the gifts bequeathed in creation and redemption and lead a divine, holy life. Similarly, Luther is inclined to emphasize the unity of God's activity and gifts by pointing out that the Holy Spirit directs us to Christ, makes him recognizable, and leads through him to God."[153]

b. Doctrina *and Core Practices:* The Holy Spirit's Modes of Actualization

Martikainen does not draw the obvious and compelling conclusion — nor does this really fall within the horizon of her study — that *doctrina* itself is to be interpreted pneumatologically. This seems the obvious thing to do, however, because the salvific-economic mission of the Holy Spirit and the function of the *doctrina* are defined identically. In its own object, namely, the person and work of Christ, *doctrina* evokes the triune economy of salvation. It has the same soteriological telos as the core practices and must thus, like the core practices themselves, be understood within the framework of the economy of salvation as the work of the Holy Spirit.

This pneumatological understanding of *doctrina* has several important consequences. First of all, one must articulate and expand the understanding of God's presence in the *doctrina evangelii* and in the core church practices with the concept of "enhypostasis" introduced earlier in connection with pneumatology. *Doctrina*[154] and the core practices are *poiemata* of the Holy Spirit in that they receive the *forma* of the object they mediate to faith, namely, Christ himself. They are not contingent "works" that remain external to the Holy Spirit, but rather participate in the being of the Spirit. They do not "exist" independently the way products do over against their producer. Rather, God himself is present in their enhypostatic participation in the being of the Spirit.

c. The Pneumatological "Enhypostasis" of Doctrina and the Core Practices

If both the core church practices as well as *doctrina* can be understood as the poiesis of the Holy Spirit that participates enhypostatically in the being of the Spirit, the next obvious question is that regarding the relation between *doctrina* and the core church practices themselves. For Luther, *both* are *poiemata* of the Spirit because, in both, the Spirit leads a person through Christ to the Father.[155] As explicated above in connection with the *communio*-ecclesiology, the church is constituted by the work of the Holy Spirit, the latter active "in, with, and among" distinct practices both constituting and marking the church. *Doctrina* is also a work of the Holy Spirit, so one must be able to speak at least of *doctrina* and the core practices being joint in the Spirit. Both refer constitutively and simultaneously to the Christian faith and to the church. Not only does the Holy Spirit call forth faith,[156] but with the *doctrina evangelii* the Spirit offers to faith its proper *forma* as well as a sphere shaped through the core practices. The Holy Spirit neither creates a faith that seeks or creates its own object, nor sanctifies independently of distinct practices. Faith is pathos precisely because its actualization is utterly determined by the work of the Holy Spirit and receives its "form" — which is its object — precisely in that determination, that is, it is "sanctified." The decisive feature of church doctrine and the core practices as *poiemata* of the Holy Spirit consists in their soteriological telos, namely, in the fact that God becomes present in both and as such is now accessible in faith.

d. The Interrelation of Doctrina and the Core Practices

The next important step is to understand how *doctrina* and the core church practices as works of the Holy Spirit are always related in an essential and mutual fashion. There is no *doctrina* without the core practices, nor any core practices without the *doctrina*. This relationship is not, however, one of "form" and "content." Rather, in the core practices one encounters in various ways the object of *doctrina*. Martikainen evokes this insight when she says that "because the object of theological doctrine is the manifest God, all the articles of faith are speaking about this God. He is present in the sacraments, in the church, in justifying faith, in love that serves one's fellow, and so on."[157] Despite references to Luther, she does not then draw the theological conclusion that the *doctrina* and the core practices belong inseparably together. Beginning with the understanding that the core practices subsist enhypostatically in the Spirit, it is only logical that Luther emphasizes God's presence in the gospel proclamation, in baptism, and in the Lord's Supper.[158]

The primary goal here is not an interpretation of Luther, however, but the theological insight that the *doctrina* and the core practices *together* actually constitute the indissoluble union of the work of Christ and of the Holy Spirit. *Doctrina* mediates in a distinct and thus binding fashion God's salvific action in the life, death, and resurrection of Jesus of Nazareth; its proclamation is itself one of the core church practices. The object of *doctrina* constitutes the "form" and thus the nature or essence of the various core practices. A practice genuinely is a core practice of the church if and only if it is "informed" by the object of *doctrina,* for at its core *doctrina* is Christology and Christology *alone*. As such, *doctrina* is manifested in each of the core practices in various ways. That is, its "life setting" is found precisely in the core practices of the church. Isolating it and abstracting it from those practices robs it of its soteriological telos; it loses its christological character and turns into ideology. There is no *doctrina* apart from gospel proclamation, faith and obedience, baptism, Lord's Supper, church discipline, ordained office, praise, catechetical instruction, and discipleship in suffering. This inherent connection between *doctrina* and the modes of actualization of the Holy Spirit makes concrete their pneumatological constitution. This explicit pneumatological understanding of *doctrina* also throws light on the question of where, in addition to the core practices, one actually encounters *doctrina,* namely, first in the biblical canon, and second in the symbols of the church as an explication of *doctrina*.[159]

e. Doctrina *and Canon*

Understanding the *doctrina evangelii* pneumatologically in this sense also requires that one interpret the biblical canon as a work of the Holy Spirit, namely, precisely in its soteriological function of disclosing the presence of God so that faith might have access to him. Precisely this is the horizon within which to view the traditional doctrine of inspiration.[160] The biblical canon participates in the salvific-economic mission of the Spirit, which in its own turn also includes the core church practices. Precisely by pointing to the God who is present, the Bible is together with the core practices a work of the Holy Spirit, and one must thus interpret the "inspiration" of Scripture in a strictly trinitarian fashion as an implication of the salvific economy. Insofar as the God of Israel, who became incarnate in Jesus Christ, is attested in Scripture, the latter participates in the mission of the Spirit. Its "perspicuity" as well as its "inerrancy" is found in this witness; these features are not inherent in it *in abstracto* — as fundamentalism would like to have it — but rather within the overall context of the core church practices.[161]

f. Doctrina *and Church Doctrine*

How does church doctrine itself participate in the *doctrina evangelii?* One obviously cannot draw a dividing line between these two, since that would contradict the character of *doctrina* itself. Because *doctrina* as *doctrina evangelii* (the preaching and teaching of the gospel) always also is *doctrina definita* (a specific teaching about Christ's person and work), it already implies church doctrine, since *doctrina definita* is always specified in the form of binding doctrinal statements and is never accessible independent of these.[162] That is, the *doctrina definita* can never be articulated apart from distinct church doctrine. There is no *doctrina definita* "as such," apart from its dogmatic formulation as church doctrine. The decisive feature here, of course, is that these formulations of church doctrine do not intend to say anything fundamentally new, but rather merely hold fast to the *doctrina definita* in concretely rejecting specific errors. The concrete reference point against which church doctrine is to be measured is the biblical canon. Church doctrine must always prove itself over against the *doctrina evangelii,* and the latter in its canonical form and in its soteriological telos remains the indispensable norm of all church doctrine. Church doctrine itself, however, precisely in its variously unique articulation and delimitation over against false doctrine, holds fast to *doctrina.* Although this "holding fast" to the *doctrina definita* may often appear to be innovation, under conceptually altered circumstances precisely this allegedly new formulation may be preserving the *doctrina definita.*

But how does church doctrine repeatedly prove itself over against *doctrina?* Precisely this is one task of theology as a church practice. Insofar as church doctrine itself remains the object of theological discourse and various aspects are repeatedly measured against the *doctrina evangelii,* church doctrine must continually prove itself over against the *doctrina evangelii* by guiding theological discourse normatively, on the one hand, and at the same time having to maintain itself over against the *doctrina evangelii* within that discourse on the other. In this way church doctrine makes theological discourse both possible in the first place and necessary. As the authoritative interpretation of the *doctrina*, it *makes discourse possible* by providing the horizon necessary for any discourse. This horizon itself is always already embodied by church doctrine in any given discourse tradition. Church doctrine makes theological discourse *necessary* because it must itself be maintained ever anew in appropriation, interpretation, and discerning application of church doctrine with regard to the *doctrina evangelii*.

g. Church Doctrine, Theological Doctrine, and Theology as Practice: Anticipatory Considerations

At this point an explicit distinction must be made between *church doctrine (doctrina definita)*, on the one hand, and *theological doctrine* (dogmatics) as a consensus phenomenon unique to the church practice of theology on the other. This distinction will allow a more subtle examination of the phenomenon of "innovation." The possibility of alleged "innovation" of church doctrine mentioned above is to be distinguished from the "innovations" within theological discourse or in theological doctrine. Even if innovations can later be accepted or even become "main-stream" theology,[163] neither in view of church doctrine nor of theological discourse does this militate for the Schleiermacherian organological-progressivistic model that reconciles orthodoxy and heterodoxy with each other as equally significant aspects for the historic course of Christianity.[164] For both aspects involve differentiating perception and judgment whose logic, rather than being organic and hermeneutical, is rather oriented toward the truth of the *doctrina definita*. The key difference between *church doctrine* on the one hand and *theological doctrine* as consensus within theological discourse on the other, is that in church doctrine the church as a totality expresses what must *unconditionally* be stated, taught, and confessed in continuing adherence to the *doctrina evangelii*, in continuity with how the church in other ages and at other places justifiably (that is, from the perspective of the *doctrina definita* of biblical canon) has adhered to the *doctrina evangelii*, and in delimitation over against concrete errors. (Under the conditions of ecclesiastical schism, of course, the question of who is to speak thus for the church is itself the object of dispute between the various churches.) By contrast, within the framework of theological discourse as a church practice, individual theologians *never* speak for the church as a whole, particularly not when critically examining church doctrine itself. Their churchly disposition, however, often manifests itself in the extent to which their presentations, in the form of interpretation and appropriation of church doctrine, under certain circumstances themselves become *theological doctrine* and thus a point of orientation[165] or a part[166] of church doctrine. Here appropriation and interpretation always represent "innovation" insofar as church doctrine must be interpreted and appropriated in consideration of a given time and a given place. This may not, however, constitute any qualitative innovation in the sense of theological poiesis. It must be concrete theological judgments that abide in the same pathos — that is, in adherence to canon, the core church practices, and church doctrine — and yet present different theological assessments (even regarding the use of any given conceptual framework) than theologies at other places and at other times.

This view understands theology as a practice necessarily belonging to the mission of the church, for the *doctrina evangelii* is to be proclaimed, interpreted, and appropriated in all ages and in all places. To accomplish this, that is, to express the *doctrina evangelii* ever "anew" without saying something "new" in the process, or to express the one truth in variously new ways, theology as a church practice needs the horizon of canon, the core practices, and doctrine. Without this normative horizon, theology lacks the unified object that must be appropriated and interpreted. The object of discursive theological practice is thus never immediately accessible; it is accessible only through the biblical canon, the core church practices, and the tradition of church doctrine. The discursive practice of theology thus also implies the "church *as* a public" insofar as every theological judgment, meaning every interpretation, appropriation, and critique of doctrine, must be justified within the horizon of canon, the core practices, and church doctrine; that is, it must be subjected to critical evaluation and assessment by other theologians. This always implies two potential borderline situations: first, that a given theology, that is, a specific configuration of theological explication and judgment, can itself become the central point of orientation for church doctrine, or indeed can even become church doctrine as such; and second, that any given theology can be identified as heterodoxy or false doctrine, that is, as a configuration of false judgments and thus as standing outside the horizon defined by canon, the core practices, and doctrine.[167] Wherever from the outset neither of these borderline cases *is able* to arise or where it ceases to arise, theology as a church practice is de facto not present, nor is it any longer serving the church as a specific public.[168]

Without being cognizant of these implications, Martikainen describes Luther's own engagement in theology as church practice.

> Luther thus approves the notion that when required, the church can indeed explicate the doctrine defined in the Bible. He himself proceeds thus in his

confession of 1528, one based on the trinity and yet containing articles of faith not found in the *Apostolikum*. He always emphasizes, however, that neither the symbols and councils nor he himself are presenting anything new beyond already obtaining doctrine. For him, the symbols constitute neither a new nor the entire doctrine, and he thus seems to believe that the church and theologians merely summarize, explicate, and teach the doctrine already given in the Bible. On the one hand, Luther does object to the notion that the church has already formulated this doctrine perfectly. On the other, this does not prevent him from quite unaffectedly both perpetuating and adhering to the praxis of the age preceding his own with his trinitarian presentation of doctrine. Hence he repeatedly emphasizes that he is representing the same doctrine found in the Bible, explicated in the symbols and by the church fathers, and confessed and believed by all true Christians.[169]

Although Martikainen has touched on a central point in Luther's thought here, one applicable to all church theology, she does not interpret the point according to its ecclesial logic. For her presentation easily leaves the impression that merely a personal idiosyncrasy prompted Luther to proceed theologically in this way rather than in another. The implicit consequence of her otherwise accurate observation, however, is that church doctrine must always prove itself in dialogue with the *doctrina* of Scripture, and must do so in continuity and critical debate with earlier explication without doing more than adhering to the *doctrina definita* in its own explication. In this process, however, it is never the entirety of church doctrine that is critically questioned, but only a single point that in a given crisis has emerged and that under specific circumstances certainly might be a central issue at stake; for Luther, this was the question of justification through grace by faith alone. Using the *doctrina* of Scripture and within the horizon of early church dogmatic consensus, that is, on the explicit basis of early church trinitarian theology and Christology, Luther rethought the *theological* doctrine of justification and pushed it to a new formulation (sola gratia *and* sola fide) that precisely maintained the *doctrina* of Scripture in light of a specific nominalist heterodoxy *(facere quod in se est)* and in light of the false theology and praxis of indulgences. In a second step — one to be strictly distinguished from Luther's *theological* teaching — his specific formulation of the doctrine of justification was ecclesially affirmed in the form of binding church doctrine whose central document is the Lutheran confessional writings as collected in the *Book of Concord*.

Three conclusions may be drawn from this. (1) A pneumatological understanding of *doctrina* first of all offers a way to overcome the antithesis between "dogma" and "confession" doctrinally fixed in Western Christendom after the Reformation and exemplified in the Peterson-Barth controversy. Karlmann Beyschlag has formulated this antithesis succinctly: "Whereas dogma in the Roman Catholic understanding is *identical* with revelation according to substance (and thus infallible, irreversible, an imperative mandate), the Protestant confession is merely *oriented* toward revelation, that is, to Holy Scripture (and thus temporally conditioned, reversible, and without an imperative mandate)."[170] The confession is meaningful as confession, however, only if it articulates the object of *doctrina* and seizes it within that very articulation itself. *Dogma* is meaningful only if it is adopted and confessed (in worship). *Dogma and confession must be understood as the two inseparable sides of the pneumatological mode of actualization of* doctrina. *The goal of a "dogma" is to be received and confessed publicly by the Christian communion, that is, precisely in the doxology of worship. A "confession" is a confession only if in any given reformulation as* doctrina definita *it still adheres to the* doctrina evangelii *and as a doctrinal truth then claims binding universal authority.*[171] "Consensus" takes place within this double movement insofar as a confession as a dogmatic confession adheres to the *doctrina evangelii*, that is, insofar as it expresses confessionally what must unconditionally be said, and insofar as church doctrine, that is, dogma, is received and publicly confessed by the Christian communion. What is decisive here is that this consensus is not established by the Christian communion or the *magisterium*, but rather emerges on the basis of common acknowledgment. "Consensus" is thus not poiesis; it is not the truth "produced" when "everyone" agrees. Rather, it is pathos: *consentire* with the truth as the consenting to truth, which is the implicate of acknowledging truth and of letting oneself by qualified by it.[172]

(2) Church doctrine — that is, the totality of biblical canon, early church trinitarian and christological dogmas, and confessional writings — must from this perspective (and here the author can speak only as a theologian of a specific ecclesia under the conditions of schism) be understood as a unique and genuine mode of actualization of *doctrina*, as a mode of actualization with both confessional and dogmatic character.

(3) The church needs a specific practice that carries this dogmatic debate forward, a practice that explicates and interprets church doctrine and provides clarity in conflicts with false doctrine or with new challenges; this clarity in its own turn prepares the way for emerging reformulation of church doctrine or confession.[173] This discursive practice must allow for the possible borderline case consisting in dogmatic self-criticism, that is, the acknowledgment that church doctrinal formulations may in some instances be erroneous or incomplete.

Church doctrine as a mode of actualization of *doctrina* thus needs theology as a church practice, and vice versa theology as a church practice takes place within the horizon of church doctrine and is always oriented toward the *doctrina* thematically formulated in church doctrine. As the binding interpretation of *doctrina,* church doctrine makes discourse possible by opening up the horizon within which such discourse becomes meaningful in the first place. This horizon can always be found already condensed into church doctrine within any given discursive tradition. The latter requires theological discourse because it must be preserved again and again and ever anew with regard to *doctrina* in the appropriation, interpretation, and judgmental application of church doctrine.

Neither *doctrina* nor church doctrine (as the mode of actualization of *doctrina*) can be isolated from its soteriological "life setting" in the core church practices. And precisely this is the point of understanding theology as a church practice; its pathos emerges from the soteriological telos attaching both to the core church practices and to *doctrina*. By wresting itself from this, its genuine pathos, Christian theology loses its object. At the beginning of Part Four, I will address the question in what way the genuine *freedom* of Christian theology as a church practice consists precisely in this pathos.

h. Conclusions

The inherent reference to the core practices and to church doctrine characterizes the pathos of church theology. *In* that pathos theology participates in the *poiemata* of the Holy Spirit — the core church practices and church doctrine — and thus in its salvific-economic mission. Church doctrine differs from theology as church practice and from theological doctrine as a consensus phenomenon within the theological practice in that, as a work of the Holy Spirit, as the *doctrina definita* authoritatively expressing the *doctrina evangelii,* it steps out of theological discourse and assumes a position juxtaposed to or over against that discourse. In this juxtaposed position church doctrine shapes the pathos of the discursive theological practice. In its core practices the church is a result of the gospel. Each of the core practices actualizes the *doctrina evangelii* in its own way, and church doctrine always adheres to this *doctrina* in explanation and definition. Both cases involve nothing other than the fulfillment of the salvific-economic mission of the Holy Spirit, its sanctifying, re-creative work that draws believers into God's triune communion.

The mission of the church must thus be identified with the mission of the Holy Spirit. This constitutes neither a reification of the Spirit nor an incorporation of the church into the deity as the fourth *hypostasis*. The church remains strictly separate from the Holy Spirit insofar as it perpetually receives what the Spirit creates in it and is thus pathically determined by the Spirit's poiesis. The eschatological salvific work of the Spirit takes place *pathically* in every historic concrete aspect of the church. As I will show in the following discussion, this gives the church its own, unique public character. Through the Holy Spirit (Pentecost!), Christ becomes "public" in the world.[174]

PART FOUR

Theology as Church Practice

I. The Pathos of Theology as Church Practice: Participation in God's Freedom and Truth

The question now is how to understand the pneumatological constitution of theology as its specific pathos. I will unfold the pathos of theology from the perspective of the concepts of *freedom* and *truth*. Here again, the association of Luther and Eastern Orthodox theology will be useful, developing further as it does the salvific-economic perspective presented in Part Three. In a first step I will examine Luther's concept of freedom in *The Bondage of the Will* (1525), since this concept makes it clear why the freedom of theology consists precisely in its pathos, to which, as already shown above, *doctrina* inherently belongs. This interpretation also provides the clue to Luther's famous statement — one found in the same writing — that the Holy Spirit speaks in assertions.[1] Finally, with a soteriologically articulated, eucharistic concept of truth of the sort John Zizioulas develops from Greek patristics, I will expand the notion that the freedom of theology is pneumatologically constituted insofar as, through the gift of the Spirit, it participates in the one true *liberum arbitrium*, the one genuinely free will there is, namely God's. This interpretation will show that by being shaped and qualified by the core church practices and *doctrina*, theology as a church practice is at once both "taken prisoner" and liberated such that freedom and truth, rather than opposing one another, need to be viewed as one.

1. The "Royal Freedom" of Christians: Participation in God's Liberum Arbitrium *in the Holy Spirit*[2]

Let me counter any misunderstanding and misinterpretation right at the outset by adducing Luther's insistence that the *liberum arbitrium* is a divine predicate attributable exclusively to God. This is why he is hesitant to ascribe *liberum arbitrium,* that is, genuinely *free* will, to anything else.[3] Hence wherever *The Bondage of the Will* refers to freedom in the full sense, the reference is to God's freedom.[4] Luther's writing directly addresses two characteristics of God's freedom. First, God's freedom consists in making and keeping promises.[5] For Luther, the logic of the promise presupposes the *liberum arbitrium* as a divine predicate. The condition for the possibility of the promise's reliability is grounded in it.[6] The other characteristic of God's freedom is its nonevident nature. Within creaturely knowledge of God's freedom, any immediate knowledge of God collapses before the eschaton. Both worldly and theological experience confront us with God's double hiddenness, first in God's utter sovereignty, and second in God's love as shown on Christ's cross.[7]

To learn more about God's freedom — the basis of an ontology of freedom in Luther — an indirect method of interpretation is necessary. Luther's arguments against the creaturely possession of a *liberum arbitrium* allow one to deduce additional characteristics associated with the divine name *liberum arbitrium*. His arguments *against* creaturely *liberum arbitrium* can be classified into two groups.

The following argument characterizes the first group. Human beings cannot step behind the concrete performance of their choice or of their freedom of decision and, as it were, themselves choose "choosing" or decide concerning "deciding." Human freedom consists simply in the "willingness" to do what one has decided to do *(libentia seu voluntas faciendi).*[8] Human beings thus have no will behind the will (no *purum et merum velle*).[9] The *purum et merum velle* is ascribed exclusively to the *liberum arbitrium,* so that God alone precedes his own determined will.

The second group of arguments involves that which can be said at most within the framework of theological anthropology about human freedom, namely, that it is a solely dispositional feature *(dispositivam qualitatem et passivam aptitudinem).* This passive *aptitudo,* however, marks the anthropological locus of genuine freedom (in the sense of *libentia)* only to the extent a person is rapt *(rapi)* into this freedom by another. That is, rather than representing an extant quality and capacity, it is one whose existence can be inferred only from the reality of actual freedom. Because this *aptitudo* is prompted and actualized by an "other," it must — via inference — be determined as *passive and relational*. The situation of persons under the condition of sin, however, is that God and Satan both are fighting over them; either God or Satan sweeps them into the "freedom of action" *(libentia)* in which they then act "willingly" or "voluntarily" in the sense of "concurrence" *(libentia seu voluntas faciendi)*. The "other" is always theologically qualified. There is no "neutral" other who might sweep a person into this limited freedom of action — indeed, precisely the other human being is excluded here because he or she participates in the same *conditio humana*.[10]

Hence for Luther, freedom of action means being "rapt" *(rapi)* into the freedom of action by an "other." This dependency applies to human beings in an unfallen creation as well; precisely *in* their freedom of action, human beings remain *dependent* on an other. Human freedom of action exists as a concretely contingent phenomenon only in a social nexus, and always presupposes the freedom of action of others who "sweep" or "rapt" us into our own action. From this passive qualification of human freedom of action, Robert Jenson persuasively concludes the passive constitution of the *liberum arbitrium* itself: "It seems justified to say: to have '*liberum arbitrium*' is to be rapt into freedom without dependence on alien freedom."[11] In this view *liberum arbitrium* means freedom from alien freedom, freedom from being bound into a social nexus in which one's own freedom, as both possibility and reality, can only be contingent freedom, *libentia*. Even this genuine freedom, however, is not simply "sovereignty" in the sense of bad omnipotence. Rather or even precisely God's '*liberum arbitrium*' is also to be understood as passively constituted — and precisely as such as *genuine* freedom. What does this mean?

This suggests the trinitarian conclusion that *liberum arbitrium* is exclusively a divine predicate; for God alone can be rapt into freedom *(rapi)* without depending on alien freedom, since God is himself the "other" who "rapts" God into freedom.[12] *Freedom is thus an exclusively divine predicate because only the triune God can encounter himself as an other and can do so such that freedom itself, as a hypostatic reality, that is, as the person of the Holy Spirit, is then God's own future.*

In accordance with this trinitarian understanding of God's *liberum arbitrium*, the latter does not become a demonic[13] principle of omnipotence "behind" God's actions, but rather God's inexhaustible freedom grounded in God's own triune life.[14] *God's freedom must thus not be conceived independently from God's economy of salvation through the Son and the Holy Spirit. Rather, it is in God's triune economy of salvation that God's* liberum arbitrium *is actualized and thus also God's self-determination through the* promissiones. *God's being, God's actions, and God's freedom must be conceived together here from a trinitarian perspective such that God's freedom as God the Holy Spirit is identical with God's salvific actions.*

Finally, one must integrate, along with Jenson, these trinitarian considerations into Luther's conception of freedom by showing how with regard to human beings, too, Luther is able to speak of "freedom," or even of "royal freedom," *regia libertas*.[15] First of all, human beings obviously possess a particular disposition making them suitable for free action. When a person genuinely makes a concrete decision and then acts in a way determined by that decision, the person is acting uncoerced and voluntarily *(lubendo)*. Luther refers to this capacity as *libentia* or as *servum arbitrium*, freedom as the concrete will to action in the weak sense.[16] In my opinion, Jenson does not emphasize enough that precisely this *libentia* is theologically, that is, *soteriologically,* utterly irrelevant, since it is through precisely this "willingness" that human beings in fact stand not between salvation and condemnation, but in the nexus of sin out of which they can only be "rapt" or torn.

Freedom in the strong sense, *libertas*, appears in *The Bondage of the Will* only as the negative freedom human beings lost under the condition of sin.[17] Under the condition of sin, only *libentia* is possible; *libentia*, however, does not lead a person out of the fateful nexus of sin, since a person does not have access to the choice of his or her choice and remains exposed to the powers of evil precisely in the concrete act of choosing.[18]

Only if God is the *raptor* in the Holy Spirit does *libertas* arise, indeed, *regia libertas*, royal freedom.[19] Jenson quite rightly concludes that God alone can as *raptor* really set a person free, for only the triune God has access to a freedom that re-creates itself ever anew and in this sense is inexhaustible such that God can grant participation in it. Ultimately, this *raptus*-relation is to be understood not at all as causal, but in the sense of enduring participation; neither the human being nor Satan can be the "other" who enduringly leads a person into *libertas,* for neither possesses it. The triune God alone can set a person free by granting to the person participation in that freedom.[20]

2. Assertiones — *the Freedom of the Holy Spirit*

A key feature of my interpretation of *The Bondage of the Will* is the pneumatological articulation of the concept of freedom. "Freedom" is not an abstract attribute of a divine subject "behind" God's concrete triune life that might be conceived as independent of the economy of salvation. Nor is it an abstract attribute of a human subject that is allegedly not in need of redemption. Rather, freedom in the substantive sense, namely, as *liberum arbitrium,* is identical with God's salvific action grounded in God's triune being. The substance of this freedom is identical with God's economy of salvation because it is to be understood as the self-determination of God's future.

God's promises as well as pneumatology must both be understood from the perspective of this freedom as conceived in light of the economy of salvation. God's *liberum arbitrium* consists in God binding himself to the *promissiones,* that is, in God determining his own future such that God remains true to himself in his own freedom. *Accordingly, the content of God's freedom is to be interpreted as God's economy of salvation, meaning that it is also to be anchored in the trinitarian economy. The hypostatic person of the Spirit is the actualization of this freedom; the Holy Spirit is God's future insofar as the triune God remains true to himself in freedom in the person and work of the Spirit.*

This notion corresponds to a basic feature in Luther's pneumatology, namely, the thesis that the Holy Spirit speaks in *assertiones.*[21] The *assertio,* the binding statement, is grounded entirely in the substance and logic of the *promissio.* The *promissio,* however, is to be understood from the perspective of the person and work of Jesus Christ, and at the same time is to be interpreted from the perspective of the trinitarian economy of salvation. The Holy Spirit speaks in *assertiones* because, as a hypostatic person, it is the actualization of God's freedom through which God has established his own future. The Holy Spirit assures us authoritatively of this future, thereby making present even now the *eschata* to faith.[22]

Here we encounter from the opposite side both *doctrina* and the church practices explicated above as the work of the Holy Spirit. They now appear as the work of the Holy Spirit because in them the *assertiones* are articulated. Put succinctly: *The* assertiones *are a characteristic feature of the definition of the core church practices and of* doctrina. The *assertiones* can thus never be encountered abstractly, but only in a given concrete embodiment which for precisely that reason is to be understood as a work of the Holy Spirit. Hence the *assertiones* are the actualization of God's freedom consisting in the determination of God's own future, that is, fellowship with a renewed creation in the eschatological reign of God. *The Spirit speaks in* assertiones *because it is in* assertiones *that God actualizes his* liberum arbitrium.

Because genuine human freedom consists in participation in God's freedom, it is to be understood as a pathic feature; it is *vita passiva.* Precisely this *vita passiva,* however, is free in that it is qualified by the core practices of the church and by *doctrina.* It enters into God's freedom, to use Luther's expression, by being "rapt" into it by the core church practices and by *doctrina.* This salvific-economic *rapi* is the actualization of the pathos of theology as well.

Theology's freedom is thus not to be understood as an abstract passivity, but as *concrete* pathos actualized in the form of a specific practice, one to be outlined in the last section of this part. It suffices at this juncture to point out that the *vita passiva* of faith and then also of theology is a participation in God's freedom insofar as it is rapt into that freedom by allowing itself to be "taken prisoner" by the work of the Holy Spirit — through enactment of the *assertiones,* that is, the core practices of the church and church doctrine. In these two, it receives the object that "in-forms" and thereby radically qualifies it.

3. The Freedom of Theology as a Church Practice

The inherent orientation toward the core practices and toward *doctrina* thus constitutes the pathos of church theology. It is only *in* this pathos that it participates in the enhypostatic reality of the core church practices and of the *doctrina* attaching to them as works of the Holy Spirit. Hence Christian theology as a church practice participates in Christian freedom only if it remains in its appropriate place, namely, in its explicit orientation toward the core practices and toward *doctrina.*

It is thus precisely from its pathos that a theologically qualified definition of the "freedom of theology" can be derived. The freedom of theology consists in nothing other than participation in the *assertiones* of the Spirit. Every other understanding of freedom might involve a theological misunderstanding, an emphasis on *libentia;* although within certain limitations such emphasis is certainly justified,[23] outside these limitations it binds theology in a theologically unreflected fashion to the *libentia,* the *servum arbitrium* itself. Only a strictly *pneumatological understanding* of the freedom of theology can overcome conceptually the hidden lack of freedom attaching to *libentia.* The freedom of theology is pneumatologically constituted in its participation in God's exclusive *liberum arbitrium.* Its freedom resides in its pathos, in being drawn into God's salvific actions as authoritatively promised by the *doctrina evangelii.* Thus can Luther say: "And this is the reason why our theology is certain: it snatches us away from ourselves and places us outside ourselves *[extra nos],* so that we do not depend on our own strength, conscience, experience, person, or works but depend on that which is outside ourselves *[extra nos],* that is, on the promise and truth of God, which cannot deceive."[24] Both the certainty and the freedom of theology are inextricably bound together because both are grounded in its concrete pathos, the *extra nos* we encounter in connection with the core church practices and *doctrina.* Only if theology is understood from the perspective of the core church practices and *doctrina* can this *ponere nos extra nos* also be effected with regard to theology, and only in this way does it as a distinct practice participate in the *ponere nos extra nos,* the certainty of God's promises grounded in the freedom of God's own triune life.

It may sound paradoxical to modern ears, but Christian theology acquires and preserves its freedom exclusively as *church* theology. Its pathos, its qualification by and connection with the core church practices and *doctrina* is to be understood as the substance of its freedom. For only in this "imprisonment" does Christian theology participate in the *assertiones* of the Holy Spirit.

In his *Heidelberg Disputation,* Luther calls the task of theology "dicere quod res est," "to call the thing what it actually is."[25] Theology can say authoritatively what the matter is only if it itself is rapt into God's freedom, that is, only if it allows itself to be "taken prisoner" by the Holy Spirit and its *assertiones,* and in so doing participates in God's freedom. This participation, however, occurs only in its pathos, in its qualification by the core church practices and by the *doctrina evangelii* in whose context the *assertiones* of the Spirit are authoritatively articulated.

4. Freedom and Truth in Theology as a Church Practice

Which concept of truth does this "imprisonment" and resulting freedom of theology imply? It must be a concept of truth not introduced abstractly from the outside but essentially determined by the soteriological telos of the *assertiones* of the Holy Spirit. Hence neither the scientific concept of truth attaching to a mastery of the world by the natural sciences and technology nor the ontological concept of truth of a metaphysical worldview can be adopted without qualification; the understanding of truth attaching to the various logics of truth cannot do justice to the "object" under discussion here. It is appropriate to the overall course of the present study to inquire here, too, concerning the trinitarian understanding of the concept of truth. I will again take as my point of orientation John Zizioulas, who in *Being as Communion* has already provided an important point of departure.[26] His reflections concerning a *eucharistic concept of truth* are important for the present discussion because they help avoid two problematic alternatives in the relation between *doctrina* and church doctrine. The first is the renewed and merely postponed reification of church doctrine in the sense that truth is conceived as the "content" of church doctrine, content which "as such" must be accepted intellectually.[27] The second is church doctrine as the hermeneutic of individual disclosure of truth according to the motto "Ultimately, what is first of all true for me is the only thing that can be true." Zizioulas's recourse to Greek patristics is of considerable relevance because the concept of truth he develops as a synthesis of the Greek-patristic tradition attempts to overcome precisely these two false alternatives between objective-abstract and subjective-experiential truth.

Zizioulas believes the Greek-patristic doctrinal tradition[28] is able to identify truth and communion because the ontology of the Greek Fathers has a trinitarian structure. Their position is that being itself, rather than being characterized by substantiality without reference,[29] is to be conceived according to God's own triune identity. As I have already shown, this identity is primarily relational; that is, God's *ousia* is composed through the concrete relation of the three *hypostaseis* of the Father, Son, and Holy Spirit. The *hypostaseis* logically precede the *ousia* and determine it. God's "being" is the communion of Father, Son, and Holy Spirit. Creation, too, is to be conceived as originally inherently relational; as creation, it is constituted through its relationality to the triune God.

Although Zizioulas never uses the term "pathos," it is appropriate to mention it here. With reference to God the Creator, creatureliness as relationality is inherently pathic existence. "Being" is not simply "being thus" or "being there" in the sense of merely existing, but rather a specifically qualified being; it is a reality whose origin, future, and present are dependent on the creative activity of the triune God and are inherently qualified by this creative activity. The pathos of creatureliness is the hypostatic reality of creation; that is, its substance is in-formed by its pathos of creatureliness.[30]

In the theology of the Greek Fathers, the fall into sin interrupts this constitutive relationality. Being and communion are torn asunder. Being is no longer relationally determined by the creative communion of the triune God. *Post lapsum,* creaturely existence becomes its own absolute or self-related point of reference, which is also the definition of idolatry. Without fail, this turns the "substance" or *ousia* of a thing into its absolute truth content when truth refers entirely to being *post lapsum.*[31]

Under the condition of sin, the world consists of objects and individuals, that is, of substances whose being precedes their relationships and whose substance is not determined by their relationality. The latter, in fact, has only accidental character: "You first *are* and then relate."[32] Similarly, the relation of love and truth is problematically determined under this *conditio humana.* One can love an object or individual only after having acquired knowledge of it. Knowledge ontologically precedes love.[33] The Greek Fathers interpret death as the ontological consequence of individualization and fragmentation of nature. Death is not, for example, punishment for an act of disobedience, but the ontological result of an individualization to which the entire cosmos is subject.[34]

This presupposes an ontological concept of person that combines conceptually both *ekstasis* and *hypostasis*.[35] The christological mystery according to its Chalcedonian definition means that redemption as truth and life is possible only through a person who is ontologically true, a person who lives in the communion of the triune God and at the same time co-constitutes that communion.[36] This, however, is not something a fallen creation can effect itself.

One consequence of developing Christology in this way, from the perspective of the trinitarian concept of person, is that Christ is not to be understood as an "individual" in the modern sense whose "substance" is fixed *in se*, but as a person, and that means strictly *relationally* from the very outset.[37] The pneumatological implications of this Christology are far-reaching. First of all, the pneumatological Christology of the Eastern Church emphasizes the poiesis of the Holy Spirit in contrast to the pneumatology of communicative "bridging." The Holy Spirit is the eschatological Creator Spirit and not the divine power bridging the historic chasm between former salvific event and present existence (in faith) in the sense of a purely epistemic manifestation. Rather, the "creative" as well as salvific economy of the Spirit overcomes the division between Christology and ecclesiology.[38] Zizioulas identifies the *Lord's Supper* as the decisive locus of this pneumatologically conceived Christology and ecclesiology: "The eucharistic community is the Body of Christ *par excellence* simply because it incarnates and realizes our communion within the very life and communion of the Trinity, in a way that preserves the eschatological character of truth while making it an integral part of history."[39] *This makes the Lord's Supper itself into the "form" of the concept of truth, a concept that now does justice to its object, namely, the salvific self-manifestation of the triune God, in the eschatologically renewed communion.*

Zizioulas identifies five consequences arising from this understanding of the Lord's Supper as the locus of truth. Although all five are of interest, only three are significant with regard to the further development of my argument, and will now be discussed briefly.

a. Because the truth of Christ is not only revealed in the Lord's Supper but also becomes reality in the eucharistic fellowship as "communion," it involves no dictate demanding subjugation. Truth emerges rather from the center of communion. The eucharistic fellowship does not, however, produce it itself in the sense of poiesis; it does not "actualize" truth on its own. Rather, it receives it as a gift. Because God mediates himself such that the communion of the Lord's Supper already participates eschatologically in the triune communion, it is ultimately ontological truth also *as* communion. This, however, makes the relation of the eucharistic fellowship to eucharistic truth a pathic one; the eucharistic fellowship receives this truth by being created by it, taken into it, and defined anew by it.[40]

b. If truth as communion cannot be separated from the ontology of the triune life, then dogmas are to be understood essentially as soteriological explanations whose goal is to free the original *eikon* of Christ (image of Christ), namely, that truth, from its various heretical distortions. Hence dogma or church doctrine inherently has a soteriological telos. To the extent that dogmas fulfill this task, they are oriented toward the truth as communion, and in fulfilling this christological and trinitarian task they also participate in the truth as communion.[41] Here Zizioulas's concept of dogma finds an important parallel in a central feature of Lindbeck's cultural-linguistic understanding of church doctrine. Dogmas are to be understood in the sense of a salvific-economic grammar authoritatively articulating the soteriological telos of *doctrina*. Here, however, the dogmas do indeed exhibit a reality in the sense of the theory of correspondence by implying an *adequatio mentis ad rem* of a unique kind; the *res* does not represent part of a universally accessible metaphysical reality, but is rather the *doctrina evangelii* attested in Scripture and proclaimed and actualized in word and sacrament.[42]

Zizioulas is also able to interpret the undeniable historicity of the dogmas *pneumatologically*. Dogmas have no "content of meaning" that might be isolated from their culturally and historically conditioned form(ulation) and then formulated "anew" under different cultural and historical conditions. This would amount to a highly problematic *historicizing of the Holy Spirit* of the sort genuinely expressed in modern hermeneutics. By contrast, Zizioulas does quite justifiably advocate the *pneumatologizing of history*. Certain forms and articulations are appropriated by the Holy Spirit at certain times, acquiring thereby a form of permanence in the life of the church.[43] Dogmatic truth is itself pathic truth in that it *remains* the poiesis of the Holy Spirit and of its eschatological work.[44]

c. Zizioulas's eucharistic concept of truth shows how truth itself becomes *freedom*. "Truth" and "freedom" are not diametrically opposed in the Spirit but rather are inherently related, since both are grounded in the communion of the triune God. This freedom is actualized in the affirmation of the congregational "amen": "The people of God gathered together in the eucharist realize their freedom under the form of affirmation alone: it is not the 'yes' and the 'no' together which God offers in Christ, but only the 'yes,' which equates to the eucharistic 'Amen' (2 Cor. 1:19-20)."[45]

Zizioulas's concept of truth coincides with the previous trinitarian exposition of the divine name *liberum arbitrium* in Luther's *The Bondage of the Will*. In the communion of the triune God and the eucharistic fellowship, a human being becomes a *nova creatura* and thus simultaneously a person in the strict sense. Human beings are free insofar as God's salvific activity constitutes and "in-forms" their relationality, that is, their hypostasis as persons; this relationality, being as person, is identical with the mode of receptivity, of pathos over against God's salvific activity. Human beings are free in abiding within this specific receptivity, within this pathos. Zizioulas calls this *epicletic* existence, existence in the Spirit. The church is the *locus of freedom* precisely insofar as it receives all of this — Scripture, sacrament, ministries — *epicletically* from the communion-event of the Lord's Supper, and makes it true, that is, delivers it over to the Holy Spirit and thus to the perpetual situation of being rapt by God into God's own freedom.[46] If we inquire after the structures of the church that point to this communion-event, here, too, Zizioulas refers us anew to the *core practices* which, as he puts it, as "channels of the Holy Spirit" begin to draw human beings into the communion of the triune God.

From the perspective of Luther, however, one can now carry Zizioulas's pneumatological understanding of the concept of truth further and understand it as *existence in faith*. For Luther, "faith" is eschatologically configured insofar as believers already "extend into heaven" and in faith already participate in God's triune communion.[47] Believing existence is ecstatic existence. In this sense, this being in faith is quite rightly to be understood in correspondence to the core practices and to *doctrina* as a work of the Holy Spirit subsisting enhypostatically in the Spirit and thus in the trinitarian communion itself. This pathically qualifies the concept of truth attaching to church doctrine. The truth of church doctrine resides in its relationality. It remains oriented toward and determined by the object of the *doctrina evangelii* and of the Lord's Supper.[48] "Truth" is thus a gift received in the *vita passiva* through the gospel proclamation and the Lord's Supper. The freedom of theology is grounded in the pathos of this reception of truth.

By understanding theological discourse as a church practice determined by the salvific-economic mission of the Holy Spirit in doctrina *and the core practices, we overcome the false alternative between freedom and being bound, between theology being self-determined or being externally determined. Only in the Holy Spirit and its genuine poiesis of communion does theology as a church practice participate in God's* liberum arbitrium. *Only by remaining bound to God's economy of salvation does it step into the "freedom of the children of God," becoming thus a discipline commensurate with its object. For only within its distinct pathos does it become capable of truth.*

II. The Church *as* Public, and Theology as the Practice Inherent to Its Telos

Whereas the previous section focused on the *pneumatological* aspect of the pathos of theology as a church practice, examining it then from the perspective of the mutually intertwined aspects of the "freedom" and "truth" of theology, this section will now focus on the *ecclesiological* aspect of this pathos, albeit without losing sight of pneumatology.

Within the framework of *communio*-ecclesiology, Part Three above examined the church as the body of Christ from the perspective of the eschatological meal instituted by Jesus of Nazareth himself, illuminating it at the same time as an emergent work of the Holy Spirit in the form of distinct core practices (themselves shaped by the *doctrina evangelii*). This examination concluded that the ecclesial *koinonia* is to be understood as a soteriological work of the Holy Spirit grounded as such in the communion of the triune God, a communion which through its own presence engages its salvific activity in the *koinonia* and indeed binds itself to the *koinonia* by beginning to draw the latter into the triune life. The "other" side of the church as a work of the Holy Spirit is also that the triune God has bound his communion to the ecclesiastical *koinonia*. Hence not only does God's poiesis shape the pathos of the church, the self-binding of the trinitarian communion to the *koinonia* also constitutes the latter's authoritative status. *The binding authoritative status of the core practices and of* doctrina *is grounded alone in God's trinitarian self-binding to the* koinonia; *that is, this authoritative status may not be understood as "reified" in se. This is also the perspective from which to understand the mission of the church. In its pathos the church is the actualizing agent of the salvific-economic mission of Christ and of the Holy Spirit. In this sense the church needs to be understood precisely as the public of the Holy Spirit.*

In this chapter I will examine the church's pneumatological as well as soteriological character as such a public. I will show first that any public possesses a telos both defining and constituting it, and then explicate how the church, given its genuine telos, is a quite specific public related to other publics in multifarious ways. Briefly, my thesis is that to the extent the church can indeed be described as a "public," its *soteriological telos* is what distinguishes it from other publics and makes it recognizable as *church*. These reflections directly build on Part Three, which explicated how the soteriological mission of the church is actually a weave of core church practices and church doctrine within which theology is to be situated as a distinct church practice. There and in the first section of Part Four, I also showed the extent to which the pneumatological-ecclesiological horizon discernible in those core practices and in the *doctrina evangelii* constitutes the *pathos* of theology as a church practice, a pathos to be understood at once also as its distinct freedom within the Spirit.

The inherent connection between the core practices, doctrine, and theology can now be examined from the ecclesiological perspective and with the aid of the concept of public. These aspects are meaningfully related only if the church is understood as the public of the Holy Spirit and thereby as a specific public. Here, rather than explicating in full all the implications of this thesis, I will develop only the pneumatological as well as ecclesiological framework itself, one that does, however, have far-reaching implications, especially for Christian social ethics.[49]

The concept of public has a long and complex history, one that cannot be examined here in full because it follows a specific sociopolitical development that in its own turn already standardizes the concept of public such that it lends legitimacy only to the one "public" of political liberalism composed as "society."[50] By contrast, in what follows I will apply a *structural concept of public* allowing for a whole multiplicity of different publics that overlap and complement one another and yet also are able to relate to one another from within positions of serious, fundamental tension. The English term "public" is heuristically especially helpful because it still resonates with the Latin *res publica*, something also reflected in the understanding with which theology or the church in the contemporary American (USA) context can be described more closely by the adjective "public," albeit in a threefold, not at all uniform fashion. The Reformed theologian William Placher summarizes these three usages by distinguishing between three different semantic directions attaching to church or theology as "public." In his view a theology or church is "public" insofar as "(1) it appeals to warrants available to any intelligent, reasonable, responsible person; (2) it understands a religion as fundamentally a public, communal activity, not a matter of the individual's experience; (3) it effectively addresses political and social issues."[51] The concern here is with the second aspect of "public." With recourse to the political theory of antiquity as explicated in an exemplary fashion by Hannah Arendt[52] as a critique of the modern destruction of the public sphere, I will identify the decisive elements characterizing this type of "public."

1. A Structural Concept of Public

Hannah Arendt orients her own understanding of the term "political" toward the theory and praxis of the polis in antiquity. On this view a "public" is a human sphere of coactivity constituted and defined by its surrounding borders and by the standards determining it. A polis in antiquity would accordingly be constituted and defined by the walls surrounding it and by the laws regulating common life among its citizenry.[53] By contrast, an unrestricted "space" such as an endless plain is not really a human sphere rendering possible the assembly of human beings for speaking and acting. *Qua* "openness," then, an undefined, essentially open space by no means constitutes a "public." Quite the contrary, general openness in all directions destroys the public. The polis itself shows paradigmatically how the "public" emerges only by way of a circumscribed locale. Nonetheless, the decisive, characteristic feature of the polis is not really geographical locale but location grounded in the mutually binding laws of the polis citizenry. "The *polis*, properly speaking, is not the city-state in its physical location; it is the organization of the people as it arises out of acting and speaking together."[54] The "mobility" of the polis Arendt elicits here does not, however, imply that the polis can be universalized in the sense of unrestricted surface extension. As polis, a polis cannot as it were be infinitely extended such as might be at least theoretically possible for an empire or a modern state founded on universal principles; rather, the polis implies a moveable or flexible locale, that is, a particular locale bound to laws and to the practices qualifying or determining it. This aspect will be important for the ecclesiological implications of the structural concept of public derived from the polis.

For the public character of the polis of antiquity, however, the key feature was not spatial identification through city architecture and its concrete demarcation, but rather two other aspects that are of central significance for the present discussion. The first was the *laws*, that is, the framework of explicit and binding regulatives making possible and circumscribing public activity and speaking within the polis. The laws constituted the precondition for the public character of the polis;[55] they were the result of *poiesis*, that is, of conscious production — so to speak, as an inherent part of the "architecture" of the polis — within which the activities of free citizens or the praxis of the polis became possible.[56] This also touches on the second central aspect, namely, *the specific telos* for whose sake the polis as a distinct public exists, namely, the common activity of the free citizenry.[57] Arendt articulates this telos of the polis in a twofold fashion.

160

The task of the *polis* was regularly to provide the opportunity through which a person could acquire "immortal fame," or to organize the opportunities through which each person might excel and in word and deed display his or her uniqueness. . . . The second task of the *polis*, one also closely related with the risks of action experienced before the emergence of the *polis* itself, was to provide a remedy for the futility endemic to acting and speaking. . . . The task of the *polis* was to provide a place where this immortal fame of great deeds and words might settle in and linger among human beings in order to free action as it were from its dependency on the productive and poetic arts.[58]

In articulating thus the telos of the polis, Arendt touches on the ancient form of an additional central feature of "public," namely, *freedom*, which in its own turn presupposes the visibility of word and deed and thus the presence of other free persons, and the abiding of this freedom through the laws and practices of the polis itself. One important constituent part of the abiding quality of this *freedom* of the polis citizenry was the perpetual *recollection* of actualized freedom in the form of glorious deeds. Freedom, however, implies taking responsibility for one's deeds before the forum of other free persons and before the perpetual possibility that these deeds may well be criticized by others.

The key consideration as far as the present discussion is concerned is that in addition to the reference to a structured sphere, both the binding nature of the laws (and of the practices thereby circumscribed) as well as a particular telos were constitutive for the public character of the polis. The laws and telos of the polis[59] constituted a distinct public defined in juxtaposition over against the *oikos*.[60] That is, this juxtaposition or contrast over against the *oikos* defined the polis as a *specific* public. The *oikos* was the "other" over against the polis, just as the "private" represents the "other" over against the public within modern society.[61]

The heuristic example of the polis suggests that a "public" in the second sense enumerated above is characterized by four constitutive features: (1) a specific telos; (2) mutually binding principles expressed in distinct practices, laws, and doctrines; (3) a "moveable" locale; and (4) the phenomenon of "freedom." These four constitutive aspects together constitute the "time-place" nexus[62] in which common action and speaking can take place.

This *structural concept of the public* has the heuristic advantage over the substantive normative concept of public attaching to political liberalism, that is, over the concept oriented toward the specific political development and phenomenon of "society," that it allows one to focus on a whole series of different publics as such. It also allows one to understand the emergence or construction of a "universal" and comprehensive (global) public as *one* specific construction of public with its sociopolitical genealogy; the structural concept of public also raises the question regarding the extent to which the phenomenon of a so-called "global public" still allows one to speak at all of "public."[63] Beyond this, it also and especially allows one to scrutinize more closely on one central aspect of what within the horizon of the public of modern liberalism is commonly called "religion." For it is essential for this structural understanding of public that the terms "public" and "political" are synonymous, that is, that the activities within each public sphere are of a "political" sort commensurate with the particular character of the public in question.[64]

With the aid of this structural concept of public, one can understand, for example, the Torah (and in particular the Decalogue) together with its attendant practices as the concrete and binding circumscription of the "time-place" nexus, that is, of the public within which the praxis of the covenantal people of Israel — the "way of the Lord" — was and is actualized. Understood thus, the Torah does not represent an idiosyncratic demarcation of what is otherwise a "free" existence. Rather, it constitutes the condition for the possibility of Israel's praxis in following the way of the Lord, and as such is the presupposition for the *freedom of Israel* as God's covenantal people.[65] The binding nature of the Torah and the perpetual recollection of God's salvific deeds for Israel effected within its framework generates the "time-space" characterizing Israel as a public.[66]

Within the public of Israel as the people of God, Pentecost as the poiesis of the Holy Spirit then initiated the eschatological public of the ecclesia, the eschatological polis (Heb. 13:14).[67] After initial struggles, it became increasingly clear that it was no longer the Torah, no longer life within the binding principles of the *mitzvoth* that constituted and characterized this public. Rather, it was constituted christologically and pneumatologically by the kerygma (the *doctrina evangelii*) and by specific core practices (especially baptism and the breaking of the bread).[68] Alongside these, it was the earliest confessions of faith, the emerging canon, and the episcopal office that came to characterize the church as an identifiable public,[69] one that quite early came into conflict with the religio-politically constituted public of the Pax Romana.[70] How is this eschatological public, this assembly of the ecclesia of the eschatological polis, to be understood? What is its unique feature? What definitively qualifies it?

In the following discussion I will examine the church as the public of God's economy of salvation. Whereas the polis was *per definitionem* the "other" of the *oikos*, in the New Testament the church by contrast is charac-

162

terized as both "polis" *and* "oikos." It is the assembly of the future polis that even now is being drawn into God's *oikonomia*. That is, precisely its *freedom* is qualified in a quite specific way. It is free *in* rather than *over against* God's *oikonomia*, free in being qualified by the core church practices and *doctrina*, and thus free in its salvific-economic pathos.

2. *Difference from the Polis: Church as "Polis"* and *"Oikos"*

The structural concept of public developed above with reference to Hannah Arendt's reconstruction of the polis of antiquity, the reference to Hebrews 13:14, and the Augustinian tradition of the two *civitates*[71] all suggest that the church itself be regarded as a polis,[72] albeit only by *analogy,* as a *challenge to the modern, monolithic concept of public advocated by political liberalism.* The key feature of this analogy is that the polis and the church represent two unique *publics*. The limits of the analogy, however, are that the church *as* public also has to assert itself in and against the public of the polis, and understands itself as a public that, rather than being conceived in radical antithesis to the *oikos*, transcends both polis and *oikos* in a revolutionary way and precisely therein also fundamentally transforms the *oikos* of antiquity. The church thus does not simply represent yet one more embodiment of the overriding genus "polis," but rather as a distinct public is a "polis sui generis." Its public character is shaped in correspondence to its christological corporeality and pneumatological creatureliness. Its eucharistic locale, its "time-space" as characterized by the core practices and by *doctrina*, and its soteriological telos all demand that one emphasize the analogous character of the church as "polis."

In articulating the crucial *difference* in such analogous reference to the "church as polis," it suffices to include in its qualification the "other" of the polis of antiquity, namely, the *oikos*, or household.[73] This distinction need not be incorporated from the outside, since it is succinctly formulated in the New Testament letter that deals most intensively with the nature of the church, namely, Ephesians.[74] Ephesians 2:19, for example, shows how the church can be articulated with reference to the constitutive political terminology of the ancient world, that is, to the dichotomy of the polis and *oikos*, without being identified with either: "So then you are no longer strangers and aliens, but you are citizens with the saints and also members of the household of God" (NRSV).[75] Taking the radical nature of this sentence seriously prompts the conclusion that by attempting to formulate its own self-understanding in the Hellenistic political terminology accessible to it, the ecclesia at least implicitly and quite early transcended the framework of the political order of antiquity, since the latter was based not least on the strict dichotomy between polis and *oikos*.[76]

Though interesting historical and sociological factors can doubtless also be adduced, ultimately it was a theological consideration that prompted the early church to employ such reference to *both* the polis *and* the *oikos*. *God's economy of salvation demands that the church understand itself on the one hand as a specific public in analogy to the polis, and on the other, simultaneously remain precisely as such the household of God. For in analogy to the* oikos, *it is constituted by a particular pathos. The triune God remains its "head of household," the resurrected Christ the "head" of its body in a one-sided and irreversible fashion quite unforeseen by the polis with regard to the relation between free citizens. In articulating the distinct public of the church, if one draws on the logic of the polis, one must in the same breath also draw on an essential aspect of the logic of the* oikos, *namely, the irreversible relational system in which relationships, rather than being freely disposed, are fixed.* The crucial *difference* over against the *oikos* of antiquity and thus the feature demonstrating that this reference is indeed analogous, is that the ecclesia involves the *oikos* of the *triune God.* God's own triune economy, God's own salvific activity, encompassing the entirety of creation itself, constitutes and structures this *"oikos"* through the economy of salvation. This radically "sublates" the concept of the *oikos* in the true Hegelian sense; that is, reference to the *oikos* remains analogously meaningful because it contains a crucial aspect of truth not expressed by its counterpart, namely, the analogy to the polis. At the same time, however, this radically calls into question the *oikos* of antiquity itself, since those who by definition were excluded from the polis of antiquity and imprisoned in the *oikos,* namely, women, children, and slaves, all similarly become through baptism "fellow citizens" *(sympolitai)* of that particular public that is entirely determined by God's own economy, God's own "household rule." It is precisely this divine economy to which Paul is referring when, in Galatians 3:27-29, he proclaims that "as many of you as were baptized into Christ have clothed yourselves with Christ. There is no longer Jew or Greek, there is no longer slave or free, there is no longer male and female; for all of you are one in Christ Jesus. And if you belong to Christ, then you are Abraham's offspring, heirs according to the promise" (NRSV).

3. The Church as the Public of the Holy Spirit

The church in this sense is thus not demarcated by "walls" even though it does have a distinct identity and character as the public sphere of the Holy

Spirit. The core practices and *doctrina* demarcate this identity and "circum-scribe" at the same time the "time-space," that is, the specific spatial and temporal locale of the church. Similar to that of the polis, this time and place is constituted by the core practices and by doctrine, and as such is both dia-chronically and synchronically "mobile." The church's diachronic universality emerges from the economy of salvation. In the Lord's Supper and in the es-chatological proclamation of the word associated with it, the eschaton itself has commenced as *opus inchoatum*, qualifying both the present and the past from the perspective of the end. At the same time, this diachronic universality is not some abstraction to be "realized" universally in the world at large; rather, it is concretely embodied in the spatially and temporally bound core practices that create the church. Nor can the synchronic spatial universality be isolated from the concrete time and place of the core practices. The church does not expand "globally" like a market or an empire; rather, within the framework of the proclamatory and missionary activity with which it is charged, it undergoes unlimited multiplication of its spatial-temporal locale "for the many" (Mark 14:24) in the core practices and *doctrina*, but without subjecting itself to an abstract universalism or an equally abstract partic-ularism. Rather, it is a universal *koinonia* of locally bound concrete churches.

The highly unique character of this public is to be understood entirely from the perspective of its soteriological telos as examined earlier. This telos prevents the church from being described according to the purely spatial logic of modern political thought, logic focused entirely on "boundaries" (and on overcoming them!), and from falling prey to modernity's uniquely normative concept of public. *As the public of the Holy Spirit, the church is con-stituted not through "boundaries" but through a "center" that in the core prac-tices creates "space" and "time" and is expressed authoritatively in* doctrina. *This center is of an utterly christological nature, and as such also does indeed de-marcate the one 'boundary' the church never transcends.*[77]

4. The Church as Public and Its Genuine Discursive Practice

The implication of the structural concept of public, one central to the present discussion and already examined against the paradigm of the polis, must now be examined in and of itself. Every public has its own unique discourse inher-ing within it as a distinct practice, specifically as a mode of actualization of the telos of that public. The characteristic feature in this regard of the polis of antiquity and for the actualization of its specific telos is political discourse, including the teaching of rhetoric and a reflection on both political discourse and the nature of the polis itself. The public of synagogal Judaism includes the rabbinic expository tradition and adjudication; that of Islam similarly includes the theological exposition of the Koran and its accompanying discourse (similarly as the practice of adjudication). The political theory and concrete political discourse of modernity are analogously to be understood as inherent features of the telos of the public of modern democracy.

Such discourse does not embody the entire telos of any given public, since this telos is to be understood as a *praxis* in the comprehensive sense while the discourse itself represents merely one *practice* subordinated to the more comprehensive praxis. Without the actualization of this inherent discursive practice, however, the telos of any given public can be realized only imperfectly, since it is only in this discursive practice that any given public becomes explicitly conscious of its own telos. This discursive practice also includes a training in the acquisition of the capacity to judge in those matters unique to every comprehensive praxis. Here the specific character of the discursive practice depends on the distinct character of the public whose inherent feature it actually represents. The political discourse of the ancient polis along with its theoretical reflection differ from modern political discourse and its theoretical reflection insofar as the two are oriented toward completely different publics (this naturally involves primarily not historical but *substantive* differences, that is, differences based on a different substantive telos). Islamic theological discourse and rabbinic discourse differ from Christian theological discourse precisely because the telos of the public they are examining thematically and reflecting differs from others in quite specific ways.

Understanding theology properly as a discursive church practice requires understanding the christological and pneumatological disposition of its corresponding public, namely, the church. This was the focus of the previous sections of this section. *The church as public and theology as the discursive church practice mutually imply one another.* If the church is indeed a public, then it requires a discourse that publicly gives account of the actualization of the core practices and of doctrine. If theology is the discursive church practice (rather than the science, philosophy, history, or philology of religion), then it presupposes the church as public. But if the church is a public, then it implies the practice of theology.

5. Theology as Discursive Church Practice — at the University?

This also provides new access to the unavoidable question regarding the place of academic theology at the modern university. I believe this question is a complex and recurring phenomenon not because theology as an academic discipline in modernity might pose a theoretical "problem" as regards the discipline itself,[78] but because the "university" itself as a specific public in modernity has increasingly become an open question and especially because the telos of the university in the larger sense has become increasingly unclear. The burden of proof regarding the appropriateness or inappropriateness of certain traditional disciplines at the modern university (jurisprudence, medicine, and theology as the "higher faculties" of the traditional university, and philosophy as the comprehensive undertaking of the "lower faculty" encompassing all contemporary "humanities" and natural sciences) is thus not to be demanded from the individual disciplines or sciences themselves. Rather, the query to these disciplines must be incorporated into the reflection on the telos of the university on the whole.[79] The question of theology's justification as a university discipline is an important but secondary one within the logic of our inquiry; in any event, the question is related to the modern university's lack of any telos encompassing and directing all disciplines and practices, and with the university's collapse as a specific public.

It is thus not at all the case that theology as a discursive church practice might as such be an enterprise inherently alien to the modern university, simply because the telos of the public we know as the "university" might contradict that of the public we know as "church." We, rather, should start thinking afresh about this question by assuming first of all a historically conditioned *plurality of universities* which, if at all, formulate their telos differently (again, for historically and contextually different reasons).[80] Nor should one neglect the question whether a university is an entity independent of the state or one subject to the state or a normative societal understanding of the public sphere.

Depending on the cultural, religious, and political context, the question of Christian theology as a university discipline involves an encounter between at least three different publics; the encounter itself can assume the form of overlapping or coexistence, confrontation, exclusion, or normative control by one of the publics. Even the mode of description already reflects the given context. One very good example of this is the leading American Catholic theologian David Tracy, who in his influential book *The Analogical Imagination*[81] introduced what has in the meantime become a widespread distinction between three publics that touch on theology: society, academy, and church. Tracy identifies normative criteria for each of these publics and relates them to one another in highly nuanced ways, but then integrates the entire undertaking into the normative framework of *one* comprehensive public, namely, that of society. He does this implicitly rather than explicitly, however, by keeping all three publics in exemplary balance[82] while yet juxtaposing them from the very outset and concealing the fundamental normative difference and potential normative conflict between these publics through the type of description itself. Tracy's sociological-descriptive use of the concept of public, however, contains a tacit normative component insofar as its sociological use must be understood within the framework of that particular normative public constituted through the binding practices and principles within which "sociology" itself already represents a meaningful enterprise, namely, within the normative overall horizon of political liberalism and of the ontology of the modern subject. That is, the sociological description itself is political insofar as liberalism as a political theory has already entered the discipline of sociology.[83] Because of Tracy's *theologically* uncritical recourse to sociological categories, the telos of civil society determines the way he understands the publics of society, church, and university as well as the role of theology — which is now "public" in a threefold sense — within the comprehensive concept of "civil society." Civil society, however, itself implies a distinct, namely, universalistic, normativity; that is, it is already oriented toward the norm of the binding practices and doctrines expressed in civil religion. European readers easily discern that in its own turn, the phenomenon and concept of "civil religion" itself is a unique product of the particular political-religious public in the USA.[84]

The key objection here is not that theology as a discursive church practice might not enter into dialogue with the discourses of other publics or might not even overlap with them in some specific way. The crucial consideration here is that *none* of the three publics of "church," "university," and "society" is "neutral" in the first place. Their presence makes it *possible* for differing and potentially even contradictory binding principles (that is, differing and in part contradictory practices and principles) to collide. Hence, although theology as a church practice certainly can and ought to move about in the publics of society and the university, it can acknowledge the binding principles constituting these publics only insofar as they can be qualified by the telos of the church. Here theology as a discursive church practice differs *per definitionem* from religious studies as a discursive practice for which the constitutive binding principles of the university are primary, and from the discursive practice of "civil religion" for which the constitutive binding principles of "society" are primary.[85]

6. Excursus: The Church and Public — or the Church as Public?

In order to make this reference to the church *as* public more precise, let me examine the socio-ethical proposal of "church *and* society" that has exerted such an influence within German-speaking Protestant discussion, and do this from the perspective of the ecclesiological concept presented above. In his comprehensive study *Kirche und Öffentlichkeit*,[86] Wolfgang Huber has presented an exhaustive inquiry as far as thoroughness and detail are concerned. At first glance the ecclesiological concept developed above seems to concur fairly extensively with Huber's own position. He emphasizes the church's public claim, its public character, and can even speak in a recent essay about the "public church within plural publics."[87] This terminology seems at first glance to be commensurate with the notion of the "church as public."

Closer examination, however, reveals that Huber is presupposing a normative horizon of "public" toward which the church has always been *oriented* and within which the church is one entity *alongside* others. The reason for this is that his own concept of public is socio-historically determined, referring thus explicitly to the understanding of public coinciding with the development of modern bourgeois society. Although his concept of public seems to be descriptive, he is borrowing it from an academic discipline (sociology) deriving from the corresponding political development and at the same time legitimizing that development in its descriptive conceptuality and terminology.[88] By orienting the church toward this concept of public and understanding the church's own public claim from its perspective, Huber subtly draws the church into the normative horizon of this allegedly all-encompassing public and its implicit political theory.

By reconstructing the modern concept of public sphere in this socio-historic fashion, and by then continuing to use this concept, Huber subjects himself to the normative implications of the concept in a way similar to David Tracy. Rather than gaining critical theological distance from the normative horizon of this political theory, he falls prey to the *modern* monolithic concept of "public," which ultimately can be only *one*. In the constellation "church *and* public," and naturally quite contrary to Huber's own intention, the church undergoes subtle political discipline and domestication insofar as its own self-understanding as a *specific* public is undermined by being oriented primarily toward a "public" not identical with itself. As long as the church is not understood explicitly *as* a public, any reference to the "public church" is merely an external perspective on the church from the perspective of the normative public of modern, differentiated liberal society that promptly effects the church's eclipse *as* a public.[89] If by contrast one understands the church first of all ecclesiologically as a public itself, one can then also consider its complex relationships with a multiplicity of other, different publics, including that of the democratically constituted modern society.

In a recent essay, however, Huber does betray a certain shift in accent. Here he is also able to assert that "the public in which common tasks are articulated and solutions to them sought is constituted through the interaction between a multiplicity of communities, all of which develop the capacity for responsible judgment and action first of all in the circumscribed sphere of 'face-to-face communities.' In this sense, the public is itself a 'community of communities,' a 'sphere of action of spheres of action,' a 'public of publics.'"[90] Huber comes very close to the understanding of church *as* public developed above when he speaks of a "public of publics" and understands the church's own status with reference to article VII of the *Augsburg Confession* as the "representative evocation of its ground": "This representative evocation takes place in the worship assembly of believers in which the gospel is proclaimed and the sacraments celebrated."[91] Close examination, however, reveals that ultimately this still is the same concept of public as used in *Kirche und Öffentlichkeit*, albeit in a more nuanced form commensurate with the development from a moderately plural to a multicultural society in the Federal Republic of Germany. Huber's theory of public now explicitly takes account of the four referential spheres of state, economy, civil society, and cultural communication. In this way he is able to show persuasively how in all four referential areas of "public" in this sense a plurality is formed in commensurately specific ways. At the same time, however, and despite this more nuanced view, the overall framework remains that of a specific, normative, substantive public whose telos is pansocietal integration: "If by contrast pluralism is to be understood as a life form in which communication between those who are different is possible, then the public as that which concerns everyone must be brought to bear and actualized."[92] Ultimately, the public is *one*, albeit with a plural structure. The contribution of the church is asked for from the perspective of the specific telos of this specific public. "Public theology" is then also quite logically a discourse deriving its criteria from the binding principles of this particular public and thus participating in the telos of this public. Precisely because the church is not developed *as* a public, the locus, identity, and mission of the "public church" ultimately remain ambivalent despite the emphasis on its ground;[93] this becomes clear both at its demarcation from the "church of society" on the one hand and from the "church as a contrast community" on the other.[94] The two alternative models, however, can be persuasively rejected only if the church itself is conceived *as* a public. Otherwise Huber cannot ultimately avoid the objection that even he has merely presented another variant of the "church of society," namely, the *critically* participating variant as opposed to the *uncritically* participating variant of the so-called "people's church" *(Volkskirche)*. If genuine criticism of the "church of society" presupposes an explicit understanding of the church as public, Huber's demarcation of church as a "contrast community" shows unequivocally that he intends to adhere to the axiom of the one, comprehensive public.[95] By contrast, such contrasting groupings can be productively integrated within the framework of a theological conception of "church as public" anchored in the *communio*-ecclesiology. At the same time, however, one must explicitly acknowledge that these groupings themselves do not as such constitute the church as a public, and that the church as a public itself is not a "contrast community."[96] That under certain circumstances the church as public can indeed or even must assume the form of a "contrast community" is a question of ecclesial *judgment*, that is, an answer — to be determined in each given case — to the question of how under changing circumstances the church can itself remain a public, and not to the question of how within a single normatively understood public the church acquires a "public character" from the perspective of that public.

Only if one puts the horse before the cart, that is, first understands the church theologically as the public of the Holy Spirit, can one speak about a "public church" such that this does not deliver the church over to an alien logic; rather, the church will then remain free even under the conditions of modernity in its relation to a specific configuration of problems that despite its, in some respects, "global" dimensions, is nonetheless really a constellation of a quite specific contextual nature. Precisely *because* one can largely concur with Huber's detailed socio-ethical analysis, one needs a thorough theological perspective on the church "from within," that is, a theological theory of the christological-pneumatological reality of the church that conceives it *as* a public.

III. The Actualization of the Pathos of Theology as Church Practice

In the following discussion I will outline the central aspects of theology as a distinct church practice from the perspective of theology's pneumatological pathos (in core practices and *doctrina*). Building directly on the preceding section, that is, on the perspective of the soteriological telos of the church as the public of the Holy Spirit, I will examine theology as a church practice in the three basic aspects in which it participates in the telos of this distinct public: (1) the discursive aspect in the theological context of justification, (2) the aspect of perception and judgment in the theological context of discovery, and (3) the presentative-communicative aspect of theology.

Beyond the Alternative of "Theory" — "Praxis" versus "Praxis" — "Theory" — "Praxis"[97]   Of course, I cannot present a complete "theory of theology as a church practice" in this final section of Part Four. Similarly, any attempt to develop theology *as* a theory which is then to be "realized" within church (or a "universal") praxis or from the perspective of which such a "praxis" were to be "shaped" would certainly fall far short of the constitutive framework of theology as a church practice as developed above. For if the *theoria* of theology is to be understood as a pathos inhering in the *vita passiva* of faith, it is first of all always *undergone* or *suffered* through participation in the core church practices and in being qualified by the *doctrina evangelii*. Hence the *theoria* of theology is utterly inaccessible without the horizon of the core practices constituting the church. Engagement in theology always presupposes and includes these core practices such that "theology" is not simply "applicable" to them in some one-track sense; rather, its engagement always transpires in connection with them and from their perspective. The *theoria* of theology is thus neither theory in the classical sense as the free perception of the divine and of the divine order,[98] nor in the early modern sense of the Cartesian knowledge of reflection,[99] nor in the emphatically *modern* sense of a Hegelian mediation of the unity of theory and praxis through historical-philosophical speculation in which world history becomes the locus of the realization of reason.[100] Rather, the *theoria* of theology always presupposes a nexus of distinct practices and is itself a distinct practice within this nexus. Yet does this mean that liberation theology is correct in its comprehensive assertion that theology represents a quite specific "moment" in a hermeneutical circle moving from "praxis" back to "praxis" in the comprehensive sense, and that "theology" thus stands between praxis and praxis such that in the genuine sense it is actually the reflection of praxis?[101]

The preceding sections included an implicit attempt to overcome — within the pneumatological as well as ecclesiological framework developed there — this classically *modern* alternative between Hegel's speculative theory[102] and its Marxist reversal[103] in political theology by understanding human beings not primarily as agents and producers, but as "*sufferers*," that is, as those who undergo the works (the *poiemata*) of the Holy Spirit.[104] God's economy of salvation finds its correspondence in the poiesis of the Holy Spirit, which is passively experienced as the *rapi*, being rapt into the freedom of life with God. The specific mode of actualization of this salvific-economic pathos thus consists in the freedom of life with God.[105] This is not, however, "abstract" freedom. It assumes concrete form in one's participation in the core church practices as well as in a network of additional practices both initiated and shaped by the original core practices. I earlier defined theology as that particular practice inhering in the telos of the church as the public of the Holy Spirit; as such, and in a way yet to be outlined, theology reflects, articulates, and presents precisely this telos.

This perspective allows us to build on certain features of the two predominately *modern* ways of understanding theology. It is indeed "theory" insofar as it is concerned with the conceptually precise disclosure of the *doctrina evangelii,* for it is received as a *doctrina* implying a grammar for speaking about God, creation, and human beings. In this context God's economy of salvation is the praxis embracing theology, the poietic praxis of the Holy Spirit toward whose works — namely, *doctrina,* biblical canon, and the core practices — theology is bindingly oriented. The line of demarcation and thus the crucial difference from the modern concept of theory as classically developed by Hegel is that theology *abides* in the pathic mode of reception. Its engagement does not aim at a theoretical penetration of *doctrina* and of the core practices; that is, it does not "conceptualize" these such that the core practices — which always precede it in any case — become "intuition" and the received *doctrina* "representation," both always essentially in need of precisely this *conceptual* penetration.[106]

The core notion of political theology, namely, that theology is disclosed as critical reflection from the perspective of "praxis" and remains oriented toward "praxis," can also be accommodated after a fashion, albeit *not* within its own overall politically determined horizon of perception,[107] but within the horizon of God's economy of salvation, the latter of which can certainly also critically address political contexts and horizons. This is the key difference as well: Within this soteriological horizon, theology is one practice alongside other distinct practices. Rather than being caught in a hermeneutical circle, it occupies a specific position within the nexus of the core church practices with relation to the telos of this particular public. The church *as* public is always in critical debate with distinct social, economic, and political constellations, all of which constitute together with other factors the irreplaceable "context of discovery"[108] for the church practice of theology. In this respect the "context" represents an inherent feature that cannot be removed from theology as a church practice. The situation is thus not such that theology as "theory" finally becomes "practical," nor that it as the critical reflection of praxis now makes a limited theoretical claim in the sense of "critical theory."[109]

This appropriation of certain features of *both* modern alternatives of relating theory and praxis (while remaining at a critical distance from both) is possible, however, only if the *proprium* of each is negated, that is, only if human beings do *not* stand at the beginning of this understanding of "theology" either as the reflecting "spirit"[110] in its conceptual penetration of divine or worldly reality, or as the productive agents in their shaping of the world. The classic-modern alternative between "theory" and "praxis" in the understanding of theology can be overcome only if human beings are understood primarily as "recipients," that is, as being pathically determined, and only if this reception is understood as the actualization of God's economy of salvation and thus as the poiesis of the Holy Spirit. The crucial point here is that this particular insight itself is emphatically *not* in its own turn to be understood as the "better" theory that is then similarly to be realized in "praxis" in order to demonstrate its "relevance." Rather, this particular angle of vision emerges from having taken seriously in a theologically explicit fashion God's economy of salvation as implied in the already existing core church practices. Were this economy of salvation negated, all the core practices would become meaningless precisely from the perspective of their center. To legitimize them within their ongoing enactment, a different "meaning" would have to be ascribed to them. They then become "signs" for all sorts of things: preaching becomes a measure relating to education, formation, or liberation; baptism a symbol of the *bonitas* of all creatures; the Lord's Supper a symbol of human fellowship; and so on. Beginning with neology,[111] this has become a recurring phenomenon in the church under the conditions of modernity. By contrast, if with Luther one takes seriously the core practices in the sense explicated above, namely, as "sacred possessions" of the Holy Spirit, that is, as organs of actualization of God's economy of salvation, one frees the meaning implicit within them and also unequivocally discloses theology in its relation to them as a distinct practice oriented in a specific way toward the telos of that salvific economy.

In the previous section I examined the extent to which theology is to be understood as a practice inhering in the public of the Holy Spirit, that is, the church, a practice serving the soteriological telos of this public by participating in this telos in a quite specific way, namely, as the actualization of its own pneumatological pathos. The pneumatological and ecclesiological grounding undertaken in Part Three as well as its initial concretion with respect to the freedom and truth of theology already suggested how the poiesis of the Holy Spirit is to be understood as the pathos of theology in the latter's dependence on the core practices and *doctrina*. The poiesis of the Holy Spirit becomes concrete for theology as a church practice in that the latter can never be "abstracted" from the *doctrina evangelii* and the core practices, and can fulfill its task only in intimate connection with or even dependence on them. The following discussion makes it clear once more that the freedom of theology consists precisely in its specific actualization of the soteriological telos of the public of the Holy Spirit, and is thus to be understood not as an antithesis to some "alienating" ecclesiastical "rule," but as the practical actualization of the pneumatological pathos.

Theology can be described in its three essential aspects: (1) as an argumentative-discursive practice, (2) as a practice of perception and judgment, and (3) as a presentative-communicative practice. It is important to remember here that these aspects do not involve a simple circle in which one might arbitrarily switch from one aspect to the next, nor some rigid, mechanical schema that might turn this practice into a "methodology" oriented toward a quasi-technical "application." There obtains rather a specific *taxis* between these inseparable aspects that emerges from the soteriological telos of the church as the public of the Holy Spirit. It is this salvific-economic *taxis* alone, grounded in the pathos of theology, that meaningfully relates the various aspects of the practice of theology to one another. Similarly, one must distinguish here between the *substantive logic* and the *teleological logic* of this *taxis*, even though the two cannot really be separated. The former refers to the order within the context of justification of theology. The presentative-communicative aspect is grounded in a specific perception and in the formation of theological judgment that in its own turn emerges and argumentatively proves itself within theological discourse. At the same time, however, this substantive logic as the order or justification is interwoven with the teleological logic of the salvific-economic *taxis* according to which the all-encompassing telos of theology as a church practice is actually the presentative-communicative aspect, to which the aspect of perception and judgment is subordinated. In its own turn, the latter is then that to which teleologically the discursive aspect is subordinated. Expressed in the reverse: The discursive aspect is always oriented toward perception and judgment, while perception and judgment are always oriented toward presentation and communication.

Whenever these three aspects of theology as a church practice are no longer oriented toward one another from the specific soteriological telos of the church as a public, they invariably collapse into isolated enterprises each of which then seeks its own telos from its specific, internal dynamic and perspective. Logically consistent and coherent argumentation, clear presentation and persuasive communication, and an abstract "orthodoxy" of binding theological principles almost inevitably become isolated ends in themselves of theological activity.[112] The key question here is then the following: How does the pathos of theology, as this situation of being qualified by the *doctrina evangelii* in connection with the core practices, come to bear in its enactment as a church practice?

175

1. *The Discursive Aspect:* Fides Quaerens Doctrinam *as "Accounting for the Ground of Hope" (1 Pet. 3:15)*

The point of departure in introducing theology as a church practice was a consistently pneumatological exposition of the core church practices and of *doctrina* within the framework of God's economy of salvation. As a result of this assessment, we found that the Holy Spirit speaks in *assertiones*, that is, in binding promises, precisely because as a hypostatic person the Spirit is at once also the actualization of God's freedom, namely, of the fact that in his promises God himself has bindingly fixed his own future. By authoritatively assuring us of these promises, the Holy Spirit makes the *eschata* present to faith even now. This binding authority is nothing other than the salvific-economic actualization of God's own freedom.[113] Here we encountered — as it were, "from the opposite side" — the core church practices and *doctrina* (as already developed in Part Three) as the work of the Holy Spirit. They are the work of the Holy Spirit in that they articulate the *assertiones*. Put succinctly: *The* assertiones *are the definition of the core church practices and of* doctrina. *They are the work of the Holy Spirit precisely because they mediate or communicate the* assertiones *in various ways and in various forms.* The *assertiones* can thus never be encountered in abstraction, but only in a given concrete incarnation which for just that reason is itself to be understood as the work of the Holy Spirit. Hence the core church practices and the *doctrina* together with the *assertiones* are to be understood as actualizations of God's freedom, freedom consisting in his determination of his own future, namely, community with a renewed creation in the consummate reign of God. *The Spirit speaks in* assertiones *because it is precisely as such that God actualizes his* liberum arbitrium.

The key feature of this understanding is that the binding nature of *doctrina* and of the core practices is *not* an abstract one that might under the conditions of modernity be unmasked and rejected as heteronomy. Rather, their authoritative nature derives immediately from God's own promissory self-binding in the Holy Spirit *through* these *poiemata* of the Spirit. Robbing them of their authoritative, binding nature means robbing them of their essential promissory identity.

This can be seen in the way the Apostle Paul, in his letter to the Romans, understands the pathos of faith as life in the freedom of grace completely from the perspective of this binding authority: Τί οὖν; ἁμαρτήσωμεν, ὅτι οὐκ ἐσμὲν ὑπὸ νόμον ἀλλὰ ὑπὸ χάριν; μὴ γένοιτο. οὐκ οἴδατε ὅτι ᾧ παριστάνετε ἑαυτοὺς δούλους εἰς ὑπακοήν, δοῦλοί ἐστε ᾧ ὑπακούετε, ἤτοι ἁμαρτίας εἰς θάνατον ἢ ὑπακοῆς εἰς δικαιοσύνην; χάρις δὲ τῷ θεῷ ὅτι ἦτε δοῦλοι τῆς ἁμαρτίας ὑπηκούσατε δὲ ἐκ καρδίας εἰς ὃν παρεδόθητε τύπον διδαχῆς, ἐλευθερωθέντες δὲ ἀπὸ τῆς ἁμαρτίας ἐδουλώθητε τῇ δικαιοσύνῃ (Rom. 6:15-18).[114] In this section of his letter to the Romans, Paul inquires concerning the nature and telos of the freedom to which Christians have been liberated. Freedom is the consequence of a concrete change of ruler that does not provide for one thing, namely, freedom as abstract self-determination *over against* the powers of sin on the one hand and God's righteousness on the other.[115] The essence of the freedom to which Christians have been liberated is rather to live in obedience to righteousness, that is, within the dominion of God's own righteousness. The telos of this freedom is to become obedient to the τύπος διδαχῆς to which Christians are entrusted precisely when they become Christians. But what does this mean?

Heinrich Schlier explicates this much-discussed τύπος διδαχῆς as follows: "Τύπος is 'form' or 'shape,' τύπος διδαχῆς is the form of teaching in the sense of a doctrine present in a specific form, resonating perhaps with the fact that a τύπος represents a pattern or model. Concretely, one might imagine the διδαχή in the form of a baptism symbol or even as catechetical formulation of doctrine in transmitted traditions (cf. 1 Cor. 11:23; 15:1ff.)."[116] By contrast, Ulrich Wilckens asks critically whether one can really be "entrusted" or "given over" (by God) to the creed in the first place. He suggests that "Paul's expression might be referring to Christ as the content of doctrine (cf. Gal. 3:1) into which Christians are baptized according to v. 3 and thus 'entrusted' when they accept the baptismal creed according to 10:9f."[117] This christological articulation brings the salvific-economic telos of the διδαχή clearly into the foreground: "If the *typos* is referring to Christ, then it is referring to him . . . as the Resurrected himself, who as such is precisely this *typos,* the key content of the baptismal 'doctrine,' such that τύπος here functions as the prototype into which Christians are transformed (cf. 2 Cor. 3:18) insofar as they are baptized into him; in this sense, the baptismal creed, that is, Christian 'doctrine' or 'teaching,' derives its prototypical reality from the person of the Resurrected himself."[118] Our pneumatological approach prevents us from having to understand the interpretations of Schlier and Wilckens in opposition to one another. Rather, we can understand the union of concrete teaching form, on the one hand, and its content, the resurrected Christ, on the other as *doctrina evangelii* actualized in the act of baptism and coming to binding expression in the baptismal creed.[119] The content of both is the Resurrected because both are works of the Holy Spirit. This is why "freedom" and "obedience" are not antitheses here. Rather, the freedom of faith is actually grounded through the actualization of baptism in obedience to the τύπος διδαχῆς, as Schlier points out: "For Paul, human life is thus always subject to and claimed by a certain power. That power is either ἡ ἁμαρτία or ἡ δικαιοσύνη. Human freedom, one admittedly acquired only in faith through baptism, consists in being able, as a baptized person, to give oneself over to obedience. And precisely this freedom of decision, or the decision of this freedom, is the χάρις one owes to God."[120] Rather than being subjected to heteronomy, this obedience is the actualization of the freedom grounded in God's own self-binding to his promises. This is the ground and content of the binding nature of *doctrina*. The *doctrina* authoritatively circumscribes the sphere of "God's righteousness" whose prototype and content is Christ and into which Christians are entrusted through baptism.

The role of the *regula fidei* in early church theology shows that this is not merely a hypothetical construction of New Testament exegesis. In an extensive and unfortunately largely neglected study, Bengt Hägglund[121] not only examined the influential role played by the *regula fidei* in early church theology, but also alluded in outline to its significance for a theology of the church. As it turns out, the *regula fidei* is of relevance because it allows theology as a church practice to actualize its own pathos in a specific way, namely, as *discurrere*, as "running along" God's economy of salvation.

This means first of all that theology always encounters the unity of Christian faith in the *regula fidei;* that is, it must not first establish it. "The *regula fidei* presupposes that the content of the Christian faith constitutes a unity from the outset. . . . For the content of faith resides originally as a totality, as a coherent 'order' coinciding with the *regula fidei* and with the divine salvific order attested in Scripture. This unity is simultaneously a unity of the two testaments."[122] It is thus *not* the poietic task of dogmatics to establish the unity of the Christian faith (e.g., from some fundamental "idea" of Christianity). Rather, its mode is basically pathic such that in its *discurrere* it moves along the order of God's economy of salvation as found in *doctrina*.[123]

The second consequence of orienting the discursive aspect of theology as a church practice toward the *regula fidei* is that *precisely because* the content of faith is from the outset fixed in the *regula fidei* and always remains the same, its portrayal or presentation can be different, depending on the situation, completeness, method, and teacher.[124] It is nothing else than this authoritative determination of the content of theology by the *regula fidei* that gives theology its freedom of movement. Because the object does not depend on its poiesis, theology is able to vary within its pathos, and precisely this, of course, makes explicit argumentation within the "movement" along God's economy of salvation really necessary.

The orientation of theology to the *regula fidei* implies as its third consequence a soteriological understanding of truth of the sort developed in section I of Part Four above. "In this context, 'truth' refers not only to 'reality' in the sense of what actually happens, but also to that which is true knowledge of God, and to the teaching that brings salvation."[125]

As a fourth consequence, Hägglund adduces a point that needs more specific examination from the perspective of *theology as a practice of judgment,* namely, its inherent distinction between true and false theological doctrine. For if this truth is indeed characterized as *regula,* this means first that, as the foundation of theology, it constitutes the point of departure for the entirety of the doctrinal tradition of the church, and second that it becomes the standard for assessing true and false doctrine:

> In the struggle against heresies, the fathers adduce the *regula* as a summary of the genuine and one true *traditio* of the church. The first thing here is thus not the heresies themselves, but the rule of faith. One can even say that only the *regula* itself makes heresies recognizable as such. Without the *regula,* there are no heretics. The rule of faith is what determines what is true and what is false doctrine. Modern theology doubtless speaks so seldom about "heresy" precisely because it knows so little about a *regula veritatis* through which reference to that which heresy is becomes meaningful in the first place.[126]

The positive task of the *regula fidei,* namely, to provide a foundation for church instruction, then also yields the other task, namely, that of distinguishing between true and false doctrine and of countering the latter. This understanding of the tasks of the *regula fidei* shows how the discursive aspect of theology as a church practice, in the exposition of *doctrina,* invariably is oriented first toward the aspect of theological judgment and then toward the presentative-communicative aspect.

One final consequence is the explicit orientation of the *regula fidei* (as church doctrine), together with theological doctrine (dogmatics), back toward God's revealed economy of salvation: "The prepositioning of a *regula fidei* before the statements of our dogmatics means that both derive their unity and their context from the concrete order of the salvific event, in the οἰκονομία. Ultimately, every true statement about this order must be grounded in the concrete event itself; as we saw, for the fathers of the early church this *regula fidei* refers to the fact of revelation."[127]

According to Hägglund, because theology deals with objects which human beings can neither give to themselves nor produce themselves, the notion of *tradere,* the expository transmission of what is received, played such a

179

central role in the early church. Transmitted doctrinal tradition, however, is *not* an independent source of truth over against Scripture. "In such 'exposition,' which itself belongs to the *tradere* of theology, the *regula fidei* plays an important role in expressing the binding of dogmatic thinking to an already existing reality and to the original witness which communicates to us knowledge of this reality."[128] This is not only an external, formal binding, however, but also an internal one. "The object is for the actual *regula*, that is, the factually given order of the salvific event, to ground the context and unity of dogmatic presentation."[129] The pathos of theology in its discursive aspect thus consists in God's economy of salvation becoming transparent in theology's *discurrere*.

a. Theological Discurrere: Unfolding God's Economy of Salvation Argumentatively

I will examine the *argumentative* aspect of this *discurrere* with reference to a theologian who seems a rather improbable choice within the framework of Protestant theology and who seems to be quite inconsequential as far as the problems of contemporary theology are concerned: Thomas Aquinas.[130] One of the most interesting results of Aquinas research during this century is the fundamental revision of reading Aquinas's thought as a *philosophia perennis* as the neo-Thomism of the nineteenth century did; one came to the realization that Aquinas was first and foremost a *theologian,* specifically: a theologian of the Holy Scriptures.[131] For Aquinas, the Holy Scriptures are the point of departure, norm, and preexisting content of theology such that one may speak of a *pathos of theology* in Aquinas constituted both materially and formally by the canon.[132] The reason for this is that the biblical canon communicates something to human beings to which they do not, *qua* experience or reason, have access through their own powers.[133] It is thus this *doctrina*, understood as *revelatio*,[134] which the *discurrere* of theology is to unfold with the aid of human *ratio* accessible to it and illuminated by faith.[135] The key feature here is that Aquinas understands the *doctrina* of Scripture from the perspective of the economy of salvation such that the task of the *sacra doctrina*, that is, of theology, is to follow this salvific-economic order itself as attested in the canon. *Sacra doctrina* is thus theological doctrine or teaching whose object is God on the basis of his *oikonomia* as communicated in the witness of Scripture. This understanding initially suggests that the task of theology is a purely presentative one, namely, to simply state the biblical *doctrina* by organizing it according to its main points and by summarizing it in its salvific-economic order (as, e.g., in large parts of early Lutheran and early Reformed theology, beginning with Melanchthon's *Loci Praecipui Theologici* and Calvin's *Institutes* as models).

In the eighth article of the first *Quaestio* on the nature of Christian theology, at the beginning of the *Summa Theologiae*, Aquinas adduces two reasons that could identify theological doctrine or teaching as an enterprise whose *discurrere* remains purely presentative. First, faith and argumentation mutually exclude one another; argumentation has no place when the issue is the doctrine or teaching of faith.[136] Second, if argumentation is engaged at all, it must be done either on the basis of authority — allegedly the weakest form of argumentation — or on the basis of reason; the latter, however, can in and of itself contribute nothing to faith.[137]

With reference to Titus 1:9, however, Aquinas then nonetheless explicates how theological doctrine is to be understood after all as a principally argumentative discipline — *albeit not* in the sense of a science of first principles, but in the sense of a derived science, a discipline that always takes as its point of departure principles already given to it. Just as other derived sciences do not argumentatively demonstrate the principles upon which they are based, so also theology. The biblical canon[138] and the articles of faith[139] constitute those particular principles of theology which theology itself does *not* reflexively retrieve and establish yet again on its own.[140] In the course of this argument, Aquinas describes the relation of *sacra doctrina* and *sacra scriptura* in analogy to that between the derived sciences (in the Aristotelian sense) and metaphysics. Whereas metaphysics explains the principles of all other disciplines, it can develop argumentative power only if its opponents or dialogue partners accept at least some of the principles on the basis of which it argues. Only then can it respond to objections. Because Scripture similarly has no discipline over it, it, like metaphysics, can develop argumentative power only if at least some of its truths are accepted. If none of the truths of Scripture are accepted, one can only respond to objections to faith but not argumentatively explicate the latter precisely because the interlocutor does not recognize any of the requisite principles.[141] The capabilities of theology understood in this sense will thus be utterly dependent on the dialogue situation. If nothing of the witness to truth of the *sacra scriptura* is recognized, theology can only respond to objections and refute them in indirect argumentation. Positive argumentative explication, however, is possible only where at least a limited and partial agreement with regard to the scriptural witness can be presupposed. This association between the argumentative explication of *doctrina* and a specific dialogue situation is characteristic for the context of justification of theology, namely, for the question of the binding witness of the *doctrina evangelii* in the debate between differing positions. That is, within the teleological logic of the salvific-economic *taxis,* the argumentative task of *discurrere* arises from the perspective of theological perception and judgment. Theological judgment arises from the perspective of a specific perception, and must prove itself theologically in the context of justification. For that reason, the argumentative *discurrere* is on the one hand *necessary* because mere presentative activity by itself can accomplish nothing; it is on the other hand *possible* because this dialogue situation always presupposes the implicit or explicit acknowledgment of at least some principles. Coherent theological argumentation thus presupposes at least punctiliar agreement; the greater such agreement, the more detailed and refined can the argumentation itself become.[142]

Interestingly, Aquinas does not speak here about the *sacra doctrina* of theology, but rather directly about the *sacra scriptura.*[143] *Sacra doctrina* is to be understood from the perspective of *sacra scriptura* and stands in its service such that the latter, in the mode of pathos, is able to become the implementing subject of the former. Here again, one clearly sees the extent to which theology is the argumentative engagement of the witness to truth expressed in the *sacra scriptura.* The *sacra doctrina* develops itself as an argumentative discipline precisely and entirely in the service of the *sacra scriptura.* The argumentative aspect is a consequence of the pathos of theology, here in the specific sense that the *discurrere* is *qualified* entirely from the perspective of that which qualifies theology as its object, and as such is *freed* precisely for argumentation. On the one hand, natural reason is indeed engaged in the service of the *sacra doctrina;* on the other, the truths of faith are unequivocally distinguished from the truths of reason that are engaged in the service of the truth of faith as probability arguments.[144] Significantly, Aquinas distinguishes thus between Scripture as the binding witness of the *doctrina evangelii,* theological doctrine as the supporting and commensurate internal argument of probability, and that which philosophy contributes as an extrinsic argument of probability.[145] Moreover, for Aquinas *discurrere* as argumentation can always implicitly and in principle be superseded or surpassed in a limited fashion, since any given theological argument can never become more than an *auctoritas* itself that argues from the perspective of Scripture on the basis of what is essential to the church. Just as theological argumentation can also draw on other significant theological voices for support whose status does not, however, transcend that of the *probabilitas,* so also does this apply to itself.[146] Even though the "inerrancy" of Scripture has in the meantime (and quite rightly) come to be viewed with considerably more flexibility, this does not fundamentally change the *theological relevance* of Aquinas's (and Augustine's) distinction between, on the one hand, what Scripture does say bindingly in its promissory statements, and on the other, what theological doctrine (not church doctrine)[147] explicates argumentatively within its own consensus in the form of specific discursive theological traditions.

Precisely because the pathos of theology is grounded in the binding nature of the *doctrina evangelii*, that is, in God's salvific-economic self-binding to his promises,[148] the *discurrere* itself, this movement along God's economy of salvation, can be developed argumentatively, and the reasons it is able to offer on the basis of the *doctrina evangelii* can be presented and explicated.[149]

The point here is not to decide between various methods, classification schemata, or approaches of dogmatics,[150] nor to advocate a "renewed renewal" of Thomism, but merely to show that *one* implicate of the reacquisition of the pathos of theology as a church practice is the argumentative element of its discourse. Though reference to Luther in connection with other, more contemporary voices from Eastern Orthodox theology has predominated through most of this inquiry, the reference to Aquinas was made at this juncture to show that a fulcral aspect of theology as a church practice could be explicated *also* from the perspective of this theological witness who is particularly central to the Roman Catholic tradition.[151] When, for example, within the horizon of historicism the historical-exegetical construction of reality becomes the normative point of reference for theology, or when, for example, within the horizon of religious subjectivism the individually or communally expressed religious consciousness becomes that normative point, it is meaningless to speak of an argumentative discourse of *theology*. Under those circumstances, theology has either a hermeneutical-descriptive function subordinated to historical research or a poietic-constructive function subordinated to the primary religious experience. In either case, argumentative discourse is *per definitionem* impossible. Political theology alone, which is mediated by the social sciences and by the theory of communicative action, still participates in discourse that is "universally" conceived, yet is no longer understood in specifically *theological* terms. What may seem an untimely reference to Thomas Aquinas clearly shows that only if theology participates in its object such that the latter authoritatively qualifies it as a distinct practice is argumentative theological discourse possible at all.[152] Within the context of modernity, this can easily *appear* to be "fundamentalism" (even though among *real* fundamentalists argumentative theological discourse is notoriously absent). This derives from the power of historicism that still largely qualifies normatively the understanding of "science" inhering in the humanities, and in its wake, from the power exerted by sociology; it also derives from the conditions constitutive of an increasingly "hypothetical civilization."[153]

183

Because the presentative-communicative task of theology looks different depending on its diachronic or synchronic aspect, and because theology requires perpetually new theological perception and judgment, so also does the *discurrere* as the argumentative development of God's economy of salvation present itself perpetually as a new task. There is a good reason why this *discurrere* moves within discursive traditions rather than always "beginning at the beginning."[154] The constructive continuation of the argumentative *discurrere* presupposes a dialogic context within which, in agreement with the fundamental first principles, the argumentative *discurrere* itself can be carried forward. The formation of "schools" in theology as well as in other disciplines does not represent primarily the formation of "cliques" or a "concentration of power" (though such can certainly *also* be the case), but the unavoidable consequence of the logic of argumentative *discurrere* itself. That is, any focused continuation of a particular discourse necessarily presupposes agreement with regard to certain principles. If such continuation is not to move about in an empty circle or become simply petrified, however, it needs the external challenge presupposed by the aspect of perception and judgment and by the communicative-presentative aspect. Whenever a particular discursive tradition of church theology seals itself off, it inevitably becomes fossilized, and that in its own turn always implies a crisis in the aspects of perception and judgment as well as with respect to the communicative-presentative aspect. Precisely within any given discursive tradition, theology itself as a church practice remains stretched out *within* its pathos between the authoritatively given, binding *doctrina evangelii* on the one hand and diverse configurations of challenge and context on the other. This stretching not only requires an *ever new* engagement of argumentative *discurrere*, it also of necessity carries forward a particular theological *discurrere* that is *already* engaged and in motion.

b. *Theological* Discurrere: *Finite, Provisional, Definite*

Does this mean that the argumentative *discurrere* of God's economy of salvation is to be understood as an endless dialectical back-and-forth from thesis to antithesis? Oswald Bayer accurately describes this technical-dialectical aspect of Schleiermacher's understanding of scientific disciplines:

Saying that statements are "scientific" is the same as saying that they are "dialectical." They move perpetually between statement and contradiction, thesis and objection, hypothesis and falsification. Thus does the never-ending dispute concerning the appropriate understanding of a given matter

184

move ever onward, the never-ending search for truth understood in the sense of the *adaequatio rei et intellectus*. "The game of science basically never ends" is the principle of Karl Popper's "logic of research," which thanks to its shared philosophical inheritance can be compared meaningfully with Schleiermacher's "dialectic."[155]

This potentially endless quality of the theological *discurrere* is possible only if a strict qualitative distinction is maintained between statements of faith and scientific-dialectical statements as implied and reflected by Schleiermacher's own transcendental-dialectical understanding of science.[156] This, however, presupposes Romanticism's experiential-expressive logic which understands faith as being pre-linguistic and pathic but its expression as linguistic-poietic. Surrendering this distinction[157] and understanding theology specifically as having a substantive-pathic disposition requires understanding the argumentative *discurrere* from the perspective of this pathos as a provisional and yet precisely as such simultaneously *definite* and thus *finite* enterprise.

The reason for this can be deduced from the double logic of the salvific-economic *taxis* of theology as a church practice in which this argumentative *discurrere* is imbedded. The teleological logic according to which the *discurrere* aims at establishing a definite, theologically accountable judgment comes to its "end" again and again in the double sense of *telos* and *finis* in the specific presentative-communicative task of theological doctrine, more specifically: in the communication and exposition of the *doctrina evangelii* in the specific configuration of ecclesial, social, and spiritual-intellectual challenges and contexts. This is one of the concrete "ends" of the argumentative *discurrere* of theology as a church practice. The other "end" is characterized by the substantive logic of this *taxis*, with the pathic relation of the *discurrere* to the canon and to church doctrine.

This double *taxis* of theology as a church practice also prevents any given discursive-theological argument from establishing (falsely) its own definitive validity. Within the framework of the *substantive* logic of this practice, theology is essentially qualified by and distinguished from *doctrina*. It is shaped by it and yet is *not* identical with it, and thus in and of itself — that is, abstracted from that which it develops argumentatively — it does *not* possess any definitive validity. Moreover, within the framework of the *teleological* logic, new challenges and contexts for the presentation and communication of the *doctrina evangelii* as well as the necessity for a new engagement of theological judgment in response to new, specific queries require that such *discurrere* be differently dispositioned. This does *not* involve automatically falsifying or considering obsolete the previous *discurrere,* but rather building precisely on what went before and, if necessary, rejecting in a limited fashion specific parts of it in accounting in a theologically responsible fashion for a specific new judgment or opinion. This is precisely why in its provisional and finite nature the *discurrere* is always simultaneously characterized by a distinct definiteness, and indeed finds its concrete "end" in it. If the argumentative *discurrere* has not yet attained such definiteness, it is as yet unconcluded, and cannot yet contribute anything to theological judgment because that judgment itself cannot be accounted for responsibly in any theologically unequivocal way. Only in the definiteness of its unique course of argumentation can any given *discurrere* attain its properly provisional *and* finite nature.

c. Conclusions

We thus find that once the argumentative-discursive aspect of theology as a church practice is understood pathically from the perspective of the *doctrina fidei,* the discursive development of the *doctrina evangelii* and the argumentative engagement of other theological articulations mutually imply one another. In the substantive logic of the salvific-economic *taxis,* the aspect of perception and judgment is always subordinated to the aspect of theology as a discursive-argumentative practice, since the former always presupposes the latter, though even here one can see that the argumentative-discursive aspect is always oriented toward a specific perception and judgment in its actual church engagement and is thus teleologically qualified by precisely that perception and judgment. In this specifically teleological sense, then, the argumentative-discursive aspect does indeed always presuppose the aspect of judgment, since one can neither explicate nor argue discursively without the perception or discernment of certain challenges and contexts and without the articulated and authoritative application of the *doctrina evangelii* to precisely these challenges and contexts.[158] Within the teleological disposition, however, what in the substantive order is actually the third aspect of theology as a church practice, namely, the presentative-communicative aspect, now precedes all the others. Both the argumentative-discursive as well as the perceptive-judgmental aspects are oriented toward the presentative-communicative aspect insofar as the latter, third aspect now brings to "fulfillment" the participative engagement of theology in the soteriological telos of the church as the public of the Holy Spirit.

The logic of argumentation already predisposes the argumentative *discurrere* to be actualized in the form of discourse traditions or "schools." Within the framework of theology as a church practice, however, this always takes place in the context of a given, specific configuration of internal theological debates and of external challenges to faith. The argumentative-discursive aspect of theology thus cannot be artificially separated from the aspect of theological perception and of theological judgment. Within the substantive logic of the salvific-economic *taxis* of theology as a church practice, however, it must be addressed first because the *doctrina evangelii*, in the form of the biblical canon, the core practices, and the specifically given church doctrine, will always precede theological perception and all theological judgment such that the latter two, because they are always already specifically shaped, can thus never simply be engaged "impartially."

2. The Aspects of Theological Perception and Theological Judgment: The Dokimazein (Rom. 12:2)

Through participating in the telos of the church, theology as a specific church practice encounters together *with* the church the most varied social, political, economic, religious, philosophical, and moral constellations; because these constellations can never be abstractly anticipated, the church accordingly must deal with them in various, specific ways over the course of its *missio Dei*. This, theology's context of discovery, one in which queries are addressed to the church and to theology both internally and externally, first of all involves theological perception and then theological judgment.

Theological perception here refers to the precise discernment of the constellation of problems inhering in any given query, discernment that always takes place from the perspective of the *doctrina evangelii* and *within* the context of the core practices; that is, it is always *pathic* rather than abstract perception and discernment. It is *free* perception and discernment precisely because it is bound and shaped in a specific way. For *within* theology as a church practice, one is standing *neither* completely in a specific context such that the latter, as the normative horizon, ultimately determines the perception itself, *nor* completely outside any and all contexts in abstract isolation. Rather, precisely because *doctrina* and the core church practices, in actualizing God's economy of salvation, are oriented toward the human world, so also is theology in its role as a specific aspect of the actualization of the telos of the public of that salvific economy. This is why the pathos of theology implies the simultaneity of "contemporaneity" and "noncontemporaneity" in practicing theological judgment.

The actualizing feature of this critical contemporaneity — contemporaneity qualified by God's own salvific work — is *theological judgment.*

Theological judgment does not mean simply to decree in the declarative sense "freely" according to the taste and personal conviction of whichever theologian happens to be involved; such would surrender the very pathos of theology. Nor does it mean simply to apply a given method in the "technical" sense to a specific situation. Rather, theological judgment involves the unique application of the *doctrina evangelii* in concurrence with church doctrine to a specific constellation of problems such that the judgment itself ultimately comes to bear precisely *in* this constellation. What does this mean? It means that the binding theological judgment as a distinct theological statement in a given, specific constellation of problems is completely transparent with regard to its telos, namely, the *doctrina evangelii,* reflecting thus a *distinction* between this particular judgment and its alternatives, alternatives that virtually obscure the *doctrina evangelii.* By bringing to expression and adhering to the *doctrina evangelii* in a binding, authoritative fashion in a specific constellation of problems, theological judgment always aims in precisely this distinction at the *consolation or comfort of the gospel itself.*

The goal of theological judgment within the framework of the teleological *taxis* of theology as a church practice is to support concretely both preaching and "instruction" in the broadest sense, areas in which the *doctrina evangelii* is proclaimed and taught in the context of a specific constellation of problems and challenges so that human beings might be able to join in praise of God's salvific work.

Because the constellations of problems in which both the church and, with it, theology as a church practice move vary from place to place, and can even change at the same place, theology is required as a *continually performed, ongoing practice of judgment.* And because God's *opus inchoatum* encounters all sorts of both internal and external resistance, and because on this side of the eschaton the church itself must thus remain *ecclesia militans,* theology as a church practice also always implies the aspect of theological *judgment.* This aspect, however, is unavoidably intertwined with the discursive-argumentative aspect. Within judgment itself, differences between those engaged in judging invariably arise, and thus the presuppositions for the given, specific judgment itself must be argumentatively clarified and fixed through an explicit course of discussion by way of a doctrinal explication of the *doctrina evangelii;* beyond this, one must also explicate and articulate the theological point within the constellation of problems that elicited the specific judgment in the first place. Because theology is a practice engaged in the public sphere that is the church, the discursive-argumentative aspect inevitably becomes intertwined with the perceptive-judgmental aspect. This perspective also shows that the substantive *taxis,* that is, the logical prepositioning of the discursive-argumentative aspect, is necessary, since judgment must be able to prove itself argumentatively within theological discourse with others over against the *doctrina evangelii* and its doctrines. The result is (1) that a specific, doctrinally explicated judgment can itself become a theological doctrine, that is, can itself become the consensus in the formation of theological judgment and as such can in the boundary situations of crisis in church doctrine also either prepare doctrinal confession or can itself function as an explicit part of such; and (2) that in the other boundary situation it must be identified as false judgment and as false theological doctrine.

Perception and distinguishing discernment in the practice of judgment is of central significance because of the third aspect of theology as a church practice, the presentative-communicative aspect, since the latter always presupposes both the first and the second aspects in the sense of the inner *taxis* of theology as a practice. The first two aspects, however, never appear without this third one as well.

3. The Presentative-Communicative Aspect: Catechesis as Ad Hoc Apologetics

The ground and specific content of the presentative-communicative aspect of theology as a church practice is found in the soteriological telos of the church. This is why within the *substantive order* of the salvific-economic *taxis* of theology it is the final aspect, and yet within the *teleological order,* the first. This is also the proper locus of the poietic aspect of theological practice *within* its comprehensive pathos. For its presentative-communicative aspect is comprehensively oriented toward the entirety of the life of faith, indeed, toward the Christians' praxis of faith as such. It is precisely here that the insights derived from Lindbeck's cultural-linguistic model of religion, albeit now with substantial theological permeation, become relevant, since this particular aspect of theology (to use Lindbeck's terminology) involves the introduction and ongoing acquisition of the "cultural-linguistic" competency in the "learning of faith." Formulated substantively from the perspective of the economy of salvation, this aspect of theology as a church practice aims at enabling human beings to praise God for God's salvific acts and for their own *peregrinatio* with God toward God, that is, for their own *life with God.* The teleological logic of theology's salvific-economic *taxis* is the immediate consequence of theology as a reflective actualization of the church's soteriological telos. Therefore, the learning of the faith remains the goal of its presentative-communicative aspect, albeit *not* its criterion for truth.

189

Within this framework of learning the faith, and in addition to the practical acquisition of faith through being drawn into the core church practices, theology emerges in a twofold fashion in its presentative-communicative aspect. Here Lindbeck's cultural-linguistic model is again helpful, since its implicit post-Constantinian ecclesiology can build on early church practices without falling into overly simplistic strategies of repristination. It is precisely in Western societies, those which increasingly no longer understand themselves as being specifically Christian, that the *explicit catechetical* process of learning the faith again becomes an urgent aspect of church life, one the theological task of communication must now address in a fashion quite similar to that in the early church itself.[159]

In this perspective the presentative-communicative aspect of theology appears in two forms: The first is the *initiatory acquisition* of the central configurations of the language and activities of the Christian faith. This acquisition of faith can be called *catechetical acquisition* and can, depending on context and the age of the participants, continue for a shorter or longer period of time and be ecclesially anchored in various ways. The key feature here is the acquisition of new, unfamiliar configurations of language and activities, at the end of which one has acquired a certain competency in language and action. It seems obvious that this catechetical learning among both young and adult candidates for baptism will assume the form of baptismal instruction ultimately leading to the praise of God's salvific actions in the confesion of faith. Luther's understanding of the catechism — in the way Oswald Bayer emphasized it most recently — also plays a significant role in this context, since the salvific-economic articulation of the *doctrina evangelii* is both the ground and the content of the imminent baptism of these candidates. This is why the one pole of the presentative-communicative aspect of theology remains the *authoritative, binding* communication of the *doctrina evangelii* itself, which is then "experienced" in faith at baptism.

The other pole of the presentative-communicative aspect of theology, however, is authoritative, binding *communication* or *mediation*. This is where *poiesis*, hitherto consistently banned from theology's context of justification, acquires its important and indeed even indispensable role *within* the pathos of theology, since catechetical theology must be able to do justice to the "context of discovery" in which it moves. The pathos of catechetical theology is poietic where one must consider the context, that is, the origin and social, cultural, and intellectual status of the catechumens. As already stated above, a catechetical theology in secularized Europe at the end of the twentieth century must look different from one in the sixteenth century at the same place, or from one in Muslim Syria in the eighth or ninth century, or in Japan in the

nineteenth century. Both the church and theology become "contemporaneous" within the context of discovery by creatively considering the cultural,
political, and social situation of the catechumens as well as their variously
specific *consciousness of truth,* albeit without allowing these factors in their
own turn to become the determinative horizon and medium of a specific "local theology."[160] Here "poietic pathos" refers to the creative exposition of the
received *doctrina evangelii* and of the core church practices with regard to a
specific cultural and social constellation. Hence catechetical theology always
exhibits a basic pragmatic-apologetic feature; it is ad hoc apologetics insofar
as it orients itself *critically in the theological sense* toward a given, specific consciousness of truth, considering this consciousness poietically without allowing it to become the normative horizon for the communication of faith.[161] It
is precisely in this *theological-critical* form of the communication of faith that
the poietic task remains pathically determined and encompassed. Catechesis
as ad hoc apologetics thus does not mean the systematic development or defense of the truth of faith within the truth consciousness of a given age, but a
creative willingness to be qualified by the *doctrina evangelii* such that precisely in the communication of the truth of faith, the truth consciousness of a
given age is drawn poietically into and qualified by the *doctrina evangelii* itself.[162] Precisely by being qualified through and through by the *doctrina
evangelii,* the communicative-presentative aspect of theology as a church
practice becomes *free* for poietic communication. This freedom is presented
as a gift into which theology, in its pathos, is rapt insofar as it must not itself
now constitute the horizon within which it moves in poietic communication.
In its pathos, that is, in being qualified by and bound to the *doctrina evangelii,*
as well as in its resultant poietic freedom of communication, Luther's theology can serve as a paradigmatic example of a catechetical theology.

The initiatory acquisition of faith is joined by a learning of faith, one
immanent to faith that begins daily anew and never ends. This involves the
development of the implications of the praxis of the Christian faith within
the most varied contexts, that is, the exposition of faith with regard to precisely these contexts and the preservation of faith within them. This ongoing
learning of faith may, of course, overlap with the initiatory acquisition, and is
perhaps best called *peregrinational learning,* that is, the learning inhering in
the Christian *peregrinatio.* Here, too, the presentative-communicative aspect
of catechetical theology is to be understood as poietic pathos, as a continual
actualization of baptismal recollection; Lindbeck refers to this as "intratextual theology," one concerned with maintaining the praxis of faith amid
the most varied contexts of life and with interpreting these life situations
within the context of the praxis of faith itself. In contradistinction to the

theological poiesis of metaphorical constructivism, peregrinational learning within the framework of catechetical theology follows a *typological logic* as described by Lindbeck:

> Typology does not make scriptural contents into metaphors for extra-scriptural realities, but the other way around. It does not suggest, as is often said in our day, that believers find their stories in the Bible, but rather that they make the story of the Bible their story. The cross is not to be viewed as a figurative representation of suffering nor the messianic kingdom as a symbol for hope in the future; rather, suffering should be cruciform, and hopes for the future messianic. More generally stated, it is the religion instantiated in Scripture which defines being, truth, goodness, and beauty, and the nonscriptural exemplifications of these realities need to be trans-formed into figures (or types or antitypes) of the scriptural ones. Intratextual theology redescribes reality within the scriptural framework rather than translating Scripture into extrascriptural categories. It is the text, so to speak, which absorbs the world, rather than the world the text.[163]

Typology refers in a specific way to the *poietic* pathos of the peregrinational aspect of catechetical theology. It is pathic insofar as it stands within the story described in the canonical Scriptures and, from the perspective of this story, then (poietically) interprets the world within the context of discovery attach-ing to theology as a church practice. The *typological logic* of catechetical the-ology as peregrinational learning thus remains determined by God's specific history as authoritatively expressed by *doctrina,* and writes itself, as it were, into that history again and again and ever anew. By contrast, the purely poietic discourse of metaphorical constructivism is concerned with the pro-duction of new metaphors with whose aid it tries to orient the praxis of faith itself ever anew toward that which the "old" biblical "metaphors" tried to ex-press in their own way and in their own "context." The pathos of the peregrinational learning of faith is thus characterized by a specific and bind-ing horizon (biblical canon and *doctrina*) and by specific and binding config-urations of language and activities (the core practices).

Within the framework of this peregrinational learning within the con-text of discovery attaching to theology as a church practice, theology makes use of certain philosophical theorems and concepts for the sake of communi-cating faith within the horizon of the truth consciousness of a given age. Within the framework of theology as a church practice, however, its context of discovery is never separated from its context of justification; hence this poietic element must always prove itself within the diachronic recollection in which theology, in the context of justification, *maintains* through ongoing exposition the theorems which bindingly formulate *church doctrine*. That is, it does not simply leave these behind, for example, as contingent "expressive forms" of a certain culture or of the truth consciousness of a certain epoch. Rather, precisely this constant recollection within the theological context of justification prevents peregrinational learning within the context of discovery from being subjected in an unreflected, uncritical fashion to the dominant philosophical, cultural, or scientific discourses of any given epoch.

As *initiatory catechesis*, the presentative-communicative aspect of theology will thus emphasize the pole of pathos within poietic pathos, and as *peregrinational catechesis*, the pole of poiesis within pathos. By always remaining cognizant of its "end," namely, the *doctrina evangelii*, theology as a church practice is able to preserve its freedom within its "new obedience" in the to-and-fro between the contexts of justification and discovery. As a distinct practice, however, it cannot do justice to this "end" in some abstract, "autonomous" freedom *over against* the church, but only by participating in the salvific-economic telos of the church as the public of the Holy Spirit such that by being qualified by and thus bindingly oriented toward the biblical canon, *doctrina*, and the core church practices, it allows itself through engagement in its own, distinct activity to be rapt ever anew into God's freedom.

Notes

Notes to the Introduction

1. J. Habermas, *Die neue Unübersichtlichkeit,* Kleine politische Schriften, vol. V. (Frankfurt am Main: Suhrkamp, 1985). Of course, this current lack of clarity in theological discourse is also connected with the global, political, social, and economic changes reflected in various ways today in both theology and the church. The Lutheran ecumenist G. Lindbeck, a proven authority on world Christianity, offers a good summary of this complex dynamic in his essay "Ecumenical Imperatives for the Twenty-First Century," *Currents in Theology and Mission* 20 (1993): 360-66, where he draws attention to the loss of the theological center in Western Christendom, a center given in and with Christology and also represented in the successful (earlier) paradigm of the ecumenical movement. Although the churches of Southeast Asia, Latin America, and Africa manage to combine a progressive political stance with the kind of orthodox theology presupposing precisely this christological center, that center is rapidly disappearing within the traditional churches of the West. With regard to the latter, Lindbeck points out that "there are, so sociologists say, fewer and fewer communities held together despite contentions by an identifiable core of shared beliefs and group loyalties. Rather, like society at large, they are becoming heterogeneous collections of special interest groups united, if at all, by bureaucratic management. Transmitting even a modicum of communal ties and creedal commitments is increasingly left to the conservatives. The center is not holding" (364). Recent studies and general experience show that what Lindbeck describes here with regard to the so-called "mainline" American churches applies to a considerable extent also to the so-called "people's churches" *(Volkskirchen)* within the German-speaking European sphere. The following study represents among other things a contribution to the theological as well as ecclesiastical task of understanding theological discourse anew as ecumenical discourse from the perspective of its christological center, and of ori-

enting it toward that center, albeit with a pneumatological-ecclesiological point of departure.

2. The third edition of *Religion in Geschichte und Gegenwart* is probably its final, great, "classical" document, while the *Theologische Realenzyklopädie*, drawing as it does its encyclopedic superabundance from every possible quarter, already seems to represent a late phenomenon.

3. In its present "postmodern" phase, modernity has by no means been overcome. Rather, it has reached an increasingly self-critical stage with a condition of intensified plurality as its central feature. One of the ironies of modernity is that the "most modern modernists" increasingly proclaim postmodernity as their most recent advance. Cf. W. Welsch, *Unsere postmoderne Moderne* (Berlin: Akademie, 1987; 4th ed., 1993), as an accessible and thoroughly typical example.

4. One important study of the creative, destructive, and ultimately inescapable reality of modernity is M. Berman, *All That Is Solid Melts into Air: The Experience of Modernity* (New York: Simon & Schuster, 1982).

Notes to Part One

1. E. Peterson, "Briefwechsel mit Adolf Harnack und ein Epilog," in Peterson, *Theologische Traktate* (Munich: Kösel, 1951), 293-321 (originally published in *Hochland* 30 [1932/33]: 111-24). Michael Hollerich has made this fascinating correspondence accessible to an English-speaking audience: "Erik Peterson's Correspondence with Adolf von Harnack: Retrieving a Neglected Critique of Church, Theology, and Secularization in Weimar Germany," *Pro Ecclesia* 2 (1993): 305-32.

2. Cf. Peterson, 295. His observation was prompted particularly by the following statement in Harnack's study: "The Old Testament, itself 'only relatively authoritative over against the New Testament, did not allow any absolute grammatolatry with regard to the Bible. The authority of the *apostolic doctrine,* which added its own organizing and restricting features to the authority of "scripture," provided a salutary corrective to biblicism' (*loc. cit.,* 141)" (295).

3. Peterson, 295f.

4. Peterson, 297.

5. Peterson, 298f.

6. "Spiritually and sociologically, the Protestant church corresponds approximately to the spiritual and sociological status of the German national *Volkspartei.* Just as the latter must of necessity ultimately break up, so also must the Protestant church necessarily break up in the future" (Peterson, 301).

7. "When you refer to theology with the paradoxical expression 'catechism instruction,' you are merely pointing out that when we speak of 'theology' or even 'catechism,' we are still basically living off past currency [both Catholic and old Protestant]. For theology, especially within the framework of a university, has always lived from the presupposition that it is more than merely catechism instruction, and the catechism in its own turn is meaningful only under the presupposition that there

is dogma or at least some form of 'pure doctrine' [i.e., formal authority]. If your thesis were taken seriously, one would have to dissolve the theological faculties at the universities. I am familiar with the elimination of catechism instruction in the Rhineland, and it is only logical that one must now also eliminate university dogmatics as 'catechism instruction'" (Peterson, 301).

8. Peterson, 303f.

9. Peterson, 303f.

10. Peterson, 305, my emphasis.

11. After much hesitation and inner struggle, Peterson converted to Roman Catholicism on December 25, 1930. Concerning this and Peterson's life and work in general, cf. the exhaustively documented study by B. Nichtweiß, *Erik Peterson. Neue Sicht auf Leben und Werk* (Freiburg im Breisgau: Herder, 1992).

12. Cf. in this regard Nichtweiß, 211-17, 512-17, 638-41.

13. Despite considerable and substantive differences, the Lutherans include Wolf, Iwand, Vogel, Gollwitzer, Diem, P. Brunner, Schlink, Althaus, and Elert, while the Reformed include E. Brunner, Weber, Kreck, and de Quervain.

14. "While Dibelius is inclined to demonstrate through increased activity the public character of the *church*, Barth wishes to demonstrate through a return to dogma and dogmatics the public character of Protestant *theology*" (Peterson, 308).

15. Peterson, 307. Peterson continues: "In principle, nothing has changed at present in the relationship between 'theology' and 'church' within Protestantism. Just as the previous generation was able to engage in a 'theology' whose historical-philological queries were not really affected by the presence of the 'territorial church,' so also is it possible to engage in 'dialectical theology' today without regard to that problematic structure which the Protestant calls 'church,' and yet whose separate life repeatedly escapes the grasp of Protestant theology" (307f.). Apart from significant exceptions, does not this observation, two generations later, remain as relevant as before, and does it not even today still articulate the heart of the problematic relationship between "church" and "theology" within Protestantism?

16. Peterson, 309f.

17. Peterson, 312f.

18. Such can include projects of "modernity," "culture," or progressive-emancipatory, national, popular, or other "movements."

19. Cf. section I in Part Three.

20. D. Bonhoeffer, *Gesammelte Schriften*, vol. 6, ed. Eberhard Bethge (Munich: Kaiser, 1974), 485f. I was directed to this passage by K.-A. Bauer's essay "Kerygma und Kirche. Der Weg Heinrich Schliers als Anfrage an die evangelische Kirche und ihre Theologie," *Evangelische Theologie* 41 (1981): 401-23, an article quite relevant for the question I am addressing here.

21. This is an appropriate time to recall Karl Barth's interesting comment, one made in the lecture "Roman Catholicism as a Question to the Protestant Church" from 1928, i.e., three years after his famous dispute with Erik Peterson (which we will discuss in detail below): "Perhaps I can clarify things a bit if I explicitly add that what I mean by this statement is the following: If today I were to be persuaded that the in-

terpretation of the Reformation along the lines of Schleiermacher-Ritschl-Troeltsch (or even -Seeberg or -Holl) were *correct*, and that Luther and Calvin really did intend it in *this* way, then tomorrow although I would perhaps not become a Catholic, I would at least take leave of the allegedly Protestant church; if I were forced to *choose* between these two evils, I would indeed rather become Catholic" (Barth, *Die Theologie und die Kirche* [Munich, 1928], 338f.; see also English translation, *Theology and Church: Shorter Writings 1920-1928* [London: SCM Press, 1962, 307-33; here 314]).

22. H. Schlier, "Kurze Rechenschaft," in Schlier, *Der Geist und die Kirche. Exegetische Aufsätze und Vorträge*, vol. 4, ed. Veronika Kubina and Karl Lehmann (Freiburg im Breisgau: Herder, 1980), 270-89.

23. Schlier, 273.

24. Schlier, 273f.

25. The essay mentioned earlier by K.-A. Bauer performed the service of drawing explicit attention to this situation as early as 1981, albeit without eliciting any significant reaction. The essay obviously represents an extremely unpleasant "recollection out of season."

26. J. Fischer, "Pluralismus, Wahrheit und die Krise der Dogmatik," *Zeitschrift für Theologie und Kirche* 91 (1994): 487-539.

27. In addition to the obvious "fall of the wall" and the reunification of Germany, involving as yet unforeseeable implications for the Protestant churches, this also especially includes the profound changes in the membership numbers of the so-called Protestant "people's churches" *(Volkskirchen)*. For a considered and discerning look at the *Volkskirche* and the "crisis" it faces, a crisis extrapolated from tendencies within society, cf. M. Welker, "Der Mythos 'Volkskirche,'" *Evangelische Theologie* 54 (1994): 180-93.

28. During the 1920s, the Protestant churches still drew their identity largely from the ecclesiastical authority of the regional sovereign and from the culture of the Wilhelmian empire. They, too, experienced the radical political upheavals of 1918/19 as a crisis and ended up feeling alienated by the new democratic culture. Something similar seems to be happening today in the German Protestant regional churches. The identity of the *Volkskirchen*, oriented as it is toward the democratic-bourgeois and largely value-conservative and homogeneous culture of the Federal Republic, is similarly experiencing the present upheavals in society and culture as a crisis, and finds itself alienated from the emerging late-modern, pluralistic, value-neutral, process-oriented culture.

29. "The individualization of religion versus institutionally authoritative religion; internal stabilization through subjectivity versus external stabilization through ecclesiastical institutions; self-referentiality in adopting religious content versus objectively asserted religious truths; a pluralism of religious views versus the exclusivity of a single truth binding for all; post-confessionality versus confessionally determined larger churches — these antithetical pairs basically circumscribe this religious change" (Fischer, "Pluralismus, Wahrheit und die Krise der Dogmatik," 506).

30. "Schleiermacher's understanding of the devout consciousness must today be

understood from the perspective of communication. *Christian faith* must be understood as a *communicative event* instead of as a form of the devout self-consciousness. Accordingly, the *task of theology* resides not in presenting or articulating the Christian consciousness in faith, but *in stimulating and critically accompanying this communicative event*" (Fischer, "Pluralismus, Wahrheit und die Krise der Dogmatik," 500, my emphasis).

31. Fischer, "Pluralismus, Wahrheit und die Krise der Dogmatik," 488.

32. Fischer, "Pluralismus, Wahrheit und die Krise der Dogmatik," 488f.

33. J. Fischer, *Leben aus dem Geist. Zur Grundlegung christlicher Ethik* (Zürich: Theologischer Verlag, 1994).

34. "It is tied to the *Volkskirche* by its function of training pastors. The standard by which it is measured is whether it is commensurate with this church reality and is able to train people adequately for the vocation of pastor under the presuppositions of the *Volkskirche*" (Fischer, "Pluralismus, Wahrheit und die Krise der Dogmatik," 529). "If dogmatics is to do justice to this reality of the *Volkskirche*, then it must focus on the church as the locus of this question addressed to Christian tradition and define its task accordingly" (530).

35. Schleiermacher defines dogmatic theology as "the science which systematizes the doctrine prevalent in a Christian Church at a given time" (*The Christian Faith*, trans. H. R. Mackintosh and J. S. Stewart from 2nd German ed. [Edinburgh: T. & T. Clark, 1928], §19).

36. Dalferth defines church doctrine as the "quintessence of a consensus obtaining at a certain time in a church concerning the common knowledge of faith employed in congregational praxis" (*Kombinatorische Theologie. Probleme theologischer Rationalität*, Quaestiones disputate 130 [Freiburg im Breisgau: Herder, 1991], 39).

37. Fischer, "Pluralismus, Wahrheit und die Krise der Dogmatik," 491f.

38. Fischer, "Pluralismus, Wahrheit und die Krise der Dogmatik," 492.

39. The question, of course, is whether one can appropriately switch from the communicative context of faith to that of reason. Is there indeed a "general" determination of the relationship between truth and communication, or is precisely such a determination itself *one* discussion within the context of "what is the case" and quite a *different* discussion within the context of faith?

40. Fischer, "Pluralismus, Wahrheit und die Krise der Dogmatik," 493.

41. Here Fischer approximates that to which I refer with the term "pathos." At issue is the element of being shaped and guided, of a quite specific *passio* "within" which that which is common, shared, the element of communication or acting with one another first becomes possible.

42. Fischer, "Pluralismus, Wahrheit und die Krise der Dogmatik," 499f.

43. Fischer, "Pluralismus, Wahrheit und die Krise der Dogmatik," 501.

44. Fischer, "Pluralismus, Wahrheit und die Krise der Dogmatik," 502, my emphasis.

45. Fischer, "Pluralismus, Wahrheit und die Krise der Dogmatik," 502. Not surprisingly, Christian religious knowledge, too, exhibits precisely this dialectical structure: "Obviously, Christian religious knowledge also exhibits the polarity just de-

scribed between concrete reference to God in communication to and about God on the one hand, and non-concrete reference to God in the experience of the spirit on the other" (503).

46. By contrast, Luther speaks of the church as the "mother of faith," that is, as a reality that itself nourishes faith but is identical neither with the content of faith nor with the nonconcrete experience of the Spirit, but rather quite precisely constitutes that "third place" independently juxtaposed over against faith and from which faith itself draws both strength and nourishment. Cf. in this regard Luther, *Weimar Ausgabe,* 40/1, 664, 18-21, and 665, 15-17. In the *Large Catechism* of 1529, Luther describes the church as "the mother that begets and bears every Christian through the Word of God" (*The Book of Concord,* trans. and ed. Theodore G. Tappert [Philadelphia: Fortress, 1959], 416); in the *Church Postille* of 1522 he observes that "therefore whosoever would find Christ must first find the church" (*Weimar Ausgabe,* 10/1, 140, 8). Cf. in this regard Part Three below.

47. Fischer, "Pluralismus, Wahrheit und die Krise der Dogmatik," 504.

48. One specific problem contributing probably to a significant extent to the alienation of dogmatics and church reality is the abstract doctrinal consensus with which Protestant dogmatics operates in departments of theology in separation from church reality. Fischer believes that dogmatics begins with an abstract consensus by simply working further with the problems already attaching to theological tradition, while at the same time becoming increasingly alienated through precisely this practice from the multiplicity of faith actually found in the church. Here Fischer addresses an *extremely* important point, albeit one that itself can be addressed within an understanding of theology as the discursive practice within the church, one distinguishing between the context of discovery and that of justification. Within the context of discovery or disclosure, theology must become considerably more flexible, and must address in a productive fashion those concrete questions arising within the framework of precisely this multiplicity of faith, and must discuss these questions critically within the horizon of the context of justification. Then, in the sense of catechetical theology, which itself is to be understood as "poietic pathos," it must formulate the soteriological essence of the Christian faith such that this formulation itself discloses that faith communicatively. This cannot be accomplished except by way of the context of justification itself (canon, dogma, discourse tradition) and the kind of theologically binding or authoritative judgment that aims at consensus and seeks to delimit its results from false doctrine. Without taking this path, this presentative task will remain nothing but pure construction. Yet without an implementation of just this presentative task, Fischer's queries quite justifiably remain open and theology does not do justice to its own churchly task as a distinct church practice that continually articulates the soteriological telos of the church itself.

49. In his study *Church and Theology: The Systematic Function of the Church Concept in Modern Theology,* trans. Reginald H. Fuller (Philadelphia: Westminster, 1971), T. Rendtorff investigates a specific aspect of this question, namely, the significance of the concept of church for systematic theological construction. His study, however, also contains an implicit perspective directly implementing certain norma-

tive ecclesiological decisions, namely, an interpretation of the Reformation that understands contemporary Protestantism as the latter's inevitable and genuine consequence. This implies a theory of Christianity that understands the modern world in all its multiplicity as a Christian world that in its own turn can no longer be reduced to any specific ecclesiastical construction. Rendtorff is thus concerned with securing the universality of the Christian religion under conditions making its ecclesiastical articulation impossible. Precisely this intention itself presupposes within its problem horizon the church concept of contemporary Protestantism, first as the implied possibility of distinguishing at all meaningfully between the Christian religion and the church, and second as the implied necessity of accepting "history" itself as the normative horizon of perception. This is why a "reality" from the perspective of which the church itself is viewed within an external perspective as a necessarily specific entity can be engaged against an "abstract" dogmatic concept of church. This alternative position, however, along with its attendant description of the problem, is possible only if one understands the church as the aggregate of believers in which devotion or piety is communicated and fostered in a context of agreement. The perception of church, the attendant self-understanding of theology, and the description of that which constitutes "history" — all these things are inevitably interconnected. If one takes "history" itself as the normative horizon of perception, then as Christian perception this always implies the ecclesiological thesis that the church is to be perceived within the horizon of history. By contrast, if one takes as one's normative horizon of perception that which makes the church a church and that on which it is based as a church, namely, God's salvific economy precisely in its ties to specific ecclesial processes and practices (a point on which the ecclesiastical self-understanding of Lutherans, Roman Catholics, and Eastern Orthodox concur in the broadest sense), then "history" as a comprehensive problem horizon becomes impossible; instead, one must address a theologically qualified multiplicity of and differences between various specific "histories." The conflict between contemporary Protestantism and dialectical (or "confessional") theology is the "second difference" at work within Protestant theology itself. This second difference must either be resolved in a theory of Christianity that takes "history" as its comprehensive problem horizon, or must be articulated and endured as an explicit difference that is conceptualized theologically and ecclesiologically. My own argumentation, of course, is just as circular as Rendtorff's; this is unavoidable because we both presuppose a different comprehensive horizon that allows us to formulate the variously "other" internally and address it thematically precisely as divergence.

W. Pannenberg's program of "revelation as history" and its explication within the framework of a comprehensive, ecumenically based systematic theology can be read as an attempt to reach a synthesis between the two mutually exclusive problem horizons. Here the neo-economic doctrine of the Trinity provides the brackets allowing one to introduce nature and history into the one divine history. This proposal's thrust must be radically ecumenical, since the "second difference," namely, the *saeculum,* is to be understood as a consequence of the "first difference" (i.e., of the inner-Christian schism). But this synthesis can succeed only if the multiplicity of churches and their practices are actually an anticipatory sign of the divine dominion, and only if the basic distinction between true and false church, true and false theology is at least set aside if not completely abandoned. This means, however, that binding doctrine as a witness to the gospel, in contrast to false doctrine, either becomes impossible in this synthesis or itself threatens the synthesis, since a gospel proclaimed within binding doctrine always constitutes an element of "difference" that cannot be integrated into the comprehensive problem horizon of "history." It can be harmonized with the comprehensive trinitarian divine history only if the latter is understood as being tied to the proclamation of the gospel and the administration of the sacraments, in which case that which actually constitutes "church" itself then enters into a status different from "history," the result being that the synthesis is already dissolved. In other words, in order to remain stabile, the synthesis itself must operate with the *anticipation* of an ecumenical church within the framework of an ecumenical theology in which all differences between true and false church and theology have already been overcome. Of course, the very *necessity* of anticipating this ecumenically unified church again delimits the existing difference. That is, an internally stabile synthesis of these two mutually exclusive problem horizons is not possible.

50. Cf. in this regard the argumentative effort with which J. Habermas, in his study *The Philosophical Discourse of Modernity: Twelve Lectures,* trans. Frederick Lawrence (Cambridge: MIT Press, 1987), believes he must hold fast, over against postmodern criticism, to modernity as what has become an explicit "project."

51. I will refer especially to J. Dunne, *Back to the Rough Ground: "Phronesis" and "Techne" in Modern Philosophy and in Aristotle* (Notre Dame: University of Notre Dame Press, 1993); R. Bernstein, *Praxis and Action: Contemporary Philosophies of Human Activity* (Philadelphia: University of Pennsylvania Press, 1971); R. Bubner, *Handlung, Sprache und Vernunft. Grundbegriffe praktischer Philosophie* (Frankfurt am Main: Suhrkamp, 1982); N. Lobkowicz, *Theory and Practice: History of a Concept from Aristotle to Marx* (Notre Dame: University of Notre Dame Press, 1967); A. MacIntyre, *After Virtue: A Study in Moral Theory,* 2nd ed. (Notre Dame: University of Notre Dame Press, 1984), and the pertinent articles in the *Historisches Wörterbuch der Philosophie* (Basel: Schwabe, 1971f.).

52. Cf. in this regard the introduction of J.-F. Lyotard, *The Postmodern Condition: A Report on Knowledge,* trans. Geoff Bennington and Brian Massumi, foreword by Fredric Jameson (Minneapolis: University of Minnesota Press, 1984); W. Welsch, *Unsere postmoderne Moderne,* 4th ed. (Berlin: Akademie, 1993); and R. Bernstein, *The New Constellation: The Ethical-Political Horizons of Modernity/Postmodernity,* 2nd ed. (Cambridge: MIT Press, 1993).

53. George Lindbeck, *The Nature of Doctrine: Religion and Theology in a Postliberal Age* (Philadelphia: Westminster, 1984). This book has in the meantime also been translated into German as *Christliche Lehre als Grammatik des Glaubens. Religion und Theologie im postliberalen Zeitalter. TB,* 90, ed. H. G. Ulrich and R. Hütter, trans. M. Müller (Gütersloh: C. Kaiser/Gütersloher Verlagshaus, 1994).

54. R. Meyer-Kalkus, "Pathos," in *Historisches Wörterbuch der Philosophie,* 7:193.

55. "'Affection' means (a) In one sense, a quality in virtue of which alteration is

possible; *e.g.,* whiteness and blackness, sweetness and bitterness, heaviness and lightness, etc. (b) The actualizations of these qualities; *i.e.,* the alterations already realized" (Aristotle, *Metaphysics* 1022b, 15; cf. also 1049a, 25; translation according to Loeb Classical Library 271; trans. Hugh Tredennick [Cambridge and London: Harvard University Press, 1933]).

56. Cf. Meyer-Kalkus, 7:193-99.

57. "We usually translate *pathos* with passion, ebullition of emotion. But *pathos* is connected with *paschein,* to suffer, endure, undergo, to be borne along by, to be determined by. It is risky, as it always is in such cases, if we translate *pathos* with tuning, by which we mean dis-position and determination. But we must risk this translation because it alone protects us from conceiving *pathos* in a very modern psychological sense. Only if we understand *pathos* as being attuned to, can we also characterize *thaumazein,* astonishment, more exactly. In astonishment we restrain ourselves *(être en arrêt).* We step back, as it were, from being, from the fact that it is as it is and not otherwise. And astonishment is not used up in this retreating from the Being of being, but, as this retreating and self-restraining, it is at the same time forcibly drawn to and, as it were, held fast by that from which it retreats. Thus, astonishment is dis-position in which and for which the Being of being unfolds. Astonishment is the tuning within which the Greek philosophers were granted the correspondence to the Being of being" (M. Heidegger, *What Is Philosophy?* translated with an introduction by William Kluback and Jean T. Wilde [London: Vision, 1958], 83ff.).

58. Heidegger, 83.

59. D. Cunningham, *Faithful Persuasion: In Aid of a Rhetoric of Christian Theology* (Notre Dame and London: University of Notre Dame Press, 1991).

60. Although he peculiarly does not refer to Ps. 8, O. Bayer does skillfully articulate this situation in his chapter "Staunen, Seufzen, Schauen. Affekte der Wahrnehmung des Schöpfers," in his book *Schöpfung als Anrede. Zu einer Hermeneutik der Schöpfung,* 2nd rev. ed. (Tübingen: J. C. B. Mohr, 1990), delineating at the same time the radical difference between the philosophical "pathos" of astonishment in the face of the cosmos and the biblical "pathos" of believing astonishment: "The astonishment of faith does not emerge from the visible as such. Nor is it directed to an invisible idea whose representation would be the visible. It is directed rather toward the word that, contrary to all appearances, promises redemption and as such is the power of resurrection and consolation. The word of the creator and that of the redeemer are one, namely, a saving word, a word of salvation" (174). With regard to Ps. 8, G. Sauter has pointed out the connection between the psalmist's astonishment and Luther's own perception of human beings. Cf. Sauter, "Die Wahrnehmung des Menschen bei Martin Luther," *Evangelische Theologie* 43 (1983): 489-503; esp. 499f. He draws attention to the following observation from Luther's *Operationes in Psalmos* (1519-21) regarding Ps. 8; here Luther articulately describes the relationship between *thaumazein* and the *passio* of God's works in faith: "Igitur grande miraculum est, hominem, qui in seipso et omnium oculis derelictus, desperatus, oblitus dei nihil minus sentit quam deum sui memorem, esse deo in memoria. Et cor hominis debet ac potest hoc capere et credere, deum esse iucundum, benevolentem, dulcem, quem non sentit nisi

iracundum, horrendum, insustentabilem. Quis non miretur? Quis non dicat, 'Quid est homo, quod memor es eius?' Opera dei sunt haec incomprehensibilia, nisi per fidem" (*Weimar Ausgabe*, 5, 270, 17-23).

61. It is not surprising that Meister Eckehart uses "pathos" in this explicitly theological sense (*Deutsche Predigten und Traktate*, trans. and ed. J. Quint [Munich: Carl Hanser, 1963], 430f.): "Our blessedness derives not from our actions, but from us suffering God" (431, 4-5). "When our actions are passive in nature, suffering, we are more perfect than when they are active" (430, 25-26). Concerning the philosophical background, cf. U. Köpf, "Passivität und Aktivität in der Mystik des Mittelalters," in *Pragmatik. Handbuch pragmatischen Denkens*, ed. H. Stachowiak, vol. 1 (Hamburg: Felix Meiner, 1985), 280-98. It would be interesting to read the works of Christian spirituality and especially the tradition of Christian mysticism with an eye on their specific embodiment of the pathos of Christian existence. A noteworthy beginning in this regard is R. Williams, *The Wound of Knowledge: Christian Spirituality from the New Testament to St. John of the Cross* (Atlanta: John Knox, 1980; 2nd ed., London, 1990).

62. Cf. Meyer-Kalkus, 7:193. Luther's higher estimation of the passive is usually explicitly oriented toward the theme of *iustificatio:* "primum petimus opus tuum, Domine. Ibi nos nihil agimus, sed tantum sumus spectatores et receptatores, sumus mere passivi. Deus ostendit nobis se et facit nos salvos suo solius opere" (*Weimar Ausgabe*, 40/3, 588, 2-4). Cf. in this regard the definitive contribution of C. Link, "Vita passiva. Rechtfertigung als Lebensvorgang," *Evangelische Theologie* 44 (1984): 315-51.

63. O. Bayer has expressed this quite succinctly: "The decisive point here is a completely new understanding of faith, which Luther did not distinguish from theology in the way we today have done quite naturally since Semler — as if theology were merely a reflection or meditation on faith — but rather identified it with theology. Theology as faith is neither a dianoetic nor a moral virtue; it is not a *virtus*, not even a disposition. Faith happens to a person as a work of God alone" (*Theologie*, Handbuch Systematischer Theologie 1 [Gütersloh: Gütersloher Verlagshaus G. Mohn, 1994], 45f.).

64. "Afterwards shall we come and also be believers when our Lord God makes us believers beforehand. Sed tamen haec etiam est gratia dei et procedit ex primo opere dei, that he alone has it *et sit dominus*" (Luther, *Weimar Ausgabe*, 40/3, 588, 7-10). Luther thus holds fast to the primacy of *passio* over any sort of human *operatio*. Here he articulates a central aspect of human creatureliness. Cf., e.g., *Weimar Ausgabe*, 9, 97, 12-16: "Nota, quod divina pati magis quam agere oportet, immo et sensus et intellectus est naturaliter etiam virtus passiva. Et Apostolus: 'Velle mihi adjacet, perficere non invenio' [Rom. 7:18], i.e. nos materia sumus pura, deus formae factor, omnia enim in nobis operatur deus" (allusion to Isa. 26:12). Or *Weimar Ausgabe* 40/1, 610, 17f.: "Nostrum agere est pati operantem in nobis Deum, qui dat verbum, quo per fidem divinitus datam apprehenso nascimur filii dei." ("Our 'activity' is to permit God to do His work in us; He gives the Word, and when we take hold of this by the faith that God gives, we are born as sons of God." *Lectures on Galatians, 1535, Luther's Works*, vol. 26, trans. and ed. Jaroslav Pelikan [St. Louis: Concordia,

1963], 401). G. Ebeling observes that for Luther, "Nostrum agere est pati deum in nobis operantem, whereby one's own *operari* really has more the character of a *rapi* and *duci*" (*Lutherstudien,* vol. 2, *Disputatio de homine,* pt. 3, *Die theologische Definition des Menschen* [Tübingen: J. C. B. Mohr, 1989], 591). W. Joest does quite rightly emphasize, however, that in this pathic existence the human self is not excluded, but rather participates to the highest degree. "This should not be overlooked in the famous metaphor immediately adjacent to the passage just cited, namely, that concerning the *humana voluntas* as *iumentum* on which either God or Satan rides (18, 635, 17ff.). There Luther says: 'si insederit Deus, *vult et vadit,* quo vult Deus. . . . Si insederit Satan, *vult et vadit,* quo vult Satan.' The 'vult et vadit' is to be understood as a genuinely personal willing and going of the self" (*Ontologie der Person bei Luther* [Göttingen: Vandenhoeck & Ruprecht, 1967], 221). Cf. in this regard also Sauter, "Die Wahrnehmung des Menschen bei Martin Luther."

65. Joest, 292f. Of course, this is not merely a matter of abstract silencing, but rather one occurring in connection with quite specific procedures, and for Luther especially in connection with the process of hearing the witness of Scripture or with that of scriptural meditation. G. Ebeling quite rightly points out that "probably no other Christian exegete shows as clearly as does Luther what understanding means in its most profound sense, namely, not just a comprehending of the text itself, but a condition of being seized by that text, with the *comprehendere* emerging from scripture rather than from the exegete. Understanding is in reality something passive, with all attendant activity coming from the text. That is, the text becomes the subject, while the person engaged in understanding actually becomes the object, a prisoner of the text. For: Scripture virtus est hec, quod non mutatur in eum, qui eam studet, sed transmutat suum amatorem in sese ac suas virtutes . . . Quia non tu me mutabis in te . . . sed tu mutaberis in me. Nec ego a te, sed tu a me denominaberis" (*Lutherstudien,* vol. 1 [Tübingen: J. C. B. Mohr, 1971], 3). Although this is doubtless the paradigmatic process in which a person "is seized," in Part Three below I will use Luther's own pneumatological ecclesiology in relating this particular "pathos" to other church core practices as well.

66. Joest, 294.

67. Cf. in this regard C. von Wolzogen, "Poiesis II," in *Historisches Wörterbuch der Philosophie,* 7:1025-26.

68. "You know that poetry [poiesis] is more than a single thing. For of anything whatever that passes from not being into being the whole cause is composing or poetry [poiesis]" (*Symposium* 205.b.8f.). Cf. also *Sophista* 265.b.8-10: "We said, if we remember the beginning of our conversation, that every power is productive [poiesis] which causes things to come into being which did not exist before."

69. "Things which people call natural are made by divine art, and things put together by men out of those as materials are made by human art" (*Sophista* 266d.2-4). Plato distinguishes productive art (poiesis) from imitative art (mimesis) with regard to both the divine and the human, in nature the thing and the image accompanying it, in the human sphere imitative art ("the thing itself, produced by the art that creates real things, and the image, produced by the image-making art," *Sophista* 266d-267b).

Artistic poiesis is thus to be understood as imitation once removed after manual poiesis. Cf. in this regard H. Koller, "Mimesis," in *Historisches Wörterbuch der Philosophie,* 5:1396-99, esp. 1398. Plato thus also uses poiesis to refer to the poetic arts and their works, and it is this meaning under which the term then acquired an identity as "poesy, poetry." Cf. D. Ewald and N. Rath, "Poesie," in *Historisches Wörterbuch der Philosophie,* 7:1000-1008.

70. J. Derbolav, "Poiesis I," in *Historisches Wörterbuch der Philosophie,* 7:1024, in reference to *Physica* 192b, 27-33.

71. "The class of things that admit of variation includes both things made and actions done. But making is different from doing (a distinction we may accept from extraneous discourses). Hence the rational quality concerned with doing is different from the rational quality concerned with making. Nor is one of them a part of the other, for doing is not a form of making, nor making a form of doing" (*Nicomachean Ethics* 1140.a.1-5). "Moreover the case of the arts is not really analogous to that of the virtues. Works of art have their merit in themselves, so that it is enough if they are produced having a certain quality of their own; but acts done in conformity with the virtues are not done justly or temperately if they themselves are of a certain sort, but only if the agent also is in a certain state of mind when he does them: first he must act with knowledge; secondly he must deliberately choose the act, and choose it for its own sake; and thirdly the act must spring from a fixed and permanent disposition of character. For the possession of an art, none of these conditions is included, except the mere qualification of knowledge; but for the possession of the virtues, knowledge is of little or no avail, whereas the other conditions, so far from being of little moment, are all-important, inasmuch as virtue results from the repeated performance of just and temperate actions" (1105.a.26–b.5).

72. Wolzogen, 7:1024.

73. Cf. in this regard Bernstein, *Praxis and Action,* 11-83, esp. 44, 59; and M. Riedel, *Theorie und Praxis im Denken Hegels. Interpretationen zu den Grundstellungen der neuzeitlichen Subjektivität* (Stuttgart: W. Kohlhammer, 1965), 128-36.

74. Ewald and Rath, 7:1000.

75. Until the eighteenth century, writers on poetics understood poesy totally as mimesis, either of nature or of antiquity. In the mid–eighteenth century this understanding of poesy radically changed. Poesy became the creative act of the subject who brings forth something new. Baumgarten, one of the pioneering aestheticians of the eighteenth century, formulates this quite pointedly: "Fictio poetica novum ita creans orbem" (A. G. Baumgarten, *Aesthetica* [1750; reprint, 1961], §518, cited after Ewald and Rath, 7:1001). The poetics of the Enlightenment still focused on the central notion of the formation or creation of possible worlds; beginning with the idea of "genius" in Romanticism, however, "poesy" was understood more pointedly as new creation. Mimetic poiesis is replaced by an original poiesis of the sort Plato attributed only to God. The culmination of this radical idealistic theory of poesy is found in Schelling and Hölderlin. For Schelling, "the human species" became in an extraordinarily radical fashion "subject of a universal poesy at once encompassing philosophy, mythology, and science" (Ewald and Rath, 7:1002).

76. "Human essence is grounded not in the non-concreteness of the spirit or of 'consciousness as such,' but in the concrete being of nature in which it objectifies itself through activity. Only then is the Hegelian non-difference replaced by that particular model of an *identity of work and action in which instead of praxis, it is poiesis that constitutes the basic character of life*: ὁ δὲ βίος ποίησις, οὐ πρᾶξις, ἐστιν. Work is not only the 'only substance of these products' and is their very 'nature,' but is also the 'productive life' as the life specific to human beings" (M. Riedel, "Hegel und Marx. Die Neubestimmung des Verhältnisses von Theorie und Praxis," in Riedel, *System und Geschichte. Studien zum historischen Standort von Hegels Philosophie* [Frankfurt am Main: Suhrkamp, 1973], 37f.).

77. Castoriadis interprets social praxis entirely from the perspective of a radical poiesis which he understands as *creatio ex nihilo* in the sense of an "absolute ontological creation." Cf. Castoriadis, *Gesellschaft als imaginäre Institution* (Frankfurt am Main, 1984), 335, 337; English translation, *The Imaginary Institution of Society,* trans. Kathleen Blamey (Cambridge: MIT Press, 1987).

78. For Romantic hermeneutics (e.g., Schleiermacher, its paradigmatic representative), all human activity becomes transparent as poiesis. This is why all "understanding" must be construed poietically; as a reconstructive implementation of the original poiesis, it is itself production. Cf. in this regard esp. H.-G. Gadamer, *Truth and Method,* trans. Joel Weinsheimer and Donald G. Marshall, 2nd ed. (New York: Crossroad, 1989), 184-97.

79. G. Picht has indirectly identified the decisive feature of poietic reason, the feature that is at the same time its genuine accomplishment, namely, design. "Every work a human being is able to complete actually becomes possible through a preceding design. . . . Because such designing is a fundamental feature of all art, thinking is then also an art if it is essentially an activity of designing" ("Die Kunst des Denkens," in Picht, *Wahrheit — Vernunft — Verantwortung. Philosophische Studien* [Stuttgart: E. Klett, 1969], 427-34; here 431f.). He then succinctly articulates the extent to which such "models" (the central concept of metaphorical constructivism) are actually designs or outlines within the framework of poietic reason: "Those who wish to make something must possess an image before their inner perception of that which is to be made. The activity of 'making' is always the actualization of a model, and in everyday language we refer to these anticipatory models as designs or outlines. The primary content of such a design would accordingly be the image, model, or schema of an inner perception" (432). Precisely this framework of production logic is decisive for metaphorical constructivism, since its most prominent representatives are indeed concerned with the production of a new, transformed reality. Cf. S. McFague, *Metaphorical Theology: Models of God in Religious Language* (Philadelphia: Fortress, 1982). Cf. also the introduction "Theology as Construction," in G. Kaufman's *magnum opus, In the Face of Mystery: A Constructive Theology* (Cambridge, Mass.: Harvard University Press, 1993), 3-93. Another prominent representative of this direction is P. Hodgson, whose theological efforts are oriented toward Hegel's philosophy of religion and are summarized in his recent systematic theology, *Winds of the Spirit: A Constructive Christian Theology* (Louisville: Westminster/John Knox, 1994). Although

these admittedly merely representative but certainly authoritative theologians do indeed differ in many points, their common point of departure is still the basically constructivist character of all theology. To that extent, all are interested in various ways in poietic "reconstruction," that is, in proposals that are self-transparent as constructions and are more commensurate with contemporary perceptions and problems than are more "traditional" and by now "obsolete" constructions.

80. During his early period, Schleiermacher was still able to "tame," as it were, his own, poietically oriented hermeneutics theologically within the framework of a reality of faith and ethics variously constituted in a concrete fashion from the perspective of the church. This enabled him to present a theologically coherent picture of the more organic "poiesis" taking place communally within an ecclesiastical community. By contrast, in carrying on the Romantic program of poiesis, "theology" inevitably itself becomes a poietic undertaking under the conditions of intensified religious pluralism and the disappearance of the state church; it is within this undertaking itself that devotion and piety are expressed both immediately and multifariously. The difference between poietic theologies and individual expressions of faith is that the former use new metaphors to invite believers to see things in a certain way and to motivate them to engage in certain kinds of behavior. Whether and to what extent such theologies are "true," that which makes them preferable to other constructions is their "success" within a horizon of meaning and values, albeit a horizon that is itself poietically construed at the same time. Cf. in this regard especially the programmatically unequivocal works of S. McFague, *Models of God: Theology for an Ecological, Nuclear Age* (Philadelphia: Fortress, 1987), and *The Body of God: An Ecological Theology* (Minneapolis: Fortress, 1993).

81. Sydney E. Ahlstrom, *A Religious History of the American People* (New Haven: Yale University Press, 1972), 605. Cf. C. West, *The American Evasion of Philosophy: A Genealogy of Pragmatism* (Madison: University of Wisconsin Press, 1989), 17. The roots of this thinking, however, do probably go back even further to the beginnings of the modern experiential sciences and their concept of theory, a concept whose problematic consequences for all of modern civilization have only gradually become noticeable. Cf. in this regard R. Spaemann, "Überzeugungen in einer hypothetischen Zivilisation," in *Abschied von Utopia? Anspruch und Auftrag der Intellektuellen,* ed. O. Schatz (Graz, Vienna, and Cologne: Styria, 1977), 311-31: "What counts is what can be reconstructed in a theory. Theory is our own free creation. It is not *theoria* in the classical sense, not perception. It is not concerned with answering the naive question, 'What is that,' but rather the question, 'How does that function.' Thomas Hobbes said that to know something means 'to know what we can do with it when we have it'" (313).

82. In his genealogy of pragmatism, C. West shows how this particular impulse runs through American pragmatism all the way to Richard Rorty, one of the leading neo-pragmatic philosophers. Rorty sees "the poet rather than the priest, the philosopher or the scientist as the paradigmatic human being. . . . the poet, in the general sense of the maker of new words, the shaper of new languages, as the vanguard of the

species" (*The American Evasion of Philosophy,* 204). Within a completely different context of tradition, Rorty makes statements recalling Hölderlin and Schelling.

83. Cf. in this regard especially N. Lobkowicz, *Theory and Practice;* G. Picht, "Der Sinn der Unterscheidung von Theorie und Praxis in der griechischen Philosophie," in Picht, *Wahrheit — Vernunft — Verantwortung,* 108-40; G. Bien, T. Kobusch, and H. Kleger, "Praxis, praktisch," in *Historisches Wörterbuch der Philosophie,* 7:1277-1307.

84. Bubner, 70.

85. Aristotle, *Nicomachean Ethics* 1098, 21f.; cf. Bubner, 70.

86. This distinction also enables one to understand, e.g., the life of Christian faith as a comprehensive praxis of faith, as the active actualization of the life of faith, albeit a life whose purpose, in its Reformation understanding, is not to bring forth "products" (precisely this is "freedom from works"); rather, the "good works" to which Christians are doubtless called are understood as the inherent actualization of precisely this praxis of faith. Eph. 2:10 reflects this distinction in an interesting way: "For we are what he has made us, created in Christ Jesus for good works, which God prepared beforehand to be our way of life" (NRSV). As God's poiesis, these works are the implication of the *nova creatura,* which itself is the work of God's re-creative salvific action, and as such constitute straightaway the actualization of the faith praxis of this *nova creatura.* "Good works" are precisely not such "products" of faith, nor are they the telos of any productive activity; as such, they remain rather the results of God's own creative action.

87. Cf. in this regard J. Ritter, "Die Lehre vom Ursprung und Sinn der Theorie bei Aristoteles," in Ritter, *Metaphysik und Politik. Studien zu Aristoteles und Hegel,* 2nd ed. (Frankfurt am Main: Suhrkamp, 1988), 9-33. In the words of G. Picht: "The ontological basis for the distinction between theory and praxis is the distinction between being and time, between the absolute and the contingent, between the God of Greek philosophy and the human being subject to mortality" ("Der Sinn der Unterscheidung," 135).

88. Dunne, 238. Two different life-forms correspond to this antithesis between theory and praxis: the βίος θεωρητικός and the βίος πρακτικός. Even though *theoria* as a perception or intuition of eternal truths and praxis as the political-social actualization of life are strictly separated such that the former cannot be transferred into the latter, theory can nonetheless be expressed in two ways within practical life contexts. First, an exclusive dedication to *theoria* involves a life-form (βίος) requiring a long period of discipline, since it does make, so to speak, "superhuman" demands on a person. The capacity for *theoria* is acquired only through *askesis,* long-term discipline. This life-form thus has practical, pedagogical implications insofar as it transforms the character of those who in the course of *askesis* do indeed engage in it. Second, not only does this educational aspect have psychological significance, but within the framework of *mimesis* the character of the "theoretician" also conforms to the object of that *theoria* itself, that is, to the order and harmony of the cosmos. Cf. Dunne, 239. Moreover, the βίος θεωρητικός also fulfills the criterion of praxis insofar as it does not bring forth any object outside itself; rather, *sophia* or *episteme* constitutes the

inherent actualization of this life-form. This explains why Aristotle operates with both an *extended (bios; praxis tis)* and a *narrower,* specific concept of praxis. Cf. again in this regard Dunne, 157.

89. MacIntyre, 187.

90. In his doctoral dissertation, "The Reappearance of the Visible Church: An Analysis of the Production and Reproduction of Christian Identity" (diss., Duke University, 1991), P. Kenneson persuasively illustrates this point. Cf. esp. 278-84.

91. It is certainly possible (though not necessary for these specific actualizations) that, commensurate with MacIntyre's own articulation, the insight into the various goals and goods can be continually expanded within each framework.

92. Every practice thus also has its own history, and successful engagement in a specific practice requires not only an introduction to and acquisition of its implicit rules, but also an introduction to its history, a history providing the backdrop against which present engagement with it is disclosed. Cf. the more detailed discussion in C. Dykstra, "Reconceiving Practice," in *Shifting Boundaries: Contextual Approaches to the Structure of Theological Education,* ed. B. Wheeler and E. Farley (Louisville: Westminster/John Knox, 1991), 35-66, and D. Kelsey, *To Understand God Truly: What's Theological about a Theological School?* (Louisville: Westminster/John Knox, 1992), 118-24.

93. Bayer, *Theologie,* 43f. Bayer may, however, be projecting a modern concept of theory back onto the theology from which Luther polemically distances himself. "Luther saw quite clearly that those for whom the gospel is a theory, a 'human poem and idea,' necessarily must demand that this gospel also be actualized in praxis. In the schema of theory and praxis, they fall into error and say, 'Faith is not enough; one must also perform works,' or put differently: sanctification must be added to justification as a second act, as the human response to God's word. Luther saw that the degree to which the word that grounds faith pales into a theory and idea is precisely the degree to which the realization of this idea in praxis must be demanded. The theoretization of faith corresponds to a moralization of life. The theoretization of faith and of the word that creates faith corresponds precisely to the demand to actualize that which one has first and beforehand allowed to pale into an idea" (*Theologie,* 48f.). This is confirmed by the context of this particular citation, one in which Bayer is taking issue with the theoretization (from the perspective of a theology of the cross) and principalization of the gospel of the sort that began with Hegel. The category of actualization is a modern one; similarly, only within the context of modernity can something "pale" into a theory. This notion would be a self-contradiction for the understanding of *theoria* in antiquity as well as for the medieval notion of *contemplatio.*

94. One critical remark is in order here, namely, that even the early church radically altered the ancient understanding of the *vita contemplativa* and the *vita activa.* It did so first by associating the two, e.g., in the Benedictine *ora et labora* or in Chrysostom's assertion that all who are baptized are actually called to the *contemplatio* of prayer; and second by radically altering its content, e.g., where the two life-forms were kept separate in the juxtaposition of monastic and general Christian life-forms. Cf. in this regard the perspective of political theory in H. Arendt, *The Hu-*

man Condition, 2nd ed.(Chicago: University of Chicago Press, 1998), 73-78, and passim, and with a positive view also J. Bethke Elshtain, *Public Man, Private Woman: Women in Social and Political Thought* (Princeton: Princeton University Press, 1981).

95. Such include at least the proclamation of the gospel, commemoration of the law, celebration of the Lord's Supper, and baptism.

96. These include among other things also theology as a church practice. By also mentioning commemoration of the saints and martyrs (so to speak, purely *gymnastikos*), I do so to point out that the classification of many practices into these categories is confessionally disputed. For example, for Catholics and Orthodox, confession belongs quite naturally in the first category; for the Reformation tradition, it belongs theologically in the second category, and as regards practical considerations of life in the third.

97. This would include especially the traditional Christmas celebration on December 25, and in particular the tradition of the Christmas tree. This particular activity of actualization enjoys questionable worldwide acceptance without in this form or at precisely this time being necessary or constitutive for the practice of the Christian faith.

98. Given the great popularity enjoyed by the concept of "process" in broad theological circles today, it is appropriate to point out that a categorical distinction obtains between a *practice* and a *process*. Practices are not processes, since the latter are an inherent constituent part of *poietic logic,* according to which any given process is evaluated from the perspective of the specific result it produces. It stands or falls with the quality of its result, a result which, quite in the sense of a product, can also exist in and for itself. By contrast, although practices do indeed under certain circumstances generate by-products, their goal is never an end product as such. The goal and purpose of every practice is and remains to perform it as well as possible.

99. Hence all practices are concerned with the *quality* of their actualization, a quality determined by the telos of the practice in question. The logic of practice itself thus already inherently distinguishes between correct and false as well as between good and bad performance or actualization. The former is concerned with *whether or not* the performance or actualization of a specific practice attains its telos, the latter with the *way* in which that telos, the telos inherent in every practice, is actually attained. The understanding of theology in Part Four as a necessary church practice thus inherently distinguishes between better and worse actualization on the one hand and false and correct actualization on the other.

Notes to Part Two

1. Cf. in this regard J.-F. Lyotard, *The Postmodern Condition: A Report on Knowledge,* trans. Geoff Bennington and Brian Massumi, foreword by Fredric Jameson (Minneapolis: University of Minnesota Press, 1984); W. Welsch, *Unsere postmoderne Moderne,* 4th ed. (Berlin: Akademie, 1993); and R. Bernstein, *The New*

Constellation: The Ethical-Political Horizons of Modernity/Postmodernity, 2nd ed. (Cambridge: MIT Press, 1993).

2. George A. Lindbeck, *The Nature of Doctrine: Religion and Theology in a Postliberal Age* (Philadelphia: Westminster, 1984); German edition, *Christliche Lehre als Grammatik des Glaubens. Religion und Theologie in einam postliberalen Zeitalter,* trans. Markus Müller, ed. H. G. Ulrich and R. Hütter, Theologische Bücherei 90 (Gütersloh: C. Kaiser/Gütersloher Verlagshaus, 1994). Concerning the discussion and reception of the book in Germany, cf. the bibliography in the German edition. The German translation has material not contained in the English original, and will be referenced as such when necessary.

3. Cf. the bibliography in *Christliche Lehre,* 205f.

4. Cf. the introduction to the German edition, pp. 7-15.

5. One can even go so far as to say that his book is inevitably misunderstood apart from this ecumenical context. So especially H. W. Frei, Lindbeck's longtime colleague at Yale University: "Without the absolute priority of that Christian-ecumenical reality, without its reality, forget the 'rule' or regulative approach, forget the cultural-linguistic theory — forget the book" (in *Theology and Dialogue,* ed. B. Marshall [Notre Dame: University of Notre Dame Press, 1990], 278).

6. Cf. in this regard C. Taylor, *Sources of the Self: The Making of Modern Identity* (Cambridge: Harvard University Press, 1989), esp. 111-210 and 305-92.

7. Cf. as representative in this regard the cross section in R. Rorty, ed., *The Linguistic Turn: Recent Essays in Philosophical Method* (Chicago: University of Chicago Press, 1967).

8. Cf. in this regard C. Geertz, *The Interpretation of Cultures: Selected Essays* (New York: Basic Books, 1973).

9. Cf. in this regard R. Bernstein, *Beyond Objectivism and Relativism: Science, Hermeneutics, and Praxis,* 2nd ed. (Philadelphia: University of Pennsylvania Press, 1985), whose insights have been theologically appropriated by R. Thiemann, *Revelation and Theology: The Gospel as Narrated Promise* (Notre Dame: University of Notre Dame Press, 1985).

10. Lindbeck, *The Nature of Doctrine,* 16.

11. A typical example of an understanding of dogma according to the experiential-expressive model is H. Jonas, "Über die hermeneutische Struktur des Dogmas," in Jonas, *Augustin und das paulinische Freiheitsproblem. Eine philosophische Studie zum Pelagianischen Streit,* appendix I, 2nd ed. (Göttingen: Vandenhoeck & Ruprecht, 1965), 80-89.

12. Lindbeck, *The Nature of Doctrine,* 17.

13. Schleiermacher offers the paradigmatic models for both alternatives, namely, the *Christian Faith* for the descriptive alternative and the *Speeches on Religion* for the radically poietic alternative. "It is not the person who believes in a holy writing who has religion, but only the one who needs none and probably could even make one for himself" (*On Religion: Speeches to Its Cultured Despisers,* trans. and ed. Richard Crouter [Cambridge: Cambridge University Press, 1996], 50). Christian propositions of faith are "accounts of the Christian religious affections set forth in speech"

(*The Christian Faith,* trans. H. R. Mackintosh and J. S. Stewart from 2nd German ed. [Edinburgh: T. & T. Clark, 1928], 76). Cf. in this regard the previous discussion (Part One) under "Poiesis" concerning metaphorical constructivism.

14. Lindbeck, *The Nature of Doctrine,* 32.

15. Lindbeck, *The Nature of Doctrine,* 33.

16. Cf. Lindbeck, *The Nature of Doctrine,* 9-12.

17. The theoretical distinction between "context of justification" and "context of discovery" derives from H. Reichenbach, *Experience and Prediction: An Analysis on the Foundations and the Structure of Knowledge* (Chicago: University of Chicago Press, 1938); *The Rise of Scientific Philosophy* (Berkeley and Los Angeles: University of California Press, 1951), and in the German context especially H. Albert, *Traktat über kritische Vernunft* (Tübingen: Mohr, 1968), 37-41. G. Sauter then introduced this distinction into theological discourse, especially in critical discussion with "contextual theology," whose quite justified concern he tried to appropriate constructively by way of this fundamental distinction on the one hand, but whose comprehensive conceptual claim to validity (beginning with the epistemological primacy of context) he was nonetheless able to restrict with the aid of just this distinction on the other. Cf. in this regard esp. Sauter, "Wie kann Theologie aus Erfahrungen entstehen?" in *Theologie im Entstehen. Beiträge zum ökumenischen Gespräch im Spannungsfeld kirchlicher Situationen,* ed. L. Vischer, Theologische Bücherei 59 (Munich: Kaiser, 1976), 99-118, and Sauter et al., *Wissenschaftstheoretische Kritik der Theologie. Die Theologie und die neuere wissenschaftstheoretische Diskussion* (Munich: Kaiser, 1973), 308-15, 356. In the process Sauter transports this theoretical distinction ultimately into a *theological* distinction between the manifold social, political, and cultural contexts in which church and theology always find themselves within contemporary circumstances on the one hand, and the context unique to them on the other, that is, the context already given and shaped by God's salvific action. He distinguishes *theologically* between a theological context of justification and various contexts of discovery of theology. With reference to 1 Pet. 3:15 (the accounting for the ground of hope demanded of all Christians), Sauter characterizes the theological context of justification in a way largely coinciding with our own understanding of the pathos of theology: "Precisely because this ground [of hope] cannot be produced by any human deed or conceptual activity, it permits a justified discourse that is just as distinct from any form of theoretical or practical self-justification or self-grounding as it is from alleged 'justifications' that are merely supposed to justify before the public forum one's own spiritual existence or the motivation of one's own behavioral choices" (*In der Freiheit des Geistes. Theologische Studien* [Göttingen: Vandenhoeck & Ruprecht, 1988], 177). To distinguish between contexts of discovery and justification means to emphasize the asymmetry and discontinuity of the two within their indissoluble juxtaposition in contemporary theological circumstances; the freedom of theology alone can keep these from being functionalized: "The theological context of justification is of a different sort than the historic, cultural, social context of discovery, for it does not present something to which theology was notoriously simply able to react, but contains rather an answer *not prefigured in the question.* . . . With the distinction between context of jus-

tification and context of discovery, I am referring to two conceptual forms of Christian theology that in the past two decades have frequently been played out against one another, often as the alternatives of 'dogmatic' and 'contextual' theology within ecumenical debates. . . . This confrontation evokes an extremely old, albeit not always clearly articulated problem encountered by theology, namely, the relationship between its 'temporally qualified' insights and the perpetual questions belonging to the character of theology itself" (*In der Freiheit des Geistes*, 180). In the following discussion I will try to integrate into the conception of theology as a church practice Sauter's *theologically* qualified distinction between the context of discovery and the context of justification of theology, and with the aid of this distinction to articulate meaningfully especially the relationship between the argumentative-discursive aspect and the aspect of perception and of judgment, and at the same time to preserve the pathos of theology from poietic functionalization.

18. Lindbeck, *The Nature of Doctrine*, 34.

19. "Rather, to become religious — no less than to become culturally or linguistically competent — is to interiorize a set of skills by practice and training. One learns how to feel, act, and think in conformity with a religious tradition that is, in its inner structure, far richer and more subtle than can be explicitly articulated" (Lindbeck, *The Nature of Doctrine*, 35).

20. Lindbeck, *The Nature of Doctrine*, 34.

21. J. Milbank, *Theology and Social Theory: Beyond Secular Reason* (Oxford and Cambridge, Mass.: B. Blackwell, 1990), 382, quite rightly points out that "[t]he subjective, therefore, is conserved not in Cartesian or Kantian interiority, but rather in a Spinozan or Leibnizian structural positionality, which makes it at once 'more objective,' and at the same time less universal, and more confined to a perspective. In consequence, the realm of feelings, affections, aspirations and experiences can no longer pose as a new site of universality, a firm 'base' in which to locate the religious, and on which to build a theology."

22. "There are numberless thoughts we cannot think, sentiments we cannot have, and realities we cannot perceive unless we learn to use the appropriate symbol systems" (Lindbeck, *The Nature of Doctrine*, 34).

23. Lindbeck, *The Nature of Doctrine*, 36f.

24. Cf. discussion below.

25. Cf. the definition of a "saint" from the Lutheran perspective in H. G. Anderson, J. F. Stafford, and J. A. Burgess, eds., *The One Mediator, the Saints and Mary*, Lutherans and Catholics in Dialogue VIII (Minneapolis: Augsburg, 1992), 39.

26. Cf. Lindbeck, *The Nature of Doctrine*, 35f., the declaration of convergence, implying precisely this point.

27. Lindbeck, *The Nature of Doctrine*, 36.

28. ". . . the language they have begun to learn *ex auditu* . . ." (Lindbeck, *The Nature of Doctrine*, 61).

29. Cf. Lindbeck, *The Nature of Doctrine*, 132f.

30. A catechetical theology in secularized Europe at the end of the twentieth century must look different from one in the sixteenth century at the same place, or

from one in Muslim Syria in the eighth or ninth century, or in Japan in the nineteenth century.

31. "Similarly, a postliberal approach need not exclude an ad hoc apologetics, but only one that is systematically prior and controlling in the fashion of post-Cartesian natural theology and of later liberalism. As Aquinas himself notes, reasoning in support of the faith is not meritorious before faith, but only afterward; or, in the conceptuality employed in this book, the logic of coming to believe, because it is like that of learning a language, has little room for argument, but once one has learned to speak the language of faith, argument becomes possible" (Lindbeck, *The Nature of Doctrine,* 131f.).

32. See discussion below, pp. 61f.

33. Not surprisingly, Roman Catholic theologians have raised vehement questions regarding just this aspect of Lindbeck's proposal. Cf. in this regard especially C. E. O'Neil, "The Rule Theory of Doctrine and Propositional Truth," *Thomist* 49 (1985): 417-42, and D. Tracy, "Lindbeck's New Program for Theology: A Reflection," *Thomist* 49 (1985): 460-72. Within the German-speaking context, two extremely interesting Catholic contributions are noteworthy, namely, W. Kasper, "Postmoderne Dogmatik? Zu einer neueren nordamerikanischen Grundlagendiskussion," in *Der Weg zum Menschen. Zur philosophischen und theologischen Anthropologie. Festschrift Alfons Deissler,* ed. R. Mosis and L. Ruppert (Freiburg im Breisgau: Herder, 1989), 265-74, and M. Knapp, "Postmoderne Dogmatik? Überlegungen zu einer Grundlagendiskussion im Anschluss an einen Vorschlag von George A. Lindbeck," *Münchener theologische Zeitschrift* 45 (1994): 1-10.

34. Here Lindbeck is referring to J. L. Austin's theory of speech acts, and especially to the latter's understanding of the performatory use of language: "A religious utterance, one might say, acquires the propositional truth of ontological correspondence only insofar as it is a performance, an act or deed, which helps create that correspondence" (Lindbeck, *The Nature of Doctrine,* 65).

35. This view corresponds exactly to his ecclesiological thesis of the church as a community of witnesses. Cf. the discussion below.

36. So, among others, Kasper, "Postmoderne Dogmatik?" and Knapp, "Postmoderne Dogmatik?"

37. Lindbeck, *The Nature of Doctrine,* 64.

38. Lindbeck, *The Nature of Doctrine,* 65.

39. George Hunsinger, "Truth as Self-Involving: Barth and Lindbeck on the Cognitive and Performative Aspects of Truth in Theological Discourse," *Journal of the American Academy of Religion* 61 (1993): 43.

40. Hunsinger, 47.

41. Hunsinger, 48.

42. Although dogmas or church doctrines are indeed to be understood primarily as regulatives, still, because they refer to the praxis of faith or to the overall life context of the church, they cannot be separated from the latter. They emerge as regulatives from the overall life context of the church and then return to it, shaping it as regulatives. As such, they always implicitly claim a correspondence with truth even

though this is not their primary function. On the other hand, neither are "first-order propositions" really concerned primarily with truth correspondence as Lindbeck implies, but rather with the *soteriological telos* of theology that itself is one with faith. Here God's salvific action comes to expression in worship, prayer, and so on, and here, too, truth correspondence, although implied, is actually secondary. The concern here is similarly with a performative moment, albeit now with the word of God that itself creates a new reality. This would be a *theological* version of the discussion of truth correspondence, a version that would evade any fixed metaphysical determination within the framework of a given ontology.

43. Lindbeck's "agnostic" reading of Aquinas's doctrine of analogy (cf. *The Nature of Doctrine*, 66f., and B. Marshall, "Thomas Aquinas as Postliberal Theologian," *Thomist* 53 [1989]: 353-402) can be understood as a theological move in this direction, as an attempt to alter the metaphysical question into a genuinely theological one. If the *res significata* and the *modus significandi* in the analogous knowledge of God are as totally different as Lindbeck's reading of Aquinas suggests, there emerges space for a theological perspective in which God's self-demonstration takes the place of the *modus significandi;* this perspective automatically raises Hunsinger's question whether God's own performance (in the sense of a Barthian *analogia fidei*) configures the *modus significandi* such that from the human perspective it can only be engaged performatively-propositionally as "poietic pathos" or as an "active undergoing" of God's own performative action.

44. A curious example in Lindbeck intends precisely this logic: "To say, for example, that marriage vows are performative, i.e., create the reality of marriage, is to deny that they are propositional, i.e., correspond to a prior reality of marriage. Yet, if the banality may be permitted, in a marriage genuinely made in heaven, the earthly promises would produce a 'propositional' correspondence of one reality to another. If this example has any merit, it suggests one way in which a statement can be conceived of as having the propositional force of an ontological truth claim about objective reality even though it does not fit the classical model of a proposition as an *adaequatio mentis ad rem*" (*The Nature of Doctrine*, 65f.).

45. Truth coherence stands in the foreground because it supports the regulatory character of doctrines, thus making possible in the first place the ecumenically initiatory discussion of the doctrinal formulations of Nicaea and Chalcedon, of the Marian dogmatic developments, and of the doctrine of infallibility. Precisely because their use in the practical context of faith and thus the question of their ontological truth is bracketed out, the grammatical sense of these doctrines can be discussed such that the doctrines themselves can be the object of consensus among all parties. Although Lindbeck sets aside for the moment the ontological truth of church doctrines, he does not exclude it. Hence, although his distinction is indeed heuristically valuable for ecumenical dialogue, the inner logic of his own model undermines it, since it implies a dialectical intertwining of truth correspondence and truth coherence which he himself cannot conceptionally carry through.

46. Lindbeck, *The Nature of Doctrine*, 69. Lindbeck does quite justifiably point out that as rules, doctrines do naturally also imply propositions, albeit second-order

propositions: "The rules formulated by the linguist or the logician, for example, express propositional convictions about how language or thought actually work. These are, however, second-order rather than first-order propositions and affirm nothing about extra-linguistic or extra-human reality" (80).

47. Lindbeck, *The Nature of Doctrine*, 74.

48. "In any case, it is not the lexicon but rather the grammar of the religion which church doctrines chiefly reflect. Some doctrines, such as those delimiting the canon and specifying the relation of Scripture and tradition, help determine the vocabulary; while others (or sometimes the same ones) instantiate syntactical rules that guide the use of this material in construing the world, community, and self, and still others provide semantic reference" (Lindbeck, *The Nature of Doctrine*, 81).

49. Lindbeck illustrates the implications of this access and its capability in a series of difficult cases from ecumenical dialogue, including the christological results of the councils of Nicaea and Chalcedon, Mariology, and the dogma of infallibility. Cf. in this regard, *The Nature of Doctrine*, 91-111.

50. Lindbeck, *The Nature of Doctrine*, 76.

51. Lindbeck, *The Nature of Doctrine*, 76.

52. Lindbeck, *The Nature of Doctrine*, 107.

53. Concerning the terminology "context of discovery" and "context of justification," cf. n. 17 in this chapter and section III in Part Four.

54. Lindbeck, *The Nature of Doctrine*, 113, my emphasis.

55. This inevitably makes these extratextual theologies into strategies of ultimate grounding.

56. Lindbeck, *The Nature of Doctrine*, 114.

57. Lindbeck, *The Nature of Doctrine*, 114f.

58. Lindbeck, *The Nature of Doctrine*, 115.

59. Lindbeck, *The Nature of Doctrine*, 117.

60. Lindbeck, *The Nature of Doctrine*, 118. Here Lindbeck is obviously referring to Luther's theological-hermeneutical principle that the Bible as Scripture interprets its reader rather than the reverse. O. Bayer has formulated this quite succinctly with reference to one of Luther's own formulations: "'Note that the power of scripture is as follows: it is not transformed into the person who studies it, but rather transforms the person who loves it into itself and into its powers.' It is not the interpreter who interprets scripture, but scripture that interprets the interpreter. Scripture thus provides for its own interpretation, is its own interpreter. *Sacra scriptura sui ipsius interpres*" (*Autorität und Kritik. Zur Hermeneutik und Wissenschaftstheorie* [Tübingen: J. C. B. Mohr, 1991], 6). Bayer's interpretation, though, does substantially intensify Luther's core hermeneutical idea. Whereas for Lindbeck hermeneutics remains a "poietic pathos" for which interpretive poiesis, that is, the process of actively drawing the world into the text, remains central as the activity of the interpreter, Bayer radicalizes this perspective. The interpreter himself or herself proves to be part of the world that is to be interpreted; in being interpreted by the Bible, the interpreter is "drawn into" the Bible. Bayer, I think, quite justifiably radicalizes this pathos over against Lindbeck. There is no place where the interpreter can engage in the poietic pathos of intra-

textual theology without himself or herself being interpreted ever anew by the biblical text.

61. The crucial difference between a typological and a metaphorical exegesis cannot be overemphasized. Cf. esp. the important essay by the Jewish exegete and religious scholar J. Levenson, who shows the decisive difference between Martin Luther King's Exodus-typology and the metaphorical use of the Exodus by the liberation theologian and exegete G. V. Pixley; cf. "Exodus and Liberation," in Levenson, *The Hebrew Bible, the Old Testament, and Historical Criticism: Jews and Christians in Biblical Studies* (Louisville: Westminster/John Knox, 1993), 127-59. Cf. in this regard also the foundational study by G. Sauter, "'Exodus' und 'Befreiung' als theologische Metaphern. Ein Beispiel zur Kritik von Allegorese und mißverstandenen Analogien in der Ethik," *Evangelische Theologie* 38 (1978): 538-59.

62. Lindbeck, *The Nature of Doctrine*, 113, my emphasis.

63. Here I am using a key concept ("einfache Gottesrede") from F. Mildenberger, who is addressing specifically this kind of intratextuality; cf. in this regard Mildenberger, *Biblische Dogmatik. Eine Biblische Theologie in dogmatischer Perspektive*, vol. 1, *Prolegomena. Verstehen und Geltung der Bibel* (Stuttgart: W. Kohlhammer, 1991), 11-30.

64. Cf. in this regard the pointed critique of Milbank, 382-88.

65. An indication of the preliminary nature of this formalism is that the author's argumentative structure nonetheless turns out to be Lutheran.

66. Cf. Milbank, 382-88.

67. Similarly Milbank, 382-88.

68. Cf. in this regard the recent work by S. Hauerwas, *Unleashing the Scripture: Freeing the Bible from Captivity to America* (Nashville: Abingdon, 1993).

69. It is worth noting in this regard that Lindbeck's interpretation of "infallibility" already implies such a practice of judgment. Cf. *The Nature of Doctrine*, 98-104.

70. The following publications by Lindbeck are of importance in this context: "Ecumenism and the Future of Belief," *Una Sancta* (Brooklyn, N.Y.) 25, no. 3 (1968): 3-17; "The Sectarian Future of the Church," in *The God Experience*, ed. J. P. Whelan, S.J. (New York: Newman, 1971), 226-43; "The Story-Shaped Church: Critical Exegesis and Theological Interpretation," in *Scriptural Authority and Narrative Interpretation: Festschrift Hans W. Frei*, ed. Garrett Green (Philadelphia: Fortress, 1987), 161-78; "The Church," in *Keeping the Faith: Essays to Mark the Centenary of Lux Mundi*, ed. G. Wainwright (Philadelphia and Allison Park: Fortress, 1988), 178-208; "The Church's Mission to a Postmodern Culture," in *Postmodern Theology: Christian Faith in a Pluralist World*, ed. F. Burnham (New York: Harper & Row, 1989), 37-55; "Ecumenical Imperatives for the Twenty-First Century," *Currents in Theology and Mission* 20 (1993): 360-66.

71. Lindbeck is not, of course, concerned with physical survival, but with the ongoing identity of the gospel and of the proclaiming and witnessing church.

72. "The referential force of this narrative code can be analyzed into distinct aspects. First, the identity and being of the church rests on God's election, not on its faithfulness. Second, as an implicate of this, the elect communities are stamped by ob-

jective marks which are both blessing and curse depending on how they are received. Eating and drinking, Paul reminds us, can be unto judgment (1 Cor. 11:29) and not only life, and the same applies to circumcision and baptism, the *shema* and the *apostolicum*. Even when the sacraments are spiritualized, as by Quakers, the profession that the Christ spoken of in Scripture is the Lord can be a publicly unmistakable brandmark of the group's election. Third, election is communal. Individuals are elect by virtue of visible membership in God's people. Last, the primary mission of this chosen people is to witness to the God who judges and who saves, not to save those who would otherwise be damned (for God has not confined his saving work exclusively to the church's ministrations). It testifies to this God whether or not it wills to do so, whether it is faithful or unfaithful. The final consummation which has begun in Christ is proleptically present in this people as nowhere else, but so also is the eschatological judgment (1 Pet. 4:17; cf. Amos 3:2 and Jer. 25:29). The church thus identified sounds Catholic in its comprehensiveness, Calvinist in the unconditionality of its chosenness, and Lutheran in its possibilities of unfaithfulness while remaining genuinely the church; but the total effect, not surprisingly, is more Jewish than anything else. . . . Also Jewish sounding is the church's mission. It is above all by the character of its communal life that it witnesses, that it proclaims the gospel and serves the world. . . . Christians have as much reason as Jews to eschew heedless invitations to outsiders . . . to bear the burdens of election. The possibilities of damnation as well as of salvation are increased within the people of God (think of the story of Ananias and Sapphira in Acts 5 or, as far as that goes, of Judas). . . . The purpose of that presence of salvation, furthermore, is witness, and it is up to God to add whom he will to the company (Acts 2:47). Churches should not imitate the Pharisees, whom Jesus condemned for compassing land and sea to make proselytes (Matt. 23:15), but should rather follow the practice that prevailed in the first centuries of prolonged catechesis. The primary Christian mission, in short, is not to save souls but to be a faithfully witnessing people" (Lindbeck, "The Church," 192-94).

73. Lindbeck, *The Nature of Doctrine*, 113.

74. Oswald Bayer, *Theologie*, Handbuch Systematischer Theologie 1 (Gütersloh: Gütersloher Verlagshaus G. Mohn, 1994), 403.

75. Oswald Bayer, *Was ist das: Theologie? Eine Skizze* (Stuttgart: Calwer, 1973); *Umstrittene Freiheit. Theologisch-philosophische Kontroversen* (Tübingen: J. C. B. Mohr, 1981); *Autorität und Kritik; Leibliches Wort. Reformation und Neuzeit im Konflikt* (Tübingen: J. C. B. Mohr, 1992).

76. Bayer, *Theologie*, Handbuch Systematischer Theologie 1 (Gütersloh: Gütersloher Verlagshaus G. Mohn, 1994).

77. In addition to the fascinating and constructive elements of his critical Luther reception, Bayer thereby simultaneously perpetuates one of the enduring weaknesses of Lutheran theology.

78. Cf. Bayer, *Theologie*, 409. "By saying that sinful humanity and the justifying God constitute the object of theology, or, put differently, the deadening word of the law and the vivifying word of the gospel, we are not saying that this object is something given in the positivistic sense; it is not a dead object about which one might

draw conclusions or make statements. The object is a living, dramatic event, one which, it seems, can be as little depicted as can a bird in flight, but which must nonetheless be taught" (410f.).

79. Bayer, *Theologie,* 413.

80. Bayer, *Theologie,* 413.

81. Bayer, *Autorität und Kritik,* 184.

82. Bayer, *Theologie,* 417. Bayer does concede the difficulty in conceiving the *usus elenchticus legis* together with the *primus usus* under the overriding term "law." "Clarity is served by understanding and emphasizing the categorially independent character of the *usus politicus legis* (which is more God's gentle presence than his fourth encounter)" (417).

83. Luther, *Weimar Ausgabe,* 5, 163, 28f. "A theologian is made through living, and even more so through death and damnation, rather than through understanding, reading, and speculating."

84. Bayer, *Theologie,* 61. I believe the decisive point of Bayer's understanding of the significance of *oratio, meditatio, tentatio* is lost if they are not understood strictly as a *practice* of pathos. For the pathos in question here, the *vita passiva,* has its own practice, albeit not a practice in which it is "realized" (this is the false production logic of theory and praxis), but rather in which it is engaged and implemented ever anew. Bayer does quite justifiably refer to the ecclesiological significance of Ps. 119 for Luther, though only in the sense that in it a petition or prayer is made for the sake of the church itself as *creatura verbi,* as "creature of the Word." The conditions of modernity, on the other hand, make it necessary to articulate explicitly the other side of the ecclesiological significance of the *oratio, meditatio, tentatio,* one that for Luther was a self-evident part of his own monastic praxis (cf. in this regard esp. M. Nicol, *Meditation bei Luther,* Forschungen zur Kirchen- und Dogmengeschichte 34 [Göttingen: Vandenhoeck & Ruprecht, 1984]), and to do this in a way Bayer does not, namely, such that the reference is to a concretely implemented *church practice* in which the entire scope of those who are baptized is to engage regularly.

85. Bayer, *Theologie,* 69.

86. "First, know that the Holy Scriptures are a book that makes the wisdom of all other books look foolish because none of them teaches about eternal life besides this one. This is why you should give up straightaway on your own sense and understanding. For you will not attain it through them, and your presumptuousness will only plunge both you and others with you down from heaven into the abyss of hell (as happened to Lucifer)" (Bayer, *Theologie,* 71, cited from Luther, *Weimar Ausgabe,* 50, 659, 5-10).

87. "You should also meditate, that is: not only in your heart, but you should also engage externally and constantly by loud reading and rereading with industrious attentiveness and reflection, what the Holy Spirit means by it. And beware lest you become bored or think you've read, heard, said it once or twice and that's enough, and that you already understand it completely. Such a person will never be much of a theologian, but will be like the unripe fruit that falls to the ground before it has even half-ripened.... For God will not give you his Spirit without the external word, so act

accordingly. For he has not commanded us for nothing to write, preach, read, hear, sing, speak, etc. externally" (Bayer, *Theologie*, 83, cited from Luther, *Weimar Ausgabe*, 50, 659, 22-35).

88. Bayer, *Theologie*, 85.

89. Bayer, *Theologie*, 86f.

90. Bayer, *Theologie*, 89.

91. Bayer, *Theologie*, 94.

92. Here he criticizes the core distinction — one adopted uncritically or even perhaps quite consciously by neo-Protestantism — of the political theory of modernity, that is, of political liberalism; then, however, he himself does not follow up on the crucial implications of this for the understanding of the church. (Cf. in this regard Milbank, esp. 9-48.) He loses this decisive perspective in ecclesiology precisely because he is not keeping in mind the concrete genealogy of this terminology. For under the conditions of modernity, which defines "private" and "public" normatively, the church is defenselessly exposed to this definition if it does not understand itself explicitly in tension and in difference to the modern distinction between "private" and "public," that is, as a reality resisting precisely this distinction, and resisting in the concreteness of its own practices. Any discussion of the church as "order of creation" (Bayer) under the conditions of modernity is possible only if one understands the church itself *ecclesiologically* completely in the sense of Bayer's own understanding of theology as a conflict discipline such that it stands in an unresolvable conflict with precisely this core distinction of political modernity, a conflict that finds its resolution in and through the concrete church practices. Cf. in this regard section II in Part Four below.

93. "For as soon as God's work arises in you, the devil will afflict you, will make you into a real scholar, and through his temptations will teach you to seek and love God's word" (Bayer, *Theologie*, 96; citation from Luther, *Weimar Ausgabe*, 50, 660, 8-10).

94. For a persuasive presentation of Luther's apocalyptic perspective, cf. H. A. Oberman, *Luther: Man between God and the Devil*, trans. Eileen Walliser-Schwarzbart (New Haven: Yale University Press, 1989).

95. Bayer, *Theologie*, 100.

96. Bayer, *Theologie*, 101. This apocalyptic understanding of *tentatio* permits him to delimit himself decisively, following Luther, from Schleiermacher's concept of experience. Both Bayer and Luther are concerned with a specific experience that cannot be separated from its object, what may be called differentiated passivity.

97. Bayer, *Theologie*, 101.

98. "The experience of scripture rather than experience as such makes the theologian into a theologian. The experience I have with Holy Scripture is that it interprets me, thus providing for its own interpretation and acting as its own interpreter — *sui ipsius interpres*, as Luther puts it succinctly in explicit connection with Psalm 119. . . . The object is to allow scripture, and with scripture also its author, the triune God, to be active within me. This is the unique passivity of the experience of faith: it is primarily *vita passiva*" (Bayer, *Theologie*, 102).

99. Anyone who prays the psalms daily is, after all, living either in Israel or in the church!

100. Cf. in this regard section II.2 in Part Three below.

101. Bayer, *Theologie,* 105f.

102. Cf. section II.3.c in Part Three below.

103. Luther, *Weimar Ausgabe,* 50, 626, 18-19.

104. Luther, *Weimar Ausgabe,* 50, 626, 19-36.

105. Luther, *Weimar Ausgabe,* 50, 627, 1-17, and 50, 643, 6-26.

106. Luther, "On the Councils and the Church," *Luther's Works,* vol. 41, *Church and Ministry* III, trans. Charles M. Jacobs, ed. E. W. Gritsch (Philadelphia: Fortress, 1966), 146. *Weimar Ausgabe,* 50, 626, 29-36.

107. For Luther, these include (1) the externally, orally proclaimed word of God; the church is recognized in the actualization of preaching, believing, confessing, and in the corresponding actions; (2) baptism and (3) Lord's Supper; (4) the power of the keys in community discipline; (5) church offices and ordination; (6) worship and instruction; and (7) discipleship in suffering and temptation. The church can also be recognized in sanctification according to the second tablet, that is, in life according to the commandments, though not as unequivocally; according to Luther, non-Christians also engage in such works, and indeed occasionally even appear more holy than Christians themselves (cf. *Weimar Ausgabe,* 50, 643, 27-37). The decisive point for Luther in the characteristics of the first tablet is the notion of publicly accessible unequivocalness.

108. An ecclesiological proposal that does justice to Luther's thick ecclesiology can, however, be found *in nuce* in Bayer, *Leibliches Wort,* 65.

109. Cf. Bayer, *Theologie,* 105.

110. Cf. Bayer, *Theologie,* 109ff.

111. Bayer, *Theologie,* 107f.

112. Cf. Bayer, *Theologie,* 110-13. "It is obvious that the catechism is not only to be learned by heart, but also inwardly practiced, prayed, and taken as the object of meditation on a daily basis if *meditatio* means nothing other than attention to God's word. . . . Nor does catechetical meditation proceed along a discursively linear path which, once found and traversed, might be left behind, preserved as information, stored, and arbitrarily retrieved from memory. Rather, this catechetical meditation, this attention to God's word in fourfold response to that word, is rumination, *ruminatio,* lifelong learning, recollection, repetition; it is to be practiced daily" (113).

113. "Sixth, the holy Christian people are externally recognized by prayer, public praise, and thanksgiving to God. Where you see and hear the Lord's Prayer prayed and taught; or psalms or other spiritual songs sung, in accordance with the word of God and the true faith; also the creed, the Ten Commandments, and the catechism used in public, you may rest assured that a holy Christian people of God are present. For prayer, too, is one of the precious holy possessions whereby everything is sanctified, as St. Paul says" (Luther, "On the Councils and the Church," 164). (Luther, *Weimar Ausgabe,* 50, 641, 20-26).

114. "Theology does, of course, want to perceive that object, and corresponds

to the object in the process. This is why its choice of object is indeed decisive, or rather, the object that offers itself to theology's vision is decisive, not what theology takes as its object, but rather what forces itself upon theology or suggests itself irrefutably to theology" (Bayer, *Autorität und Kritik*, 183f.).

115. Cf. in this regard section III.2 of Part One.

116. Cf. O. Bayer, *Promissio. Geschichte der reformatorischen Wende in Luthers Theologie*, Forschungen zur Kirchen- und Dogmengeschichte 24 (Göttingen: Vandenhoeck & Ruprecht, 1971).

117. Bayer, *Was ist das: Theologie?* 28.

118. Cf. Bayer, *Theologie*, 444: "Luther understands the *verbum efficax* to be a linguistic act that itself generates communication, an act that both liberates and gives a person assurance: an active, efficacious word. . . . They [the linguistic acts] are the concrete mode in which Christ is present: definite and unequivocal — unequivocally liberating and providing unequivocal assurance."

119. Bayer, *Autorität und Kritik*, 184.

120. Cf. in this regard esp. O. Bayer, *Schöpfung als Anrede. Zu einer Hermeneutik der Schöpfung*, 2nd rev. ed. (Tübingen: J. C. B. Mohr, 1990).

121. Bayer, *Leibliches Wort*, 307.

122. Cf. Bayer, *Was ist das: Theologie?* 25ff.

123. ". . . the celebration of the Lord's Supper is the summary presentation of that . . . which grounds Christian faith, of that toward which it is directed, and of that which directs the actions of the congregation. It is thus from the perspective of this event . . . that it shapes and defines itself as theology. The Lord's Supper is a succinct formulation of the entire gospel, its 'compendium,' its 'sum'" (Bayer, *Leibliches Wort*, 306).

124. "It is a word of performance or of actualization. An excellent example of such a performative word is the communicative word bequeathed precisely in the words of the Lord's Supper. Theology as linguistics analyzes the 'performance' of this gift and explicates the efficacious 'competence' within it" (Bayer, *Leibliches Wort*, 307f.).

125. Cf. Bayer, *Leibliches Wort*, 307.

126. Cf. Bayer, *Was ist das: Theologie?* 24-39; Bayer, *Autorität und Kritik*, 144f., 149, 187ff.; Bayer, *Theologie*, 123-26.

127. "For anyone accepting Pauline and Reformational hermeneutics, that which makes a theological discipline into theology in the first place is a much more powerful reference point than some 'reference to church government,' namely, the acknowledgment of the utter dependency on the linguistic acts described above as the proper activity of theology, and the imperative and will to function within those acts. Whoever takes them as reference points has already begun to be a theologian. Although all Christians have already begun, precisely as Christians, to become theologians, the academic theologian differs from others merely (and this is the unique vocation of such a person) in having to render an account of this reference in the scholarly medium of language, that is, in sentences articulated as precisely as possible. . . . *What makes this theological discipline into theology is its orientation toward these el-*

ementary linguistic acts in which law and gospel concretely come to bear as both binding and liberating; this reference is expressed in the confession to be utterly dependent on them and in the will to be active within them. . . . What makes the theological discipline into an academic discipline is that it is executed within the forum of the scholarly methodologies of its time; although these methodologies neither legitimate nor constitute the affairs of theology, they do regulate one's reflected and reflective interaction with these affairs, interaction necessary not least for dealing with heresy" (Bayer, *Theologie,* 497f., 500).

128. Cf. Bayer, *Theologie,* 334f., and section III in Part One above.

129. Cf. in this regard Bayer, *Theologie,* 403-7.

130. The proximity to Lindbeck's understanding of doctrine as the grammar of faith is obvious here, though, as we will see below, the place occupied by doctrine for Lindbeck is occupied by theology for Bayer. Both, however, do distinguish clearly between the theology inhering in the actualization of faith itself on the one hand and "theology in the narrower sense" (Bayer, *Theologie,* 439) on the other, namely, as a second-order discourse. "Theology in the narrower sense, as a specialized and specific conceptual undertaking, participates in its object but is not itself identical with that object. It is related to that object in the same way Ordinary Language Philosophy is related to ordinary language" (439). *"As the analytic of the language of proclamation, theology halts the connecting thread of all theological inquiry precisely at the place whence it derives and to which it returns"* (440).

131. Bayer, *Theologie,* 493.

132. Concerning this difficult and extremely out-of-season complex of problems, cf. J. Wirsching, *Kirche und Pseudokirche. Konturen der Häresie* (Göttingen: Vandenhoeck & Ruprecht, 1990), who has addressed this topic with considerable prudence and with an eye on the christological core of the issue at stake in heresy.

133. This is not a matter of "scientific freedom of opinion" in the sense of liberalism, but rather of public debate, of the mode of establishing truth; during Luther's time the locus of this was still the public *disputatio.* This discussion, however, is possible and is genuinely plural only if it transpires in a place or within a horizon that is itself *not* a matter of debate. Strictly speaking, church doctrine opens up this space in which the disputed search for truth is possible in the first place. Cf. in this regard section III in Part Four below.

134. The difference between the *Barmen Declaration* as an ecclesiastically binding confession (and thus of church doctrine) and the theologies of Asmussen and Barth illustrates this decisive distinction. Another example is the difference between, on the one hand, the Pannenberg/Lehmann volume on lifting the mutual condemnations of the Reformation period and the contemporary theological debate concerning this proposal, and on the other, an ecclesiastically binding implementation of this proposal as the recent *Joint Declaration on Justification* signed by the Roman Catholic church and by the churches of the Lutheran World Federation.

135. See Part Three below.

136. Cf. Bayer, *Theologie,* 27-31, 500.

137. I am indebted to D. Yeago, who provided the formative impulse for this critique of Bayer's interpretation of Austin.

138. J. L. Austin, *How to Do Things with Words*, 2nd ed. (Oxford: Clarendon, 1975).

139. Bayer, *Theologie*, 441f.

140. Austin, 150.

141. Austin, 147.

142. Cf. Bayer, *Theologie*, 442.

143. "If the concern of theology is the assurance just described, then two negative elements attach to the problem of verification. First, an assurance that is not already an affirmative clause cannot be transformed into one. Were it already an affirmative clause, one would have to be able to test it against that which it states" (Bayer, *Theologie*, 446).

144. Austin, 150.

145. Bayer, *Theologie*, 443.

146. Otherwise, the entirety of the later university disputations — disputations of great importance to Luther — would be meaningless.

147. Luther, *Weimar Ausgabe*, 39, I and II. Cf. in this regard the recent study by G. White, *Luther as Nominalist: A Study of the Logical Methods Used in Martin Luther's Disputations in the Light of Their Medieval Background*, Schriften der Luther-Agricola-Gesellschaft (Finland) 30 (Helsinki: Finnische Theologische Literaturgesellschaft, 1994). White shows quite persuasively that Luther is intensely interested in what Austin would call the "locutionary content" and illocutionary role of the gospel, and clarifies this with the help of a semantic-grammatical and logical analysis quite in keeping with scholastic analytical methodology.

148. It transcends the alternative between apophantic speech and performative speech act insofar as its *doctrina* is concerned with the *Christus praesens*, who can only demonstrate himself. Cf. in this regard "*Doctrina* in Luther" in Part Three below.

149. Luther, *A Brief Instruction on What to Look for and Expect in the Gospels*, in *Luther's Works*, vol. 35, *Word and Sacrament*, ed. and trans. E. T. Bachman (Philadelphia: Muhlenberg, 1960), 117f. (*Weimar Ausgabe*, 10/1, 9,11–10,8).

150. Luther, *A Brief Instruction*, 120f. (*Weimar Ausgabe*, 10/1, 13,19–14,9).

151. "Theology is not the establishment of agreement with itself in matters of faith within the confines of its own space; it is a conflict discipline. It is constituted only by addressing objections and challenges. For in the arena of understanding and thought, one cannot gloss over something that challenges one's personal faith. He whose message is 'I am the Lord, your God, you shall have no other gods before me,' will inevitably be involved in conflict" (Bayer, *Theologie*, 505; cf. also 511). Theology "is constituted only by addressing objections and challenges," and arises from within the temptations accompanying living faith. "Nor can thought itself transcend this situation of conflict and struggle; indeed, it must prove itself *within* that very situation" (Bayer, *Autorität und Kritik*, v).

152. In contradistinction to the agonistic horizon of modernity (cf. in this regard Milbank, 9-48), Bayer's agonistic horizon is characterized by Luther's apocalyp-

tic perspective. God's intervention in the old world generates a conflict that cannot be resolved under the conditions of this world.

153. Bayer, *Leibliches Wort*, 6.

154. Bayer, *Leibliches Wort*, 7. Although Bayer does indeed address the theme of *church* here by referring to concrete spheres of church activity, the peculiar way in which he does so simultaneously neutralizes these spheres in juxtaposition with "history" and "nature," as if they are not also or even especially involved with history and nature. Bayer's insistence on adducing immediate "dealings with nature and history in the larger sense," as it were, "independent" of and alongside spheres of church activity, shows that he does not understand the church as a nexus of *practices* in and through which Christians are indeed involved "with nature and history in the larger sense"; rather, he conceives them externally such that dealings with history and nature become conceivable *in abstracto*. He perpetuates the problem by consistently understanding the "communicative form of judgment" not as a practice inhering within the church, that is, not as discourse practice, but as the doctrine of justification transformed into method: "The 'communicative form of judgment' that must prove itself in this conflict emerges from that particular event in which the old person becomes new, though this new person must indeed relate to the old" (*Theologie*, 518). Understanding this *bona fide* presupposes at least baptism, Lord's Supper, and gospel proclamation. With reference to the core practices, however, the "communicative form of judgment" remains at most only implicitly a practice unto itself.

155. Cf. Bayer, *Theologie*, 521.

156. This is the sense of "metaschematism"; cf. the following section.

157. Bayer, *Theologie*, 494.

158. Bayer, *Theologie*, 493f.

159. The example Bayer adduces to illustrate the method of communicative judgment shows especially well that he is *not* understanding theology here as a discursive *church* practice. He suggests that Paul's dealings with the Corinthians exemplify quite well this method of communicative judgment: "Paul does not really carry on a 'dialogue' with the Corinthians. Rather, having in freedom made himself their slave (1 Cor. 9:19), he engages them such that he puts himself in their position: 'I have applied (μετεσχημάτισα) all this to Apollos and myself for your benefit, brothers and sisters, so that you may learn through us . . .' (1 Cor. 4:6). Carrying on a 'dialogue' is something different than engaging others in this figure of 'metaschematism' to the point of the kind of intercession in solidarity attested in Rom. 9:3" (*Leibliches Wort*, 7). Even though Bayer introduces "communicative judgment" here in a theologically "dense" fashion, he revealingly does *not* seem to ascribe any significance to the fact that Paul's debate with the Corinthians deals with a conflict focusing decidedly on the *church* itself — and not with Paul's dealings with the pagan-Hellenistic world around him as such in any immediate way, but rather in a way mediated precisely by the church. By adducing this particular example for the communicative form of judgment as the "method" of critical mediation between modernity and Reformation, Bayer shows that his debate with modernity has covertly itself become an ecclesial/inner-church debate, and that without noticing and despite gestures of distancing himself from

such (cf. *Autorität und Kritik,* 148, 177), he moves surprisingly close to T. Rendtorff's understanding of the structural adaptation of Christianity to modern self-understanding. At the same time, his understanding of "metaschematism" does offer an excellent point of departure for understanding theology substantively as an ecclesial practice of judgment in the face of substantial disagreements, namely, as an engagement for those separated from each other within the church. Moreover, this also naturally suggests the notion of free, (self-)critical dealings with modernity (more recently: with late- or postmodernity), albeit *not* in any abstractly immediate way that ignores the concrete practices of the church. Bayer also calls this "communicative form of judgment" "*diaconia* of thought" (*Leibliches Wort,* 10). In order to orient itself concretely as such "*diaconia* of thought," however, it needs church *diaconia* as a concrete practice.

160. Rather, Bayer is able to integrate this critique into his own concept of theology. He can appropriate modern criticism critically as "metacritical wisdom," that is, without turning it into a new dogmatism. This critical appropriation is made possible by a theological self-perception on the part of theology that takes the first commandment as its point of orientation and at the same time finds the perception of world as also attaching to the personal relationship between God and human beings. This yields a threefold *subjectum theologiae,* namely, God, human being, and world indissolubly intertwined (cf. *Theologie,* 432). Here Bayer gains a theological perspective that as a metacritique of modernity simultaneously contains both pre- and postmodern motifs. Postmodern features might include the surrender of any notion of unity and an emphasis on the historicity of reason and of its "other" in human sensuousness and corporeality. The decisive premodern features are what Bayer, with Hamann, calls the "oldest aesthetics," namely, "to fear and love God above all else and to trust him alone" (433). It is at precisely this juncture, however, that he must refer in a roundabout way ("communicative community of the justified sinner" [434]) to the church as the necessary locus at which this understanding of the world and self arises through the hearing, reading, and vivifying transmission of the Old and New Testaments. The "concrete historical apriori" (434) of the Bible also finds its concrete historical locus here, though Bayer can address it only indirectly and implicitly, as he also does, for example, by applying it to theology itself when distinguishing between law (in the sense of *primus usus legis*) and gospel. "A Christian's knowledge and action remain bound to the place of worship — essentially: to the place of the event of word and faith — and cannot be understood as a universal principle of knowledge and action that might also be expected of the non-believer. God's life-preserving law in the sense of the *usus politicus legis* is at work whenever a non-believer — happily — has moments of insight into the gospel that motivate that person's thinking and action" (436). Bayer then quite rightly points out that hermeneutics and any theory of science or knowledge need to take sin seriously (437); unless one takes the epistemologically or ontologically "self-evident nature of sin" as one's point of departure, however, precisely this position again makes the church necessary as the concrete place at which one learns first of all nothing other than to be a "sinner"!

161. Cf. Bayer, *Autorität und Kritik,* 53ff.

162. This can be seen especially in the way he does indeed precisely articulate the difference between theology and philosophy in Luther, but then fails to explicate the political implication of this thesis: "Luther vehemently denies 'that this is true in all [areas],' and emphasizes the inner-historically fixed distinction between philosophy and theology, *forum politicum* and *forum theologicum, iustitia civilis* and *iustitia dei*" (Bayer, *Theologie,* 125f.). Bayer adopts this distinction, one conceived within the horizon of the *corpus Christianum,* for his own understanding of theology as a conflict discipline without explicitly considering that under the altered conditions of modernity, this distinction can be maintained only if the *forum theologicum* is independently constituted precisely as a *forum,* that is, as a public sphere (something that occurs only through the explicit practices of the church). The new feature of modernity is that the *forum politicum* has in the meantime developed its own "theology" (cf. in this regard Milbank, 51-143). Under the conditions of modernity, a "public" is by no means a self-evident entity, and rather is vehemently disputed and contested. The *forum politicum* and the *forum theologicum* are no longer incorporated into a common sociopolitical-ecclesiastical horizon, as was the case during Luther's time; rather, they refer to different "citizenries." The *forum theologicum* is constituted by the public attaching to the *civitas Dei,* concretely inhering in its practices — or there is no *forum theologicum.* Similarly, the *forum politicum* has developed its own "theologies" with which Christian theology is in conflict. Only an ecclesiology that is at once also a political theory of the church enables one to maintain a *forum theologicum* under the conditions of modernity that itself stands in conflict with the *forum politicum* and yet is not monopolized with the latter's comprehensively inclusive horizon as the "public theology" of a civil religion.

163. Bayer, *Autorität und Kritik,* 6.

164. Bayer, *Autorität und Kritik,* 6, my emphasis.

165. To say that all who study Scripture also love it would be to conclude from the smaller to the larger. Whoever loves Scripture does indeed also study it. Although full adherence to the Torah does also include studying the Torah, studying the Torah does not yet imply adherence to the Torah.

166. Bayer, *Autorität und Kritik,* 7, my emphasis.

167. Bayer, *Autorität und Kritik,* 149, my emphasis.

168. An additional impulse in this direction is found in Bayer, *Leibliches Wort,* 65, where he says in regard to Luther's seven marks of the church: "These 'external' signs do not, however, refer to something internal that might be distinguished from them; rather, the church is not only recognized, but is indeed constituted in, with, and among these signs. That is, these distinguishing features of the church are also its essential features." Here Bayer decisively departs from all neo-Protestant "aggregate notions" by presenting an outline understanding the church as a reality that is always antecedent to individuals and which those individuals then encounter in word and sacrament. Luther expressed this central ecclesiological insight in several different places and with unmistakable clarity. In the *Large Catechism* of 1529, Luther refers to the church as "the mother that begets and bears every Christian through the Word of God" (*Large Catechism, The Book of Concord,* trans. and ed. Theodore G. Tappert

[Philadelphia: Fortress, 1959], 416). In the *Church Postille* of 1522 he writes that "whoever would find Christ must first find the church" (*Weimar Ausgabe*, 10/1, 140, 8). Cf. also *Lectures on Galatians, 1535, Luther's Works*, vol. 26, trans. and ed. Jaroslav Pelikan (St. Louis: Concordia, 1963), 441: "Therefore Sarah, or Jerusalem, our free mother, is the church, the bride of Christ who gives birth to all. She goes on giving birth to children without interruption until the end of the world, as long as she exercises the ministry of the Word, that is, as long as she preaches and propagates the Gospel; for this is what it means for her to give birth." Here Luther envisions the church not as *creatura verbi*, but as the mother of all believers who begets these believers through the proclamation of the gospel. Although faith comes through hearing, the subject of that gospel proclamation is the church. Furthermore: "She teaches, cherishes, and carries us in her womb, her bosom, and her arms; she shapes and perfects us to the form of Christ, until we grow into perfect manhood (Eph. 4:13). Thus everything happens through the ministry of the Word" (*Lectures on Galatians, 1535*, 441f.). Similarly, the service of the word also includes this motherly activity of the church, its rearing, caressing, carrying within its womb, at its breast, and in its arms, its forming and perfecting of believers "to the measure of the full stature of Christ" (Eph. 4:13 NRSV). Hence precisely Luther's understanding of the motherly activity of the church suggests that this service of the word is developed in a series of practices that are themselves ecclesiologically constitutive.

169. Bayer, *Autorität und Kritik*, 149, my emphasis.

170. Bayer, *Autorität und Kritik*, 149.

171. Bayer, *Autorität und Kritik*, 151.

172. Bayer, *Autorität und Kritik*, 152, my emphasis.

173. Bayer, *Autorität und Kritik*, 153.

174. Bayer, *Leibliches Wort*, 6.

175. Bayer, *Theologie*, 493.

176. This coincides with the Protestant development of departments of theology into a de facto magisterium.

177. It was still decisive for the theology of early Protestantism (and rightly so) to demonstrate the catholicity of its position with reference to the dogma of the early church and to the patristic fathers. It could not afford to concentrate exclusively on Luther. One particularly good example in this regard is Johann Gerhard's *Confessio Catholica* (1634-37).

178. This can be resolved only within the framework of an explicit ecclesiology and in the relation between binding doctrine, church, and theology; early Protestantism still realized this.

179. Reference is made neither to Lindbeck's ecumenically extremely relevant proposal nor to the Lehmann/Pannenberg initiative; cf. K. Lehmann and W. Pannenberg, eds., *The Condemnations of the Reformation Era: Do They Still Divide?* trans. Margaret Kohl (Minneapolis: Fortress, 1990), and with regard to the ensuing discussion J. Baur, *Einig in Sachen Rechtfertigung? Zur Prüfung des Rechtfertigungskapitels der Studie des Ökumenischen Arbeitskreises evangelischer und katholischer Theologen: Lehrverurteilungen — kirchentrennend?* (Tübingen: J. C. B. Mohr, 1989); H. Schütte,

ed., *Einig in der Lehre von der Rechtfertigung! Mit einer Antwort an Jörg Baur,* with contributions by Horst Georg Pöhlmann, Vinzenz Pfnür, and Heinz Schütte (Paderborn: Bonifatius, 1990); U. Kühn and O. H. Pesch, *Rechtfertigung im Disput. Eine freundliche Antwort an Jörg Baur* (Tübingen: J. C. B. Mohr, 1991); neither is there any debate with the ongoing American (USA) dialogue between Lutherans and Roman Catholics, not to speak of the international dialogue between Lutherans and Roman Catholics. Cf. in this regard *Growth in Agreement: Reports and Agreed Statements of Ecumenical Conversations on a World Level,* ed. H. Meyer, H. J. Urban, and L. Vischer (New York: Paulist, 1984 [Geneva: World Council of Churches, 1984]). Concerning the already lengthy Lutheran–Roman Catholic dialogue in the United States of America, cf. the common dialogue documentation and positions in Lutherans and Catholics in Dialogue I-III *(The Status of the Nicene Creed as Dogma of the Church; One Baptism for the Remission of Sins; The Eucharist as Sacrifice),* ed. P. C. Empie and T. A. Murphy (Minneapolis: Augsburg, 1967); IV *(Eucharist and Ministry),* ed. P. C. Empie and T. A. Murphy (Minneapolis: Augsburg, 1970); V *(Papal Primacy and the Universal Church),* ed. P. C. Empie and T. A. Murphy (Minneapolis: Augsburg, 1974); VI *(Teaching Authority and Infallibility in the Church),* ed. P. C. Empie, T. A. Murphy, and J. Burgess (Minneapolis: Augsburg, 1978); VII *(Justification by Faith),* ed. H. G. Anderson, T. A. Murphy, and J. Burgess (Minneapolis: Augsburg, 1985); VIII *(The One Mediator, the Saints and Mary),* ed. H. G. Anderson, J. F. Stafford, and J. Burgess (Minneapolis: Augsburg, 1992).

180. Although he does indeed and quite justifiably take early Protestantism as a point of reference, he simultaneously moves into tension with it by losing the ongoing reference to and debate with Catholicism. Bayer's critical debate with neo-Protestantism is explicit and welcome, but early Protestantism itself lived in an *ecclesial* debate without which it is inconceivable. Cf. Martin Chemnitz, *Examination of the Council of Trent* (1564-73), and Johann Gerhard, *Confessio Catholica* (1634-37). One fine example that this is also possible in the present and within the context of the *ecumene* is A. C. Piepkorn, *The Church: Selected Writings of Arthur Carl Piepkorn,* ed. M. Plekon and W. Wiecher (Delhi, N.Y., and New York: ALPB Books, 1993), for whom ecclesiological reflection, constant reference to the church fathers, and an ongoing explicit debate with Catholicism belong together. The decisive feature here is not whether this reference is directed toward delimitation within a theologically controversial context or toward establishing ecumenical accord, but rather *that* it takes place as an activity *inherent* within Protestant theology itself. The absence of such activity can be explained only by an ecclesiological deficit of the sort consistently characterizing, for example, neo-Protestantism.

Notes to Part Three

1. Cf. in this regard the detailed historical presentation in B. Nichtweiß, *Erik Peterson. Neue Sicht auf Leben und Werk* (Freiburg im Breisgau: Herder, 1992), 499-721.

2. Karl Barth, "The Word of God and the Task of the Ministry," in *The Word of*

God and the Word of Man (English translation) (Boston and Chicago: Hodder & Stoughton, 1928), 183-217.

3. O. Bayer accurately describes this dialectical movement in Barth's early theology: "This [dialectical path] moves back and forth in continual oscillation between the thesis and antithesis without ever establishing a synthesis. The point is to relate *mutually, one to the other*, these two poles, position and negation, to throw the yes into relief against the no, the no into relief against the yes, without ever lingering more than an instant in a rigid yes or no . . ." (*Theologie*, Handbuch Systematischer Theologie 1 [Gütersloh: Gütersloher Verlagshaus G. Mohn, 1994], 313).

4. Peterson, from G. Sauter, ed., *Theologie als Wissenschaft. Aufsätze und Thesen*, Theologische Bücherei 43 (Munich: Kaiser, 1971), 134. Peterson's tractate "What Is Theology?" as well as Barth's rejoinder, "Church and Theology," are cited according to this German edition. Cf. also the English translation of Barth, "Church and Theology," in *Theology and Church: Shorter Writings, 1920-1928* (London: SCM Press, 1962), 286-306.

5. From the perspective of the heuristic categories developed in Part One above, Peterson's critical query can be understood precisely as a criticism of the seriousness of the poietician. This echoes in O. Bayer's later critique of Barth when he finds predominating in Barth's own hermeneutics a modern subjectivity that assimilates all that is other or foreign (cf. Bayer, 332-35). The decisive point here is that the subject follows the movement of the object, and yet the expressed dialectic remains the engagement of the theologian, a diastasis that must be *established* or *produced ever anew* by the theologian's own thinking and speaking. That is, it exists only in the actual performance or enactment of its production, only in the event itself of theologizing; outside itself it has no reality or capacity for juxtaposition, for constituting an "other."

6. "In contradistinction to myth, three things are presupposed and at work in theology, namely, that there is revelation, faith, and obedience. But this also means that there can be no theology in the form of dialectics, and that dialectical reference to God may very well be part of the non-binding features of a mythical narrative, but not of theology, which demands obedience" (Peterson, in *Theologie als Wissenschaft*, 135f.).

7. "The sacrament does not continue the incarnation directly, but rather such that the sacrament itself is *instituted*. And dogma does not continue Christ's own discourse about God directly, but rather such that there is now a teaching authority Christ has conferred upon the church in which dogma appears" (Peterson, in *Theologie als Wissenschaft*, 149).

8. The background here is Peterson's own distinction between discourse, saying, and speaking: "Theology does not 'say' God's word; to do so would be to forget that the prophets appeared. Nor does theology 'discourse' about God; to do so would be to forget that Christ was revealed. There can be theology only if one presupposes the authority of the prophets and of Christ — in other words, *the authority manifesting itself in theology is derived authority*" (in *Theologie als Wissenschaft*, 143). The revelation of Christ that has continued itself into and within dogma thus makes it impossible to "speak" or "discourse" in a christological-theological fashion "about God."

Dogma alone is the binding discourse about God that continues Christ's discourse, and theology is the interpretation dependent on and oriented toward it.

9. "Dogma continues the situation in which Christ has pressed up hard against the very body of human beings. The gospel is not good news directed 'to everyone' — else how could it be distinguished from the Communist Manifesto? — but rather is God's positive legal claim that from the body of Christ affects every one of us concretely, and does so *iure divino*. It is a *positive* legal claim grounded in the concrete event of Christ's death and resurrection and continuing on in dogma and sacrament" (Peterson, in *Theologie als Wissenschaft*, 146f.).

10. Peterson, in *Theologie als Wissenschaft*, 150.

11. Peterson, in *Theologie als Wissenschaft*, 143.

12. Peterson, in *Theologie als Wissenschaft*, 147.

13. Peterson, in *Theologie als Wissenschaft*, 147f.

14. Peterson, in *Theologie als Wissenschaft*, 149. Cf. also 150: "Just as there has been dogma and the church only since the ascension, so also has there been theology only from this particular point on. One cannot answer the question 'what is theology' if one forgets that God's word became flesh and spoke about God. Nor can one answer the question 'what is theology' if one forgets the other aspect as well, namely, that Christ ascended to heaven and that there is now dogma."

15. Peterson, in *Theologie als Wissenschaft*, 145f.

16. "There *is* no theology among Jews and pagans. There *is* theology only in Christianity and only presupposing that the incarnate word of God has spoken. Though Jews may well also engage in exegesis, and pagans in mythology and metaphysics, theology in the genuine sense has come about only since the incarnate spoke about God" (Peterson, in *Theologie als Wissenschaft*, 145).

17. "Deferring honor to Christ means to defer in the objective intellectual world to the dogma belonging to Christ. In theology, this means honoring the logos by participating in the logos's discourse about God mediated through dogma. We ourselves, however, cannot honor Christ; he must leave it to us, must leave it to us in some objective fashion, namely, in dogma" (Peterson, in *Theologie als Wissenschaft*, 149).

18. "But not in the form of a discipline like all others, but in the form of a discipline of all disciplines. Theology is the *first* discipline. This is not spoken from a position of human arrogance, but rather simply out of acknowledgement that dogma has subordinated all human knowledge" (Peterson, in *Theologie als Wissenschaft*, 151).

19. Peterson's Protestant critics delighted in citing the following passage, so I will also reference it at this time: "The objective and concrete expression of God having pressed up hard against the very body of human beings in the incarnation is dogma. It is such an appropriate expression for this situation that every turn against dogma, such as that of the *heretic*, logically should also result in *corporeal* punishment of that person" (Peterson, in *Theologie als Wissenschaft*, 146). One must emphasize in this context that this is a statement of the Protestant and not the Catholic Peterson for which one can unfortunately find sufficient documented parallels from the Reformation period, especially over against the Baptists. Cf. in this regard the sad witnesses in

P. Wappler, *Die Stellung Kursachsens und des Landgrafen Philipp von Hessen zur Täuferbewegung* (Münster: Aschendorff, 1910), a chapter in the history of the Reformation critics of Peterson are too inclined to overlook.

20. I have borrowed this term from R. Jenson, "You Wonder Where the Spirit Went," *Pro Ecclesia* 2 (1993): 296-304.

21. Peterson, in *Theologie als Wissenschaft*, 149. Cf. also 147 n. 21: "In this sense, pneumatic exegesis and proclamation are not at all the kind of *activity* that are dogma and theology."

22. For additional biographical details and developments, cf. Nichtweiß, *Erik Peterson.*

23. Here one must agree with Karl Barth's evaluation and approach: "I consider it neither justified nor appropriate to react to Peterson's argument with the impulsive response that, after all, its presuppositions and consequences are all Roman Catholic in any event and are thus to be passed over in silence as being beyond discussion. Although I, too, share the opinion that they are not only Catholic, but in some aspects even hyper-Catholic, still, I do think that this facile assessment carries no real polemical weight and that one is ill-advised to reject substantive discussion of this and similar arguments merely on the basis of such an assessment" (Barth, in *Theologie als Wissenschaft*, 153). Cf. "Church and Theology," 287.

24. Cf. in this regard the Harnack-Peterson correspondence discussed in Part One above.

25. Cf. in this regard D. Bonhoeffer's and H. Schlier's remarks in Part One above concerning the delicate relation between theology, church doctrine, and church in the Confessing Church.

26. One ecclesiological point of contention remains unresolved here, namely, whether theology itself as binding doctrine is an interpretation of dogma, or as argumentative interpretation always *also* refers to binding doctrine.

27. Peterson, in *Theologie als Wissenschaft*, 146.

28. Cf. Nichtweiß, 512-17, for a detailed description of the attendant circumstances. Peterson's attack was also of great significance for Barth's own development from dialectics to analogy, a development E. Jüngel has examined in great detail in his study "Von der Dialektik zur Analogie. Die Schule Kierkegaards und der Einspruch Petersons," in Jüngel, *Barth-Studien* (Zürich and Cologne: Benziger; Gütersloh: Gütersloher Verlagshaus G. Mohn, 1982), 127-79. Cf. in this regard also H. U. von Balthasar, *The Theology of Karl Barth*, trans. Edward T. Oakes, S.J. (San Francisco: Ignatius Press, 1992), 64-113, even though part of Barth scholarship understands this development more as a shift in accentuation for which the figure of dialectics still remains fundamental. Thus R. Prenter, "Dietrich Bonhoeffer und Karl Barths Offenbarungspositivismus," in *Die Mündige Welt*, vol. 3 (Munich: Kaiser, 1960), 11-41, esp. 34f.; R. Jenson, *God after God: The God of the Past and the Future as Seen in the Work of Karl Barth* (Indianapolis: Bobbs-Merrill, 1969); W. Härle, *Sein und Gnade. Die Ontologie in Karl Barths Kirchlicher Dogmatik* (Berlin: Walter de Gruyter, 1975); recently also Bayer, 310-90, esp. 372f.; and in a historically detailed and nuanced fashion also B. McCormack, *Karl Barth's Critically Realistic Dialectical Theology: Its Gene-*

sis and Development, 1909-1936 (Oxford: Clarendon, 1995). The most exhaustive recent dissenting voice is G. Hunsinger, *How to Read Karl Barth: The Shape of His Theology* (Oxford: Oxford University Press, 1991).

29. Lecture delivered on October 7, 1925, at the Göttingen Fall Conference and on October 23, 1925, during the Theological Week at Elberfeld. First published in *Zwischen den Zeiten* 4 (1926): 18-40, reprinted in K. Barth, *Die Theologie und die Kirche* (Munich, 1928), 302-28; cited here according to Sauter, *Theologie als Wissenschaft*, 153-75. Cf. *Theology and Church: Shorter Writings, 1920-1928*, 286-306.

30. Barth, in *Theologie als Wissenschaft*, 156. Cf. "Church and Theology," 289.

31. Barth considers the following hierarchy to be constitutive for concrete authority under which Roman Catholic dogmatics operates: (1) biblical reference, (2) the theology of the church fathers, (3) church dogma, and (4) papal promulgations.

32. "One very essential presupposition of the misery in which our own contemporary theology finds itself is that when we engage in theology, we have no church behind us with the courage to say unequivocally to us 'this or that is — to the extent we are to speak as well — dogma *in concretissimo*.' If the churches do not tell us that, and yet simultaneously demand that we both learn and teach 'dogmatics,' then truly, they are like King Nebuchadnezzar, who not only wanted his wisemen to tell him what his dreams meant, but also what he dreamt in the first place. The embarrassment one can cause Peterson with the question '*which* dogma,' merely reflects the embarrassment in which our own Protestant church finds itself. It alters not a thing in the veracity of the statement that there can be no theology without concrete authority or dogma" (Barth, in *Theologie als Wissenschaft*, 157). Cf. "Church and Theology," 290.

33. "It is not dogma alone that constitutes the concrete authority to which theology is to render concrete obedience, but the statements of the church regarding the canon and the canonical text of scriptural revelation, regarding certain more or less unanimously accepted principles of church proclamation grounded on that revelation, explicated by the Fathers, and finally the need of the moment (similarly to be understood ecclesially); it is these three or four aspects together, aspects residing, as one can see, on completely different levels and significant in completely different ways" (Barth, in *Theologie als Wissenschaft*, 158). Cf. "Church and Theology," 291.

34. Barth, in *Theologie als Wissenschaft*, 161f. Cf. "Church and Theology," 294f.

35. Barth, in *Theologie als Wissenschaft*, 161f. Cf. "Church and Theology," 294.

36. "This spoken and written word into which the logos-revelation has entered in order to go out into the world is as such the *principle of all concrete representative evocation of that revelation, the origin and limit of all such representative evocation,* the standard by which everything the church 'says' in the name of its Lord is measured and is always to be measured. We must add: insofar as God, the Holy Spirit confesses to this word of the witness as to its own word, insofar as he repeatedly makes it incomparably true and efficacious, and insofar as in the hearts of his believers he brings about and implements his decisions by means of this word" (Barth, in *Theologie als Wissenschaft*, 163, my emphasis). Cf. "Church and Theology," 295f.

37. Cf. in this regard the discussion below.

38. Barth, in *Theologie als Wissenschaft,* 164. Cf. "Church and Theology," 296.

39. Barth, in *Theologie als Wissenschaft,* 165. Cf. "Church and Theology," 297f.

40. Barth, in *Theologie als Wissenschaft,* 168f. Cf. "Church and Theology," 301.

41. Barth, in *Theologie als Wissenschaft,* 170. Cf. "Church and Theology," 302.

42. Barth, in *Theologie als Wissenschaft,* 170. Cf. "Church and Theology," 302.

43. The eschatological definition of "dogma" in Barth's *Church Dogmatics* I/1 shows quite clearly how the "center" of the "mediate forms" disassembles into a diastatic juxtaposition of eschatological dogma as God's eschatological self-attestation on the one hand, and church "dogmas" as witnessing reference to this epiphany on the other. That "dogma" is for Barth a "concept of relation" (*Church Dogmatics,* I/1, 268) confirms this essentially dialectical understanding for which this distinction and simultaneous relation is virtually constitutive. "Thus the real results of dogmatics, even when they have the form of the most positive statements, can themselves only be new questions, questions to and fro between what the Church seems to proclaim and the Bible seems to want proclaimed, questions which can be put only with the greatest modesty and with a sense of supreme vulnerability if they are perhaps serious and important questions. If questioning ceased, dogma itself came on the scene instead of dogmas and dogmatic propositions, if the agreement of specific Church proclamation with the Word of God and therefore the Word of God itself in this specific Church proclamation could be demonstrated, then dogmatics would be at an end along with the *ecclesia militans* and the kingdom of God would have dawned. The second possibility of the appearing of dogma or the Word of God itself can only be that of great illusions and prolepses. To this extent one may call dogma an 'eschatological concept'" (*Church Dogmatics,* I/1, 268-69). Regarding the overall complex of problems involving eschatology and dogma in Barth, and particularly in his *Christliche Dogmatik im Entwurf,* cf. the discerning study by G. Sauter, "Dogma — ein eschatologischer Begriff," in Sauter, *Erwartung und Erfahrung. Predigten, Vorträge und Aufsätze,* Theologische Bücherei 47 (Munich: Kaiser, 1972), 16-46.

44. W. Härle discloses the substantive relation between dialectics and analogy in Barth, and with reference to Erich Przywara suggests that "analogy is accordingly ameliorated dialectics; dialectics is radicalized analogy" (200 n. 135).

45. Cf. in this regard the instructive essay by Prenter, "Dietrich Bonhoeffer und Karl Barths Offenbarungspositivismus."

46. Karl Barth, *The Word of God and the Word of Man* (English translation) (Boston and Chicago: Hodder & Stoughton, 1928), 183-217. Cf. esp. the concluding passage: "All my thoughts circle about the one point which in the New Testament is called Jesus Christ. Whoever can say 'Jesus Christ' need not say 'It *may* be'; he can say 'It *is.*' But which of us is capable, of himself, of saying, 'Jesus Christ'? Perhaps *we* may find satisfaction in the evidence that his first witnesses did say Jesus Christ. In that case our task would be to believe in their witness to the promise, and so to be witnesses of their witness, ministers of the *Scripture.* But my premises in this address have been the Old Testament and the tradition of the Reformed Churches. As a Reformed Churchman — and not only, I think, as such — I must keep my sure distance from the Lutheran *est* and the Lutheran type of *assurance of salvation.* Can theology,

should theology, pass beyond *prolegomena* to Christology? It may be that everything is said in the prolegomena" (216-17).

47. Cf. in this regard my *Evangelische Ethik als kirchliches Zeugnis. Interpretationen zu Schlüsselfragen theologischer Ethik in der Gegenwart,* Evangelium und Ethik 1. (Neukirchen-Vluyn: Neukirchener, 1993), 92-105.

48. D. Bonhoeffer already criticized Barth's formal understanding of freedom grounded in the subjective aspect of God. Over against a formal understanding of freedom, he brings to bear one based on content: "In revelation, it is a question less of God's freedom on the far side from us, i.e., his eternal isolation and aseity, than of his forth-proceeding, his *given* Word, his bond in which he has bound himself, of his freedom as it is most strongly attested in his having freely bound himself to historical man, having placed himself at man's disposal. God is not free *of* man but *for* man. Christ is the Word of his freedom. God is *there,* which is to say: not in eternal non-objectivity but (looking ahead for a moment) 'haveable,' graspable in his Word within the Church" (*Act and Being,* trans. Bernard Noble [New York: Harper, 1961], 90-91).

49. Barth, *Church Dogmatics,* I/1, 449.

50. Barth, *Church Dogmatics,* I/1, 450f., my emphasis.

51. Cf. in this regard *Church Dogmatics,* IV/3.1, §69.1, 2, which ultimately anchors the objectivity of proclamation *pro nobis* in Christ's resurrection. The Holy Spirit cannot transcend this subjectivity, and has no unique work of its own. Pentecost, however, is the concrete counterargument, a work of the Holy Spirit, a new beginning in the overall context of the trinitarian salvific economy. Cf. in this regard at the end of this section N. Nissiotis as a typical representative from the Eastern Church for this early church position. Cf. in this regard also *Church Dogmatics,* IV.3.2, 757-62. We again encounter the Chalcedonian logic between God and human beings transferred to the logic of action, whose realization is the work of the Holy Spirit; for Barth, the mode of being or the person of the Spirit coincides with the activity or work: "The Holy Spirit is the power, and His action the work, of the co-ordination of the being of Jesus Christ and that of His community as distinct from and yet enclosed within it" (*Church Dogmatics,* IV/3.2, 760). "The work of the Holy Spirit, however, is to bring and to hold together that which is different and therefore, as it would seem, necessarily and irresistibly disruptive in the relationship of Jesus Christ to His community, namely, the divine working, being and action on the one side and the human on the other, the creative freedom and act on the one side and the creaturely on the other, the eternal reality and possibility on the one side and the temporal on the other. His work is to bring and to hold them together, not to identify, intermingle nor confound them, not to change the one into the other nor to merge the one into the other, but to co-ordinate them, to make them parallel, to bring them into harmony and therefore to bind them into a true unity" (*Church Dogmatics,* IV/3.2, 761).

52. Cf. in this regard my study *Evangelische Ethik als kirchliches Zeugnis,* 92-105.

53. "Diskussion auf dem Leuenberg 1973," in B. Klappert, *Promissio und Bund. Gesetz und Evangelium bei Luther und Barth,* Forschungen zur systematischen und ökumenischen Theologie 34 (Göttingen: Vandenhoeck & Ruprecht, 1976), 239-89, here 272.

54. P. Brunner, *Pro Ecclesia. Gesammelte Aufsätze zur dogmatischen Theologie,* vol. 1, 3rd ed. (Fürth, 1990; Berlin: Lutherisches Verlagshaus, 1962), 222f.

55. Jenson, "You Wonder Where the Spirit Went."

56. "Precisely in that the inner-trinitarian relations do gloriously become concrete and alive in Barth, so that the Father and the Son *confront* one another, the actuality of a *vinculum* between the two parties Father and Son must be their I-thou relation itself. Thus the very reality of the Spirit excludes his appearance as a *party* in the triune actuality" (Jenson, "You Wonder," 301).

57. Cf. the lengthy citation above from *Church Dogmatics,* I/1, 450f. (see p. 109 above).

58. A paradigmatic formulation from *Church Dogmatics* IV/3.2 documents this nicely: "Just as the Holy Spirit, as Himself an eternal divine 'person' or mode of being, as the Spirit of the Father and the Son *(qui ex Patre Filioque procedit),* is the bond of peace between the two, so in the historical work of reconciliation He is the One who constitutes and guarantees the unity of the *totus Christus. . . .* This co-ordination and unity is the work of the active grace of God" (760).

59. Cf. Barth, *Church Dogmatics,* III/2, §45.

60. Jenson articulates this succinctly when he suggests that "[t]he Spirit is the capacity of God as archetype, at whatever ontological level, to evoke an echo in some subjectivity. When does the Spirit disappear from Barth's pages? Whenever he would appear as someone rather than as something. We miss the Spirit at precisely those points where Bible or catechism have taught us to expect him to appear as someone *with* capacities, rather than as sheer capacity — in the archetype/image scheme, as himself an archetype" ("You Wonder," 304).

61. Cf. in this regard the justified criticism of W. Pannenberg in his essay "Die Subjektivität Gottes und die Trinitätslehre. Ein Beitrag zur Beziehung zwischen Karl Barth und der Philosophie Hegels," in Pannenberg, *Grundfragen systematischer Theologie* II (Göttingen: Vandenhoeck & Ruprecht, 1980), 96-111, and esp. his constructive views in "The Outpouring of the Spirit, the Kingdom of God, and the Church," in Pannenberg, *Systematic Theology,* trans. Geoffrey W. Bromiley, vol. 3 (Grand Rapids: Wm. B. Eerdmans Publishing Co., 1998), 1-27.

62. N. A. Nissiotis, *Die Theologie der Ostkirche im ökumenischen Dialog. Kirche und Welt in orthodoxer Sicht* (Stuttgart: Evangelisches Verlagswerk, 1968), 74f. P. Brunner's forty-five theses, "Der Geist und die Kirche," in Brunner, *Pro Ecclesia,* 1:220-24, show quite effectively how taking this explicit reference to Eastern Church pneumatology does not necessarily take us away from the ground of Protestant theology.

63. Cf. in this regard J.-L. Leuba, who begins his study *New Testament Pattern: An Exegetical Enquiry into the "Catholic" and "Protestant" Dualism,* trans. Harold Knight (London: Lutterworth, 1953), with the following statement: "At the ecumenical conference of Amsterdam (1948), it appeared that the knottiest of theological problems in regard to the reunion of the churches arose from the doctrinal opposition between Catholicism and Protestantism. The catholic position implies the continuity of the Church, its institutional character and the many consequences which re-

sult from that fact — a sacramental idea of the ministry, the value of tradition, the emphasis (no doubt under various forms) on apostolical succession. The protestant position stresses, on the other hand, the liberty of the Holy Spirit, the ever-renewed initiatives by which God in His Word judges, corrects, sustains, recreates and consoles His Church, the universal priesthood and the charismatic nature of all forms of the ministry" (7). The thesis of the important study by R. Jenson, *Unbaptized God: The Basic Flaw in Ecumenical Theology* (Minneapolis: Fortress, 1992), is that this "Western" "either-or" is not only ecumenically still unresolved but also highly relevant and at the same time grounded in a deficient doctrine of the Trinity. The following reflections presuppose Jenson's analysis and try to adopt his manner of creatively incorporating Eastern Orthodox theology in overcoming precisely this alternative, and to make it fruitful for addressing the problem of the relation between church, church doctrine, and theology as church practice.

64. A small but paradigmatic example in this regard is the volume *Spirit of God, Spirit of Christ: Ecumenical Reflections on the Filioque Controversy,* ed. Lukas Vischer (London: SPCK, 1981) [Geneva: World Council of Churches, 1981].

65. Cf. in this regard the works of W. Kasper, T. F. Torrance, J. Moltmann, W. Pannenberg, R. Jenson, C. Gunton, C. LaCugna, G. Wainwright, et al.

66. John D. Zizioulas, *Being as Communion: Studies in Personhood and the Church,* Contemporary Greek Theologians 4 (Crestwood, N.Y.: St. Vladimir's Seminary, 1985; 2nd ed., 1993); "Die pneumatologische Dimension der Kirche," *IKZ Communio* 2 (1973): 133-47; "The Mystery of the Church in Orthodox Tradition," *One in Christ* 24 (1988): 294-303.

67. Nikos A. Nissiotis, *Die Theologie der Ostkirche im ökumenischen Dialog;* Nissiotis, "Der pneumatologische Ansatz und die liturgische Verwirklichung des neutestamentlichen νῦν," in *Oikonomia. Heilsgeschichte als Thema der Theologie. Festschrift Oskar Cullmann,* ed. F. Christ (Hamburg and Bergstedt: Reich, 1967), 302-9.

68. Dimitru Staniloae, *Theology and the Church* (Crestwood, N.Y.: St. Vladimir's Seminary, 1980).

69. Vladimir Lossky, *The Mystical Theology of the Eastern Church* (Crestwood, N.Y.: St. Vladimir's Seminary, 1976).

70. For general orientation, cf. the extremely helpful and instructive introduction to more recent Orthodox theology by K. C. Felmy, *Die orthodoxe Theologie der Gegenwart. Eine Einführung* (Darmstadt: Wissenschaftliche Buchgesellschaft, 1990), and most recently the very important account of the thought of the Eastern Fathers from the time of the Apostles to the end of the Byzantine era by Boris Bobrinskoy, *The Mystery of the Trinity: Trinitarian Experience and Vision in the Biblical and Patristic Tradition,* trans. Anthony P. Gythiel (Crestwood, N.Y.: St. Vladimir's Seminary Press, 1999).

71. This *communio*-ecclesiology enjoys widespread ecumenical acceptance, and in very different ways has already been adopted in various churches, often in accommodation to a presupposed, normative ecclesial self-understanding. Cf. in this regard the instructive overview by the Institute for Ecumenical Research, *Communio/*

Koinonia: A New Testament–Early Christian Concept and Its Contemporary Appropriation and Significance (Strassbourg, 1990), and the brief but highly instructive presentation of and debate with the Roman Catholic reception of *communio*-ecclesiology, especially since Vatican II, in Pannenberg, *Systematic Theology*, 3:104-8. Let me also refer expressly to one particular, impressive ecumenical document in which the *communio*-ecclesiology together with a trinitarian grounding of the church plays a central role in an agreement between Lutherans and Roman Catholics: Lutheran–Roman Catholic Joint Commission, *Church and Justification: Understanding the Church in the Light of the Doctrine of Justification* (Geneva: Lutheran World Federation, 1994). I believe the commission's agreement in key theological points confirms my own trinitarian and ecclesiological explications in what follows.

72. Cf. in this regard the works of K. Rahner, W. Pannenberg, J. Moltmann, T. F. Torrance, R. Jenson, C. Gunton, C. LaCugna, L. Boff, et al.

73. Cf. in this regard the detailed and precise presentation in Zizioulas, *Being as Communion*, 27-65.

74. T. F. Torrance articulates this concern with respect to Gregory of Nazianzus in the following passage: "[A]s he understood them the relations between the divine Persons are not just modes of existence but substantial relations which belong intrinsically to what Father, Son and Holy Spirit are in themselves as distinctive hypostatic realities as well as in their objective reciprocal relations with one another. The relations between them are just as substantial as what they unchangeably are in themselves and by themselves. Thus the Father *is* Father precisely in his indivisible ontic relation to the Son and the Spirit, and the Son and the Spirit *are* what they are as Son and Spirit precisely in their indivisible ontic relations to the Father and to one another" (*The Trinitarian Faith: The Evangelical Theology of the Ancient Catholic Church* [Edinburgh: T. & T. Clark, 1988], 321). Of course, this entire issue is considerably more complicated than can be demonstrated here. As Torrance clearly shows, even the Cappadocian Fathers debated whether the *monarchia* was to be attributed only to the person of the Father as the *archē* of the deity, or to the communion of the trinitarian persons precisely in their unity. Even contemporary Orthodox theology exhibits explicit differences of opinion on this point. Western theologians (Torrance, Pannenberg, Moltmann, Boff, et al.) tend to follow Gregory of Nazianzus, while the most important representatives of contemporary Eastern Orthodox theology advocate the *monarchia* of the Father following Basil the Great and Gregory of Nyssa (Lossky, Staniloae, Zizioulas). (Cf. in this regard Felmy, 40-49.) Both options, however, support the priority of the hypostatic identity of person consisting in the specific inner-trinitarian relationality. The contested issue involves an important aspect of this relationality itself between the trinitarian persons.

75. Wolfhart Pannenberg, *Systematic Theology*, vol. 1, trans. Geoffrey W. Bromiley, 3 vols. (Grand Rapids: Wm. B. Eerdmans Publishing Co., 1991f.), 428.

76. Cf. in this regard Lossky, 217-35.

77. This term derives from Luther. Cf. in this regard n. 104 below.

78. Cf. in this regard Zizioulas, *Being as Communion*, 110ff. and 123-42; Staniloae, 11-44.

79. Cf. Zizioulas, "Die pneumatologische Dimension der Kirche," 134: "Christology and pneumatology must exist simultaneously rather than as separate or sequential stages of God's relation to the world. According to Irenaeus, this contemporaneity also applies with regard to creation, in which Christ and the Spirit are simultaneously at work as God's two hands."

80. Zizioulas, "Die pneumatologische Dimension der Kirche," 135. Cf. in this regard the considerable substantive agreement of the Lutheran P. Brunner: "The body and blood of Christ are not separate from the Spirit in their essence, but as it were are permeated by the Spirit *(pneuma)* through and through. Jesus Christ's humanity was produced at its very origin in Mary's womb by the Spirit. The human being Jesus is the bearer of the Spirit unlike any prophet, apostle, or Christian, but rather such as only the eschatological redeemer of the world can be the bearer of the Spirit (Mark 1:10f.). Through the eschatological transformation in the resurrection at Easter (Rom. 8:11), Jesus' humanity was released for the essence and work of the Spirit such that the Lord and the Spirit are one in 'dynamic identification' (2 Cor. 3:17; 1 Cor. 15:45)" ("Zur Lehre vom Gottesdienst der im Namen Jesu versammelten Gemeinde," in *Leiturgia. Handbuch des evangelischen Gottesdienstes,* vol. 1, *Geschichte und Lehre des evangelischen Gottesdienstes,* ed. Karl Ferdinand Müller and Walter Blankenburg [Kassel: n.p., 1954], 353ff., here 355; cf. the English edition, *Worship in the Name of Jesus,* 305).

81. "It is the Spirit that makes the reality relational, and this applies equally or even especially to Christ" (Zizioulas, "Die pneumatologische Dimension der Kirche," 136).

82. "Both the Bible and tradition circumscribe the activity of the Spirit . . . especially as 'giver of life' and *'communio.'* . . . Paul and nearly all the Fathers see the Spirit's activity in the light of these two concepts. 'Giver of life' and *'communio'* are, after all, essentially identical, since the divine life the Spirit bestows consists in a life of *communio* of persons, and in this sense the Spirit brings about power and dynamic existence as well as healing, miracles, prophecies, and truth revelation; it establishes the preposition 'in' in which all this occurs" (Zizioulas, "Die pneumatologische Dimension der Kirche," 135f.).

83. Zizioulas, "Die pneumatologische Dimension der Kirche," 137. Cf. also Zizioulas, "The Mystery," 294-303.

84. It is appropriate at this point to recall that these reflections emphasize the pneumatological *dimension* of ecclesiology; that is, they implicitly presuppose a *trinitarian ecclesiology.* The goal is thus *not* to ground ecclesiology exclusively pneumatologically through some process of questionable reduction, but only to examine the unique features of the pneumatological dimension. For explicit advances toward a trinitarian understanding of the church from an ecumenical perspective, cf. recently G. Larentzakis, "Trinitarisches Kirchenverständnis," in *Trinität. Aktuelle Perspektiven der Theologie,* ed. W. Breuning, Quaestiones disputatae 101 (Freiburg im Breisgau: Herder, 1984), 73-96, and H. Schütte, "Kirche des dreieinigen Gottes. Zur trinitarischen Entfaltung der Ekklesiologie als Aufgabe," in *Im Gespräch mit dem*

dreieinigen Gott. Elemente einer trinitarischen Theologie. Festschrift Wilhelm Breuning,
ed. M. Böhnke and H. P. Heinz (Düsseldorf: Patmos, 1985), 361-75.

85. Cf. in this regard Felmy, 146-68.

86. Zizioulas, "Die pneumatologische Dimension der Kirche," 137. Cf.
Zizioulas, *Being as Communion,* 181-88, and Felmy, 240-46.

87. Zizioulas, "Die pneumatologische Dimension der Kirche," 136f. Concerning the "eschatological character of memory," cf. also Felmy, 192ff.

88. The congregational "amen" and the congregational confession of faith constitute the response to the proclamation of the word, and both conclude and complete that proclamation; only as a congregational celebration is the Lord's Supper really the "Lord's Supper." In this respect, P. Brunner's monograph "Zur Lehre vom Gottesdienst" represents the considerable achievement of developing Christology, pneumatology, and eschatology in the horizon of God's economy of salvation as the doctrine of worship. He, like Zizioulas, believes that the eschaton itself enters our purview in the Christ-anamnesis. "The worship service of the church, however, already contains in a unique, anticipatory fashion the still outstanding future of God's salvific economy. The pneuma-epiphany of the body of Jesus is already the actual commencement of God's reign in this world. In the worship service of the church, the pneuma and its gifts proleptically and representatively evoke God's coming reign. In particular, the Lord's Supper effects an advance manifestation of Jesus' eschatological meal fellowship with his followers in God's kingdom" (159; cf. the English edition, *Worship in the Name of Jesus,* 81).

89. The in-breaking of the eschaton is already reflected spatially in Orthodox churches, especially in the icon-screen. Cf. Felmy, 194.

90. Cf. in this regard the immediately following excursus.

91. Zizioulas, "Die pneumatologische Dimension der Kirche," 145.

92. Cf. W. Pannenberg, "Was ist Wahrheit?" in Pannenberg, *Grundfragen systematischer Theologie* (Göttingen, 1967), 202-22 (no English translation), the comprehensive treatment in L. Kugelmann, *Antizipation. Eine begriffsgeschichtliche Untersuchung,* Forschungen zur systematischen und ökumenischen Theologie 50 (Göttingen: Vandenhoeck & Ruprecht, 1986), and the critical views of I. Schoberth, *Erinnerung als Praxis des Glaubens,* Öffentliche Theologie 3 (Munich: Kaiser, 1992), 53ff.

93. Johannes Fischer, *Leben aus dem Geist. Zur Grundlegung christlicher Ethik* (Zürich: Theologischer Verlag, 1994), 172.

94. Cf. in this regard Luther's eschatological understanding of existence "in faith" in the third Antinomian Disputation, *Weimar Ausgabe,* 39/1, 521, 5-10: "Homo credens in Christum est reputatione divina iustus et sanctus, versatur estque iam in coelo, circumdatus coelo, misericordiae. Sed dum hic ferimur in sinu patris vestiti veste optima, pedes nostri mihi extra pallium descendunt, quos quantum potest mordet sathan, dar zappelt das Kindelein et clamat et sentit, se adhuc carnem et sanguinem habere et diabolum adhuc adesse."

95. This is already evident in the final sections of his great study, *Anthropology in Theological Perspective,* trans. Matthew J. O'Connell (Philadelphia: Westminster,

1985), where he adduces Eastern Orthodox theologians (Yannaras, Zizioulas) in trying to combine impulses from philosophy and from the human and social sciences regarding human identity on the one hand, with a pneumatologically articulated concept of person on the other: "History as a formative process is the way to the future to which the individual is destined. As long as the journey is incomplete, it can only be described in terms anticipatory of its end and goal. . . . For the human person as historical being is not only the goal but also the movement of the history that leads to the goal. This movement, however, derives its unity from the future by which it will be completed. Therefore only through anticipation of this future can human beings presently exist as themselves. . . . If the person is thus the presence of the self in the instant of the ego, personality is to be understood as a special instance of the working of the spirit, a special instance of the anticipatory presence of the final truth of things" (527f.).

96. Pannenberg, *Systematic Theology*, 3:6.

97. Pannenberg, *Systematic Theology*, 3:7.

98. Several striking formulations emphasize the passivity of the believing subject: "Believers, in whom Jesus is glorified as the Son (John 17:10), *are drawn by him* into his relation to the Father and hence into the glory that he receives from the Father (17:22). In the act of the glorifying of Jesus as the Son, which also glorifies the Father in the Son, believers share in the fellowship of the Son with the Father, and therefore in the glory of God by which their own lives *are changed* into imperishable fellowship with the eternal God" (Pannenberg, *Systematic Theology*, 3:11, my emphasis). This is actually comprehensible only within the horizon of pathos.

99. Cf. in this regard my study *Evangelische Ethik als kirchliches Zeugnis*, 101-5.

100. "The imparting of the Spirit as gift thus characterizes the distinctiveness of the soteriological phase of his work in the event of reconciliation. The form of the gift does not mean that the Spirit comes under the control of creatures but that he comes into them and thus makes possible our independent and spontaneous entry into God's action of reconciling the world and our participation in the movement of his reconciling love toward the world. As the Spirit who 'indwells' believers (Rom. 8:9ff.; 1 Cor. 3:16) lifts them above their own particularity, he is always surely more than simply gift, namely, the quintessence of the ecstatic movement of the divine life" (Pannenberg, *Systematic Theology*, 3:12).

101. Pannenberg, *Systematic Theology*, 3:274f.

102. This is why the expression is radical and clearly eschatological in the liturgy of St. Chrysostom, while the concept of "anticipation" remains ambivalent. Cf. in this regard Felmy, 193f., and Zizioulas, "Die pneumatologische Dimension der Kirche," 136f.

103. This is the difference between a practical theodicy in doxology and in witness, and Pannenberg's impressive and yet already conceptually resolved theoretical theodicy.

104. Cf. in this regard the succinct formulation in P. Brunner: "The church's worship occurs in the pneuma; that is, it occurs in the body of Jesus appearing on earth in the church. *Because the church's worship occurs in the pneuma, it occurs in*

Christ. The church's worship is thus participation in the one, never-ending worship service of the Crucified-Exalted before God's throne, a service that redeems the world" ("Zur Lehre vom Gottesdienst," 157, my emphasis; cf the English edition, *Worship in the Name of Jesus*, 79). So also W. Pannenberg's formulation, one more strongly differentiated with regard to the Trinity itself: "The christological constitution and the pneumatological constitution of the church do not exclude one another but belong together because the Spirit and the Son mutually indwell one another as trinitarian persons" (*Systematic Theology,* 3:16f.). In his *Large Catechism,* Luther characterized this eschatological work of the Holy Spirit as *opus inchoatum,* as a work already begun: "Meanwhile, since holiness has begun and is growing daily, we await the time when our flesh will be put to death, will be buried with all its uncleanness, and will come forth gloriously and arise to complete and perfect holiness in a new, eternal life" (*Large Catechism, The Book of Concord,* trans. and ed. Theodore G. Tappert [Philadelphia: Fortress, 1959], 418).

105. Cf. in this regard Luther's sermon on Sunday *Cantate* (May 14, 1536) on James 1: "Whence, then, do you derive sonship? Not from your own will, not from your own powers or efforts. . . . It is secured, James says, 'of his will.' For it never entered into the thought of any man that so should we be made children of God. The idea did not grow in our gardens; it did not spring up in our wells. But it came down from above, 'from the Father of lights,' by Word and Spirit revealed to us and given into our hearts through the agency of his apostles and their successors, by whom the Word has been transmitted to us. Hence we did not secure it through our efforts or merits. Of his Fatherly will and good pleasure was it conferred upon us; of pure grace and mercy he gave it. James says, 'That we would be a kind of first-fruits of his creatures'; that is, the newly-begun creature, or work, of God. By this phrase the apostle distinguishes the creatures of God from the creatures of the world, or creatures of men. . . . But new creatures are found with God. They are styled 'creatures of God' because he has created them as his own work, independently of human effort or human power. And so the Christian is called a 'new creature of God,' a creature God himself has made, aside from all other creatures and higher than they. At the same time, such creation of God is only in its initial stage. He still daily operates upon it until it becomes perfect, a wholly divine creature, as the very sun in clearness and purity, without sin and imperfection, all aglow with love divine" (*Weimar Ausgabe,* 41/1, 586,33–587,33; translation according to *Sermons of Martin Luther,* vol. 7, trans. and ed. J. N. Lenker [Grand Rapids: Baker, 1909; reprint, 1983], 296f.).

106. Cf. in this regard the way the Eastern Orthodox tradition intends this with the easily misunderstood concept *synergeia,* Felmy, 140ff.

107. The Lutheran theologian B. Marshall, "The Church in the Gospel," *Pro Ecclesia* 1 (1992): 27-41, has shown persuasively that the church is an implicate of the gospel if the latter is understood as the promising proclamation of the trinitarian history of God's salvific actions in the life, death, and resurrection of Jesus. Here Marshall refers to the new Finnish Luther research (especially Mannermaa) and Eastern Orthodox theologians (Lossky, Florovski), and presupposes the christological hermeneutic — one based on the concept of "realistic narrative" — of his own teacher H. W.

Frei, who was strongly influenced both by Barth's theology as well as by the classic work of the literary historian E. Auerbach, *Mimesis: The Representation of Reality in Western Literature*, trans. Willard R. Trask (Princeton: Princeton University Press, 1968).

108. Zizioulas quite rightly points out in *Being as Communion* that the notion of "institution" is qualified by pneumatological constitution: "In a christological perspective alone we can speak of the Church as *in-stituted* (by Christ), but in a pneumatological perspective we have to speak of it as *con-stituted* (by the Spirit). Christ *in-stitutes* and the Spirit *con-stitutes*. The difference between these two prepositions: *in-* and *con-* can be enormous ecclesiologically. The 'institution' is something presented to us as a fact, more or less a *fait-accomplit* [*sic*]. As such, it is a provocation to our freedom. The 'con-stitution' is something that involves us in its very being, something we accept freely, because we take part in its very emergence" (140).

109. Cf. Apology of the Augsburg Confession, *The Book of Concord,* trans. and ed. Theodore G. Tappert (Philadelphia: Fortress, 1959), 171: "We are not dreaming about some Platonic republic, as has been slanderously alleged, but we teach that this church actually exists, made up of true believers and righteous men scattered throughout the world. And we add its marks, the pure teaching of the Gospel and the sacraments. This church is properly called 'the pillar of truth' (I Tim. 3:15), for it retains the pure Gospel and what Paul calls the 'foundation' (I Cor. 3:12), that is, the true knowledge of Christ and faith."

110. Luther succinctly articulates this connection between trinitarian communion and ecclesial *koinonia* in a weekly sermon (October 17, 1528) on John 16–20, interpreting John 17:21: "Here he touches again on the high article of his deity which we discussed several times above, makes himself and the Father into a parable and example to explain what kind of unity he means. I and you are one (he is saying) in one divine being and majesty. According to the same example, they are also to be one and the same among themselves, that precisely the same unity is one in us that is incorporated into me and you, *summa,* that they are all one and purely one in us both, [baked] like one single cake, that they may have everything you and I can, hence that we, too, can partake of the divine nature, as St. Peter says (2 Pet. 1). For even if the Father and Christ are one in an incomprehensible way as a result of the divine essence, we nonetheless know that it is ours and that we can partake of him. . . . *Summa,* you cannot despise, revile, persecute, or use violence against any Christian, or, on the other hand, honor and do good things for no Christian without also doing it to God himself. . . . For everything God has, he has attached to our Lord Christ; Christ, however, is his bride; thus every Christian is attached to that bride just like one of that bride's limbs. And everything is connected together like a chain, forming a completely round circle, indeed, a beautiful crown" (*Weimar Ausgabe,* 28, 183,26–184,34).

111. P. Brunner associates the events at Pentecost with worship in articulating the soteriological telos of the church as public presence: "Something new happens at Pentecost. This Pentecostal outpouring of the Spirit did not occur in the Old Covenant, nor even in Jesus' own earthly ministry, nor also in the epiphanies of the resurrected Jesus during the forty days. With this outpouring of the Holy Spirit at Pente-

cost, Jesus, albeit corporeally invisible, comes as the pneuma both to and into his followers. Jesus' epiphany in the pneuma is the fruit of his cross and of his exaltation and thus also the fruit of God's entire previous salvific economy. . . . The outpouring of the Spirit brings to Jesus' body its final, pneumatic release, its pneumatic presence through which it now reaches for individual human beings and draws them into himself in a pneumatic and yet concretely historic event. The eschatologically new gift of Pentecost is this ontic-real corporeality and interiority of precisely this inclusion and incorporation. . . . The outpouring of the Spirit thus makes it possible for what happened to the body of Christ in death and resurrection to be concretely realized and actualized in the person seized by the pneuma. The events of Pentecost are thus the epiphany of the crucified, resurrected body of Jesus on this earth, a body that fills the All and is present before God's own throne. Pentecost is thus the epiphany of the church on earth" ("Zur Lehre vom Gottesdienst," 155f.; cf. the English edition, *Worship in the Name of Jesus*, 77f.).

112. Given the absence of church unity, one must find a way between the Scylla of a simple identification of the Spirit's activity with church doctrine and praxis, on the one hand, and the Charybdis of a pneumatological agnosticism on the other. The relation between church doctrine and praxis on the one hand and the activity of the Holy Spirit on the other should be posed as a *guiding ecumenical question*. That is, which core practices and which doctrinal formulations embody, foster, and evoke the unity of the church, and which become anew, in the form of an ecumenical *metanoia*, vessels for the teaching and recollection of the Holy Spirit?

113. Cf. in this regard the theological introduction to the writing by A. Sperl, in H. H. Borcherdt and G. Merz, eds., *Martin Luther. Ausgewählte Werke*, Ergänzungs-reihe, vol. 7, 3rd ed. (Munich: Kaiser, 1963), 139-46. Translations here according to "On the Councils and the Church," in *Luther's Works*, vol. 41, *Church and Ministry III*, ed. E. W. Gritsch (English translation) (Philadelphia: Fortress, 1966). On antinomianism cf. Steffen Kjeldgaard-Pedersen, "Antinomian Controversies." In *The Encyclopedia of Christianity* (Grand Rapids and Cambridge: Eerdmans; Leiden, Boston, and Cologne: Brill, 1999f.), 1:80f.

114. "*Ecclesia*, however, should mean the holy Christian people, not only of the days of the apostles, who are long since dead, but to the end of the world, so that there is always a holy Christian people on earth, in whom Christ lives, works, and rules, *per redemptionem*, 'through grace and the remission of sin,' and the Holy Spirit, *per vivificationem et sanctificationem*, 'through daily purging of sin and renewal of life,' so that we do not remain in sin but are enabled and obliged to lead a new life, abounding in all kinds of good works, as the Ten Commandments or the two tables of Moses' law command, and not in old, evil works" (Luther, "On the Councils," 144). For a very important contemporary actualization of Luther's widely forgotten ecclesiology of the "seven marks of the church" cf. Carl E. Braaten and Robert W. Jenson, eds., *Marks of the Body of Christ* (Grand Rapids: Eerdmans, 1999).

115. Luther, "On the Councils," 145.

116. Luther, "On the Councils," 147.

117. "We are speaking of the external word, preached orally by men like you

and me, for this is what Christ left behind as an external sign, by which his church, or his Christian people in the world, should be recognized. . . . Now, wherever you hear or see this word preached, believed, professed, and lived, do not doubt that the true *ecclesia sancta catholica,* 'a Christian holy people' must be there, even though their number is very small. For God's word 'shall not return empty' (Isa. 55:11)" (Luther, "On the Councils," 149-50).

118. "Second, God's people or the Christian holy people are recognized by the holy sacrament of baptism, wherever it is taught, believed, and administered correctly according to Christ's ordinance. That too is a public sign and a precious, holy possession by which God's people are sanctified" (Luther, "On the Councils," 151).

119. "Third, God's people, or Christian holy people, are recognized by the holy sacrament of the altar, wherever it is rightly administered, believed, and received, according to Christ's institution. This too is a public sign and a precious, holy possession left behind by Christ by which his people are sanctified so that they also exercise themselves in faith and openly confess that they are Christian, just as they do with the word and with baptism" (Luther, "On the Councils," 152).

120. "Now where you see sins forgiven or reproved in some persons, be it publicly or privately, you may know that God's people are there. If God's people are not there, the keys are not there either; and if the keys are not present for Christ, God's people are not present. Christ bequeathed them as a public sign and a holy possession, whereby the Holy Spirit again sanctifies the fallen sinners redeemed by Christ's death, and whereby the Christians confess that they are a holy people in this world under Christ. And those who refuse to be converted or sanctified again shall be cast out from this holy people, that is, bound and excluded by means of the keys, as happened to the unrepentant Antinomians" (Luther, "On the Councils," 153). Cf. on this dangerously neglected mark of the church the important contribution by D. Yeago, "The Office of the Keys: On the Disappearance of Discipline in Protestant Modernity," in Braaten and Jenson, eds., *Marks of the Body of Christ,* 95-122.

121. "Fifth, the church is recognized externally by the fact that it consecrates or calls ministers, or has offices that it is to administer. There must be bishops, pastors, or preachers, who publicly and privately give, administer, and use the aforementioned four things or holy possessions in behalf of and in the name of the church, or rather by reason of their institution by Christ, as St. Paul states in Ephesians 4:8, 'He received gifts among men . . .' — his gifts were that some should be apostles, some prophets, some evangelists, some teachers and governors, etc." (Luther, "On the Councils," 154).

122. "Sixth, the holy Christian people are externally recognized by prayer, public praise, and thanksgiving to God. Where you see and hear the Lord's Prayer prayed and taught; or psalms or other spiritual songs sung, in accordance with the word of God and the true faith; also the creed, the Ten Commandments, and the catechism used in public, you may rest assured that a holy Christian people of God are present" (Luther, "On the Councils," 164).

123. "Seventh, the holy Christian people are externally recognized by the holy possession of the sacred cross. They must endure every misfortune and persecution, all kinds of trials and evil from the devil, the world, and the flesh (as the Lord's Prayer

indicates) by inward sadness, timidity, fear, outward poverty, contempt, illness, and weakness, in order to become like their head, Christ. And the only reason they must suffer is that they steadfastly adhere to Christ and God's word, enduring this for the sake of Christ" (Luther, "On the Councils," 164f.).

124. Luther, "On the Councils," 165f.

125. Here we encounter a pendant to the Eastern Orthodox insight that theosis leads right through the middle of "asceticism" (i.e., the actualization of concrete Christian life) rather than past it. Cf. in this regard Felmy, 117ff., 121-25.

126. U. Kühn, *Kirche,* Handbuch Systematischer Theologie 10 (Gütersloh: Gütersloher Verlagshaus G. Mohn, 1980), 26. Concerning Luther's understanding of the church being both concealed and recognizable, cf. 25ff.

127. This distinction was merely erroneously modernized through identification with the distinction between externality and interiority in the modern sense.

128. Within the context of modern secular life in Europe and North America, Christian existence often takes place separated and far removed from these activities, or these activities themselves are functionalized within the framework of accommodated, substitutionary vehicles of meaning. The result is that for many people, Christian existence has become simply incomprehensible, an abstraction that must be filled with mysticism, activism, or moralism.

129. Viewed in this light, the Eastern Orthodox view that through baptism a person already enters an ecclesiastical ordo — and not, for example, only through ordination — seems ecumenically quite cogent. Cf. in this regard Zizioulas, *Being in Communion,* 216 and passim.

130. Cf. in this regard section III.3 in Part One above, "Praxis and Practice," and especially A. MacIntyre's explication of the term "practice." In a word: a "practice" differs from "praxis" insofar as it refers to a specific, teleologically directed nexus of acivities, while "praxis" refers to activities in the more comprehensive or collective sense.

131. "For Christian holiness, or the holiness common to Christendom, is found where the Holy Spirit gives people faith in Christ and thus sanctifies them . . . that is, he renews heart, soul, body, work, and conduct, inscribing the commandments of God not on tables of stone, but in hearts of flesh" (Luther, "On the Councils," 145).

132. Ordained office illustrates the unequivocal passivity of these practices. The ordained person is taken into service by the Holy Spirit through a unique practice, namely, ordination itself, that the person might take an "active" role together with the Spirit in at least five of the seven core practices, albeit in a continuing mode of a particular passivity constituting this office itself pneumatologically. By securing the pathos of the concrete performance of the first five marks, the ordained office throws into relief the soteriological character of gift attaching to all of the Spirit's practices. (The first five practices can be wrested from the soteriological poiesis of the Spirit and from the human pathos inherent to that poiesis only if "office," as a pure element of order and organization, is rationalistically functionalized.) This does not in any way, of course, involve the establishment of *superior* pastoral privileges or anything similar, but rather a strictly theological definition. Integrating these thoughts into the

communio-ecclesiology, we see clearly that all five marks imply the active participation of the congregation, even the notion of office itself and the rite of ordination grounding it. The ordained person merely stands — albeit in a decisive position — for the poiesis of the Holy Spirit, thereby "actively" securing the congregational pathos specifically required by the first five marks in personal representation. The sixth and seventh marks are to be understood differently in this respect. The practices Luther loosely subsumes under the sixth mark refer less to public worship than to forms of domestic worship and prayer, congregational and domestic Bible reading, and catechetical instruction. These practices, however, are tied to specific texts and forms whose telos similarly is sanctification, that is, growth in faith. The final mark focuses on the overall life of all who are baptized, here specifically under the aspect of discipleship in temptation. The suffering of Christians as confessors and as martyrs occupies the central position here. At issue is pathos in the elementary-physical sense, in being qualified by Christ through his Spirit even unto death, that is, to approximate Christ, the *forma fidei,* so closely that suffering for the sake of Christ and his truth becomes the ultimate fulfillment of this practice. This "final" activity of the Holy Spirit marks the limit of our analogous reference to "practice" with regard to Luther's seven "holy possessions" of the Holy Spirit, for here the practice itself dissolves into pure *passio* and is simultaneously nonetheless the greatest, albeit usually hidden, human *actio* in the confession of Christ.

133. The impetus to use this formulation came from G. Hansen, whose study "The Doctrine of the Trinity and Liberation Theology: A Study of the Trinitarian Doctrine and Its Place in Latin American Liberation Theology" (Diss., Lutheran School of Theology at Chicago, 1994) carries forward one of G. Gutierrez's central ideas in understanding Christian praxis in the comprehensive sense as subsisting enhypostatically in the Spirit. Cf. Hansen, 862-70. Hansen uses a comprehensive concept of praxis rather than one differentiated into specific practices; although he does allude to the concrete ecclesiological understanding of this praxis, he does not fully explicate it.

134. Concerning the concept of "enhypostasis" within the framework of Chalcedonian and post-Chalcedonian Christology, cf. W. Pannenberg, *Jesus — God and Man,* trans. Lewis L. Wilkins and Duane A. Priebe, 2nd ed. (Philadelphia: Westminster, 1977) 337-44; A. Grillmeier, *Christ in Christian Tradition. II/2: From the Council of Chalcedon (451) to Gregory the Great (540-609),* trans. John Bowden, 2nd rev. ed. (Atlanta: John Knox, 1995), 181-312; S. Otto, *Person und Subsistenz. Die philosophische Anthropologie des Leontios von Byzanz. Ein Beitrag zur spätantiken Geistesgeschichte* (Munich: W. Fink, 1968). Regarding the specific philosophical and christological use of the term, I am following John of Damascus, *The Philosophical Chapters,* trans. Frederic H. Chase, Jr., Fathers of the Church, vol. 37 (New York: Fathers of the Church, 1958), 7-110, chaps. 43-46, and John of Damascus, *The Orthodox Faith,* trans. Frederic H. Chase, Jr., Fathers of the Church, vol. 37 (New York: Fathers of the Church, 1958), 165-406, III, 9 and III, 11.

135. The analogous use of this christological term in pneumatology needs some explanation. Two very good objections can be raised *against* using it to refer to the

core church practices: (1) Strictly speaking, practices are not hypostasized in any event, and rather represent the activities of hypostases. (2) Use of this term in reference to practices excludes the *presence* of human agency, since its christological use intends specifically to exclude any hypostasis of Christ's human nature different from the logos. Both objections justifiably prohibit any strict, univocal application of the term "enhypostasis" to pneumatology. By contrast, its *analogous* use seems both possible and promising. Practices do doubtless involve specific kinds of activities that in their own turn presuppose human agency and agency its embodiment in the performance. The core church practices, however, are defined as *poiemata* of the Holy Spirit through which the latter implements its salvific-economic mission. The principle of the individual existence of these distinct practices thus consists immediately in the person and salvific-economic mission of the Holy Spirit. Quite apart from their nature as "holy possessions" of the Holy Spirit, of course, these activities do still embody human agency. In the strict, univocal sense, no "anhypostasis" can be asserted for them, since they do after all exist "in and for themselves." Without their soteriological telos, however, these core church practices become utterly meaningless; that is, taken "in and for themselves," they lose precisely that which constitutes them. In that sense one can very well speak *analogously* about the "anhypostasis" of the core church practices. Hence, in the following discussion references to the "enhypostasis of the core church practices in the Holy Spirit" evoke *per analogiam* the notion of "existing in another" within the framework of pneumatology. (Here my own analogous use draws from the definition of *enhypostaton* presented by John of Damascus in his *Philosophical Chapters*, 69: "Again, that nature is called *enhypostaton* which has been assumed by another hypostasis and in this has its existence.") Although the core church practices *qua* practices naturally always include the "presence" of human action, the latter is neither causatively nor constitutively that which makes these practices into the core church practices, or, using Luther's terminology, into the "holy possessions" of the Holy Spirit. Notwithstanding their independent status as human acts, the Holy Spirit remains the bearer of the soteriological features and efficacy of the core church practices. (The Palamite notion of *henosis kat'energeian* grounding a perichoresis of divine and human action may be more appropriate for a pneumatological grounding of the core church practices; unfortunately, its introduction and explication would require considerably more effort.)

This analogous use of "enhypostasis" is an attempt to carry forward logically the neo-economic doctrine of the Trinity and the *communio*-ecclesiology. If the hypostatic identity of the Holy Spirit cannot be distinguished from its economic mission, then the activities through which the Holy Spirit fulfills that mission are to be understood entirely from the perspective of that mission. That is, their telos and thus that which makes them into constitutive church practices exists *only* in the person and work of the Holy Spirit. Positing a hypostasis strictly unique to the core church practices, that is, a reality subsisting utterly "in itself," amounts to understanding them primarily from an anthropological theory of action after all, in which case they cannot be called *practices*. "In and for themselves," they lack the goal constituting their teleological structure. Analogous reference to a pneumatological enhypostasis is what first renders the "holy possessions" comprehensible as practices of the Holy Spirit.

This pneumatological grounding of the core church practices does not yet say anything about the activity of the Spirit in the larger sense. The ecclesiological pneumatology developed here does not allow the *e silentio* conclusion implying that the Holy Spirit and its eschatological work are, for example, absent in the rest of creation.

136. Eeva Martikainen, *Doctrina. Studien zu Luthers Begriff der Lehre,* Schriften der Luther-Agricola-Gesellschaft (Finland) A 26 (Helsinki: Finnische Theologische Literaturgesellschaft, 1992). Cf. also Eeva Martikainen, "Die Lehre und die Anwesenheit Gottes in der Theologie Luthers," in *Luther und Theosis. Vergöttlichung als Thema der abendländischen Theologie,* ed. Simo Peura and Antti Raunio, Schriften der Luther-Agricola-Gesellschaft (Finland) A 25 (Helsinki: Finnische Theologische Literaturgesellschaft, 1990), 215-32.

137. Cf. in this regard her debate with the philosophical understanding in Seeberg, Ritschl, Herrmann, Ebeling, and Iwand in *Doctrina,* 5-21. Her criticism of Ebeling can stand representatively for virtually the entire modern Protestant Luther-research and for its distinct philosophical perspective: "The theological modification of the so-called transcendental method also influences the understanding of the character of doctrinal statements. Because the nature of faith is always shaped from the perspective of the subject, and because this subject does not give in to the criteria of objective reality, the statements expressing this cannot be made objective. As far as statements about God are concerned, this means that one can speak about God (the pure transcendental ego) only on the basis of his actions or relation to the finite subject. . . . The influence of the transcendental method shaped not only the Ritschl-school and the Luther-interpretation drawing from existential thinking, but also the Luther-interpretation deriving from Karl Barth (Iwand), which in opposition to neo-Protestant theology believes it has reintroduced into modern theology the concept of doctrine used by Luther himself. This, too, is based on a fundamental anti-metaphysical posture" (16).

138. "Theologically, the conceptual point of departure for modern Luther-scholarship is the Kantian transcendental method. This method's critique of classical metaphysics also directs itself against classical theology insofar as one assumes the latter is also *eo ipso* metaphysically shaped. The result is that the concept of doctrine, like the entirety of theology, is evaluated and classified as metaphysical. Modern Luther-scholarship believes that the classical concept of doctrine presupposes an ontological mode of thinking requiring that theological concepts also be interpreted on the basis of *one* concept of being. Wherever the conceptual point of departure of modern Luther-scholarship has tied the classical concept of doctrine to the metaphysics of being, the criticism of the latter has also been directed against the concept of doctrine itself" (Martikainen, *Doctrina,* 16). Concerning the problem of transcendentalism in contemporary Protestant Luther scholarship, cf. the comprehensive treatment of R. Saarinen's study, *Gottes Wirken auf uns. Die transzendentale Deutung des Gegenwart-*

Christi-Motivs in der Lutherforschung, Veröffentlichungen des Instituts für Europäische Geschichte Mainz 137 (Stuttgart: Steiner Verlag Wiesbaden, 1989).

139. Martikainen, *Doctrina,* 22-28; cf. also Martikainen, "Die Lehre und die Anwesenheit Gottes in der Theologie Luthers," 218f.: "Luther's renunciation of theology based on metaphysics thus is not rejecting the assertion of a genuinely present God. In fact, quite the contrary is the case. Correct theology presupposes the God who is present. My hypothesis is thus that for Luther, theology is an independent discipline with a real object, namely, God as the God who is present. God as the object of theology thus cannot be derived from the object of any other discipline; he is neither the being of metaphysics nor the goal of the will in moral philosophy."

140. Martikainen, *Doctrina,* 89.

141. Luther adheres to the nominalist position in beginning with the radical incommensurability of objects from different disciplines, but not with the radical incommensurability of language and object, a philosophical position characteristic only of modernity.

142. Cf. Martikainen, *Doctrina,* 29-44.

143. Martikainen, *Doctrina,* 56f. Here Martikainen is referring especially to the following citation from Luther's *Lectures on Galatians* (1535): "[W]e say in opposition that faith takes hold of Christ and that He is the form that adorns and informs faith as color does the wall. Therefore Christian faith is not an idle quality or an empty husk in the heart, which may exist in a state of mortal sin until love comes along to make it alive. But if it is true faith, it is a sure trust and firm acceptance in the heart. It takes hold of Christ in such a way that Christ is the object of faith, or rather not the object but, so to speak, the One who is present in the faith itself [in ipsa fide Christus adest]" (*Luther's Works,* vol. 26, 129). Cf. in this regard especially T. Mannermaa, "In ipsa fide Christus adest. Der Schnittpunkt zwischen lutherischer und orthodoxer Theologie," in Mannermaa, *Der im Glauben gegenwärtige Christus. Rechtfertigung und Vergottung. Zum ökumenischen Dialog,* Arbeiten zur Geschichte und Theologie des Luthertums, n.s., 8 (Hanover: Lutherisches Verlagshaus, 1989), 11-94.

144. Cf. in this regard the discussion of pathos and poiesis, praxis and practice in section III of Part One above.

145. Martikainen, *Doctrina,* 57.

146. Martikainen, *Doctrina,* 58.

147. Martikainen, *Doctrina,* 64.

148. Martikainen, *Doctrina,* 63.

149. This is why it is fully intentional rather than accidental that the Lutheran confessional writings begin with the Apostolic, Nicaean-Constantinopolitan, and Athanasian symbols. These three early church symbols constitute the normative horizon within which the doctrinal statements of the *Book of Concord* are to be understood. Various scholars have pointed out that patristic theology played a decisive role for Luther especially in his early period. Cf. W. Maurer, "Die Einheit der Theologie Luthers," and especially "Die Anfänge von Luthers Theologie," in Maurer, *Kirche und Geschichte. Gesammelte Aufsätze,* vol. 1, *Luther und das evangelische Bekenntnis,*

ed. E.-W. Kohls and G. Müller (Göttingen: Vandenhoeck & Ruprecht, 1970), 11-21, 22-37. For a discussion of the debate surrounding this understanding of early church confessions in Protestant theology, cf. U. Kühn, "Evangelische Rezeption altkirchlicher Bekenntnisse. Am Beispiel des Projektes der Kommission für Glauben und Kirchenverfassung 'Auf dem Weg zu einem gemeinsamen Ausdruck des apostolischen Glaubens heute,'" in *Vernunft des Glaubens. Wissenschaftliche Theologie und kirchliche Lehre. Festschrift Wolfhart Pannenberg*, ed. J. Rohls and G. Wenz (Göttingen: Vandenhoeck & Ruprecht, 1988), 652-69.

150. Cf. in this regard the generally instructive volume, *Luther und Theosis*, and especially the introductory article by T. Mannermaa, "Theosis als Thema der finnischen Lutherforschung," 11-26; also Mannermaa, *Der im Glauben gegenwärtige Christus*, and *Thesaurus Lutheri. Auf der Suche nach neuen Paradigmen der Luther-Forschung*, ed. T. Mannermaa et al., Schriften der Luther-Agricola-Gesellschaft (Finland) A 24 (Helsinki: Finnische Theologische Literaturgesellschaft, 1987). Cf. in particular the introductory article by T. Mannermaa, "Grundlagenforschung der Theologie Luthers und die Ökumene," 17-36. For a very instructive and accessible introduction to the new Finnish Luther research, cf. most recently *Union with Christ: The New Finnish Interpretation of Luther*, ed. Carl E. Braaten and Robert W. Jenson (Grand Rapids: Eerdmans, 1998).

151. Cf. in this regard the instructive presentation by H. J. Iwand, "Der moderne Mensch und das Dogma," in Iwand, *Nachgelassene Werke*, vol. 2, ed. Helmut Gollwitzer and Walter Kreck (Munich: Kaiser, 1966), 91-105: "Dogma executes the same movement that human beings do precisely because God's word does not execute this movement, since God's word remains stable in its status as the center toward which all else is directed" (99). "Dogma is always assigned to human effort. The ultimate, however, namely, the gospel itself, does not derive from human beings; to use Pauline terminology: here things are not 'in a human way'" (104). At the same time, any trinitarian grounding of *doctrina* must consider Iwand's justified caveat: "Some misuse dogma by isolating it from its ultimate goal and purpose and then deal with it as if these were holy possessions in and for themselves. . . . Dogma can obviously result in people defending it with fanatical zeal such that it becomes an end in itself, a 'letter,' and such that they overlook the difficult, but only true and salient relation between letter and Spirit" (96f.). "Only now can it happen that the right use of dogma is replaced by what one calls 'orthodoxy'; that cost what it may, correct doctrine is enthroned such that one does not worry whether this is effecting any decisions of faith as such, or whether this actually addresses the human being of our time or age, namely, our brothers and sisters, the actual human beings in this world here and now with their thousand questions and concerns, but that it is dictated: This is the correct doctrine, and this is what you are to believe" (97f.).

152. Cf. in this regard the still important study by R. Prenter, *Spiritus Creator*, trans. John M. Jensen (Philadelphia: Muhlenberg, 1953).

153. Martikainen, *Doctrina*, 65; cf. also 68: "According to Luther, doctrine not only offers statements that are to be considered true, but also leads a person to God. To believe in Christ thus means basically nothing other than to believe in the same

God. Faith in God, however, is possible only in Christ, to whom the Holy Spirit points and to whom it leads."

154. Martikainen, *Doctrina,* 64: "At its core, theological doctrine is always salvific doctrine, and in its specific meaning and most characteristic parts refers to the present Christ and to the God at work in him, the dispenser and creator of all that is good, the victor over death and sin, the initiator of faith, and the dispenser of love." Precisely this is the enhypostatic being of *doctrina* in the Holy Spirit; precisely as such, it is a work of the Spirit.

155. "Hic est peculiaris modus huius Doctoris, quem Spiritus sanctus hoc in loco ostendere voluit, cum Patri tribuit vocem et tamen hunc Regem Doctorem esse ostendit. Vult enim, sicut Christus quoque facit, per Christum adducere nos ad Patrem" (Luther, *Weimar Ausgabe,* 40/2, 254, 23-26).

156. Cf. Martikainen, *Doctrina,* 65f., and Martikainen, "Die Lehre und die Anwesenheit Gottes in der Theologie Luthers," 220f.: "In all points, doctrine refers to the God who is present, and is of great significance for the emergence and growth of justifying faith. Doctrine shows faith the God who is present, the God faith then seizes and to which it holds fast in trust."

157. Martikainen, *Doctrina,* 63.

158. Martikainen, *Doctrina,* 63, refers especially to expressions in Luther's sermons, e.g., *Weimar Ausgabe,* 36, 80, 4-7; 36, 522, 1-5; 36, 530, 1; 37, 179, 22; 37, 191, 19-20, 23-24; 37, 282, 1-2.

159. Cf. in this regard D. Yeago, "The New Testament and the Nicene Dogma: A Contribution to the Recovery of Theological Exegesis," *Pro Ecclesia* 3 (1994): 152-64, and the entire study of J. Koopmans, *Das altkirchliche Dogma in der Reformation,* Beiträge zur evangelischen Theologie 22 (Munich: Kaiser, 1955).

160. This is also the direction R. Slenczka seems to take in developing the inspiration of Scripture from the perspective of pneumatology in *Kirchliche Entscheidung in theologischer Verantwortung. Grundlagen — Kriterien — Grenzen* (Göttingen: Vandenhoeck & Ruprecht, 1991), 47ff.

161. In recent exegesis, B. Childs's canonical proposal especially emphasizes this unity of Scripture deriving from its object, namely, from the self-mediating God. Cf. most recently B. Childs, *Biblical Theology of the Old and New Testaments: Theological Reflection on the Christian Bible* (Minneapolis: Fortress, 1992). This proposal itself needs a stronger explicit theological hermeneutic of the sort presented, for example, by F. Mildenberger in his three-volume *Biblische Dogmatik* (Stuttgart: W. Kohlhammer, 1991-93). The overall disposition of his mutual distinction and association of theology and economy implies the same trinitarian framework that would need to be explicated here, namely, an understanding of Scripture from the perspective of the economy of salvation and pneumatology. Mildenberger approximates this in his reference to Scripture as the means of grace. A pneumatological and salvific-economic understanding of the canon would also eliminate having to choose between a reifying insistence on an abstract principle of *sola scriptura,* on the one hand, and the historical-critical undercutting of this principle and a socio-historic reconstruction of the canon on the other. For the principle *sola scriptura* as the authority transcending all

church doctrine obtains not independent of, but rather *in,* the church. The Reformation formula *sola scriptura* is accordingly a *pneumatological* formula coming to bear only in connection with the core church practices themselves, for only here does "what promotes Christ" and what is mediated as *doctrina definita* emerge clearly in Scripture. Hence all church doctrine is subordinated to the canon in its Christian form precisely because the canonical witness preserves the *doctrina definita* in its soteriological telos in a way that was binding for all subsequent ecclesial doctrinal formation. Cf. in this regard S. Hauerwas, "The Politics of the Bible: *Sola Scriptura* as Heresy?" in Hauerwas, *Unleashing the Scripture: Freeing the Bible from Captivity to America* (Nashville: Abingdon, 1993), 15-44, and my objections on 153, 157. It is again P. Brunner who articulates precisely this inherent connection between economy of salvation, pneumatology, and canonical authority, precisely also in its relation to church doctrine: "The acceptance or exclusion of a writing into or from the canon is a process analogous to the formation of dogma. In the delimitation of canon, the Spirit is working through the medium of the apostolic gospel in a way analogous to that in delimitation through dogma. . . . Scripture exercises its unique authority in the simultaneous activities of the four instruments effected by the Spirit. Scripture exercises this authority only where faith actually seizes the apostolic gospel attested in it, namely, only *in* the church. Scriptural authority refers to all proclamation of the church, its preaching, instruction, liturgy, doctrine, postcanonical dogmas and confessions. . . . Scriptural authority focuses on one thing: preserving the substantive identity of the present proclamation of the church with the proclamation of the apostles. Scripture is thus an authority *for* the church" (*Pro Ecclesia,* 1:43f.).

162. Precisely because the canon itself is already to be understood as a form of church doctrine, namely, as the authoritative establishment of the textual framework of the scriptural witness itself, one sees that the *doctrina evangelii* is never accessible without *church doctrine.*

163. Consider merely in Roman Catholic theology Thomas Aquinas, or more recently the French *nouvelle theologie,* or Gutierrez and the mainstream of liberation theology.

164. Cf. F. Schleiermacher, *Kurze Darstellung des theologischen Studiums zum Behuf einleitender Vorlesungen,* ed. H. Scholz (Darmstadt: Wissenschaftliche Buchgesellschaft, 1961), §§195-231, esp. 203-8. English translation: *Brief Outline on the Study of Theology,* trans. Terrence N. Tice (Richmond: John Knox, 1966), 71-82, esp. 74-75.

165. Examples in the most general sense include the Cappadocians, Maximus Confessor, John of Damascus, and Gregory Palamas for the Eastern churches; Augustine and Thomas Aquinas for the Western churches, in the more specific sense Thomas Aquinas for post-Tridentine Roman Catholicism, especially since the encyclical *Aeterni Patris* of Leo XIII; the Reformation thinkers Luther, Melanchthon, Calvin, and Zwingli for the various Reformation churches; or John Wesley for Methodism. More recently, one might mention the significance of Karl Rahner's theology and of the French *nouvelle theologie* for Vatican II, and of Karl Barth's theology for the Barmen Declaration.

166. Examples here include the writings of Luther and Melanchthon, which became part of the Lutheran confessional writings within the framework of the *Book of Concord,* or the forty instructional sermons of John Wesley, which became part of the explicit church doctrine of the Methodist church.

167. Let me mention as a formality that this conclusion by no means implies or must imply inquisition, banishment, burning at the stake, and so on.

168. I will examine the church *as* such a public in Part Four below.

169. Martikainen, *Doctrina,* 70f.

170. K. Beyschlag, *Grundriß der Dogmengeschichte,* vol. 1, *Gott und Welt* (Darmstadt: Wissenschaftliche Buchgesellschaft, 1982), 18. Concerning the concept of dogma in the larger sense, cf. 1-28.

171. Cf. in this regard the presentation in E. Gritsch and R. Jenson, "An Ecumenical Proposal of Dogma," in Gritsch and Jenson, *Lutheranism: The Theological Movement and Its Confessional Writings* (Philadelphia: Fortress, 1976), 2-15; and Zizioulas, *Being as Communion,* 118. The antitheses "timeless/atemporal-temporal" and "irreversible/reversible" would have to be rethought from the perspective of pneumatology. One important step toward overcoming ecumenically the first antithesis is Jenson, *Unbaptized God,* 107-18, and a step toward overcoming ecumenically the second antithesis is G. Lindbeck, *The Nature of Doctrine: Religion and Theology in a Postliberal Age* (Philadelphia: Westminster, 1984), 79-111, though the latter does lack an explicit pneumatological-ecclesiological reflection of his extremely fertile ecumenical proposal. Cf. in this regard the analysis and critique of Lindbeck's proposal in Part Two above.

172. Cf. in this regard G. Sauter, "Confessio — Konkordie — Consensus. Perspektiven des Augsburger Bekenntnisses für das Bekennen und Lehren der Kirche heute," *Evangelische Theologie* 40 (1980): 478-94, and G. Sauter, "Consensus," in *Theologische Realenzyklopädie,* 8:182-89, where Sauter asks whether "we human beings are able to choose our consensus freely[.] Luther denied this, finding in consensus rather the sign of the new human being created by God in faith: Consensus concurs with God's reality (cf. *Weimar Ausgabe* 8, 113-15)" (8:183). Cf. also Slenczka, 273.

173. O. Weber precisely formulates this. In his view dogmatics questions *extant* dogma *today* so that the church is capable of making *new* decisions *tomorrow* (*Foundations of Dogmatics,* vol. 1, trans. and ann. by Darrell L. Guder [Grand Rapids: Eerdmans, 1981], 43).

174. "Pentecost is thus the epiphany of the church on earth" (Brunner, "Zur Lehre vom Gottesdienst," 156).

Notes to Part Four

1. Cf. in this regard K. Schwarzwäller, "Delectari assertionibus. Zur Struktur von Luthers Pneumatologie," *Luther-Jahrbuch* 38 (1971): 26-58.

2. In the following discussion, I am drawing on the recent brief but extremely dense interpretation of Luther's *The Bondage of the Will* by R. Jenson, "An Ontology

of Freedom in the *De Servo Arbitrio* of Luther," *Modern Theology* 10 (1994): 247-52. Jenson persuasively understands Luther's writing as a trinitarian ontology of freedom that can be combined with the doctrine of the Trinity implied within the *communio*-ecclesiology. More precisely, by interpreting Luther's writing from a strictly trinitarian perspective, Jenson uncovers its implicit *ontology of freedom*, one far transcending the controversy with Erasmus of Rotterdam. His reading by no means claims to be the last word in the history of interpretation of this profound work. He attempts rather to read Luther "against the grain" with an eye on his real object, namely, to comprehend God's freedom not as an abstraction, but from the perspective of God's economy of salvation. So in a certain, quite specific sense, Jenson deals with Luther in an "Eastern Orthodox" fashion; rather than simply attributing the *liberum arbitrium* as an abstraction to the *deus ipse,* he discloses the soteriological center of the *liberum arbitrium* from the perspective of the *deus praedicatus* such that it becomes clear just why God is able to grant participation in his own freedom. Concerning this topic as a whole, cf. H. Vorster, *Das Freiheitsverständnis bei Thomas von Aquin und Martin Luther,* Kirche und Konfession 8 (Göttingen: Vandenhoeck & Ruprecht, 1965), esp. 286-313.

3. Cf. Luther, "The Bondage of the Will," in *Luther's Works,* vol. 33, *Career of the Reformer III,* trans. and ed. Philip S. Watson (Philadelphia: Fortress, 1972), 68: "It follows now that free choice is plainly a divine term, and can be properly applied to none but the Divine Majesty alone; for he alone can do and does (as the psalmist says [Ps. 115:3]) whatever he pleases in heaven and on earth. If this is attributed to men, it is no more rightly attributed than if divinity itself also were attributed to them, which would be the greatest possible sacrilege. Theologians therefore ought to have avoided this term when they wished to speak of human ability, leaving it to be applied to God alone. They should, moreover, have removed it from the lips and language of men, treating it as a kind of sacred and venerable name for their God. And if they attributed any power at all to men, they should teach that it must be called by another name than free choice, especially as we know and clearly perceive that the common people are miserably deceived and led astray by that term, since they hear and understand it in a very different sense from that which the theologians mean and discuss."

4. Cf. Jenson, 248.

5. Jenson, 248, defines *promissio* as follows: "A promise is a communicated decision not to decide otherwise later, and so is an exercise of decision covering the whole of the promiser's future, which in God's case is all the future there is. And for someone always to *keep* his promises, he must be sovereign over all contingencies (*Weimar Ausgabe,* 18, p. 619)."

6. Cf. Luther, "The Bondage of the Will," 42: "For if you doubt or disdain to know that God foreknows all things, not contingently, but necessarily and immutably, how can you believe his promise and place a sure trust and reliance on them? For when he promises anything, you ought to be certain that he knows and is able and willing to perform what he promises." And accordingly: "Therefore, Christian faith is entirely extinguished, the promises of God and the whole gospel are completely destroyed, if we teach and believe that it is not for us to know the necessary fore-

knowledge of God and the necessity of the things that are to come to pass. For this is the one supreme consolation of Christians in all adversities, to know that God does not lie, but does all things immutably, and that his will can neither be resisted nor changed nor hindered" (43).

7. Cf. Luther, "The Bondage of the Will," 139f., esp.: "God must therefore be left to himself in his own majesty, for in this regard we have nothing to do with him, nor has he willed that we should have anything to do with him. . . . But God hidden in his majesty neither deplores nor takes away death, but works life, death, and all in all. For there he has not bound himself by his word, but has kept himself free over all things."

8. Jenson, 249. Cf. Luther, "The Bondage of the Will," 64, esp.: "And this readiness or will to act he cannot by his own powers omit, restrain, or change, but he keeps on willing and being ready; and even if he is compelled by external force to do something different, yet the will within him remains averse and he is resentful at whatever compels or resists it. He would not be resentful, however, if it were changed and he willingly submitted to the compulsion."

9. "The positing of a *merum velle*, an actual but uncommitted will, is a 'dialectical figment,' resulting from 'ignorance of realities and attention to words' *(ignorantia rerum et observantia vocabulorum)*, from the metaphysician's besetting sin of assuming that things are always 'disposed in reality as they are in words'" (Jenson, 249).

10. Hence Luther can say that every human is like a mount on which either God or the devil is riding — but which never is without a rider (cf. Luther, "The Bondage of the Will," 65f.). Concerning Luther's use of the metaphor of the mount, cf. B. Wannenwetsch, "Zwischen Schindmähre und Wildpferd. Luthers Reittier-Metapher ethisch betrachtet," *Luther* 65 (1994): 22-35. Cf. also Vorster, 415-18.

11. Jenson, 250.

12. "God is rapt by another without dependence on an other than God. He can intelligibly be said to be this as the Spirit, as the lively future of God, is himself the very same God" (Jenson, 250). Jenson's trinitarian understanding of the *liberum arbitrium* implicitly draws from the theses of the most recent Finnish Lutheran scholarship. Cf. in this regard especially T. Mannermaa, "Hat Luther eine trinitarische Ontologie?" in *Luther und die trinitarische Tradition. Ökumenische und philosophische Perspektiven*, ed. J. Henbach, 43-60. Veröffentlichungen der Luther-Akademie Ratzeburg 23. Erlangen: Martin-Luther-Verlag, 1994, and in general T. Mannermaa, *Der im Glauben gegenwärtige Christus. Rechtfertigung und Vergottung. Zum ökumenischen Dialog*, Arbeiten zur Geschichte und Theologie des Luthertums, n.s., 8 (Hanover: Lutherisches Verlagshaus, 1989). For a recent and very accessible introduction to this school of Luther interpretation cf. Carl E. Braaaten and Robert W. Jenson, eds., *Union with Christ: The New Finnish Interpretation of Luther* (Grand Rapids: Eerdmans, 1998).

13. Cf. in this regard K. Barth, *Church Dogmatics* II/1 (English translation) (Edinburgh: T. & T. Clark, 1957), 524: "Power in itself is not merely neutral. Power in itself is evil. It is nothing less than freedom from restraint and suppression; revolt and domination. If power by itself were the omnipotence of God it would mean that God was evil, that He was the spirit of revolution and tyranny *par excellence*."

14. Because Jenson radically grounds God's freedom economically, in the rela-

tion of Jesus to his Father, God's freedom becomes identical with the person of the Spirit.

15. Cf. Luther, "The Bondage of the Will," 65. Here Luther is picking up a key concept from *The Freedom of a Christian* (1520) and introducing it at a decisive juncture in his treatise on *The Bondage of the Will.*

16. Cf. in this regard Vorster, 308ff. and 380-85.

17. "For if God is in us, Satan is absent, and only a good will is present; if God is absent, Satan is present, and only an evil will is in us. Neither God nor Satan permits sheer unqualified willing in us, but as you have rightly said, having lost our liberty, we are forced to serve sin, that is, we will sin and evil, speak sin and evil, do sin and evil" (Luther, "The Bondage of the Will," 115). This is precisely the freedom Erasmus ascribes to human beings. Thus H. J. Iwand: "Erasmus defined the 'free will' as the 'power with which a person can cling to or turn away from that which is necessary for salvation.' The *liberum arbitrium* is the free, responsible decision in which a person stands between good and evil, salvation and damnation" ("Theologische Einführung," in *Daß der freie Wille nichts sei. Antwort D. Martin Luthers an Erasmus von Rotterdam*. Martin Luther, *Ausgewählte Werke*, Supplement series, vol. 1, ed. Hans Hermann Borcherdt and Georg Merz, 3rd ed. [Munich: Kaiser, 1962], 253-64; here 256).

18. Cf. Luther, "The Bondage of the Will," 64f. I will risk adducing an explicatory analogy here. An alcoholic can exercise his or her *libentia* without further ado, that is, can "freely" choose between various kinds of alcohol. That person cannot, however, freely decide concerning the addiction *itself*. Here a person can only "*become* free," that is, be *liberated* by being led by others into freedom from addiction. A *liberum arbitrium,* that is, a completely free disposition over oneself, is not — *per definitionem,* so to speak — at the disposal of the alcoholic. So also, according to Luther, is the situation of human beings in their relation to God under the condition of sin. *Libentia* simply cannot accomplish anything here; indeed, it can only occasion the fateful illusion of false "freedom" over against God *(coram Deo).*

19. "But if a Stronger One comes who overcomes him and takes us as His spoil, then through his Spirit we are again slaves and captives — though this is royal freedom — so that we readily will and do what he wills" (Luther, "The Bondage of the Will," 65).

20. "Therefore when God 'enraptures us' *(nos rapiat),* he frees us by sharing with us his own freedom, his *liberum arbitrium.* Human freedom, in the only sense Luther wants to talk about, is nothing less than participation in God's own triune rapture of freedom. We pick up the last thread: Luther's usage in *de servo arbitrium* [*sic*] is invariant that God frees us 'by the Spirit,' by that personhood in which he is his own freedom" (Jenson, 252).

21. One of these famous formulations is found right at the beginning of *The Bondage of the Will:* "Permit us to be assertors, to be devoted to assertions and delight in them, while you stick to your Skeptics and Academics till Christ calls you too. The Holy Spirit is no Skeptic, and it is not doubts or mere opinions that he has written on our hearts, but assertions more sure and certain than life itself and all experience"

(*The Bondage of the Will*, 24). Cf. in this regard Schwarzwäller, "Delectari assertionibus."

22. The enormous substantive concurrence with Eastern Orthodox *communio*-
ecclesiology becomes immediately apparent when we consider Zizioulas's understanding of freedom: "We must free ourselves of the notion that freedom consists in
arbitrariness, and must rather understand freedom as a movement toward the
communio. The Spirit does indeed give us freedom, but it is the freedom of God himself, which is not merely the capacity to choose between various possibilities, and certainly not between good and evil as in the freedom of created existence. The freedom
given by the Spirit consists in being free from selfishness and individualism, something the Spirit gives us in the church; and this in its own turn lets it simultaneously
become the Spirit of freedom and the creator of the congregation" ("Die
pneumatologische Dimension der Kirche," *IKZ Communio* 2 [1973]: 142).

23. This is the justified, precisely delimited place for the discussion of the academic freedom of theology.

24. Luther, *Lectures on Galatians, 1535, Luther's Works*, vol. 26, trans. and ed.
Jaroslav Pelikan (St. Louis: Concordia, 1963), 387. "Ideo nostra theologia est certa, quia
ponit nos extra nos: non debeo niti in conscientia mea, sensuali persona, opere, sed in
promissione divina, veritate, quae non potest fallere" (*Weimar Ausgabe*, 40/1, 589, 8ff.).

25. That this statement is made with reference to the *theologia crucis* in its antithesis to the *theologia gloriae* is also of significance for the present context, since
Christ's suffering, cross, and resurrection stand at the center of the entire salvific
economy. Cf. the entire citation in Luther, "Heidelberg Disputation," *Luther's Works,
vol. 31, Career of the Reformer I*, ed. Harold J. Grimm (Philadelphia: Muhlenberg,
1957), 40: "19. That person does not deserve to be called a theologian who looks
upon the invisible things of God as though they were clearly perceptible in those
things which have actually happened [Rom. 1:20]. 20. He deserves to be called a theologian, however, who comprehends the visible and manifest things of God seen
through suffering and the cross. 21. A theology of glory calls evil good and good evil.
A theology of the cross calls the thing what it actually is."

26. I will refer in this context to the second chapter of John D. Zizioulas, *Being
as Communion: Studies in Personhood and the Church*, Contemporary Greek Theologians 4 (Crestwood, N.Y.: St. Vladimir's Seminary, 1985; 2nd ed., 1993), "Truth and
Communion," 67-122. For the most recent presentation and engagement of
Zizioulas's eucharistic ecclesiology from a Protestant perspective cf. the important
study by M. Volf, *After Our Likeness: The Church as the Image of the Trinity* (Grand
Rapids: Eerdmans, 1998), 73-123.

27. This reification involves a separation of the intellectual content of church
doctrine from its soteriological telos, not a challenge to the notion that doctrine does
indeed refer to an object and thus has "content." The *sacrificium intellectus* this
prompts is thus the surrender to a "truth" whose reference is no longer God's salvific
economy, but an abstraction separated off from it. Church doctrine that remains focused on its soteriological telos is always simultaneously a *consoling, comforting* doc-

trine insofar as for the sake of those in need of redemption it holds fast to the *doctrina* of the gospel in demarcation from false doctrine.

28. Here Zizioulas draws especially from the theology of Maximus Confessor, which carries on the theological work of the Cappadocians Basil, Gregory of Nazianzus, and Gregory of Nyssa. Cf. *Being as Communion*, 89-101.

29. Concerning the theology of the Cappadocians and especially their transformation of Hellenistic natural theology, cf. J. Pelikan, *Christianity and Classical Culture: The Metamorphosis of Natural Theology in the Christian Encounter with Hellenism* (New Haven and London: Yale University Press, 1993).

30. Hence *creatio ex nihilo;* the hypostatic reality of creatureliness is not preceded by any substance *in se.*

31. "The only alternative to this would be to make communion *constitutive* of being, but in this case a denial of the fall — or a redemption from it — would be implied" (Zizioulas, *Being as Communion*, 102).

32. Zizioulas, *Being as Communion*, 103.

33. Zizioulas, *Being as Communion*, 104. Luther provides an interesting point of reference here insofar as he understands God's love as being the exact opposite of human love under the *conditio* of sin: "The love of God does not find, but creates, that which is pleasing to it. The love of man comes into being through that which is pleasing to it" ("Heidelberg Disputation," 41, Thesis 28).

34. "To be saved from the fall, therefore, means essentially that truth should be fully applied to existence, thereby making life something *true,* i.e. undying. For this reason the Fourth Gospel identifies eternal life, i.e. life without death, with truth and knowledge. But it can be accomplished only if the individualization of nature becomes transformed into communion — that is, if communion becomes identical with being. Truth, once again, must be communion if it is to be life" (Zizioulas, *Being as Communion*, 105).

35. "We saw above that the theme of *ekstasis* was a key idea in the Greek patristic concept of truth, but in its application to the idea of 'person' it needs to be completed by another theme, that of *hypostasis*. While *ekstasis* signifies that a person is a revelation of truth by the fact of being in communion, *hypostasis* signifies that in and through his communion a person affirms his own identity and his particularity; he 'supports his own nature' (ὑπό-στασις) in a particular and unique way" (Zizioulas, *Being as Communion*, 106).

36. "The only way for a true person to exist is for being and communion to coincide. The triune God offers in Himself the only possibility for such an identification of being with communion; He is the revelation of true personhood" (Zizioulas, *Being as Communion*, 107).

37. "When we make the assertion that He is the truth, we are meaning His *whole personal existence,* . . . that is, we mean *His relationship* with His body, the Church, ourselves. In other words, when we now say 'Christ' we mean a person and not an individual; we mean a relational reality existing 'for me' or 'for us'" (Zizioulas, *Being as Communion*, 110).

38. "Here the Holy Spirit is not one who *aids* us in bridging the distance be-

tween Christ and ourselves, but he is the person of the Trinity who actually realizes in history that which we call Christ, this absolutely relational entity, our Savior.... The Holy Spirit, in making real the Christ-event in history, makes real *at the same time* Christ's personal existence as a body or community. Christ does not exist *first* as truth and *then* as communion; He is both at once. All separation between Christology and ecclesiology vanishes in the Spirit.... So we can say without risk of exaggeration that Christ *exists only pneumatologically,* whether in His distinct personal particularity or in His capacity as the body of the Church and the recapitulation of all things. Such is the great mystery of Christology, that the Christ-event is not an event defined in itself ... but is *an integral part of the economy of the Holy Trinity*" (Zizioulas, *Being as Communion,* 110f.).

39. Zizioulas, *Being as Communion,* 114.

40. Here Zizioulas draws on a key notion from Maximus Confessor: "In one notable text, Maximus Confessor calls the things of the New Testament 'image' *(eikon),* and the *eschata* he calls 'truth' *(aletheia).* Because the tradition of the Greek fathers understands the word *eikon* to refer to nothing other than true reality, use of the term 'truth' for the *eschata* merely points out that history contains truth only insofar as the eschaton enters into it, and this happens only in the Spirit. Thus truth becomes something sacramental in history; it brings about sanctification (John 17:17-19) and life (John 3:21; 8:44) because the Spirit of truth is also the Spirit of sanctification and communion. This is what makes truth into an inseparable part of the mystery of the church" (Zizioulas, "Die pneumatologische Dimension der Kirche," 142f.).

41. "The final intention of all this is to lead to communion with the life of God, to make truth into communion and life. This is why the ancient councils ended their definitions with anathemas, as if the main aim of the council were not so much definition as anathema. Excommunication had from then on a pastoral basis, that of protecting the community from distortions of the εἰκών of truth, so as not to endanger the truth's soteriological content. If communion was no longer possible after a council's definition and anathema, it was because the eucharist requires a common vision (εἰκών) of Christ. The councils' aim was eucharistic communion, and in producing or adopting creeds the intention was not to provide material for theological reflection, but to orientate correctly the eucharistic communities. Thus it may be said that the credal definitions carry no relationship with truth in themselves, but only in their being doxological acclamations of the worshiping community" (Zizioulas, *Being as Communion,* 117). Zizioulas's succinct explication of this soteriological, salvific-economic telos of the dogmatic results of ecumenical councils provides a bridge to G. Lindbeck, whose cultural-linguistic model of church doctrine might also meaningfully and substantively be interpreted from the perspective of the soteriological, salvific-economic telos of dogma and thereby anchored in worship.

42. Zizioulas's eucharistic concept of truth thus discloses the *iconic* character of church doctrine, whose soteriological telos characterizes it as a work of the Holy Spirit. Here Zizioulas understands the iconological terminology of the Fathers in a strictly eschatological fashion from the perspective of the apocalyptic tradition rather than Platonically. "This tradition presents truth not as a product of the mind, but as a

261

'visit' and a 'dwelling' . . . of an eschatological reality entering history to open it up in a communion-event. This creates a *vision* of truth . . . as picturing a new set of relationships, a new 'world' adopted by the community as its final destiny. So, through its apocalyptic roots, iconological language liberates truth from our 'conception,' 'definition,' 'comprehension,' of it and protects it from being manipulated and objectified. . . . *Eikon* is the final truth of being communicated in and through an event of communion (liturgical or sacramental), anticipating the 'end' of history from within its unfolding" (*Being as Communion,* 100f.).

43. "What happens in a dogmatic formulation, as it passes through the charismatic process of a council, is that certain historical and cultural elements become elements of communion, and thus acquire a sacred character and a permanence in the life of the Church. Here, history and culture are accepted but at the same time eschatologized, so that truth shall not be subjugated through being incarnated in history and culture" (Zizioulas, *Being as Communion,* 117f.).

44. "This means that any breaking of the bond between dogma and community amounts to a breaking of the bond between truth and communion. Dogmas, like ministries, cannot survive as truth outside the communion-event created by the Spirit. It is not possible for a concept or formula to incorporate the truth within itself, unless the spirit gives life to it in communion. Academic theology may concern itself with doctrine, but it is the communion of the Church which makes theology into truth" (Zizioulas, *Being as Communion,* 118). Here Zizioulas touches on the central distinction between church doctrine and (academic) theology, or theology as a church practice. Church doctrine itself is never discourse; in the double sense, it is the "end" of *theological* discourse. Together with the core practices, it constitutes the horizon making theological discourse possible as a distinct church practice. For every practice presupposes a normative horizon without which it cannot function. Hence church doctrine is also the object of discursive theological practice in appropriation, exposition, and application of judgment.

45. Zizioulas, *Being as Communion,* 121.

46. "Man is free only within communion. If the Church wishes to be the place of freedom, she must continually place all the 'objects' she possesses, whatever they may be (Scripture, sacraments, ministries, etc.) within the communion-event to make them 'true' and to make her members free in regard to them as objects, as well as in them and through them as channels of communion. Christians must learn not to lean on objective 'truths' as securities for truth, but to live in an *epicletic* way, i.e. leaning on the communion-event in which the structure of the Church involves them. Truth liberates by placing beings in communion" (Zizioulas, *Being as Communion,* 122).

47. Cf. in this regard Luther's impressive image from the third Antinomian Disputation, *Weimar Ausgabe,* 39/1, 521, 5-10, cited above in section II of Part Three, n. 94.

48. That is, church doctrine, as the grammar of faith, does indeed have an objective point of reference, albeit not referring to a reality universally accessible to human reason but rather to God's own economy of salvation. As long as it remains characterized by this soteriological telos, it remains "commensurate" with its object.

49. The broad and detailed debate concerning the very nature of the "public" being carried on in political theory, sociology, and Christian social ethics cannot be discussed here in detail. Cf. in this regard the discerning and highly nuanced discussion presented recently by B. Wannenwetsch in his *Gottesdienst als Lebensform — Ethik für Christenbürger* (Stuttgart: W. Kohlhammer, 1997).

50. Concerning the history of the concept of the public or the public sphere, cf. W. Huber, *Kirche und Öffentlichkeit*, Forschungen und Berichte der Evangelischen Studiengemeinschaft 28 (Stuttgart: E. Klett, 1973); concerning Huber's own conception, cf. the excursus in the final section of Part IV.

51. W. Placher, "Revisionist and Postliberal Theologies and the Public Character of Theology," *Thomist* 49 (1985): 407.

52. Hannah Arendt, *Vita Activa oder Vom Tätigen Leben* (Munich: R. Piper, 1967; 5th ed., 1987) (*The Human Condition*, 2nd ed. [Chicago and London: University of Chicago Press, 1998]).

53. Arendt, *The Human Condition*, 192-99. Cf. in this regard my *Evangelische Ethik als kirchliches Zeugnis. Interpretationen zu Schlüsselfragen theologischer Ethik in der Gegenwart*, Evangelium und Ethik 1 (Neukirchen-Vluyn: Neukirchener, 1993), 263f., and "The Church as Public: Dogma, Practice, and the Holy Spirit," *Pro Ecclesia* 3 (1994): 347-52.

54. Arendt, *The Human Condition*, 198.

55. Arendt, *The Human Condition*, 194-95.

56. In contradistinction to modern politics, such laws were the means, and the praxis of the free citizenry the goal of the polis, rather than the reverse.

57. Arendt, *The Human Condition*, 197.

58. Arendt, *Vita Activa*, 190. Cf. Arendt, *The Human Condition*, 197. The quotation is a translation from the German version of Arendt's book, in which she, interestingly, added phrases and short sections which do not exist in the English version.

59. "Of all the activities necessary and present in human communities, only two were deemed to be political and to constitute what Aristotle called the *bios politikos*, namely action *(praxis)* and speech *(lexis)*, out of which rises the realm of human affairs (*ta tōn anthrōpōn pragmata*, as Plato used to call it) from which everything merely necessary or useful is strictly excluded" (Arendt, *The Human Condition*, 24-25).

60. Cf. J. Milbank, *Theology and Social Theory: Beyond Secular Reason* (Oxford and Cambridge, Mass.: B. Blackwell, 1990), 364, and Arendt, *The Human Condition*, 28-33, esp. 30-31.

61. In this context, the *oikos* was as fundamentally different from the modern notion of "privacy" as the polis was from modern society.

62. This conceptual association needs some explication. For the *structural concept of the public* developed from the paradigm of the polis, not only is a specific "moveable locale" constitutive, but also a specific "temporality," albeit one which, like the locale, can be quite different depending on the specific features of the public under discussion. In the case of the polis, for example, the concern was with the "sphere of manifestation" of free actions and speaking and with the "eternal nature" of im-

mortal glory, that is, with the enduring recollection of these glorious deeds in the further course of the polis. If, as I will briefly show, one understands Israel, for example, as a public, the *spatial* and *temporal* features of this specific public are naturally quite different from those of the polis; the same applies to the church.

63. Cf. in this regard Arendt, *The Human Condition*, 22-78, and especially Milbank, 9-48. In modern developments "society" has monopolized the concept of the public and thus also of the political by understanding itself as the definitive and normative public. One ironic result of this development is that "political theology," by trying to "politicize" the church, that is, to make it "relevant" within the framework of this public that understands itself as normative, has only deepened the irrelevance of the church itself and undermined its character precisely *as* a public or public sphere by subjecting the church to the political understanding and normative public claims of society and then reconditioning it within society. As early as the 1930s Peterson, together with Barth and Bonhoeffer, came out against this sort of "politicization" of the church. Precisely the assertion that the church *as* a public implies "theological politics" sui generis casts an extremely problematical light on those political theologies that already determine "politics" by a comprehensive and normative concept of public. Cf. in this regard, in addition to Milbank's analysis, A. Rasmusson's comprehensive study, *The Church as Polis: From Political Theology to Theological Politics as Exemplified by Jürgen Moltmann and Stanley Hauerwas*, rev. ed. (Notre Dame: University of Notre Dame Press, 1995).

64. One interesting contemporary phenomenon in this respect is the "encounter" between Islam and Western modernity, one in whose conflict-laden center one encounters precisely the problem of "public." One can read the conflict between Islam and Western modernity as one between distinct publics, albeit as a conflict whose outcome has already been decided beforehand on both sides, first within the framework of the self-declared normative (global) public of Western liberalism by way of the conceptual weaponry of "fundamentalism," and second within the framework of the similarly self-declared normative and comprehensive "house of Islam" by way of the satanization of the "West." Cf. in this regard J. Esposito, *The Islamic Threat: Myth or Reality?* (New York and Oxford: Oxford University Press, 1992), and A. Ahmed, *Postmodernism and Islam: Predicament and Promise* (London and New York: Routledge, 1992).

65. Cf. in this regard F. Crüsemann, *Bewahrung der Freiheit. Das Thema des Dekalogs in sozialgeschichtlicher Perspektive* (Munich: Kaiser, 1983), more recently his *The Thora: Theology and Social History of Old Testament Law*, trans. Allan W. Mahuke (Minneapolis: Fortress, 1996), and my interpretation in *Evangelische Ethik als kirchliches Zeugnis. Interpretationen zu Schlüsselfragen theologischer Ethik in der Gegenwart*, Evangelium und Ethik 1 (Neukirchen-Vluyn: Neukirchener, 1993), 261f. As a public, it was not essential that Israel be constituted as a state; under certain circumstances it was certainly possible and even plausible, while under others it was counterproductive. Israel always underwent a fulcral crisis whenever repression, persecution, or the pressure of assimilation called into question its character as a public. For Israel's life

as the people of God, it was crucial that it be a genuine public constituted by the Torah and by the latter's binding practices and the tradition of its interpretation.

66. Let me remark in passing that this public character naturally also includes
its own inherent discursive practice, namely, the rabbinic exposition of the Torah.

67. This is unfortunately not the place for a detailed exegetical discussion, neither with regard to Luke's portrayal of the events at Pentecost nor of the multilayered
and differentiated ecclesiology of the New Testament in the larger sense. Concerning
the former, cf. J. Roloff, *Die Apostelgeschichte*, Das Neue Testament Deutsch 5, 2nd ed.
(Göttingen: Vandenhoeck & Ruprecht, 1988), and J. Roloff, *Die Kirche im Neuen Testament*, Grundrisse zum Neuen Testament 10 (Göttingen: Vandenhoeck & Ruprecht,
1993), 62-68, 198-201; concerning the latter, cf. Roloff, *Die Kirche im Neuen Testament*, and Roloff, "ἐκκλησία," in *Exegetical Dictionary of the New Testament* I, trans.
James W. Thompson (Grand Rapids: Wm. B. Eerdmans Publishing Co., 1990), 410-
15. In my opinion, P. Brunner has succinctly articulated the theologically key point by
explicitly establishing the relation between the events at Pentecost on the one hand
and worship on the other, thus disclosing the soteriological telos of the church as the
public of the Holy Spirit. Cf. P. Brunner, *Worship in the Name of Jesus*, trans. Martin H. Bertram (St. Louis: Concordia, 1968), 77ff.

68. Cf. Roloff, *Die Kirche im Neuen Testament*, 58-85.

69. Cf. K. Beyschlag, *Grundriß der Dogmengeschichte*, vol. 1, *Gott und Welt*
(Darmstadt: Wissenschaftliche Buchgesellschaft, 1982), 149-72.

70. Cf. K. Wengst, *Pax Romana and the Peace of Jesus Christ*, trans. John Bowden
(Philadelphia: Fortress, 1987).

71. Cf. in this regard J. Milbank's *"re-lecture"* of Augustine's *De civitate Dei* in
Milbank, 259-438.

72. Cf., e.g., Rasmusson, *The Church as Polis*, and S. Hauerwas, *In Good Company: The Church as Polis*, rev. ed. (Notre Dame: University of Notre Dame Press,
1995).

73. Concerning the juxtaposition of polis and *oikos*, cf. Hannah Arendt's presentation in *The Human Condition*, and also J. Bethke Elshtain, *Public Man, Private
Woman: Women in Social and Political Thought* (Princeton: Princeton University
Press, 1981), 19-54, and the extensive application to theological political ethics in
Wannenwetsch, *Gottesdienst als Lebensform — Ethik für Christenbürger*. J. Milbank
has succinctly articulated this (mis)relationship between the *oikos* and polis: "However, virtue means participation in the *polis*, and the *polis* itself, as I shall show below,
was partly constituted as a machine for minimizing the *oikos*, or as a kind of cultural
bypass operation to disassociate continuity and succession from wombs and domestic
nurture" (364).

74. Cf. in this regard Roloff, *Die Kirche im Neuen Testament*, 231-49.

75. Ἄρα οὖν οὐκέτι ἐστὲ ξένοι καὶ πάροικοι ἀλλὰ ἐστὲ συμπολῖται τῶν ἁγίων καὶ
οἰκεῖοι τοῦ θεοῦ.

76. Here is not the place to examine this complex situation. Cf. in this regard
the socio-historic study of W. Meeks, *The First Urban Christians: The Social World of
the Apostle Paul* (New Haven and London: Yale University Press, 1983); *The Moral*

World of the First Christians (Philadelphia: Westminster, 1986); *The Origins of Christian Morality: The First Two Centuries* (New Haven and London: Yale University Press, 1993), and with regard to the German-speaking discussion, Wannenwetsch, *Gottesdienst als Lebensform — Ethik für Christenbürger.* It is worth noting that precisely here the central difference emerges between H. Arendt's critique of Christianity in *The Human Condition* and J. Bethke Elshtain's defense of Christianity in *Public Man, Private Woman.* To me this suggests that only in a quite specific configuration of political theory do "politics" and "religion" (to use the typically modern terms) have either "nothing" or only peripherally "something" to do with each other, namely, in the theory of political liberalism. The emergence of the church radically called and continues to call into question the very nature of "politics." Milbank, 9-48, has persuasively shown that the *saeculum* — now reinterpreted as a separate "sphere" — with its independent nature is a modern invention, one that in a post-Christian fashion, and thus radically different from antiquity, makes "politics" and especially also "economy" possible again, albeit by basically having to privatize "Christianity" in the process. The church that in the West managed to resist this development the longest was the Roman Catholic Church, as a result of which even today it is the church that liberal political theory reviles most ruthlessly. In the Roman Catholic Church, however, and increasingly also in Islam, the concealed dogmatism of liberal theory is prompting a counterpart in whose characterization it does indeed unmask itself as such.

77. The often polemically adduced alternative between "open" versus "closed" church ultimately says nothing in either instance as long as these two attributes are not filled out and precisely articulated from the perspective of the christological ground and soteriological telos of the church. Doing just that, however, immediately makes it clear that the "open" and "closed" nature of the church in truth represents no alternative at all from the perspective of its ground and telos; the reference is rather to a variously specific "open" quality or to a variously specific "closed" quality. That is, these attributes are not accessible on the same level in any case.

78. This question was already being discussed in the thirteenth century at the University of Paris, and should *always* be discussed. Wherever it is no longer discussed, theology has already turned into religious studies.

79. A particularly impressive discussion of the problem of the university as a public sphere is A. MacIntyre's Gifford Lectures, *Three Rival Versions of Moral Enquiry: Encyclopaedia, Genealogy, and Tradition: Being Gifford Lectures Delivered in the University of Edinburgh in 1988* (Notre Dame: University of Notre Dame Press, 1990), esp. 216-36, chap. 10, "Reconceiving the University as an Institution and the Lecture as a Genre."

80. Thus the constructive proposal of MacIntyre, *Three Rival Versions of Moral Enquiry.*

81. David Tracy, *The Analogical Imagination: Christian Theology and the Culture of Pluralism* (New York: Crossroad, 1981), 3-46.

82. Tracy, 31.

83. This has been persuasively demonstrated by Milbank, 51-146.

84. In his book *No Offense: Civil Religion and Protestant Taste* (New York:

Seabury Press, 1978), the sociologist J. M. Cuddihy has explicated the normative and domesticating character of the discourse of "civil religion" in the USA in an interesting way. His presentation and analysis found that "civil religion" involves not some neutral entity, but the normative process of reshaping churches into denominations, that is, the disciplining and accommodation of former publics into the normative and all-encompassing public of liberal society. Cuddihy shows how in a unique process of assimilation, leading Protestant, Catholic, and Jewish theologians accommodate the "church" to this normative public of civil society. The object of this explicit and normative process of assimilation is for churches to learn "good manners," that is, that they not understand themselves as publics; rather, they are to acknowledge the sole public claim of society and accommodate themselves to it within the framework of a specific "acculturation" through the appropriation of a denominational self-understanding. The normative horizon of acculturated theology in the USA is "America," whose religious aspect comes to expression in the Christian and Jewish denominations. By accepting a "public *claim*" within the one normative public of the project "America," these denominations all become "civil religion." Cuddihy's contextual analysis confirms the basic premise that every public possesses its own binding interpretive framework, and that precisely in the case of so-called "neutral" sociological descriptions one must inquire critically concerning the silently presupposed binding principles within such descriptions. (I am indebted to Michael Cartwright for pointing me to Cuddihy's work.)

85. "Public theology" needs to answer the critical question whether Christian theology must not perhaps understand itself here as a discourse inhering in the telos of the specific public of modern society, that is, whether the *primary* commitments of "public theology" are not to be found in the normative practices and doctrines (that is, the "reality") of modern society, and only *secondarily* in the binding principles of church and university. W. Huber articulates the real issue in drawing on the formulations of Wolfgang Vögele and asserting that "by 'public theology' I understand . . . critical reflection on the activities and influence of Christianity on the public of society and dialogical participation in reflection on the identity and crises, goals and tasks of society" ("Öffentliche Kirche in pluralen Öffentlichkeiten," *Evangelische Theologie* 54 [1994]: 175). The Christian intention of this concern is to be applauded; Huber also offers a brief normative explication of reality in the light of one's relationship to God in an attempt to avoid the danger of succumbing to the logic of a comprehensive definition of church as the religious sector of "society." It is doubtful, however, whether the church can do justice to precisely this highly demanding "public commission" if it is not explicated ecclesiologically beforehand *as* a public (in the sense of *logical* priority). Cf. in this regard the following, more detailed discussion of Huber's proposal.

86. Wolfgang Huber, *Kirche und Öffentlichkeit,* Forschungen und Berichte der Evangelischen Studiengemeinschaft 28 (Stuttgart: E. Klett, 1973).

87. Huber, "Öffentliche Kirche in pluralen Öffentlichkeiten."

88. Cf. in this regard Milbank, 51-143.

89. This often happens in a very subtle fashion simply when the "church" is

conceptually "framed," that is, is conceived conceptually. An interesting example is Huber's assertion that "any consideration of the church's participation in plural publics must begin with the acknowledgment that reference to the 'church' in the singular is possible only by way of abstraction. Historically, churches exist in the plural. Their public role in Germany has been shaped essentially by their plurality" ("Öffentliche Kirche in pluralen Öffentlichkeiten," 172). Of course, here Huber is indeed addressing an obvious situation within the context of the socio-historic and political categories of modernity. His assertion that reference to "the" church involves a (presumably "theological") abstraction is problematic, since this subjects him quite uncritically to the normative claim of those particular concepts which fix "reality," from which one then abstracts (again: presumably "theologically"). Such an assertion, however, already presupposes that Huber is moving discursively within the normative horizon of that particular public that already tells authoritatively what "reality" is in the first place and what is to be "abstracted" from it. Within the framework of theological logic, reference to the "church" is a *concretion* in the sense of its christological-pneumatological constitution and its eucharistic locus over against reference to the "churches," which involves a sociological *abstraction* from this reality.

90. Huber, "Öffentliche Kirche in pluralen Öffentlichkeiten," 170.

91. Huber, "Öffentliche Kirche in pluralen Öffentlichkeiten," 174.

92. Huber, "Öffentliche Kirche in pluralen Öffentlichkeiten," 172.

93. Cf. in this regard the enumeration in Huber, "Öffentliche Kirche in pluralen Öffentlichkeiten," 174, with which I basically concur.

94. Cf. Huber, "Öffentliche Kirche in pluralen Öffentlichkeiten," 158f.

95. Although Huber's demarcation from the ecclesiological model of the so-called "contrast community" is consistent, it is regrettable insofar as it contributes little to clarifying the complex ecclesiological issues involved. Concerning the theological and politological background of the alternatives, the "contrasting model of prophetic avant-garde" (paradigm: Moltmann) and the "contrasting model of the holiness avant-garde" (paradigm: Hauerwas), cf. Rasmusson, *The Church as Polis*.

96. The concept of "community" here is already a problem, as is the concept of "contrast," which exhibits a basically reactive meaning; that is, it logically depends on whatever constitutes its contrasting counterpart. If the term represents primarily an auxiliary construction, however, one based on an explicit theological interior perspective, then it can — as it were, *gymnastikos* — certainly be meaningful. Cf. in this regard the presentation of the ecclesiological conception of G. Lohfink and my own discussion in *Evangelische Ethik als kirchliches Zeugnis*, 153-85, esp. 176-81.

97. Here I am building on and carrying forward O. Bayer's initiative. Cf. O. Bayer, *Autorität und Kritik. Zur Hermeneutik und Wissenschaftstheorie* (Tübingen: J. C. B. Mohr, 1991), 133f.

98. Cf. in this regard J. Ritter, "Die Lehre vom Ursprung und Sinn der Theorie bei Aristoteles," in Ritter, *Metaphysik und Politik. Studien zu Aristoteles und Hegel* (Frankfurt am Main: Suhrkamp, 1977; 2nd ed., 1988), 9-33; G. Picht, "Der Sinn der Unterscheidung von Theorie und Praxis in der griechischen Philosophie," in Picht,

Wahrheit — Vernunft — Verantwortung. Philosophische Studien (Stuttgart: E. Klett, 1969), 108-40.

99. Cf. in this regard W. Schulz, *Philosophie in einer veränderten Welt* (Pfullingen: G. Neske, 1972), 257-62.

100. M. Riedel points out that Hegel advocates this position on the basis of the epochal significance he ascribes to the French Revolution and its attendant positive rendering of law: "On the ground of modernity, the world has become philosophical, philosophy worldly, and only thus really total, that is, the one and whole philosophy in which the problems of theory and praxis left behind by Plato and Aristotle are resolved and put to rest. According to Hegel, the philosophy of history is the rehearsal for practical philosophy as the theory of law, state, and political constitution" (*System und Geschichte. Studien zum historischen Standort von Hegels Philosophie* [Frankfurt am Main: Suhrkamp, 1973], 14f.). Concerning the complexity of the discussion of the relation between theory and praxis in Hegel, cf. the thorough and critical review essay by M. Theunissen, *Die Verwirklichung der Vernunft. Zur Theorie-Praxis-Diskussion im Anschluss an Hegel,* Philosophische Rundschau Beiheft 6 (Tübingen: J. C. B. Mohr, 1970).

101. The classic formulation is by G. Gutierrez, *A Theology of Liberation: History, Politics, and Salvation* (Maryknoll, N.Y.: Orbis, 1973), 3-19, and J. Miguez Bonino, *Doing Theology in a Revolutionary Situation* (Philadelphia: Fortress, 1975), 86-105. For an introduction to the concern and history of "political theology," cf. S. Wiedenhofer, *Politische Theologie* (Stuttgart: W. Kohlhammer, 1976); for a more detailed explication of the relation of theology and praxis, cf. C. Boff, *Theology and Praxis: Epistemological Foundations,* trans. Robert R. Barr (Maryknoll, N.Y.: Orbis, 1987).

102. M. Theunissen does, however, find a fundamental and unresolved tension in Hegel's concept of theory between theory as end-in-itself, that is, of "pure" theory in the classical sense, and the practical engagement of theory, that is, of theory as embraced by praxis. Cf. Theunissen, *Die Verwirklichung der Vernunft,* 87ff., and M. Theunissen, *Hegels Lehre vom absoluten Geist als theologisch-politischer Traktat* (Berlin: Walter de Gruyter, 1970), 323-447. By contrast, M. Riedel, *Theorie und Praxis im Denken Hegels. Interpretationen zu den Grundstellungen der neuzeitlichen Subjektivität* (Stuttgart: W. Kohlhammer, 1965), 140, persuasively shows that Hegel does conceptually articulate theory and praxis in an emphatically modern sense, namely, as the "concept of human freedom in being, of a self-willing of subjectivity." Hegel understands this freedom as being basically *poietic;* Riedel continues: "This human 'need' to become its own work within being unites the perceiving and positing act in the center of a subjectivity that seeks to both 'perceive' and 'enjoy' itself within being."

103. Riedel, *Theorie und Praxis im Denken Hegels,* 128-36, shows that this reversal does in any event presuppose a point common to both Hegel and Marx, namely, the poietically understood freedom of the will attaching to subjectivity.

104. O. Bayer's important contribution is having clearly explicated for contemporary Protestant theology this fundamentally pathic understanding of human beings as the core of theological anthropology, his point of departure being the differ-

ence between Luther and the modern poietic self-understanding of human beings. Despite any critique of his failure to anchor his conception of theology ecclesiologically as discussed in Part Two above, this central anthropological point is nonetheless completely worthy of our concurrence. Cf. also G. Sauter, "Die Wahrnehmung des Menschen bei Martin Luther," *Evangelische Theologie* 43 (1983): 489-503 (esp. 500), who draws attention in this respect to a central statement from Luther's *Lectures on Galatians* (1535): "Our 'activity' is to permit God to do His work in us; He gives the Word, and when we take hold of this by the faith that God gives, we are born as sons of God" (*Luther's Works*, vol. 26, 401). Not: in acting, we suffer or undergo God; that would exactly render the modern poietic understanding. Rather: the only thing we really can *do* is be still and accept God's actions. *Agere* and *pati* here are related such that *agere* is qualifed by *pati*. That is, this suffering is utter passivity, utterly a state of being created, albeit one in which we are indeed "there" or "present," that is, we *accept* it, which specifically can only mean that we answer God's salvific acts with praise, confession, and obedience. In this precise sense, Mary, the Mother of God, is the paradigmatic human being, something Luther impressively formulates in his exposition of the Magnificat (1521). Cf. Luther, *Luther's Works*, vol. 21, 297-355, esp. 318-322; *Weimar Ausgabe*, 7, 544-603, esp. 565-68.

105. Cf. H. Schlier, "Zur Freiheit gerufen. Das paulinische Freiheitsverständnis," in *Freiheit im Leben mit Gott. Texte zur Tradition evangelischer Ethik,* ed. H. G. Ulrich, Theologische Bücherei 86 (Gütersloh: Kaiser; Gütersloher Verlagshaus, 1993), 42-59, here 48: "According to Paul, human beings as creatures actualize the freedom they have from God through freely binding themselves to God and his creation. They actualize it in thanksgiving. They 'owe' themselves to God in thanksgiving; that is their freedom, since as such they are simultaneously both away from and with themselves."

106. Cf. G. W. F. Hegel on the relation between representation and concept in the last section of his *Phenomenology of Mind*, "Absolute Knowledge": "Thus, then, what was in religion content, or a way of imagining *(Vorstellen)* an other, is here the action proper of the self. The notion is the connecting principle securing that the content is the action proper of the self. For this notion is, as we see, the knowledge that the action of the self within itself is all that is essential and all existence, the knowledge of this Subject as Substance and of the Substance as this knowledge of its action. . . . This last embodiment of spirit — spirit which at once gives its complete and true content the form of self, and thereby realizes its notion, and in doing so remains within its own notion — this is *Absolute Knowledge*. It is spirit knowing itself in the shape of spirit, it is knowledge which comprehends through notions. Truth is here not merely *in itself* absolutely identical with certainty; it has also the shape, the character of certainty of self; or in its existence — i.e. for spirit knowing it — it is in the *form* of knowledge of itself. Truth is the content, which in religion is not as yet at one with its certainty. This identification, however, is secured when the content has received the shape of self. By this means, what constitutes the very essence, viz. the notion, comes to have the nature of existence, i.e. assumes the form of what is objective to consciousness. Spirit, appearing before consciousness in this element of existence, or, what is here the same thing, produced by it in this element, is systematic Science"

(*The Phenomenology of Mind,* trans. J. B. Baillie, 2nd ed. [London: George Allen & Unwin; New York: Humanities Press, 1931], 797f.). Cf. also the more extensive discussion of the relation between religion and philosophy in his *Lectures on the Philosophy of Religion* I, trans. R. F. Brown et al., ed. Peter C. Hodgson (Berkeley: University of California Press, 1984), 115-32, and the relation between representation and concept: "Thus it is that the representation resolves into the form of thought, and the determination of *form* is what philosophical knowledge of truth adds. This, however, shows that philosophy is concerned with nothing less than overthrowing religion and with asserting, for example, that the content of religion by itself cannot be truth; rather, religion is the true content, only in the form of representation, and it is not philosophy's place first to supply the substance of that truth, nor has humanity had to wait for philosophy in order to receive consciousness of the truth" (*Vorlesungen über die Philosophie der Religion* I, Theorie Werkausgabe [Frankfurt am Main: Suhrkamp, 1969], 150f.). Cf. *Lectures on the Philosophy of Religion,* 250f. Concerning the complex role of the concept of "representation" in Hegel, cf. V. Westhelle, "Religion and Representation: A Study of Hegel's Critical Theories of *Vorstellung* and Their Relevance for Hegelianism and Theology" (Diss., Lutheran School of Theology at Chicago, 1984). G. Sauter has succinctly articulated the key difference between theology in the sense explicated in this inquiry and an understanding of theology along the lines of a philosophy of religion, i.e., as the conceptual articulation and penetration of religious perception: "Dogmatics articulates what people are 'given' to believe, and does so by constructing and explicating the concepts providing access to this 'gift' as event and promise. The object language of theology begins with the fact that God has communicated or 'given' himself; insofar as dogmatics is mindful of this and focuses on the promise in this communication, it is *discursive.* Christian dogmatics operates discursively because God's final revelation in Jesus Christ and the promise of its eschatological perfection, universality, and evidence (1 Cor. 15:28) provides dogmatics with a time-place nexus which dogmatics can bring to expression only through a series of statements. . . . Its concepts are finite formulations of what is believed in faith (*fides quae creditur* [believed faith]). This is why the concepts of Christian dogmatics are . . . not concepts of reflection. Rather, they articulate what happens in promise between God and human beings" ("Dogmatik. I. Enzyklopädischer Überblick und Dogmatik im deutschsprachigen Raum," in *Theologische Realenzyklopädie* [Berlin: Walter de Gruyter, 1976f.], 9:50).

107. The essential feature of political theology and of liberation theology is their comprehensive political paradigm from whose perspective both God's salvific activity in history as well as the church's actions are interpreted. This paradigm is usually introduced and defended from a historico-philosophical perspective (as, e.g., in J. B. Metz within the framework of the "modern history of freedom," in *Faith in History and Society: Toward a Practical Fundamental Theology,* trans. David Smith [New York: Seabury Press, 1980], 14-31, 32-48). Concerning the historico-philosophical option (modernity as "end time") as the normative horizon of political theology, cf. Wiedenhofer, 53ff. Precisely this positive adoption of the theological-philosophical self-understanding of modern secularization is addressed by J. Milbank's comprehen-

sive criticism in *Theology and Social Theory;* in summary, Milbank suggests that "the initial *theological* decision is not to embrace Marxism, but to embrace secularization, and the horizon of the political; later, a way is sought whereby one can still subscribe to socialist views, despite the fact that these can no longer be drawn from Christianity itself, but must be taken instead from the immanent principles of secularization and politics. Yet these processes manifestly favour only capitalism, instrumental freedom and bureaucracy" (243). The following discussion presupposes Milbank's critical destruction of political theology as an uncritical adaptation of Christian theology to the historico-philosophical and thus implicitly *theological* self-understanding of modernity. Cf. the skeptical view of O. Marquard's criticism of modern philosophy of history and its theological implications in Marquard, *Schwierigkeiten mit der Geschichtsphilosophie,* 2nd ed. (Frankfurt am Main: Suhrkamp, 1982), 37-82.

108. Concerning the introduction of the concepts "context of discovery" and "context of justification," cf. n. 17 in Part Two, section I.

109. Concerning the understanding of "critical theory" inherently related to social and political praxis, cf. M. Horkheimer, "Traditional and Critical Theory," in *Critical Theory: Selected Essays,* trans. Matthew J. O'Connell and others (New York: Herder & Herder, 1972), 188-243.

110. Cf. in this regard M. Welker's noteworthy critique of the understanding of spirit in Aristotle and Hegel as the classic and most influential basic conceptions of the Western "spirit," albeit conceptions irreconcilable with the "Holy Spirit" (*Gottes Geist. Theologie des Heiligen Geistes,* 2nd ed. [Neukirchen-Vluyn: Neukirchener, 1993], 262-79). Cf. Welker, *God the Spirit,* trans. John F. Hoffmeyer (Minneapolis: Fortress, 1994), 283-302.

111. Cf. in this regard K. Aner, *Die Theologie der Lessingzeit* (Hildesheim: Georg Olms, 1964 = reprint of the Halle edition, 1929).

112. This applies in a preliminary sense already to the production of historical knowledge in the treadmill of constantly rotating angles of inquiry with which disciplines try to attain legitimacy in a society oriented toward accomplishment and production. This *taxis* naturally also implies a certain relationship between the various academic subjects of theology. An abstract "equality" of all subjects or even the establishment of utterly independent disciplines can only obscure or even undermine this salvific-economically understood *taxis.*

113. Cf. in this regard section I in Part Four above.

114. My emphasis in the Greek text. The NRSV translates the passage as follows: "(15) What then? Should we sin because we are not under law but under grace? By no means! (16) Do you not know that if you present yourselves to anyone as obedient slaves, you are slaves of the one whom you obey, either of sin, which leads to death, or of obedience, which leads to righteousness? (17) But thanks be to God that you, having once been slaves of sin, *have become obedient from the heart to the form of teaching to which you were entrusted,* (18) and that you, having been set free from sin, have become slaves of righteousness" (my emphasis). Both H. Schlier, *Der Römerbrief,* Herders theologischer Kommentar zum Neuen Testament 7, 2nd ed. (Freiburg im Breisgau: Herder, 1979), 205, and U. Wilckens, *Der Brief an die Römer,* Evangelisch-

katholischer Kommentar zum Neuen Testament VI/1-3 (Zürich: Benziger Verlag; Neukirchen-Vluyn: Neukirchener Verlag, 1978-82), here VI/2 (1980), 33, also translate τύπος διδαχῆς as "form of teaching."

115. Cf. in this regard my interpretation of Luther's *The Bondage of the Will* in section I of Part Four above.

116. Schlier, *Der Römerbrief,* 209. Cf. also Schlier's argument, 209f., contra Bultmann's suggestion that τύπος διδαχῆς actually represents a gloss.

117. Wilckens, 36.

118. Wilckens, 37.

119. Cf. in this regard also Basil the Great (of Caesarea), who in his writing *De Spiritu Sancto* understands both baptismal event and baptismal doctrine to be related with regard to the τύπος διδαχῆς: "What makes us Christians? Faith, one says. How are we saved? Obviously through being born again in the grace of baptism. For how else? After we have seen that this, our salvation, is effected through the Father and the Son and the Holy Spirit, will we betray what we have received as the 'form of teaching' (Rom. 6:17)? . . . Those who do not perpetually adhere to the confession we made at our initiation, when we came over from idols to the living God (cf. 1 Thess. 1:9), and do not cling to it their entire lives as to a secure shelter — they will exclude themselves from God's promises (cf. Eph. 2:12) by setting themselves in opposition to that which they personally signed when they made the confession of faith" (*De Spiritu Sancto. Vom Heiligen Geist,* Germ. trans. by H. J. Sieben, S.J., Fontes christiani 12 [Freiburg im Breisgau, Basel, and Vienna, 1993], 147, 149). Cf. *On the Holy Spirit,* trans. David Anderson (Crestwood, N.Y.: St. Vladimir's Seminary Press, 1980), 46f. Sieben remarks in this context: "Basil conceives baptism as a real 'handing over' (παράδοσις) of Father, Son, and Holy Spirit to the person baptized. What happens here in the mystery, the confession of the person baptized brings to expression through the naming of the three 'persons.' Confession and reception of the reality expressed in the confession belong inseparably together" (148). Aquinas interprets this as being "handed over" into the *fides catholica: "In eam formam doctrinae,* idest in doctrinam catholicae fidei: 2 Tim. 1:13: Formam habens sanorum verborum quae a me audisti: *in quam traditi estis;* idest cui vos totaliter subdidistis" (*Epistola ad Romanos,* Caput VI, Lectio III; *Sancti Thomae Aquinitatis Doctoris Angelici Ordinis Praedicatorum Opera Omnia Tomus XIII* [Parmae, 1862; reprint, New York, 1949], 63). In his *Commentary on the Epistle to the Romans* (1515/16), Luther is more inclined to emphasize "being handed over/entrusted" to *doctrina* as becoming like it, that is, as coming to believe in it truly and with all one's heart: "Hence 'to which you were committed' is a better interpretation than 'which was delivered to you.' For even to the ungodly the doctrine of the Gospel has been delivered, but they do not deliver themselves over to it or conform themselves to it; but they have not been delivered into it because they do not really believe it from the heart. Very similar is the statement to the Corinthians (cf. I Cor. 13:12; Gal. 4:9): 'Then you have come to know, even as you have come to be known.' And here, too, he could have said: 'Which was delivered to you, or rather, to which you were committed,' because this is characteristic of believers and saints" (Luther, *Lectures on Romans, Luther's Works,* vol. 25, trans. Walter G. Tillmanns and Jacob A. O.

Preus, ed. Hilton C. Oswald (St. Louis: Concordia, 1972), 317-18. In Basil's understanding, the two aspects remain together and are not to be separated artificially. The
fides quae creditur and the *fides qua creditur* are the two inseparable aspects of the one
pathos of faith and thus also of theology.

120. Schlier, *Der Römerbrief,* 208.

121. Bengt Hägglund, "Die Bedeutung der 'regula fidei' als Grundlage
theologischer Aussagen," *Studia theologica* (Lund) 12 (1958): 1-44.

122. Hägglund, "Die Bedeutung der 'regula fidei,'" 35.

123. "There is, so to speak, a 'natural' order of dogmatics, one grounded not in
a common idea, but in the unity of the Old and New Testaments. . . . Not only is it a
formal schema for the theological presentation of doctrine, but also is completely determined as regards content. Thus it coincides with the *regula,* and the *regula fidei* is
at the same time a witness to this original order grounded in the facts of salvation history" (Hägglund, "Die Bedeutung der 'regula fidei,'" 36f.).

124. Cf. Hägglund, "Die Bedeutung der 'regula fidei,'" 37.

125. Hägglund, "Die Bedeutung der 'regula fidei,'" 37. "'Truth' in the theological sense is that which brings salvation and life. It is the knowledge of God that reveals
the real God to human beings" (38).

126. Hägglund, "Die Bedeutung der 'regula fidei,'" 39.

127. Hägglund, "Die Bedeutung der 'regula fidei,'" 40f.

128. Hägglund, "Die Bedeutung der 'regula fidei,'" 41.

129. Hägglund, "Die Bedeutung der 'regula fidei,'" 41.

130. Still, a small group of Protestant theologians has considered the *doctor
communis* worthy of extensive study in this century, among whom one may representatively mention U. Kühn, H. Vorster, P. E. Persson, and recently also M. Bieler, B.
Marshall, and E. F. Rogers, Jr.

131. As a professor, he was first and foremost a *magister in sacra pagina,* that is,
was responsible for scriptural interpretation. Cf. M.-D. Chenu, *Toward Understanding
Saint Thomas,* translated with authorized corrections and bibliographical additions
by A. M. Landry and D. Hughes (Chicago: H. Regnery Co., 1964), 242-60, and P. E.
Persson, *Sacra Doctrina: Reason and Revelation in Aquinas,* trans. Ross Mackenzie
(Philadelphia: Fortress, 1970), 3-11. On the issue of theology (or "sacra doctrina") as
"scientia," as academic discipline, I have guided by Eugene F. Rogers, Jr. *Thomas Aqui-
nas and Karl Barth: Sacred Doctrine and the Natural Knowledge of God* (Notre Dame:
University of Notre Dame Press, 1995), 17-70.

132. Cf. in this regard Persson, 49-59.

133. Holy Scripture and revelation do not coincide in Aquinas's understanding,
though the Bible does contain and communicate God's truth as given in the event of
revelation. Cf. Persson, 49f.: "Accordingly, for Thomas holy scripture does not coincide with revelation, since he does not understand revelation as a spoken or written
word but regards it primarily as an event which takes place in the depths of the soul.
Nevertheless, the Bible contains and communicates the divine truth given in and with
this event. If the content of revelation had not been defined in this way once and for
all, it would have been wholly inaccessible to us — *ea enim quae ex sola Dei voluntate*

proveniunt, supra omne debitum creaturae, NOBIS INNOTESCERE NON POSSUNT NISI QUATENUS IN SACRA SCRIPTURA TRADUNTUR, *per quam divina voluntas innotescit* (such things as spring from God's will, and beyond the creature's due, can be made known to us only through being revealed in sacred scripture, in which the divine will is made known to us)" (Persson is citing here from *Summa Theologiae* 3 ql a3 resp.).

134. Concerning the complexity of Aquinas's concept of revelation, cf. Persson, 42f. For Aquinas, *doctrina* refers in the broadest sense to *teaching,* specifically as engagement and content: "There is for Thomas no fundamental difference at this point between preaching and teaching, preaching being essentially instruction in revealed truth; hence he can use both words as synonyms and speak of *praedicatio vel doctrina.* We should note that in Thomas *doctrina* does not have the more precise meaning which it has for us of a fixed and formal system of teaching, or 'doctrine.' As used by Thomas it has an *active* meaning which corresponds most closely to what we mean by 'teaching,' hence it denotes at the same time both the act of teaching and the knowledge communicated in teaching" (43f.).

135. In his presentation of Aquinas, Persson (285-90) mentions the borderline case of the conceptual corrective of the revelatory witness, something Persson believes Aquinas undertakes especially in his doctrine of the incarnation. A debate with Persson's not entirely unproblematical critique of Aquinas would lead too far afield here. To the extent that his critique of Aquinas is indeed justified, however, it points to the fundamental and yet utterly unavoidable danger residing in the conceptual disclosure of the *doctrina* of Scripture.

136. "For St Ambrose says, *Away with arguments where faith is at stake.* Now faith is the principal quest of this teaching, according to St John: *These things are written that you may believe.* Therefore it is not probative" (Aquinas, *Summa Theologiae* 1 ql a8 obj. 1).

137. "Again, were it to adance arguments, they would be either from authority or from the evidence of reason. If from authority, then the process would be unbefitting the dignity of this teaching, for, according to Boëthius, authority is the weakest ground of proof. If from the evidence of reason, then the process would not correspond with its purpose, for according to St Gregory, *Faith has no merit where the reason presents actual proof from experience.* Well then, holy teaching does not attempt proofs" (Aquinas, *Summa Theologiae* 1 ql a8 obj. 2).

138. For Aquinas, the scriptural canon itself is the *regula fidei.* Cf. in this regard Persson, 52: "The idea of the canon as the norm by which the scriptures are distinguished from all other documents of faith is a characteristic of Thomas and may be concisely expressed in the definition which is to be found in his commentary on the Gospel of St. John: SOLA CANONICA SCRIPTURA EST REGULA FIDEI (canonical scripture alone is the rule of faith)."

139. The confessions of faith such as the Apostolic and Nicaean Creeds are for Aquinas succinct summaries of the *doctrina* of canonical Scripture: "What is given in the creed is a summary of what scripture means when it is correctly interpreted. Since the articles of faith, *articuli fidei,* and the canonical scriptures are identical in content

when they are seen in this way, anything that may be said of the one can also apply to the other — hence Thomas can state that the articles of the creed, which constitute the *principia* of theology, have been given *immediate a Deo per revelationem* (directly from God through revelation). Furthermore, because of their identity of content both the articles of the creed and the scripture itself may be termed the *regula fidei*. This normative function of the creed is based in the last resort upon the fact that it is derived from the truth given in the biblical writings, of which it is itself a summary. Even in the earliest creeds it is thus scripture, Thomas holds, and scripture alone, that is the *regula fidei*" (Persson, 59f.).

140. "Reply: As the other sciences do not argue to prove their premises, but work from them to bring out other things in their field of inquiry, so this teaching does not argue to establish its premises, which are the articles of faith, but advances from them to make something known" (Aquinas, *Summa Theologiae* 1 q1 a8 resp.).

141. "So sacred Scripture, which has no superior science over it, disputes the denial of its principles; it argues on the basis of those truths held by revelation which an opponent admits, as when, debating with heretics, it appeals to received authoritative texts of Christian theology, and uses one article against those who reject another. If, however, an opponent believes nothing of what has been divinely revealed, then no way lies open for making the articles of faith resonably credible; all that can be done is to solve the difficulties against faith he may bring up. For since faith rests on unfailing truth, and the contrary of truth cannot really be demonstrated, it is clear that alleged proofs against faith are not demonstrations, but charges that can be refuted" (Aquinas, *Summa Theologiae* 1 q1 a8 resp.). Here Aquinas clearly shows that he associates the argumentative *discurrere* with the presentative-communicative aspect of theology.

142. The tendency toward a formation of schools and the development of larger discursive traditions can be understood as an implicate of the logic of argumentation itself. Cf. in this regard MacIntyre, *Three Rival Versions of Moral Enquiry*.

143. Persson suggests that Aquinas is able to use *sacra scriptura* and *sacra doctrina* synonymously because theology itself is essentially bound to the scriptural witness: "Theology is not to be regarded here as an addition to scripture, nor a study which may be pursued independently of scripture: in Thomas's view it is rather the extension of scriptural teaching through the ages, the *traditio* of imparting doctrine which must always be found within the church. Since it is the content of scripture which is being transmitted, *sacra doctrina* and *sacra scriptura* may be used interchangeably as synonyms. This means for Thomas that the subject of theology is preeminently *biblical theology*, and *sacra doctrina* may be regarded, to use an apt expression of Etienne Gilson, as 'holy scripture received in a human intellect'" (Persson, 89).

144. Here, in the argumentative *discurrere* of God's economy of salvation, is the locus of the constructive and unique, theologically irreplaceable contribution of historical-critical exegesis as well as that of sociological, linguistic, and archaeological studies. Precisely as probability arguments, they may develop scientific hypotheses within their own genus. The key question is whether these disciplines acquire a superior status and thus hypothesize *doctrina* (and ultimately the status of being a Chris-

tian), or whether their enlightening, emancipatory truth claims become theologically relativized by being characterized as that which they essentially are, namely, probability arguments in the sense of the modern experiential sciences. The alternative here is thus not that between "fundamentalism" and "critical disciplines" (which does indeed also exist), but between, on the one hand, Christian knowledge becoming merely the object of such disciplines and thus comprehensively hypothetical as a result of being normatively subjected to the understanding of truth entertained by historical research, and on the other, scientific exegesis within the context of a comprehensive theological *discurrere* of God's economy of salvation *guided* by the *doctrina evangelii*. Concerning the danger of reducing all human life relationships hypothetically by subsuming them comprehensively under such "critical" disciplines, cf. R. Spaemann, "Überzeugungen in einer hypothetischen Zivilisation," in *Abschied von Utopia? Anspruch und Auftrag der Intellektuellen,* ed. O. Schatz (Graz, Vienna, and Cologne: Styria, 1977), 311-31. One example of how historical-critical and archaeological research can be engaged within the framework of theological-biblical reflection *without* becoming the determinative horizon of that reflection is B. Childs's canonical proposal for a biblical theology, explicated most comprehensively in Childs, *Biblical Theology of the Old and New Testaments: Theological Reflection on the Christian Bible* (Minneapolis: Fortress, 1992).

145. A fundamental problem surfaces here. Now and then, the suggestion is made that contemporary theology should address *en détail* the modern sciences in the same way Aquinas did Aristotelian philosophy and science. The alleged goal is a comprehensive "synthesis" between Christian reflection and the most scientifically advanced worldview of a given age. This proposal generally overlooks two things. First, it forgets that Aquinas was neither a philosopher nor a "systematic theologian" in the modern sense, but a theologian of the Holy Scriptures; for him, exposition of the *doctrina* mediated by the Holy Scriptures was of primary importance rather than some "synthesis" between religion and philosophy. Second, it ignores the far more important qualitative distinction between the premodern understanding of science and the discourses of rhetoric, grammar, and logic, on the one hand, and the modern understanding of science and the self-understanding of modern philosophical and scholarly discourse in the humanities in the larger sense on the other. Distinctly modern discourses can no longer be engaged in service as were those of antiquity; a dogmatically antitheological self-understanding already inheres constitutively in them as a result of their distinct genesis, one already critical toward Christianity and the church from the outset. Milbank, 9-143, esp. 246ff., has demonstrated this with the utmost clarity. If theology is not itself to be "reconstructed" by these discourses and become thus a different entity entirely, it must assume a critical theological posture over against them when drawing on their results. Milbank formulates this insight as a question: "Can there be *theology, tout court,* without mediation by the social sciences? Because only if the answer is yes (as I hold) can one go on upholding the fundamentally historical character of salvation: in other words, orthodoxy" (246). This caveat is not advocating a hostile, anti-intellectual posture toward these disciplines and discourses, nor is it suggesting that theological discourse seal itself off from them in a

fundamentalist fashion; it is advocating merely a *theologically* reflected engagement with them. The debate concerning the correct, theologically considered use of these disciplines versus the reconstruction of Christianity within them has been under way in Protestant theology basically since the time of neology and is carried on anew within various configurations in every generation. The critical posture of the Enlightenment prompted church theology to establish explicit clarity regarding its own theological principles (under penalty of becoming completely sealed off), while that same critical posture was inclined on the one hand to moralize its own dogmatism and, on the other, to raise the charge of "fundamentalism" (which is modernity's notion for heresy) against those who did not subject themselves to these disciplines' comprehensive claim to validity. "After neology," a theological enlightenment of the Enlightenment has thus been the new task for each generation.

146. Aquinas, *Summa Theologiae* 1 ql a8 ad2: "Yet holy teaching employs such authorities only in order to provide as it were extraneous arguments from probability. Its own proper authorities are those of canonical Scripture, and these it applied with convincing force. It has other proper authorities, the doctors of the Church, and these it looks to as its own, but for arguments that carry no more than probability. For our faith rests on the revelation made to the Prophets and Apostles who wrote the canonical books, not on a revelation, if such there be, made to any other teacher. In this sense St Augustine wrote to St Jerome; *Only to those books or writings which are called canonical have I learnt to pay such honour that I firmly believe that none of their authors have erred in composing them. Other authors, however, I read to such effect that, no matter what holiness and learning they display, I do not hold what they say to be true because those were their sentiments."*

147. Concerning Aquinas's distinction between theological and church doctrine, cf. Persson, 46: "Though he frequently associates the term *traditio* in this way with the apostles, nowhere, it appears, does Thomas refer the word to the fathers or doctors of the church and their teachings. On the other hand, he can at times speak of a *traditio Ecclesiae* — as when he refers to the doctrine of original sin — or he can state that the two natures of Christ are in accordance with *catholicae fidei traditio*, and here it is quite clear that the traditions to which he refers are *traditiones credendae* and relate to what belongs to the very substance of the faith." And: "Ordinarily Thomas uses statements of the fathers purely as illustrations of the general drift of his argument, which sometimes means that they are introduced in a context which bears little relation to the idea which they were originally designed to express. Thus they have obviously a different function in his writings from what they have in the scholasticism of the Roman Catholic Church which was formulated during and after the events of the Reformation. This is connected with the fact that for Thomas *auctoritates doctorum* do not in the last resort represent the revelation which is the ground and object of faith, and therefore no proof can be sought in them which is theologically conclusive. Such proof can be found only in the *auctoritates canonici scripturae*" (66).

148. Cf. Part Three above.

149. This point could just as easily have been made with regard to Luther. Despite the obvious and much-discussed positional and methodological differences be-

tween these two key theologians of Western Christianity, they do nonetheless agree over against a theology understanding itself hermeneutically or constructivistically in the modern sense that *argumentation* is indeed possible precisely on the basis of the pathos of theology. The essential difference between Aquinas and Luther is their radically different assessment of the value of Aristotelian philosophy for theology. Cf. in this regard B. Hägglund, *Theologie und Philosophie bei Luther und in der ockhamistischen Tradition,* Lunds universitets arsskrift, n.f., avd. 1, bd. 51, nr. 4 (Lund: C. W. K. Gleerup, 1955), and Luther's *Disputatio contra scholasticam theologiam* (1517), *Weimar Ausgabe,* 1, 224-28. Luther's criticism is certainly appropriate wherever the Aristotelian conceptual framework obstructs the exposition of the witness of revelation of Holy Scripture. This turn against a specific conceptual instrument within the argumentative *discurrere* of the *doctrina evangelii,* however, is to be understood as precisely such an aspect itself.

150. Cf. in this regard the comprehensive article by G. Sauter, "Dogmatik. I. Enzyklopädischer Überblick und Dogmatik im deutschsprachigen Raum," in *Theologische Realenzyklopädie* (Berlin: Walter de Gruyter, 1976f.), 9:41-77.

151. This point could also have been exemplified, albeit with considerable effort, with regard to Luther's theology, since Luther understands faith as an acknowledgment of the truth of the *assertiones* of the Holy Spirit as communicated in the apostolic witness of Holy Scripture. Beginning with these *assertiones* as the *principia* of theology, the latter is certainly possible as a discursive-argumentative practice. Especially the sermons on 1 Cor. 15 from the years 1532-33 clearly show that the promissory statements of the scriptural witness, seized in faith through concurrence with them, constitute the point of departure and foundation of their argumentative-discursive development through theology. Like Aquinas, Luther also adheres to the notion that nothing can be accomplished discursively-argumentatively against unbelief; on the other hand, once the witness of faith is presupposed, it can indeed be demonstratively-argumentatively explicated such that from one article of the *doctrina evangelii* others can be deduced. Cf. in this regard Luther, "Commentary on I Corinthians 15," *Luther's Works,* vol. 28, ed. Hilton C. Oswald (St. Louis: Concordia, 1973), 93-100, esp. 95-97, from which the following excerpt is taken: "But I stated that this is primarily a sermon for Christians, who believe the article about Christ's resurrection and know its power and understand why He arose, namely, to overcome death and to rescue us from death and enable us to live with Him eternally. For since He is our Head, and we His body and members, He must through His resurrection also resurrect us and transplant us into a new life etc., as He often declares elsewhere. However, lest someone find fault with his argumentation, Paul continues and strengthens his viewpoint. He intertwines and interlaces his argumentation to make it cogently conclusive. He makes proper use of that device of dialectics which is known as *reducere per impossible.* He wants to say: "Whoever denies this article must simultaneously deny far more, namely, first of all, that you believe properly; in the second place, that the Word which you believed has been true; in the third place, that we apostles preach correctly and that we are God's apostles; in the fourth place, that God is truthful; in brief, that God is God" ("Commentary on I Corinthians 15," 95). In the meantime,

some scholars maintain that Luther was familiar with Aquinas's *Summa Theologiae*. Cf. D. Janz, *Luther on Thomas Aquinas: The Angelic Doctor in the Thought of the Reformer,* Veröffentlichungen des Instituts für Europäische Geschichte Mainz 140 (Stuttgart: Franz Steiner Verlag Wiesbaden, 1989), 96-113. If this is indeed the case, one might suspect that Luther was possibly thinking of *Summa Theologiae* q1 a8 when preaching on 1 Cor. 15, so obvious are the argumentative parallels. Like Aquinas in *Summa Theologiae* ql a8 resp., Luther, too, finds that there can be no argumentative discourse with those who dispute the witness of God's word in its entirety: "For we have nothing to do with him who believes nothing at all, who denies everything that is said about God and about God's Word. Therefore this is also taught in the schools: *Contra negantem prima principia non est disputandum. . . .* But we are addressing people who regard God as a true God, who is truthful and does not lie, people who regard the apostles as His ambassadors and witnesses, as men who proclaim His Word and who must be heard as He Himself is heard. As Christ says (Luke 10:16): "'He who hears you hears Me,' and he who hears Me hears My Father." Those are our *principia,* the bases and the chief article on which the entire Christian doctrine is founded. For all of scripture asserts solely of that God and of His Son and apostles that their proclamation constitutes the right Word of God, and that whoever believes this will be saved" ("Commentary on I Corinthians 15," 96). This was brought to my attention by D. Yeago, who discusses this aspect in detail in his in-progress work on Luther's theology.

152. Of course, Hegel's project was to accomplish exactly this *under the conditions of modernity,* that is, by equating the universal and particular spirit to conceive and develop this theological-argumentative discourse in the self-realization of the absolute spirit. Under the conditions of modernity, this was the last attempt to reconcile the difference between the claim of totality of modernity with the universal claim of the Christian message. "After Hegel," this will be possible only with an explicit consciousness of the difference between theology as a church practice and what in the horizon of modernity establishes itself normatively as discourse. Cf. in this regard O. Bayer, "Theologie als Konfliktwissenschaft," in *Autorität und Kritik,* 156-68, and Milbank, 147-76, 380-438. The other alternative, one whose inner consistency and intellectual rigor is worthy of note, is W. Pannenberg's program in which Christian truth is brought into a stable relationship with the modern concept of truth and understanding of reality by way of a universal-historical, eschatological schema. The place of argumentative *discurrere,* however, is assumed here by theology's systematic task of integration, namely, to make both Christian truth and the truth of the secular natural sciences, human sciences, and humanities transparent with regard to their comprehensive universal horizon.

153. Concerning the former, cf. E. Troeltsch, "Rückblick auf ein halbes Jahrhundert der theologischen Wissenschaft," in *Theologie als Wissenschaft. Aufsätze und Thesen,* ed. G. Sauter, Theologische Bücherei 43 (Munich: Kaiser, 1971), 73-104, and Troeltsch, "Über historische und dogmatische Methode in der Theologie," in *Theologie als Wissenschaft,* 105-27; also the paradigmatic correspondence between A. von Harnack and K. Barth, in *The Beginnings of Dialectic Theology,* ed. James M. Rob-

inson, trans. Keith R. Crim (Richmond: John Knox, 1968), 165-87. Concerning the latter, cf. Spaemann, "Überzeugungen in einer hypothetischen Zivilisation."

154. A. MacIntyre has persuasively articulated the logic of discourse tradition in his Gifford Lectures, *Three Rival Versions of Moral Enquiry.*

155. O. Bayer, *Theologie,* Handbuch Systematischer Theologie 1 (Gütersloh: Gütersloher Verlagshaus G. Mohn, 1994), 488.

156. Cf. in this regard Bayer, *Theologie,* 463-74, 488ff.

157. Cf. in this regard Parts Two and Three above.

158. This is then also the locus of the distinction between true and false doctrine. This distinction, however, is ultimately fixed only in a specific ecclesial doctrinal formulation; the distinction between true and false theological doctrine is expressed in the church confession (of church doctrine) and then applied in boundary situations of doctrinal disciplinary procedure. Addressing here the question of the relation between church doctrine and doctrinal discipline would transcend the scope of the present study. Although the conclusion may seem untimely that Protestant doctrine and theology cannot exist without the possible boundary situation of such public theological doctrinal demarcation, or that such public demarcation is in fact already implied in the concept of the *doctrina evangelii,* it is nonetheless a necessary implicate of Reformation theology. Cf. in this regard the complexity of these problems within the horizon of contemporary Protestant theology as exemplified in J. Baur, "Lehre, Irrlehre, Lehrzucht," in Baur, *Einsicht und Glaube. Aufsätze* (Göttingen: Vandenhoeck & Ruprecht, 1978), 222-48; E. Herms, "Die Lehre im Leben der Kirche," *Zeitschrift für Theologie und Kirche* 82 (1985): 192-230; W. Huber, "Die Schwierigkeit evangelischer Lehrbeanstandung. Eine historische Erinnerung aus aktuellem Anlaß," in Huber, *Konflikt und Konsens. Studien zur Ethik der Verantwortung* (Munich: Kaiser, 1990), 44-66; E. Jüngel, "Was ist die theologische Aufgabe evangelischer Kirchenleitung?" *Zeitschrift für Theologie und Kirche* 91 (1994): 189-209; T. Koch, "Die Freiheit der Wahrheit und die Notwendigkeit eines kirchenleitenden Lehramtes in der evangelischen Kirche," *Zeitschrift für Theologie und Kirche* 82 (1985): 231-50; H. Stoevesandt, "Verbindliche Lehre," *Glaube und Lernen* 3 (1988): 130-43. This logic can also function in the opposite direction, namely, that of mutual retraction of condemnation. Of interest here are the ecclesiological implications of church doctrine that (still) understands itself in opposition to another doctrine and yet (already) is able to recognize in that other doctrine the *doctrina evangelii.* If this really is the case, then understood *bona fide,* this involves differences in *theological* doctrine rather than of *church* doctrine; as such, it is the object of *theological* debate within dogmatic discourse that can be argumentatively engaged but is not ecclesiastically schismatic. Cf. in this regard K. Lehmann and W. Pannenberg, eds., *The Condemnations of the Reformation Era: Do They Still Divide?* trans. Margaret Kohl (Minneapolis: Fortress, 1990).

159. The key here is to understand that this sort of catechesis is meaningful only within a network of church practices, that is, one in which the actualization of the Christian life of faith itself constitutes the horizon within which theological catechetical engagement takes place. In this sense catechesis does not "translate" "belief" into the "modern understanding of self and world" in order to make it "compre-

hensible" or "acceptable" in some abstract sense. Rather, catechetical engagement is the intellectual process of being drawn into God's economy of salvation, the acquisition of a new language, the thinking of new thoughts — *in the context* of the new obedience in which Christian life as the actualization of the church practices is itself similarly learned and acquired. Cf. Robert W. Jenson, "Catechesis for Our Time," in *Marks of the Body of Christ*, ed. Carl E. Braaten and Robert W. Jenson (Grand Rapids: Eerdmans, 1999), 137-49, and L. Gregory Jones, "Baptism, Dramatic Journey into God's Dazzling Light: Baptismal Catechesis and the Shaping of Christian Practical Wisdom," in *Knowing the Triune God: The Work of the Spirit in the Practices of the Church*, ed. James J. Buckley and David Yeago (Grand Rapids: Eerdmans, forthcoming).

160. The justified concern with the acculturation of the Christian faith within the framework of so-called "local theologies" derives from its *perception* of specific situations of Christians as well as of their catechetical communicative intentions, *not* in the comprehensive claim on *how* theology is to be engaged within the framework of a comprehensive, pluralistically conceived theory of culture.

161. In this context one might consider the concern of J. Fischer with communicating the Christian faith within the horizon of communication of those who are present as an orientation aid for life and meaning; such strategy must, of course, remain strictly limited to the context of discovery attaching to the theological task, and its context of justification must not be reconstructed by this specific constellation of problems attaching to the circumstances of communication.

162. O. Bayer articulates as follows this procedural mode as one of Luther's own concerns: "A theologian is someone who is interpreted by the Holy Scripture, allows himself or herself to be interpreted by it, and as someone interpreted by it interprets it for others who are troubled or afflicted" (*Theologie*, 61). This is also the locus of the explicit *actualization* of the pathos of faith in the catechetical practice itself as articulated by Bayer with reference to Luther: "The culture of catechesis with which Luther wanted to preserve the truth of the monastic life form is necessary for the salvation of every human being. . . . Knowledge of the catechism and attention to it are necessary for salvation. Faith clings to the word, to its literality. Rhythm and linguistic form are not external, but belong rather constitutively together" (*Theologie*, 107f.).

163. George A. Lindbeck, *The Nature of Doctrine: Religion and Theology in a Postliberal Age* (Philadelphia: Westminster, 1984), 118.

Bibliography

Ahmed, Akbar S. *Postmodernism and Islam: Predicament and Promise.* London and New York: Routledge, 1992.

Albert, Hans. *Traktat über kritische Vernunft.* Tübingen: Mohr, 1968.

Anderson, H. George, J. Francis Stafford, and Joseph A. Burgess, eds. *The One Mediator, the Saints and Mary.* Lutherans and Catholics in Dialogue VIII. Minneapolis: Augsburg, 1992.

Anderson, H. George, T. A. Murphy, and Joseph A. Burgess, eds. *Justification by Faith.* Lutherans and Catholics in Dialogue VII. Minneapolis: Augsburg, 1985.

Aner, Karl. *Die Theologie der Lessingzeit.* Halle, 1929. Reprint, Hildesheim: Georg Olms, 1964.

Arendt, Hannah. *The Life of the Mind.* One-volume edition. San Diego, New York, and London: Harcourt Brace Jovanovich, 1978.

———. *Vita Activa oder Vom Tätigen Leben.* Munich: R. Piper, 1967; 5th ed., 1987; English: *The Human Condition.* Chicago and London: University of Chicago Press, 1958, 2nd ed., 1998.

Aristotle. *Metaphysics.* Translated by Hugh Tredennick. Loeb Classical Library 271. Cambridge and London: Harvard University Press, 1933.

———. *Nicomachean Ethics.* Translated by H. Rackham. Loeb Classical Library 73. Cambridge and London: Harvard University Press, 1926.

———. *Politics.* Translated by H. Rackham. Loeb Classical Library 264. Cambridge and London: Harvard University Press, 1932.

Arndt, A. "Produktion, Produktivität. II. Ökonomisch." In *Historisches Wörterbuch der Philosophie,* 7:1427-32. Basel: Schwabe, 1971f.

Asendorf, Ulrich. "Die Trinitätslehre als integrales Problem der Theologie Martin Luthers." In *Luther und die trinitarische Tradition. Ökumenische und*

283

philosophische Perspektiven, edited by Joachim Heubach, 113-30. Veröffent-lichungen der Luther-Akademie Ratzeburg 23. Erlangen: Martin-Luther-Verlag, 1994.

Auerbach, Erich. *Mimesis: The Representation of Reality in Western Literature.* Translated by Willard R. Trask. Princeton: Princeton University Press, 1968.

Austin, John L. *How to Do Things with Words.* Oxford: Clarendon, 1962; 2nd ed., 1975.

Balthasar, Hans Urs von. *The Theology of Karl Barth. Exposition and Interpretation.* 2nd ed., 1975. Translated by Edward T. Oakes, S.J. San Francisco: Ignatius Press, 1992.

Barth, Karl. *Die christliche Dogmatik in Entwurf. Vol. 1: Die Lehre vom Worte Gottes. Prolegomena zur christlichen Dogmatik.* Edited by Gerhard Sauter. Zürich: Theologischer Verlag, 1982.

————. "Church and Theology." In *Theology and Church: Shorter Writings 1920-1928.* Translated by Louise Pettibone Smith. With an Introduction by T. F. Torrance, 286-306. London: SCM Press, 1962.

————. *Church Dogmatics.* Edited by G. W. Bromiley and T. F. Torrance. Edinburgh: T. & T. Clark, 1936-77.

————. *The Epistle to the Romans.* Translated from the 6th edition by Edwyn C. Hoskyns. London, Oxford, New York: Oxford University Press, 1933.

————. "Das Geschenk der Freiheit. Grundlegung evangelischer Ethik." In *Freiheit im Leben mit Gott. Texte zur Tradition evangelischer Ethik,* edited by Hans G. Ulrich, 336-62. Theologische Bücherei 86. Gütersloh: Kaiser; Gütersloher Verlagshaus, 1993.

————. "Der römische Katholizismus als Frage an die protestantische Kirche." In *Die Theologie und die Kirche. Gesammelte Vorträge,* 2:329-63. Munich: Kaiser, 1928. See also English translation by Louise Pettibone Smith: "Roman Catholicism: A Question to the Protestant Church." In *Theology and Church: Shorter Writings 1920-1928,* 307-33. London: SCM Press, 1962.

————. "Das Wort Gottes als Aufgabe der Theologie." In *Das Wort Gottes und die Theologie. Gesammelte Vorträge,* 1:156-78. Munich: Kaiser, 1925. English translation by Douglas Horton, "The Word of God and the Task of the Ministry." In *The Word of God and the Word of Man,* 183-217. Boston and Chicago: Hodder & Stoughton, 1928.

Barth, Karl, and Adolf von Harnack. "Wissenschaftliche Theologie oder Theologie der Offenbarung Gottes? Ein Briefwechsel zwischen Karl Barth und Adolf von Harnack." In *Anfänge der dialektischen Theologie,* edited by Jürgen Moltmann, 1:323-47. Theologische Bücherei 17. 4th ed. Munich: Kaiser, 1977. See also English translation, *The Beginnings of Dialectic Theology.* Edited by James M. Robinson. Translated by Keith R. Crim. Richmond: John Knox, 1968.

Basil the Great of Caesarea. *De Spiritu Sancto. Vom Heiligen Geist.* Translated and introduced by Hermann Josef Sieben, S.J. Fontes christiani 12. Freiburg im Breisgau, Basel, and Vienna, 1993. English translation: *On the Holy Spirit.* Translated by David Anderson. Crestwook, N.Y.: St. Vladimir's Seminary Press, 1980.

Bauer, Karl-Adolf. "Kerygma und Kirche. Der Weg Heinrich Schliers als Anfrage an die evangelische Kirche und ihre Theologie." *Evangelische Theologie* 41 (1981): 401-23.

Baur, Jörg. *Einig in Sachen Rechtfertigung? Zur Prüfung des Rechtfertigungskapitels der Studie des Ökumenischen Arbeitskreises evangelischer und katholischer Theologen: Lehrverurteilungen — kirchentrennend?* Tübingen: J. C. B. Mohr, 1989.

———. "Freiheit und Bindung. Zur Frage der Verbindlichkeit kirchlicher Lehre." In Baur, *Einsicht und Glaube. Aufsätze,* 249-68. Göttingen: Vandenhoeck & Ruprecht, 1978.

———. "Kirchliches Bekenntnis und neuzeitliches Bewußtsein." In Baur, *Einsicht und Glaube. Aufsätze,* 269-89. Göttingen: Vandenhoeck & Ruprecht, 1978.

———. "Lehre, Irrlehre, Lehrzucht." In Baur, *Einsicht und Glaube. Aufsätze,* 222-48. Göttingen: Vandenhoeck & Ruprecht, 1978.

Bayer, Oswald. *Autorität und Kritik. Zur Hermeneutik und Wissenschaftstheorie.* Tübingen: J. C. B. Mohr, 1991.

———. *Freiheit als Antwort. Zur theologischen Ethik.* Tübingen: J. C. B. Mohr, 1995.

———. *Leibliches Wort. Reformation und Neuzeit im Konflikt.* Tübingen: J. C. B. Mohr, 1992.

———. "Luthers Verständnis des Seins Jesu Christi im Glauben." In *Luther und Ontologie. Das Sein Christi im Glauben als strukturierendes Prinzip der Theologie Luthers,* edited by Anja Ghiselli, Kari Kopperi, and Rainer Vinke, 94-113. Schriften der Luther-Agricola-Gesellschaft (Finland) 31/Veröffentlichungen der Luther-Akademie Ratzeburg 21. Helsinki and Erlangen: Finnische Theologische Literaturgesellschaft; Martin-Luther-Verlag, 1993.

———. *Promissio. Geschichte der reformatorischen Wende in Luthers Theologie.* Forschungen zur Kirchen- und Dogmengeschichte 24. Göttingen: Vandenhoeck & Ruprecht, 1971.

———. *Schöpfung als Anrede. Zu einer Hermeneutik der Schöpfung.* Tübingen: J. C. B. Mohr, 1986. 2nd rev. ed., 1990.

———. *Theologie.* Handbuch Systematischer Theologie 1. Gütersloh: Gütersloher Verlagshaus G. Mohn, 1994.

———. *Umstrittene Freiheit. Theologisch-philosophische Kontroversen.* Tübingen: J. C. B. Mohr, 1981.

———. *Was ist das: Theologie? Eine Skizze.* Stuttgart: Calwer, 1973.

Beiner, Ronald. *Political Judgment.* London: Methuen, 1983.

Die Bekenntnisschriften der Evangelisch-Lutherischen Kirche. Herausgegeben im

Gedenkjahr der Augsburgischen Konfession 1930. 8th ed. Göttingen: Vandenhoeck & Ruprecht, 1979.

Berman, Marshall. *All That Is Solid Melts into Air: The Experience of Modernity.* New York: Simon & Schuster, 1982.

Bernstein, Richard J. *Beyond Objectivism and Relativism: Science, Hermeneutics, and Praxis.* 2nd ed. Philadelphia: University of Pennsylvania Press, 1985.

─────. *The New Constellation: The Ethical-Political Horizons of Modernity/ Postmodernity.* 2nd ed. Cambridge: MIT Press, 1993.

─────. *Praxis and Action: Contemporary Philosophies of Human Activity.* Philadelphia: University of Pennsylvania Press, 1971.

Beyschlag, Karlmann. *Grundriß der Dogmengeschichte.* Vol. 1, *Gott und Welt.* Darmstadt: Wissenschaftliche Buchgesellschaft, 1982.

Bieler, Martin. *Freiheit als Gabe. Ein schöpfungstheologischer Entwurf.* Freiburger theologische Studien 145. Freiburg im Breisgau: Herder, 1991.

Bien, G., T. Kobusch, and H. Kleger. "Praxis, praktisch." In *Historisches Wörterbuch der Philosophie,* 7:1277-1307. Basel: Schwabe, 1971f.

Bienert, Wolfgang A. "Die Reformation als dogmengeschichtliches Ereignis. Ein Beitrag zur Geschichte des pneumatologischen Dogmas." In *Der Heilige Geist. Ökumenische und reformatorische Untersuchungen,* edited by Joachim Heubach, 35-56. Veröffentlichungen der Luther-Akademie Ratzeburg 25. Erlangen: Martin-Luther-Verlag, 1996.

Birmelé, André. "Ökumenische Überlegungen zu Pneumatologie und Ekklesiologie." In *Der Heilige Geist. Ökumenische und reformatorische Untersuchungen,* edited by Joachim Heubach, 169-88. Veröffentlichungen der Luther-Akademie Ratzeburg 25. Erlangen: Martin-Luther-Verlag, 1996.

Bobrinskoy, Boris. "The *Filioque* Yesterday and Today." In *Spirit of God, Spirit of Christ: Ecumenical Reflections on the Filioque Controversy,* edited by Lukas Vischer, 133-48. London: SPCK, 1981. [Geneva: World Council of Churches, 1981].

─────. *The Mystery of the Trinity: Trinitarian Experience and Vision in the Biblical and Patristic Tradition.* Translated by Anthony P. Gythiel. Crestwood, N.Y.: St. Vladimir's Seminary Press, 1999.

Boff, Clodovis. *Theology and Praxis: Epistemological Foundations.* Translated by Robert R. Barr. Maryknoll, N.Y.: Orbis, 1987.

Boff, Leonardo. *Trinity and Society.* Translated by Paul Burns. Maryknoll, N.Y.: Orbis, 1988.

Bonhoeffer, Dietrich. *Act and Being.* Translated by Bernard Noble. New York: Harper, 1961.

─────. *Gesammelte Schriften.* Vol. 6. Edited by Eberhard Bethge. Munich: Kaiser, 1974.

The Book of Concord: The Confessions of the Evangelical Lutheran Church. Translated and edited by Theodore G. Tappert. Philadelphia: Fortress Press, 1959.

Braaten, Carl E. *Mother Church. Ecclesiology and Ecumenism.* Minneapolis: Fortress, 1998.

————, and Robert Jenson, eds. *Marks of the Body of Christ.* Grand Rapids: Eerdmans, 1999.

————, and Robert W. Jenson, eds. *Union with Christ: The New Finnish Interpretation of Luther.* Grand Rapids: Eerdmans, 1998.

Brunner, Peter. *Bemühungen um die einigende Wahrheit. Aufsätze.* Göttingen: Vandenhoeck & Ruprecht, 1977.

————. *Pro Ecclesia. Gesammelte Aufsätze zur dogmatischen Theologie.* Vol. 1. 3rd ed. Fürth, 1990 (Berlin: Lutherisches Verlagshaus, 1962).

————. *Pro Ecclesia. Gesammelte Aufsätze zur dogmatischen Theologie.* Vol. 2. 2nd ed. Fürth, 1990 (Berlin: Lutherisches Verlagshaus, 1965).

————. "Zur Lehre vom Gottesdienst der im Namen Jesu versammelten Gemeinde." In *Leiturgia. Handbuch des evangelischen Gottesdienstes,* vol. 1, *Geschichte und Lehre des evangelischen Gottesdienstes,* edited by Karl Ferdinand Müller and Walter Blankenburg, 83-364. Kassel: Johannes Stauda-Verlag, 1954; English: *Worship in the Name of Jesus.* Translated by Martin H. Bertram. St. Louis: Concordia, 1968.

Bubner, Rüdiger. *Handlung, Sprache und Vernunft. Grundbegriffe praktischer Philosophie. Neuausgabe mit einem Anhang.* Frankfurt am Main: Suhrkamp, 1982 (1976).

Buckley, James J. "Doctrine in the Diaspora." *Thomist* 49 (1985): 443-59.

————. "Liberal and Conservative — or Catholic and Evangelical? Some Limits to the Debate over the Public Character of Theology." *Pro Ecclesia* 3 (1994): 324-33.

Cartwright, Michael C. "Practices, Politics, and Performance: Toward a Communal Hermeneutic for Christian Ethics." Diss., Duke University, 1988.

Casanova, José. *Public Religions in the Modern World.* Chicago: University of Chicago Press, 1994.

Castoriadis, Cornelius. *The Imaginary Institution of Society.* Translated by Kathleen Blamey. Cambridge: MIT Press, 1987.

Certeau, Michel de. *The Practice of Everyday Life.* Translated by Steven Rendall. Berkeley: University of California Press, 1985.

Chemnitz, Martin. *Examination of the Council of Trent.* 4 vols. Translated by Fred Kramer. St. Louis: Concordia, 1971-86.

Chenu, Marie-Dominique, O.P. *Toward Understanding Saint Thomas.* Translated with authorized corrections and bibliographical additions by A. M. Landry and D. Hughes. Chicago: H. Regnery Co., 1964.

Childs, Brevard S. *Biblical Theology of the Old and New Testaments: Theological Reflection on the Christian Bible.* Minneapolis: Fortress, 1992.

Crüsemann, Frank. *Bewahrung der Freiheit. Das Thema des Dekalogs in sozialgeschichtlicher Perspektive.* Munich: Kaiser, 1983.

————. *The Thora: Theology and Social History of Old Testament Law.* Translated by Allan W. Mahnke. Minneapolis: Fortress, 1996.

Cuddihy, John Murray. *No Offense: Civil Religion and Protestant Taste.* New York: Seabury Press, 1978.

Cunningham, David S. "Coercion or Persuasion? In Search of the Authority of Dogma." *Pro Ecclesia* 3 (1994): 307-23.

————. *Faithful Persuasion: In Aid of a Rhetoric of Christian Theology.* Notre Dame and London: University of Notre Dame Press, 1991.

Dalferth, Ingolf U. *Kombinatorische Theologie. Probleme theologischer Rationalität.* Quaestiones disputatae 130. Freiburg im Breisgau: Herder, 1991.

Davies, Brian. *The Thought of Thomas Aquinas.* Oxford: Clarendon; New York: Oxford University Press, 1992.

Derbolav, J. "Poiesis I." In *Historisches Wörterbuch der Philosophie,* 7:1024f. Basel: Schwabe, 1971f.

Dieter, Theodor. "'Du mußt den Geist haben!' Anthropologie und Pneumatologie bei Luther." In *Der Heilige Geist. Ökumenische und reformatorische Untersuchungen,* edited by Joachim Heubach, 65-88. Veröffentlichungen der Luther-Akademie Ratzeburg 25. Erlangen: Martin-Luther-Verlag, 1996.

Dressler, S. "Pathisch, Pathik." In *Historisches Wörterbuch der Philosophie,* 7:177-81. Basel: Schwabe, 1971f.

Dunne, Joseph. *Back to the Rough Ground: "Phronesis" and "Techne" in Modern Philosophy and in Aristotle.* Notre Dame: University of Notre Dame Press, 1993.

Dykstra, Craig. "Reconceiving Practice." In *Shifting Boundaries: Contextual Approaches to the Structure of Theological Education,* edited by Barbara G. Wheeler and Edward Farley, 35-66. Louisville: Westminster/John Knox, 1991.

Ebeling, Gerhard. *Lutherstudien.* Vol. 1 [without special title]. Tübingen: J. C. B. Mohr, 1971.

————. *Lutherstudien.* Vol. 2, *Disputatio de homine.* Part 1, *Text und Traditions hintergrund.* Tübingen: J. C. B. Mohr, 1977.

————. *Lutherstudien.* Vol. 2, *Disputatio de homine.* Part 2, *Die philosophische Definition des Menschen.* Tübingen: J. C. B. Mohr, 1982.

————. *Lutherstudien.* Vol. 2, *Disputatio de homine.* Part 3, *Die theologische Definition des Menschen.* Tübingen: J. C. B. Mohr, 1989.

————. *Lutherstudien.* Vol. 3, *Begriffsuntersuchungen — Textinterpretation — Wirkungsgeschichtliches.* Tübingen: J. C. B. Mohr, 1985.

————. "Das rechte Unterscheiden. Luthers Anleitung zu theologischer Urteilskraft." *Zeitschrift für Theologie und Kirche* 85 (1988): 219-58.

Eckehart, Meister. *Deutsche Predigten und Traktate.* Translated and edited by Josef Quint. Munich: Carl Hanser, 1963. 2nd ed., 1979.

Elshtain, Jean Bethke. *Public Man, Private Woman: Women in Social and Political Thought*. Princeton: Princeton University Press, 1981.

Empie, Paul C., and T. A. Murphy, eds. *The Status of the Nicene Creed as Dogma of the Church. One Baptism for the Remission of Sins. The Eucharist as Sacrifice.* Lutherans and Catholics in Dialogue I-III. Minneapolis: Augsburg, 1967.

Esposito, John L. *The Islamic Threat: Myth or Reality?* New York and Oxford: Oxford University Press, 1992.

Ewald, D., and N. Rath. "Poesie." In *Historisches Wörterbuch der Philosophie*, 7:1000-1008. Basel: Schwabe, 1971f.

Fee, Gordon D. *God's Empowering Presence: The Holy Spirit in the Letters of Paul*. Peabody, Mass.: Hendrickson, 1994.

Felmy, Karl Christian. *Die orthodoxe Theologie der Gegenwart. Eine Einführung*. Darmstadt: Wissenschaftliche Buchgesellschaft, 1990.

Fischer, Johannes. *Leben aus dem Geist. Zur Grundlegung christlicher Ethik*. Zürich: Theologischer Verlag, 1994.

———. "Pluralismus, Wahrheit und die Krise der Dogmatik." *Zeitschrift für Theologie und Kirche* 91 (1994): 487-539.

Fortin-Melkevik, Anne. "Théologie, université et espaces publics. Quelle théologie pour quelle culture?" *Théologiques* 2 (1994): 127-39.

Forum für Philosophie Bad Homburg, ed. *Philosophie und Begründung*. Frankfurt am Main: Suhrkamp, 1987.

Frei, Hans W. *The Eclipse of Biblical Narrative: A Study in Eighteenth and Nineteenth Century Hermeneutics*. New Haven and London: Yale University Press, 1974.

———. *The Identity of Jesus Christ: The Hermeneutical Bases of Dogmatic Theology*. Philadelphia: Fortress, 1975.

———. *Theology and Narrative: Selected Essays*. Edited by George Hunsinger and William C. Placher. Oxford and New York: Oxford University Press, 1993.

———. *Types of Christian Theology*. Edited by George Hunsinger and William C. Placher. New Haven: Yale University Press, 1992.

Gadamer, Hans-Georg. *Truth and Method*. Translated by Joel Weinsheimer and Donald G. Marshall. 2nd ed. New York: Crossroad, 1989.

Geertz, Clifford. *The Interpretation of Cultures: Selected Essays*. New York: Basic Books, 1973.

Gerhard, Johann. *Confessio Catholica in qua Doctrina Catholica et Evangelica quam Ecclesiae Augustanae Confessioni Addictae Profitentur ex Romano-Catholicorum Scriptorum Suffragiis Confirmatur*. 4 vols. Francofurti et Lipsiae, 1679.

Ghiselli, Anja, Kari Kopperi, and Rainer Vinke, eds. *Luther und Ontologie. Das Sein Christi im Glauben als strukturierendes Prinzip der Theologie Luthers*. Schriften der Luther-Agricola-Gesellschaft (Finland) 31. Veröffentlichungen der Luther-Akademie Ratzeburg 21. Helsinki and Erlangen: Martin-Luther-Verlag, 1993.

Grillmeier, Alois. *Christ in Christian Tradition. II/2: From the Council of Chalcedon (451) to Gregory the Great (540-609)*. Translated by John Bowden. 2nd rev. ed. Atlanta: John Knox, 1995.

Gritsch, Eric W., and Robert W. Jenson. *Lutheranism: The Theological Movement and Its Confessional Writings*. Philadelphia: Fortress, 1976.

Gunton, Colin E. *Enlightenment and Alienation: An Essay towards a Trinitarian Theology*. Grand Rapids: Wm. B. Eerdmans Publishing Co., 1985.

————. *The One, the Three, and the Many: God, Creation, and the Culture of Modernity*. Cambridge and New York: Cambridge University Press, 1993.

————. *The Promise of Trinitarian Theology*. Edinburgh: T. & T. Clark, 1991.

Gutiérrez, Gustavo. "Freedom and Salvation: A Political Problem." In Gutierrez and Richard Shaull, *Liberation and Change*, edited and introduced by Richard H. Stone, 3-94. Atlanta: John Knox, 1977.

————. *A Theology of Liberation: History, Politics, and Salvation*. Maryknoll, N.Y.: Orbís, 1973.

Habermas, Jürgen. *Die neue Unübersichtlichkeit*. Kleine politische Schriften, vol. V. Frankfurt am Main: Suhrkamp, 1985.

————. *The Philosophical Discourse of Modernity: Twelve Lectures*. Translated by Frederick Lawrence. Cambridge: MIT Press, 1987.

————. *The Theory of Communicative Action*. Translated by Thomas McCarthy. Vol. 1, *Reason and the Rationalization of Society*. Vol. 2, *Lifeworld and System: A Critique of Functionalist Reason*. Boston: Beacon, 1984f.

Hägglund, Bengt. "Die Bedeutung der 'regula fidei' als Grundlage theologischer Aussagen." *Studia theologica* (Lund) 12 (1958): 1-44.

————. *Theologie und Philosophie bei Luther und in der ockhamistischen Tradition*. Lunds universitets arsskrift, n.f., avd. 1, bd. 51, nr. 4. Lund: C. W. K. Gleerup, 1955.

Hansen, Guillermo C. "The Doctrine of the Trinity and Liberation Theology: A Study of the Trinitarian Doctrine and Its Place in Latin American Liberation Theology. " Diss., Lutheran School of Theology at Chicago, 1994.

Härle, Wilfried. *Sein und Gnade. Die Ontologie in Karl Barths Kirchlicher Dogmatik*. Berlin: Walter de Gruyter, 1975.

Hauerwas, Stanley. *In Good Company: The Church as Polis*. Notre Dame: University of Notre Dame Press, 1995.

————. *Unleashing the Scripture: Freeing the Bible from Captivity to America*. Nashville: Abingdon, 1993.

Hegel, Georg Wilhelm Friedrich. *Lectures on the Philosophy of Religion* I. Translated by R. F. Brown et al. Edited by Peter C. Hodgson. Berkeley: University of California Press, 1988.

————. *Phenomenology of Mind.* Translated by J. B. Baillie. 2nd ed. London: George Allen & Unwin; New York: Humanities Press, 1931.

————. *Vorlesungen über die Philosophie der Religion* I. Theorie Werkausgabe. Frankfurt am Main: Suhrkamp, 1969.

Heidegger, Martin. *What Is Philosophy?* Translated with an introduction by William Kluback and Jean T. Wilde. London: Vision, 1958.

Heinrichs, Johannes. "Dialogik I. Philosophie." In *Theologische Realenzyklopädie,* 8:697-703. Berlin: Walter de Gruyter, 1981.

Herms, Eilert. "Die Lehre im Leben der Kirche." *Zeitschrift für Theologie und Kirche* 82 (1985): 192-230.

————. "Überlegungen zum Wesen des Gottesdienstes. Aus Anlaß des Entwurfes für eine 'Erneuerte Agende.'" *Kerygma und Dogma* 40 (1994): 219-47.

Heron, Alasdair I. C. "The *Filioque* in Recent Reformed Theology." In *Spirit of God, Spirit of Christ: Ecumenical Reflections on the Filioque Controversy,* edited by Lukas Vischer, 110-17. London: SPCK, 1981. [Geneva: World Council of Churches, 1981].

————. *The Holy Spirit: The Holy Spirit in the Bible, the History of Christian Thought, and Recent Theology.* Philadelphia: Westminster, 1983.

————. "The Person of Christ." In *Keeping the Faith: Essays to Mark the Centenary of Lux Mundi,* edited by Geoffrey Wainwright, 99-123. Philadelphia and Allison Park: Fortress, 1988.

Heubach, Joachim, ed. *Der Heilige Geist. Ökumenische und reformatorische Untersuchungen.* Veröffentlichungen der Luther-Akademie Ratzeburg 25. Erlangen: Martin-Luther-Verlag, 1996.

————, ed. *Luther und die trinitarische Tradition. Ökumenische und philosophische Perspektiven.* Veröffentlichungen der Luther-Akademie Ratzeburg 23. Erlangen: Martin-Luther-Verlag, 1994.

Hodgson, Peter C. *Winds of the Spirit: A Constructive Christian Theology.* Louisville: Westminster/John Knox, 1994.

Hollerich, Michael. "Erik Peterson's Correspondence with Adolf von Harnack: Retrieving a Neglected Critique of Church, Theology, and Secularization in Weimar Germany." *Pro Ecclesia* 2 (1993): 305-32.

Horkheimer, Max. "Traditional and Critical Theory." In *Critical Theory: Selected Essays,* translated by Matthew J. O'Connell and others, 188-243. New York: Herder & Herder, 1972.

Huber, Wolfgang. *Kirche und Öffentlichkeit.* Forschungen und Berichte der Evangelischen Studiengemeinschaft 28. Stuttgart: E. Klett, 1973.

————. "Öffentliche Kirche in pluralen Öffentlichkeiten." *Evangelische Theologie* 54 (1994): 157-80.

————. "Die Schwierigkeit evangelischer Lehrbeanstandung. Eine historische Erinnerung aus aktuellem Anlaß." In Huber, *Konflikt und Konsens. Studien zur Ethik der Verantwortung,* 44-66. Munich: Kaiser, 1990.

————. "Die Spannung zwischen Glaube und Lehre als Problem der Theologie." In Huber, *Konflikt und Konsens. Studien zur Ethik der Verantwortung,* 15-43. Munich: Kaiser, 1990.

Hunsinger, George. *How to Read Karl Barth: The Shape of His Theology.* Oxford: Oxford University Press, 1991.

————. "Truth as Self-Involving: Barth and Lindbeck on the Cognitive and Performative Aspects of Truth in Theological Discourse." *Journal of the American Academy of Religion* 61 (1993): 41-56.

Hütter, Reinhard. "The Church as Public: Dogma, Practice, and the Holy Spirit." *Pro Ecclesia* 3 (1994): 334-61.

————. "The Church's Peace beyond the 'Secular': A Postmodern Augustinian's Deconstruction of Modernity and Postmodernity." *Pro Ecclesia* 2 (1993): 106-16.

————. *Evangelische Ethik als kirchliches Zeugnis. Interpretationen zu Schlüsselfragen theologischer Ethik in der Gegenwart.* Evangelium und Ethik 1. Neukirchen-Vluyn: Neukirchener, 1993.

Institute for Ecumenical Research. *Communio/Koinonia: A New Testament–Early Christian Concept and Its Contemporary Appropriation and Significance.* Strasbourg, 1990.

Iwand, Hans Joachim. "Der moderne Mensch und das Dogma." In Iwand, *Nachgelassene Werke.* Vol. 2, edited by Helmut Gollwitzer and Walter Kreck, 91-105. Munich: Kaiser, 1966.

————. "Theologische Einführung." In *Daß der freie Wille nichts sei. Antwort D. Martin Luthers an Erasmus von Rotterdam.* Martin Luther, *Ausgewählte Werke,* Supplement Series. Vol. 1, edited by Hans Hermann Borcherdt and Georg Merz, 253-64. 3rd ed. Munich: Kaiser, 1962.

Janz, Denis. *Luther on Thomas Aquinas: The Angelic Doctor in the Thought of the Reformer.* Veröffentlichungen des Instituts für Europäische Geschichte Mainz 140. Stuttgart: Franz Steiner Verlag Wiesbaden, 1989.

Jenson, Robert W. "Catechesis for Our Time." In *Marks of the Body of Christ,* 137-49. Edited by Carl E. Braaten and Robert W. Jenson. Grand Rapids: Eerdmans, 1999.

————. *God after God: The God of the Past and the Future as Seen in the Work of Karl Barth.* Indianapolis: Bobbs-Merrill, 1969.

————. *The Knowledge of Things Hoped For: The Sense of Theological Discourse.* Oxford and New York: Oxford University Press, 1969.

————. "An Ontology of Freedom in the *De Servo Arbitrio* of Luther." *Modern Theology* 10 (1994): 247-52.

————. *Systematic Theology.* 2 vols. New York: Oxford University Press, 1997-99.

————. "Die trinitarische Grundlegung der Theologie. Östliche und westliche Trinitätslehre als ökumenisches Problem." In *Luther und die trinitarische Tradition. Ökumenische und philosophische Perspektiven,* edited by Joachim

Heubach, 9-24. Veröffentlichungen der Luther-Akademie Ratzeburg 23. Erlangen: Martin-Luther-Verlag, 1994.

————. *The Triune Identity.* Philadelphia: Fortress, 1982.

————. *Unbaptized God: The Basic Flaw in Ecumenical Theology.* Minneapolis: Fortress, 1992.

————. "What Would a Full Doctrine of the Spirit Mean for the Doctrine of the Church?" In *Der Heilige Geist. Ökumenische und reformatorische Unter-suchungen,* edited by Joachim Heubach, 105-14. Veröffentlichungen der Lu-ther-Akademie Ratzeburg 25. Erlangen: Martin-Luther-Verlag, 1996.

————. "You Wonder Where the Spirit Went." *Pro Ecclesia* 2 (1993): 296-304.

Joest, Wilfried. *Ontologie der Person bei Luther.* Göttingen: Vandenhoeck & Ruprecht, 1967.

John of Damascus. *The Orthodox Faith.* In *Writings,* 165-406. Translated by Frederic H. Chese, Jr. The Fathers of the Church, vol. 37. New York: Fathers of the Church, 1958.

————. *The Philosophical Chapters.* In *Writings,* 7-110. Translated by Frederic H. Chese, Jr. The Fathers of the Church, vol. 37. New York: Fathers of the Church, 1958.

Jonas, Hans. "Über die hermeneutische Struktur des Dogmas." In Jonas, *Augustin und das paulinische Freiheitsproblem. Eine philosophische Studie zum Pelagianischen Streit,* appendix I, 80-89. Göttingen: Vandenhoeck & Ruprecht, 1930. 2nd ed., 1965.

Jones, L. Gregory. "Baptism: A Dramatic Journey into God's Dazzling Light: Bap-tismal Catechesis and the Shaping of Christian Practical Wisdom." In *Knowing the Triune God: The Work of the Spirit in the Practices of the Church,* edited by James J. Buckley and David Yeago. Grand Rapids: Eerd-mans, forthcoming.

Jüngel, Eberhard. *God as the Mystery of the World: On the Foundation of the Theol-ogy of the Crucified One in the Dispute between Theism and Atheism.* Trans-lated by Darrell L. Guder. Grand Rapids: Eerdmans, 1983.

————. "Von der Dialektik zur Analogie. Die Schule Kierkegaards und der Einspruch Petersons." In Jüngel, *Barth-Studien,* 127-79. Zürich and Co-logne: Benziger; Gütersloh: Gütersloher Verlagshaus G. Mohn, 1982.

————. "Was ist die theologische Aufgabe evangelischer Kirchenleitung?" *Zeitschrift für Theologie und Kirche* 91 (1994): 189-209.

————. *Wertlose Wahrheit. Zur Identität und Relevanz des christlichen Glaubens.* Beiträge zur evangelischen Theologie 107. Munich: Kaiser, 1990.

Kallis, Anastasios. "Communio Sanctorum. Vielfalt und Entfaltung der Kirchen-struktur aus orthodoxer Sicht." In *Unsichtbare oder sichtbare Kirche? Beiträge zur Ekklesiologie,* edited by Martin Hauser et al., 83-95. Ökumen-ische Beihefte zur Freiburger Zeitschrift für Philosophie und Theologie 20. Freiburg, Switzerland: Universitätsverlag, 1992.

Kasper, Walter. "'Einer aus der Trinität . . .' Zur Neubegründung einer spirituellen Christologie in trinitätstheologischer Perspektive." In *Im Gespräch mit dem dreieinigen Gott. Elemente einer trinitarischen Theologie. Festschrift Wilhelm Breuning,* edited by Michael Böhnke and Hanspeter Heinz, 316-33. Düsseldorf: Patmos, 1985.

———. *Der Gott Jesu Christi.* 2nd ed. Mainz: Matthias-Grünewald-Verlag, 1983.

———. "Postmoderne Dogmatik? Zur einer neueren nordamerikanischen Grundlagendiskussion." In *Der Weg zum Menschen. Zur philosophischen und theologischen Anthropologie. Festschrift Alfons Deissler,* edited by Rudolf Mosis and Lothar Ruppert, 265-74. Freiburg im Breisgau: Herder, 1989.

Kasper, Walter, and Gerhard Sauter. *Kirche. Ort des Geistes.* Freiburg im Breisgau: Herder, 1976.

Kaufman, Gordon D. *An Essay on Theological Method.* Missoula, Mont.: Scholars Press, 1975.

———. *In the Face of Mystery: A Constructive Theology.* Cambridge: Harvard University Press, 1993.

Kaulbach, F. "Produktion, Produktivität: I. Philosophie." In *Historisches Wörterbuch der Philosophie,* 7:1418-26. Basel: Schwabe, 1971f.

Kelsey, David H. *Between Athens and Berlin: The Theological Education Debate.* Grand Rapids: Wm. B. Eerdmans Publishing Co., 1993.

———. *To Understand God Truly: What's Theological about a Theological School?* Louisville: Westminster/John Knox, 1992.

Kenneson, Philip D. "The Reappearance of the Visible Church: An Analysis of the Production and Reproduction of Christian Identity." Diss., Duke University, 1991.

Kerr, Fergus. *Theology after Wittgenstein.* Oxford and New York: Blackwell, 1986.

Kjeldgaard-Pedersen, Steffen. "Antinomian Controversies." In *The Encyclopedia of Christianity,* 1:80f. Grand Rapids and Cambridge: Eerdmans; London, Boston, and Cologne: Brill, 1999f.

Klappert, Berthold. *Promissio und Bund. Gesetz und Evangelium bei Luther und Barth.* Forschungen zur systematischen und ökumenischen Theologie 34. Göttingen: Vandenhoeck & Ruprecht, 1976.

Knapp, Markus. "Postmoderne Dogmatik? Überlegungen zu einer Grundlagendiskussion im Anschluß an einen Vorschlag von George A. Lindbeck." *Münchener theologische Zeitschrift* 45 (1994): 1-10.

Koch, Traugott. "Die Freiheit der Wahrheit und die Notwendigkeit eines kirchenleitenden Lehramtes in der evangelischen Kirche." *Zeitschrift für Theologie und Kirche* 82 (1985): 231-50.

Koller, H. "Mimesis." In *Historisches Wörterbuch der Philosophie,* 5:1396-99. Basel: Schwabe, 1971f.

König, R. "Produktion, Produktivität. III. Kunst." In *Historisches Wörterbuch der Philosophie,* 7:1432-38. Basel: Schwabe, 1971f.

Koopmans, Jan. *Das altkirchliche Dogma in der Reformation.* Beiträge zur evangelischen Theologie 22. Munich: Kaiser, 1955.

Köpf, Ulrich. "Passivität und Aktivität in der Mystik des Mittelalters." In *Pragmatik. Handbuch pragmatischen Denkens,* vol. 1, edited by Herbert Stachowiak, 280-98. Hamburg: Felix Meiner, 1985.

Kort, Wesley A. *Bound to Differ: The Dynamics of Theological Discourses.* University Park: Pennsylvania State University Press, 1992.

Kugelmann, Lothar. *Antizipation. Eine begriffsgeschichtliche Untersuchung.* Forschungen zur systematischen und ökumenischen Theologie 50. Göttingen: Vandenhoeck & Ruprecht, 1986.

Kühn, Ulrich. "Evangelische Rezeption altkirchlicher Bekenntnisse. Am Beispiel des Projektes der Kommission für Glauben und Kirchenverfassung 'Auf dem Weg zu einem gemeinsamen Ausdruck des apostolischen Glaubens heute.'" In *Vernunft des Glaubens. Wissenschaftliche Theologie und kirchliche Lehre. Festschrift Wolfhart Pannenberg,* edited by Jan Rohls and Gunther Wenz, 652-69. Göttingen: Vandenhoeck & Ruprecht, 1988.

―――. *Kirche.* Handbuch Systematischer Theologie 10. Gütersloh: Gütersloher Verlagshaus G. Mohn, 1980.

Kühn, Ulrich, and Otto Hermann Pesch. *Rechtfertigung im Disput. Eine freundliche Antwort an Jörg Baur.* Tübingen: J. C. B. Mohr, 1991.

Lacugna, Catherine M. *God for Us: The Trinity and Christian Life.* San Francisco: Harper, 1991.

Larentzakis, Grigorios. "Die Teilnahme am trinitarischen Leben. Die Bedeutung der Pneumatologie für die Ökumene heute." In *Der Heilige Geist. Ökumenische und reformatorische Untersuchungen,* edited by Joachim Heubach, 225-44. Veröffentlichungen der Luther-Akademie Ratzeburg 25. Erlangen: Martin-Luther-Verlag, 1996.

―――. "Trinitarisches Kirchenverständnis." In *Trinität. Aktuelle Perspektiven der Theologie,* edited by Wilhelm Breuning, 73-96. Quaestiones disputatae 101. Freiburg im Breisgau: Herder, 1984.

Lehmann, Karl, ed. *Justification by Faith: Do the Sixteenth-Century Condemnations Still Apply?* Translated by Michael Root and William G. Rusch. New York: Continuum, 1997.

Lehmann, Karl, and W. Pannenberg, eds., *The Condemnations of the Reformation Era: Do They Still Divide?* Translated by Margaret Kohl. Minneapolis: Fortress, 1990.

Leuba, Jean-Louis. "Die Ekklesiologie Karl Barths." In *Unsichtbare oder sichtbare Kirche? Beiträge zur Ekklesiologie,* edited by Martin Hauser et al., 59-82. Ökumenische Beihefte zur Freiburger Zeitschrift für Philosophie und Theologie 20. Freiburg, Switzerland: Universitätsverlag, 1992.

―――. *New Testament Pattern: An Exegetical Enquiry into the "Catholic" and*

"Protestant" Dualism. Translated by Harold Knight. London: Lutterworth, 1953.

Levenson, Jon D. *The Hebrew Bible, the Old Testament, and Historical Criticism: Jews and Christians in Biblical Studies.* Louisville: Westminster/John Knox, 1993.

Lindbeck, George A. "The Church." In *Keeping the Faith: Essays to Mark the Centenary of Lux Mundi,* edited by Geoffrey Wainwright, 178-208. Philadelphia and Allison Park: Fortress, 1988.

———. "The Church's Mission to a Postmodern Culture." In *Postmodern Theology: Christian Faith in a Pluralist World,* edited by Frederic B. Burnham, 37-55. New York: Harper & Row, 1989.

———. "Ecumenical Imperatives for the Twenty-First Century." *Currents in Theology and Mission* 20 (1993): 360-66.

———. "Ecumenism and the Future of Belief." *Una Sancta* (Brooklyn, N.Y.) 25, no. 3 (1968): 3-17.

———. *The Future of Roman Catholic Theology: Vatican II — Catalyst for Change.* Philadelphia: Fortress, 1970.

———. "Martin Luther and the Rabbinic Mind." In *Understanding the Rabbinic Mind: Essays on the Hermeneutic of Max Kadushin,* edited by Peter Ochs, 141-64. South Florida Studies in the History of Judaism 14. Atlanta: Scholars Press, 1990.

———. *The Nature of Doctrine: Religion and Theology in a Postliberal Age.* Philadelphia: Westminster, 1984.

———. "The Sectarian Future of the Church." In *The God Experience,* edited by J. P. Whelan, S.J., 226-43. New York: Newman, 1971.

———. "The Story-Shaped Church: Critical Exegesis and Theological Interpretation." In *Scriptural Authority and Narrative Interpretation: Festschrift Hans W. Frei,* edited by Garrett Green, 161-78. Philadelphia: Fortress, 1987.

———. "Theologische Methode und Wissenschaftstheorie." *Theologische Revue* 74 (1978): 266-80.

Link, Christian. "Vita passiva. Rechtfertigung als Lebensvorgang." *Evangelische Theologie* 44 (1984): 315-51.

Lints, Richard. "The Postpositive Choice: Tracy or Lindbeck?" *Journal of the American Academy of Religion* 61 (1993): 655-77.

Lobkowicz, Nicholas. *Theory and Practice: History of a Concept from Aristotle to Marx.* Notre Dame: University of Notre Dame Press, 1967.

Lonergan, Bernard, S.J. *Method in Theology.* New York: Herder & Herder, 1972.

Lossky, Vladimir. *The Mystical Theology of the Eastern Church.* Translated by members of the Fellowship of St. Alban and St. Sergius. London: J. Clarke, 1957; Crestwood, N.Y.: St. Vladimir's Seminary, 1976.

Luther, Martin. *Ausgewählte Werke.* Edited by Hans Hermann Borcherdt and Georg Merz. 3rd ed. Munich: Kaiser, 1948-65.

———. *Luther's Works.* Vol. 21, *The Sermon on the Mount (Sermons) and The*

Magnificat. Sermon on the Mount translated by Jaroslav Pelikan and Magnificat translated by A. T. W. Steinhaeuser. Edited by Jaroslav Pelikan. St. Louis: Concordia, 1956.

———. *Luther's Works.* Vol. 25, *Lectures on Romans.* Translated by Walter G. Tillmanns and Jacob A. O. Preus and edited by Hilton C. Oswald. St. Louis: Concordia, 1972.

———. *Luther's Works.* Vol. 26, *Lectures on Galatians, 1535, Chapters 1–4.* Translated and edited by Jaroslav Pelikan. St. Louis: Concordia, 1963.

———. *Luther's Works.* Vol. 28, *Commentaries on I Corinthians 7 and I Corinthians 15; Lectures on I Timothy.* Edited by Hilton C. Oswald. St. Louis: Concordia, 1973.

———. *Luther's Works.* Vol. 31, *Career of the Reformer I.* Edited by Harold J. Grimm. Philadelphia: Muhlenberg, 1957.

———. *Luther's Works.* Vol 33, *Career of the Reformer III.* Translated and edited by Philip S. Watson. Philadelphia: Fortress, 1972.

———. *Luther's Works.* Vol. 35, *Word and Sacrament I.* Edited and translated by E. T. Bachman. Philadelphia: Muhlenberg, 1960.

———. *Luther's Works.* Vol. 41, *Church and Ministry III.* Edited by Eric W. Gritsch, with an introduction by E. Gordon Rupp. Philadelphia: Fortress, 1966.

———. *Sermons of Martin Luther.* Vol. 7. Translated and edited by J. N. Lenker. Grand Rapids: Baker, 1909. Reprint, 1983.

———. *(Weimar Ausgabe) Werke. Kritische Gesamtausgabe.* Weimar: Herman Böhlau, 1883ff.

Lutheran–Roman Catholic Joint Commission. *Church and Justification: Understanding the Church in the Light of the Doctrine of Justification.* Geneva: Lutheran World Federation, 1994.

Lyotard, Jean-François. *The Postmodern Condition: A Report on Knowledge.* Translated by Geoff Bennington and Brian Massumi. Foreword by Fredric Jameson. Minneapolis: University of Minnesota Press, 1984.

MacIntyre, Alasdair. *After Virtue: A Study in Moral Theory.* Notre Dame: University of Notre Dame Press, 1981. 2nd ed., 1984.

———. *Three Rival Versions of Moral Enquiry: Encyclopaedia, Genealogy, and Tradition: Being Gifford Lectures Delivered in the University of Edinburgh in 1988.* Notre Dame: University of Notre Dame Press, 1990.

Mannermaa, Tuomo. "Hat Luther eine trinitarische Ontologie?" In *Luther und die trinitarische Tradition. Ökumenische und philosophische Perspektiven,* edited by Joachim Heubach, 43-60. Veröffentlichungen der Luther-Akademie Ratzeburg 23. Erlangen: Martin-Luther-Verlag, 1994.

———. *Der im Glauben gegenwärtige Christus. Rechtfertigung und Vergottung. Zum ökumenischen Dialog.* Arbeiten zur Geschichte und Theologie des Luthertums, n.s., 8. Hanover: Lutherisches Verlagshaus, 1989.

Mannermaa, Tuomo, Anja Ghiselli, and Simo Peura, eds. *Thesaurus Lutheri. Auf der Suche nach neuen Paradigmen der Luther-Forschung.* Schriften der Luther-Agricola-Gesellschaft (Finland) A 24. Helsinki: Finnische Theologische Literaturgesellschaft, 1987.

Marquard, Odo. *Schwierigkeiten mit der Geschichtsphilosophie. Aufsätze.* Frankfurt am Main: Suhrkamp, 1973. 2nd ed., 1982.

Marshall, Bruce D. "The Church in the Gospel." *Pro Ecclesia* 1 (1992): 27-41.

———. "Faith and Reason Reconsidered: Aquinas and Luther on Deciding What Is True." *Thomist* 63 (1999): 1-48.

———. "Lindbeck on What Theology Is." *Dialog* 31 (1992): 44-47.

———. "Thomas Aquinas as Postliberal Theologian." *Thomist* 53 (1989): 353-402.

———, ed. *Theology and Dialogue: Essays in Conversation with George Lindbeck.* Notre Dame: University of Notre Dame Press, 1990.

Martikainen, Eeva. "Der Doctrina-Begriff in Luthers Theologie." In *Thesaurus Lutheri. Auf der Suche nach neuen Paradigmen der Luther-Forschung,* edited by Tuomo Mannermaa et al., 205-19. Schriften der Luther-Agricola-Gesellschaft (Finland) A 24. Helsinki: Finnische Theologische Literaturgesellschaft, 1987.

———. *Doctrina. Studien zu Luthers Begriff der Lehre.* Schriften der Luther-Agricola-Gesellschaft (Finland) A 26. Helsinki: Finnische Theologische Literaturgesellschaft, 1992.

———. *Evangelium als Mitte. Das Verhältnis von Wort und Lehre in der ökumenischen Methode Hans Joachim Iwands.* Arbeiten zur Geschichte und Theologie des Luthertums, n.s., 9. Hanover: Lutherisches Verlagshaus, 1989.

———. "Die Lehre und die Anwesenheit Gottes in der Theologie Luthers." In *Luther und Theosis. Vergöttlichung als Thema der abendländischen Theologie,* edited by Simo Peura and Antti Raunio, 215-32. Schriften der Luther-Agricola-Gesellschaft (Finland) A 25. Helsinki: Finnische Theologische Literaturgesellschaft, 1990.

Martikainen, Jouko. "Christologische und trinitätstheologische Aporien der östlichen Kirche aus der Sicht Luthers." In *Luther und die trinitarische Tradition. Ökumenische und philosophische Perspektiven,* edited by Joachim Heubach, 71-94. Veröffentlichungen der Luther-Akademie Ratzeburg 23. Erlangen: Martin-Luther-Verlag, 1994.

Maurer, Wilhelm. "Die Anfänge von Luthers Theologie." In Maurer, *Kirche und Geschichte. Gesammelte Aufsätze.* Vol. 1, *Luther und das evangelische Bekenntnis,* edited by Ernst-Wilhelm Kohls and Gerhard Müller, 22-37. Göttingen: Vandenhoeck & Ruprecht, 1970.

———. "Die Einheit der Theologie Luthers." In Maurer, *Kirche und Geschichte. Gesammelte Aufsätze.* Vol. 1, *Luther und das evangelische Bekenntnis,* edited by Ernst-Wilhelm Kohls and Gerhard Müller, 11-21. Göttingen: Vandenhoeck & Ruprecht, 1970.

McCormack, Bruce. *Karl Barth's Critically Realistic Dialectical Theology: Its Genesis and Development, 1909-1936.* Oxford: Clarendon, 1995.

McFague, Sallie. *The Body of God: An Ecological Theology.* Minneapolis: Fortress, 1993.

———. *Metaphorical Theology: Models of God in Religious Language.* Philadelphia: Fortress, 1982.

———. *Models of God: Theology for an Ecological, Nuclear Age.* Philadelphia: Fortress, 1987.

Meeks, Wayne A. *The First Urban Christians: The Social World of the Apostle Paul.* New Haven: Yale University Press, 1983.

———. *The Moral World of the First Christians.* Philadelphia: Westminster, 1986.

———. *The Origins of Christian Morality: The First Two Centuries.* New Haven and London: Yale University Press, 1993.

Metz, Johann Baptist. *Faith in History and Society: Toward a Practical Fundamental Theology.* Translated by David Smith. New York: Seabury Press, 1980.

Meyer, Harding, Hans Jörg Urban, and Lukas Vischer, eds. *Growth in Agreement: Reports and Agreed Statements of Ecumenical Conversations on a World Level.* New York: Paulist, 1984. [Geneva: World Council of Churches, 1984].

Meyer-Kalkus, R. "Pathos." In *Historisches Wörterbuch der Philosophie,* 7:193-99. Basel: Schwabe, 1971f.

Miguez Bonino, José. *Doing Theology in a Revolutionary Situation.* Philadelphia: Fortress, 1975.

Milbank, John. *Theology and Social Theory: Beyond Secular Reason.* Oxford and Cambridge, Mass.: B. Blackwell, 1990.

Mildenberger, Friedrich. *Biblische Dogmatik. Eine Biblische Theologie in dogmatischer Perspektive.* Vol. 1, *Prolegomena. Verstehen und Geltung der Bibel.* Stuttgart: W. Kohlhammer, 1991.

———. *Biblische Dogmatik. Eine Biblische Theologie in dogmatischer Perspektive.* Vol. 2, *Ökonomie als Theologie.* Stuttgart: W. Kohlhammer, 1992.

———. *Biblische Dogmatik. Eine Biblische Theologie in dogmatischer Perspektive.* Vol. 3, *Theologie als Ökonomie.* Stuttgart: W. Kohlhammer, 1993.

———. *Theorie der Theologie. Enzyklopädie als Methodenlehre.* Stuttgart: Calwer, 1972.

Moltmann, Jürgen. *History and the Triune God: Contributions to Trinitarian Theology.* Translated by John Bowden. New York: Crossroad, 1992.

———. *The Trinity and the Kingdom: The Doctrine of God.* Translated by Margaret Kohl. Minneapolis: Fortress, 1993.

Müller, Gerhard Ludwig. "Enhypostasie." In *Lexikon für Theologie und Kirche,* 3:673f. 3rd ed. Freiburg im Breisgau: Herder, 1993-.

Murphy, Nancey. *Theology in the Age of Scientific Reasoning*. Ithaca, N.Y.: Cornell University Press, 1990.

Nichtweiß, Barbara. *Erik Peterson. Neue Sicht auf Leben und Werk*. Freiburg im Breisgau: Herder, 1992.

Nicol, Martin. *Meditation bei Luther*. Forschungen zur Kirchen- und Dogmengeschichte 34. Göttingen: Vandenhoeck & Ruprecht, 1984.

Nissiotis, Nikos A. "Is There a Church Ontology in Martin Luther's Ecclesiology?" In *Luther et la réforme allemande dans une perspective oecumenique*, 403-26. Les études théologiques de Chambésy 3. Chambésy-Geneva: Centre orthodoxe du Patriarcat oecuménique, 1983.

———. "Kirchliche Theologie im Zusammenhang der Welt." In *Theologie im Entstehen. Beiträge zum ökumenischen Gespräch im Spannungsfeld kirchlicher Situationen*, edited by Lukas Vischer, 119-44. Theologische Bücherei 59. Munich: Kaiser, 1976.

———. "Der pneumatologische Ansatz und die liturgische Verwirklichung des neutestamentlichen νῦν." In *Oikonomia. Heilsgeschichte als Thema der Theologie. Festschrift Oskar Cullmann*, edited by Felix Christ, 302-9. Hamburg and Bergstedt: Reich, 1967.

———. *Die Theologie der Ostkirche im ökumenischen Dialog. Kirche und Welt in orthodoxer Sicht*. Stuttgart: Evangelisches Verlagswerk, 1968.

Oberman, Heiko A. *Luther: Man between God and the Devil*. Translated by Eileen Walliser-Schwarzbart. New Haven: Yale University Press, 1989.

O'Neil, Colman E. "The Rule Theory of Doctrine and Propositional Truth." *Thomist* 49 (1985): 417-42.

Otto, Stephan. *Person und Subsistenz. Die philosophische Anthropologie des Leontios von Byzanz. Ein Beitrag zur spätantiken Geistesgeschichte*. Munich: W. Fink, 1968.

Pannenberg, Wolfhart. *Anthropology in Theological Perspective*. Translated by Matthew J. O'Connell. Philadelphia: Westminster, 1985.

———. *Basic Questions in Theology: Collected Essays*. Translated by George H. Kehm. 2 vols. Philadelphia: Fortress, 1970-71.

———. *Grundfragen systematischer Theologie*. II. Göttingen: Vandenhoeck & Ruprecht, 1980.

———. *Jesus — God and Man*. Translated by Lewis L. Wilkins and Duane A. Priebe, 2nd ed. Philadelphia: Westminster, 1977.

———. *Systematic Theology*. Translated by Geoffrey W. Bromiley. 3 vols. Grand Rapids: Wm. B. Eerdmans Publishing Co., 1991f.

———. *Theology and the Philosophy of Science*. Translated by Francis McDonagh. Philadelphia: Westminster, 1976.

———, ed. *Lehrverurteilungen — kirchentrennend?* Vol. 3, *Materialien zur Lehre von den Sakramenten und vom kirchlichen Amt*. Dialog der Kirchen 6. Freiburg im Breisgau: Herder; Göttingen: Vandenhoeck & Ruprecht, 1990.

Pelikan, Jaroslav. *Christianity and Classical Culture: The Metamorphosis of Natural Theology in the Christian Encounter with Hellenism.* New Haven and London: Yale University Press, 1993.

Persson, Per Erik. *Sacra Doctrina: Reason and Revelation in Aquinas.* Translated by Ross Mackenzie. Philadelphia: Fortress, 1970.

Pesch, Otto Hermann. *Hinführung zu Luther.* Mainz: Mattias-Grünewald-Verlag, 1982. 2nd ed., 1983.

————. *Die Theologie der Rechtfertigung bei Martin Luther und Thomas von Aquin.* Walberberger Studien der Albertus-Magnus-Akademie 4. Mainz: Mattias-Grünewald-Verlag, 1967.

Peters, Albrecht. *Gesetz und Evangelium.* Handbuch Systematischer Theologie 2. Gütersloh: Gütersloher Verlagshaus G. Mohn, 1981.

Peterson, Erik. "Briefwechsel mit Adolf Harnack und ein Epilog." In Peterson, *Theologische Traktate,* 293-321. Munich: Kösel, 1951.

————. "Die Kirche." In Peterson, *Theologische Traktate,* 409-29. Munich: Kösel, 1951. Originally *Die Kirche.* Munich: C. H. Beck, 1929.

————. "Die Kirche aus Juden und Heiden." In Peterson, *Theologische Traktate,* 239-92. Munich: Kösel, 1951.

————. "Was ist Theologie?" In Peterson, *Theologische Traktate,* 9-43. Munich: Kösel, 1951. Reprinted in *Theologie als Wissenschaft. Aufsätze und Thesen,* edited by Gerhard Sauter, 132-51. Theologische Bücherei 43. Munich: Kaiser, 1971. Originally *Was ist Theologie?* Bonn: F. Cohen, 1926.

————. "Zeuge der Wahrheit." In Peterson, *Theologische Traktate,* 165-224. Munich: Kösel, 1951.

Peura, Simo. "Die Kirche als geistliche communio bei Luther." In *Der Heilige Geist. Ökumenische und reformatorische Untersuchungen,* edited by Joachim Heubach, 131-56. Veröffentlichungen der Luther-Akademie Ratzeburg 25. Erlangen: Martin-Luther-Verlag, 1996.

————. *Mehr als ein Mensch? Die Vergöttlichung als Thema Martin Luthers von 1513 bis 1519.* Veröffentlichungen des Instituts für Europäische Geschichte Mainz 152. Mainz: P. von Zabern, 1994.

Peura, Simo, and Antti Raunio, eds. *Luther und Theosis. Vergöttlichung als Thema der abendländischen Theologie.* Schriften der Luther-Agricola-Gesellschaft (Finland) A 25. Helsinki: Finnische Theologische Literaturgesellschaft, 1990.

Picht, Georg. "Die Kunst des Denkens." In Picht, *Wahrheit — Vernunft — Verantwortung. Philosophische Studien,* 427-34. Stuttgart: E. Klett, 1969.

————. "Der Sinn der Unterscheidung von Theorie und Praxis in der griechischen Philosophie." In Picht, *Wahrheit — Vernunft — Verantwortung. Philosophische Studien,* 108-40. Stuttgart: E. Klett, 1969.

Piepkorn, Arthur Carl. *The Church: Selected Writings of Arthur Carl Piepkorn,* edited by Michael P. Plekon and William S. Wiecher. Delhi, N.Y., and New York: ALPB Books, 1993.

Placher, William C. "Revisionist and Postliberal Theologies and the Public Character of Theology." *Thomist* 49 (1985): 392-416.

―――. *Unapologetic Theology: A Christian Voice in a Pluralistic Conversation.* Louisville: Westminster/John Knox, 1989.

Plathow, Michael. "Der Geist hilft unserer Schwachheit auf. Ein aktualisierender Forschungsbericht zu M. Luthers Rede vom Heiligen Geist." *Kerygma und Dogma* 40 (1994): 143-69.

Plato. *Lysis; Symposium; Gorgias.* Translated by W. R. M. Lamb. Loeb Classical Library 166. Cambridge: Harvard University Press, 1983.

―――. *Theaetetus; Sophist.* Translated by Harold North Fowler. Loeb Classical Library 123. Cambridge: Harvard University Press; London: W. Heinemann, 1977.

Prenter, Regin. "Dietrich Bonhoeffer und Karl Barths Offenbarungspositivismus." In *Die Mündige Welt,* vol. 3, 11-41. Munich: Kaiser, 1960.

―――. *Spiritus Creator.* Translated by John M. Jensen. Philadelphia: Muhlenberg, 1953.

Rahner, Karl. "Der dreifaltige Gott als transzendenter Urgrund der Heilsgeschichte." In *Mysterium Salutis. Grundriß heilsgeschichtlicher Dogmatik,* edited by Johannes Feiner and Magnus Löhrer, 2:317-401. Einsiedeln: Benziger, 1967.

Rasmusson, Arne. *The Church as Polis: From Political Theology to Theological Politics as Exemplified by Jürgen Moltmann and Stanley Hauerwas.* Rev. ed. Notre Dame: University of Notre Dame Press, 1995.

Ratschow, Carl Heinz. *Der angefochtene Glaube. Anfangs- und Grundprobleme der Dogmatik.* Gütersloh: Gütersloher Verlagshaus G. Mohn, 1957.

Ratzinger, Joseph Cardinal. *The Nature and Mission of Theology: Essays to Orient Theology in Today's Debates.* Translated by Adrian Walker. San Francisco: Ignatius, 1995.

Raunio, Antti. "Sein und Leben Jesu Christi im Glauben bei Luther. Korreferat zum Vortrag von Oswald Bayer." In *Luther und Ontologie. Das Sein Christi im Glauben als strukturierendes Prinzip der Theologie Luthers,* edited by Anja Ghiselli, Kari Kopperi, and Rainer Vinke, 114-41. Schriften der Luther-Agricola-Gesellschaft (Finland) 31/Veröffentlichungen der Luther-Akademie Ratzeburg 21. Helsinki and Erlangen: Finnische Theologische Literaturgesellschaft; Martin-Luther-Verlag, 1993.

Reichenbach, Hans. *Experience and Prediction: An Analysis on the Foundations and the Structure of Knowledge.* Chicago: University of Chicago Press, 1938.

―――. *The Rise of Scientific Philosophy.* Berkeley and Los Angeles: University of California Press, 1951.

Rendtorff, Trutz. *Church and Theology: The Systematic Function of the Church*

Concept in Modern Theology. Translated by Reginald H. Fuller. Philadelphia: Westminster, 1971.

Riedel, Manfred. "Hegel und Marx. Die Neubestimmung des Verhältnisses von Theorie und Praxis." In Riedel, *System und Geschichte. Studien zum historischen Standort von Hegels Philosophie*, 9-39. Frankfurt am Main: Suhrkamp, 1973.

―――. *Theorie und Praxis im Denken Hegels. Interpretationen zu den Grundstellungen der neuzeitlichen Subjektivität.* Stuttgart: W. Kohlhammer, 1965.

Ritschl, Dietrich. *The Logic of Theology: A Brief Account of the Relationship between Basic Concepts in Theology* (English translation). Philadelphia: Fortress, 1987.

Ritter, Joachim. "Die Lehre vom Ursprung und Sinn der Theorie bei Aristoteles." In Ritter, *Metaphysik und Politik. Studien zu Aristoteles und Hegel*, 9-33. Frankfurt am Main: Suhrkamp, 1977. 2nd ed., 1988.

Rogers, Eugene F., Jr. *Thomas Aquinas and Karl Barth: Sacred Doctrine and the Natural Knowledge of God.* Notre Dame: University of Notre Dame Press, 1995.

Roloff, Jürgen. *Die Apostelgeschichte.* Das Neue Testament Deutsch 5. 2nd ed. Göttingen: Vandenhoeck & Ruprecht, 1988.

―――. "ἐκκλησία." In *Exegetical Dictionary of the New Testament*, translated by James W. Thompson, 1:410-15. Grand Rapids: Wm. B. Eerdmans Publishing Co., 1990.

―――. *Exegetische Verantwortung in der Kirche.* Edited by Martin Karrer. Göttingen: Vandenhoeck & Ruprecht, 1990.

―――. *Die Kirche im Neuen Testament.* Grundrisse zum Neuen Testament 10. Göttingen: Vandenhoeck & Ruprecht, 1993.

Roloff, Jürgen, and Hans G. Ulrich, eds., *Einfach von Gott reden. Ein theologischer Diskurs. Festschrift Friedrich Mildenberger.* Stuttgart: W. Kohlhammer, 1994.

Root, Michael. "Truth, Relativism, and Postliberal Theology." *Dialog* 25 (1986): 175-80.

Rorty, Richard. *Contingency, Irony, and Solidarity.* Cambridge: Cambridge University Press, 1989.

―――, ed. *The Linguistic Turn: Recent Essays in Philosophical Method.* Chicago: University of Chicago Press, 1967.

Rosato, Philip J. *The Spirit as Lord: The Pneumatology of Karl Barth.* Edinburgh: T. & T. Clark, 1981.

Saarinen, Risto. *Gottes Wirken auf uns. Die transzendentale Deutung des Gegenwart-Christi-Motivs in der Lutherforschung.* Veröffentlichungen des Instituts für Europäische Geschichte Mainz 137. Stuttgart: Steiner Verlag Wiesbaden, 1989.

―――. "Die moderne Theologie und das pneumatologische Defizit. Eine ökumenische Situationsbestimmung." In *Der Heilige Geist. Ökumenische und reformatorische Untersuchungen,* edited by Joachim Heubach, 245-63. Veröffentlichungen der Luther-Akademie Ratzeburg 25. Erlangen: Martin-Luther-Verlag, 1996.

Sauter, Gerhard. "Confessio — Konkordie — Consensus. Perspektiven des Augsburger Bekenntnisses für das Bekennen und Lehren der Kirche heute." *Evangelische Theologie* 40 (1980): 478-94.

———. "Consensus." In *Theologische Realenzyklopädie,* 8:182-89. Berlin: Walter de Gruyter, 1976f.

———. "Dialogik. II. Theologisch." In *Theologische Realenzyklopädie,* 8:703-9. Berlin: Walter de Gruyter, 1976f.

———. "Dogma — ein eschatologischer Begriff." In Sauter, *Erwartung und Erfahrung. Predigten, Vorträge und Aufsätze,* 16-46. Theologische Bücherei 47. Munich: Kaiser, 1972.

———. "Dogmatik. I. Enzyklopädischer Überblick und Dogmatik im deutsch-sprachigen Raum." In *Theologische Realenzyklopädie,* 9:41-77. Berlin: Walter de Gruyter, 1976f.

———. "'Einfaches Reden von Gott' als Gegenstand der Dogmatik." In *Einfach von Gott reden. Ein theologischer Diskurs. Festschrift Friedrich Mildenberger,* edited by Jürgen Roloff and Hans G. Ulrich, 159-71. Stuttgart: W. Kohlhammer, 1994.

———. "'Exodus' und 'Befreiung' als theologische Metaphern. Ein Beispiel zur Kritik von Allegorese und mißverstandenen Analogien in der Ethik." *Evangelische Theologie* 38 (1978): 538-59.

———. *In der Freiheit des Geistes. Theologische Studien.* Göttingen: Vandenhoeck & Ruprecht, 1988.

———. "Kirchenleitung als Theologie." *Glaube und Lernen* 2 (1987): 47-60.

———. "Theologie als Wissenschaft. Historisch-systematische Einleitung." In *Theologie als Wissenschaft. Aufsätze und Thesen,* edited by Gerhard Sauter, 9-72. Theologische Bücherei 43. Munich: Kaiser, 1971.

———. "Verbindlichkeit als Lehre?" *Glaube und Lernen* 3 (1988): 120-30.

———. *Vor einem neuen Methodenstreit in der Theologie?* Theologische Existenz heute, n.s., 164. Munich: Kaiser, 1970.

———. "Die Wahrnehmung des Menschen bei Martin Luther." *Evangelische Theologie* 43 (1983): 489-503.

———. "Wie kann Theologie aus Erfahrungen entstehen?" In *Theologie im Entstehen. Beiträge zum ökumenischen Gespräch im Spannungsfeld kirchlicher Situationen,* edited by Lukas Vischer, 99-118. Theologische Bücherei 59. Munich: Kaiser, 1976.

———, ed. *Theologie als Wissenschaft. Aufsätze und Thesen.* Theologische Bücherei 43. Munich: Kaiser, 1971.

Sauter, Gerhard, and Jürgen Courtin, Hans-Wilfried Haase, Gisbert König,

Wolfgang Raddatz, Gerolf Schultzky, and Hans G. Ulrich. *Wissenschafts-theoretische Kritik der Theologie. Die Theologie und die neuere wissenschaftstheoretische Diskussion.* Munich: Kaiser, 1973.

Schleiermacher, Friedrich. *Brief Outline on the Study of Theology.* Translated, with introductions and notes, by Terrence N. Tice. Richmond: John Knox, 1966.

———. *The Christian Faith.* Translated by H. R. Mackintosh and J. S. Stewart from 2nd German ed. Edinburgh: T. & T. Clark, 1928.

———. *On Religion: Speeches to Its Cultured Despisers.* Translated and edited by Richard Crouter. Cambridge and New York: Cambridge University Press, 1996.

Schlier, Heinrich. "Kurze Rechenschaft." In Schlier, *Der Geist und die Kirche. Exegetische Aufsätze und Vorträge,* vol. 4, edited by Veronika Kubina and Karl Lehmann, 270-89. Freiburg im Breisgau: Herder, 1980.

———. *Der Römerbrief.* Herders theologischer Kommentar zum Neuen Testament 7. Freiburg im Breisgau: Herder, 1977.

———. *Die Zeit der Kirche. Exegetische Aufsätze und Vorträge.* 2nd ed. Freiburg im Breisgau: Herder, 1958.

———. "Zur Freiheit gerufen. Das paulinische Freiheitsverständnis." In *Freiheit im Leben mit Gott. Texte zur Tradition evangelischer Ethik,* edited by Hans G. Ulrich, 42-59. Theologische Bücherei 86. Gütersloh: Kaiser; Gütersloher Verlagshaus, 1993.

Schlink, Edmund. *Ökumenische Dogmatik. Grundzüge.* Göttingen: Vandenhoeck & Ruprecht, 1983.

Schmid, Heinrich. *Die Dogmatik der evangelisch-lutherischen Kirche. Dargestellt und aus den Quellen belegt,* newly edited by Horst Georg Pöhlmann. 9th ed. Gütersloh: Bertelsmann, 1979. English translation: *The Doctrinal Theology of the Evangelical Lutheran Church.* Translated by Charles A. Hay and Henry E. Jacobs. 5th ed., revised by Henry E. Jacobs and Charles A. Hay. Philadelphia: United Lutheran Publication House, 1899.

Schmidt, Kurt Dietrich. "Luthers Lehre vom Heiligen Geist." In *Schrift und Bekenntnis. Zeugnisse lutherischer Theologie,* edited by Volkmar Herntrich and Theodor Knolle, 145-64. Hamburger Theologische Studien 1. Hamburg and Berlin: Im Furche, 1950.

Schoberth, Ingrid. *Erinnerung als Praxis des Glaubens.* Öffentliche Theologie 3. Munich: Kaiser, 1992.

Schulz, Walter. *Philosophie in einer veränderten Welt.* Pfullingen: G. Neske, 1972.

Schütte, Heinz. "Kirche des dreieinigen Gottes. Zur trinitarischen Entfaltung der Ekklesiologie als Aufgabe." In *Im Gespräch mit dem dreieinigen Gott. Elemente einer trinitarischen Theologie. Festschrift Wilhelm Breuning,* edited by Michael Böhnke and Hanspeter Heinz, 361-75. Düsseldorf: Patmos, 1985.

———, ed. *Einig in der Lehre von der Rechtfertigung! Mit einer Antwort an Jörg*

Baur. With contributions by Horst Georg Pöhlmann, Vinzenz Pfnür, and Heinz Schütte. Paderborn: Bonifatius, 1990.

Schwarzwäller, Klaus. "Delectari assertionibus. Zur Struktur von Luthers Pneumatologie." *Luther-Jahrbuch* 38 (1971): 26-58.

Slenczka, Reinhard. *Kirchliche Entscheidung in theologischer Verantwortung. Grundlagen — Kriterien — Grenzen.* Göttingen: Vandenhoeck & Ruprecht, 1991.

Soden, Hans von. "Was ist Wahrheit? Vom geschichtlichen Begriff der Wahrheit." In Soden, *Urchristentum und Geschichte. Gesammelte Aufsätze und Vorträge,* edited by Hans von Campenhausen, 1:1-24. Tübingen: J. C. B. Mohr, 1951.

Spaemann, Robert. "Die christliche Religion und das Ende des modernen Bewußtseins." *IKZ Communio* 8 (1979): 251-70.

————. "Überzeugungen in einer hypothetischen Zivilisation." In *Abschied von Utopia? Anspruch und Auftrag der Intellektuellen,* edited by Oskar Schatz, 311-31. Graz, Vienna, and Cologne: Styria, 1977.

Sparn, Walter. *Wiederkehr der Metaphysik. Die ontologische Frage in der lutherischen Theologie des frühen 17. Jahrhunderts.* Calwer theologische Monographien: series B, Systematische Theologie und Kirchengeschichte 4. Stuttgart: Calwer, 1976.

Staniloae, Dimitru. "The Procession of the Holy Spirit from the Father and His Relation to the Son, as the Basis of Our Deification and Adoption." In *Spirit of God, Spirit of Christ: Ecumenical Reflections on the Filioque Controversy,* edited by Lukas Vischer, 174-86. London: SPCK, 1981. [Geneva: World Council of Churches, 1981].

————. *Theology and the Church.* Crestwood, N.Y.: St. Vladimir's Seminary, 1980.

Stell, Stephen L. "Hermeneutics in Theology and the Theology of Hermeneutics: Beyond Lindbeck and Tracy." *Journal of the American Academy of Religion* 61 (1993): 679-703.

Stoevesandt, Hinrich. "Verbindliche Lehre." *Glaube und Lernen* 3 (1988): 130-43.

Taylor, Charles. *Sources of the Self: The Making of Modern Identity.* Cambridge: Harvard University Press, 1989.

Theunissen, Michael. *Hegels Lehre vom absoluten Geist als theologisch-politischer Traktat.* Berlin: Walter de Gruyter, 1970.

————. *Die Verwirklichung der Vernunft. Zur Theorie-Praxis-Diskussion im Anschluß an Hegel.* Philosophische Rundschau Beiheft 6. Tübingen: J. C. B. Mohr, 1970.

Thiemann, Ronald F. "Revelation and Imaginative Construction." *Journal of Religion* 61 (1981): 242-63.

————. *Revelation and Theology: The Gospel as Narrated Promise.* Notre Dame: University of Notre Dame Press, 1985.

Thomas Aquinas. *Expositio in S. Pauli Epistolam ad Romanos, in Sancti Thomae*

Aquinitatis Doctoris Angelici Ordinis Praedicatorum Opera Omnia ad Fidem Optimarum Editionum, Tomus XIII, 3-156. Parmae, 1862. Reprint, New York, 1949.

————. *St. Thomas Aquinas Summa Theologiae.* Vol. 1, *Christian Theology (1a.1), Latin Text, English Translation: Introduction, Notes, Appendices, and Glossary by Thomas Gilby OP.* New York and London: McGraw-Hill, 1964.

————. *Summa Theologiae I-III.* Biblioteca de autores cristianos. Madrid, 1951. 4th ed., 1978.

Torrance, Thomas F. *The Trinitarian Faith: The Evangelical Theology of the Ancient Catholic Church.* Edinburgh: T. & T. Clark, 1988.

————. *Trinitarian Perspectives: Toward Doctrinal Agreement.* Edinburgh: T. & T. Clark, 1994.

Tracy, David. *The Analogical Imagination: Christian Theology and the Culture of Pluralism.* New York: Crossroad, 1981.

————. "Lindbeck's New Program for Theology: A Reflection." *Thomist* 49 (1985): 460-72.

Troeltsch, Ernst. "Rückblick auf ein halbes Jahrhundert der theologischen Wissenschaft." In *Theologie als Wissenschaft. Aufsätze und Thesen,* edited by Gerhard Sauter, 73-114. Theologische Bücherei 43. Munich: Kaiser, 1971.

————. "Über historische und dogmatische Methode in der Theologie." In *Theologie als Wissenschaft. Aufsätze und Thesen,* edited by Gerhard Sauter, 105-27. Theologische Bücherei 43. Munich: Kaiser, 1971.

Trowitzsch, Michael. "Die nachkonstantinische Kirche, die Kirche der Postmoderne — und Martin Luthers antizipierende Kritik." *Berliner theologische Zeitschrift* 13 (1996): 3-35.

Ulrich, Hans G. *Eschatologie und Ethik. Die theologische Theorie der Ethik in ihrer Beziehung auf die Rede von Gott seit Friedrich Schleiermacher.* Beiträge zur Evangelischen Theologie 104. Munich: Kaiser, 1988.

————. "Was heißt: Von Gott reden lernen? Zugleich Bemerkungen zum Verhältnis von Dogmatik und Ethik." In *Einfach von Gott reden. Ein theologischer Diskurs. Festschrift Friedrich Mildenberger,* edited by Jürgen Roloff and Hans G. Ulrich, 172-89. Stuttgart: W. Kohlhammer, 1994.

————, ed. *Freiheit im Leben mit Gott. Texte zur Tradition evangelischer Ethik.* Theologische Bücherei 86. Gütersloh: Kaiser; Gütersloher Verlagshaus, 1993.

Vilmar, August Friedrich Christian. *Dogmatik. Akademische Vorlesungen.* Gütersloh: C. Bertelsmann, 1874.

Vischer, Lukas, ed. *Spirit of God, Spirit of Christ: Ecumenical Reflections on the Filioque Controversy.* London: SPCK, 1981. [Geneva: World Council of Churches, 1981].

————, ed. *Theologie im Entstehen. Beiträge zum ökumenischen Gespräch im*

Spannungsfeld kirchlicher Situationen. Theologische Bücherei 59. Munich: Kaiser, 1976.

Volf, Miroslav. *After Our Likeness: The Church as the Image of the Trinity.* Sacra Doctrina, vol. 1. Grand Rapids: Eerdmans, 1998.

Vorster, Hans. *Das Freiheitsverständnis bei Thomas von Aquin und Martin Luther.* Kirche und Konfession 8. Göttingen: Vandenhoeck & Ruprecht, 1965.

Wainwright, Geoffrey. "Ecumenical Dimensions of George Lindbeck's *Nature of Doctrine.*" *Modern Theology* 4 (1988): 121-32.

―――, ed. *Keeping the Faith: Essays to Mark the Centenary of Lux Mundi.* Philadelphia and Allison Park: Fortress, 1988.

Wannenwetsch, Bernd. *Gottesdienst als Lebensform — Ethik für Christenbürger.* Stuttghart: W. Kohlhammer, 1997.

―――. "Zwischen Schindmähre und Wildpferd. Luthers Reittier-Metapher ethisch betrachtet." *Luther* 65 (1994): 22-35.

Wappler, Paul. *Die Stellung Kursachsens und des Landgrafen Philipp von Hessen zur Täuferbewegung.* Münster: Aschendorff, 1910.

Weber, Otto. *Foundations of Dogmatics.* 2 vols. Translated and annotated by Darrell L. Guder. Grand Rapids: Eerdmans, 1981-83.

Welker, Michael. *God the Spirit.* Translated by John F. Hoffmeyer. Minneapolis: Fortress, 1994.

―――. "Der Mythos 'Volkskirche.'" *Evangelische Theologie* 54 (1994): 180-93.

Wellmer, Albrecht. *Zur Dialektik von Moderne und Postmoderne. Vernunftkritik nach Adorno.* Frankfurt am Main: Suhrkamp, 1985. 2nd ed., 1993.

Welsch, Wolfgang. *Ästhetisches Denken.* Stuttgart: Reclam, 1990. 2nd ed., 1991.

―――. *Unsere postmoderne Moderne.* Berlin: Akademie, 1987. 4th ed., 1993.

Wengst, Klaus. *Pax Romana and the Peace of Jesus Christ.* Translated by John Bowden. Philadelphia: Fortress, 1987.

West, Cornel. *The American Evasion of Philosophy: A Genealogy of Pragmatism.* Madison: University of Wisconsin Press, 1989.

Westhelle, Vítor. "Religion and Representation: A Study of Hegel's Critical Theories of *Vorstellung* and Their Relevance for Hegelianism and Theology." Diss., Lutheran School of Theology at Chicago, 1984.

White, Graham. *Luther as Nominalist: A Study of the Logical Methods Used in Martin Luther's Disputations in the Light of Their Medieval Background.* Schriften der Luther-Agricola-Gesellschaft (Finland) 30. Helsinki: Finnische Theologische Literaturgesellschaft, 1994.

Wiedenhofer, Siegfried. *Politische Theologie.* Stuttgart: W. Kohlhammer, 1976.

Wilckens, Ulrich. *Der Brief an die Römer.* Evangelisch-katholischer Kommentar zum Neuen Testament VI/1-3. Zürich: Benziger Verlag; Neukirchen-Vluyn: Neukirchener Verlag, 1978-82.

Williams, Rowan. *The Wound of Knowledge: Christian Spirituality from the New*

Testament to St. John of the Cross. Atlanta: John Knox, 1980. 2nd ed., London, 1990.

Wirsching, Johannes. *Kirche und Pseudokirche. Konturen der Häresie.* Göttingen: Vandenhoeck & Ruprecht, 1990.

Wolzogen, C. von. "Poiesis II." In *Historisches Wörterbuch der Philosophie,* 7:1025f. Basel: Schwabe, 1971f.

Yannaras, Christos. *Person und Eros. Eine Gegenüberstellung der Ontologie der griechischen Kirchenväter und der Existenzphilosophie des Westens.* Forschungen zur systematischen und ökumenischen Theologie 44. Göttingen: Vandenhoeck & Ruprecht, 1982.

Yeago, David S. "The New Testament and the Nicene Dogma: A Contribution to the Recovery of Theological Exegesis." *Pro Ecclesia* 3 (1994): 152-64.

———. "The Office of the Keys: On the Disappearance of Discipline in Protestant Modernity." In *Marks of the Body of Christ,* edited by Carl E. Braaten and Robert W. Jenson, 95-122. Grand Rapids: Eerdmans, 1999.

Zizioulas, John D. *Being as Communion: Studies in Personhood and the Church.* Contemporary Greek Theologians 4. Crestwood, N.Y.: St. Vladimir's Seminary, 1985. 2nd ed., 1993.

———. "The Mystery of the Church in Orthodox Tradition." *One in Christ* 24 (1988): 294-303.

———. "Die pneumatologische Dimension der Kirche." *IKZ Communio* 2 (1973): 133-47.

Index